AF540250

BEING AS CONSCIOUSNESS

Being as Consciousness

Yogācāra Philosophy of Buddhism

FERNANDO TOLA
CARMEN DRAGONETTI

MOTILAL BANARSIDASS PUBLISHERS
PRIVATE LIMITED • DELHI

First Edition: Delhi, 2004

ISBN: 81-208-1967-5

MOTILAL BANARSIDASS
41 U.A. Bungalow Road, Jawahar Nagar, Delhi 110 007
8 Mahalaxmi Chamber, 22 Bhulabhai Desai Road, Mumbai 400 026
236, 9th Main III Block, Jayanagar, Bangalore 560 011
120 Royapettah High Road, Mylapore, Chennai 600 004
Sanas Plaza, 1302 Baji Rao Road, Pune 411 002
8 Camac Street, Kolkata 700 017
Ashok Rajpath, Patna 800 004
Chowk, Varanasi 221 001

Printed in India
BY JAINENDRA PRAKASH JAIN AT SHRI JAINENDRA PRESS,
A-45 NARAINA, PHASE-I, NEW DELHI 110 028
AND PUBLISHED BY NARENDRA PRAKASH JAIN FOR
MOTILAL BANARSIDASS PUBLISHERS PRIVATE LIMITED,
BUNGALOW ROAD, DELHI 110 007

PREFACE

First of all we want to thank the institutions and persons who have made possible for us to compose this book: The *Reiyukai* and its academic branch *The International Institute for Buddhist Studies* IIBS (Tokyo), Dr. Tsugunari Kubo, President of both institutions, and Dr. Akira Yuyama, former Director of the Institute: the fellowship they granted us allowed us to stay six months in Tokyo in 1989 and to collect great part of the bibliographical material we needed in the excellent library of the Institute; the *Nyingma Institute* at Berkeley, California, Ven. Tarthang Tulku Rinpoche, Founder and Head of that Institute, Dr. Leslie Bradburn and Dr. Jack Petranker, Research Directors of *Yeshe De Buddhist Research and Translation Project* who invited us in 1996 as visiting scholars at the *Nyingma Institute* and *Odiyan Buddhist Center* in California, giving us the possibility to complete there our work, Ralph McFall, Dean of the Institute, and the staff of the *Nyingma Institute* and the Odiyan community who gave us all the cooperation we needed for our work; the University of California at Berkeley, and the *Flora Lamson Hewlett Library of the Graduate Theological Union,* that generously authorized us to freely use their libraries; and Miss Gabriela Dobler, secretary of our *Institute of Buddhist Studies* in Argentina, who patiently prepared the successive drafts of the original text of this book.

Our work is intended to be an introduction to the study of the Yogācāra Buddhist philosophy; its commentaries and notes have the purpose to help the reader to understand in a more complete way the contents of the three texts we edit and translate. In the *References*, we have limited to indicate the works we have utilized. Cf. for more bibliographical information the following books:

Shinshō Hanayama, *Bibliography on Buddhism*, Tokyo: The Hokuseido Press, 1961.

Pierre Beautrix, *Bibliographie du Bouddhisme, Volume I, Editions de textes*, Bruxelles: Institut Belge des Hautes Études Bouddhiques, 1970.

Hajime Nakamura, *Indian Buddhism, A Survey with Bibliographical Notes*, Delhi: Motilal Banarsidass, 1987.

Karl H. Potter, *Bibliography of Indian Philosophies*, Delhi: Motilal Banarsidass, 1970 (first edition).

Karl H. Potter, *Encyclopedia of Indian Philosophies. Bibliography*, Delhi: Motilal Banarsidass, 1983 (second revised edition).

John Powers, *The Yogācāra School of Buddhism, A Bibliography*, Metuchen, N.J. and London: The American Theological Library Association and The Scarecrow Press, 1991.

Frank Bandurski, "Übersicht über die Göttinger Sammlungen der von RĀHULA SĀṄKṚTYĀNA in Tibet aufgefundenen buddhistichen Sanskrit-Texte (Funde buddhistischer Sanskrit-Handschriften, III)", in *Untersuchungen zur buddhistischen Literatur*, Bearbeitet von Frank Bandurski, Bhikkhu Pāsādika, Michael Schmidt, Bangwei Wang, Göttingen: Vandenhoeck & Ruprecht, 1994.

E. Steinkellner und M.T. Munch, *Texte der erkenntnistheoretischen Schule des Buddhismus*, Göttingen: Vandenhoeck und Ruprecht, 1995.

We have put Dignāga's treatise in the first place, because we consider it a brief and clear introduction to the fundamental tenet of the Yogācāra School : the *cittamātra* theory.

Buenos Aires,
January 2001.

FERNANDO TOLA
CARMEN DRAGONETTI

CONTENTS

Part II

Part III

GENERAL INTRODUCTION

The Initial Philosophical Position in Buddhism: Realism

Between the epoch during which Buddha (566-486 B.C.)[1] preached his Doctrine and *circa* second century of the Christian Era the philosophical position of Buddhism was exclusively *realism*.

This period includes what is designated as Early Buddhism, and the first centuries of development of what is designated as Hīnayāna Buddhism. Early Buddhism extends from the moment the Buddha began teaching his *Dharma* until *circa* 350 B.C. (more or less one hundred years after His *Parinirvāṇa*), when the original Buddhist Community started dividing itself in different schools or sects (*nikāya*). From *circa* 350 B.C. until *circa* the beginning of the Christian Era, Buddhism is solely represented by a series of schools or sects: Sthaviravādins (= Theravādins in Pali), Lokottaravādins, Prajñaptivādins, Sautrāntikas, Sarvāstivādins, Haimavatas, Caityaśailas, Pūrvaśailas, Aparaśailas, Mahīśāsakas, Vātsīputrīyas, Dharmaguptakas, Kāśyapīyas, Mahāsāṅghikas, Bahuśrutīyas, etc. These specific names came from the doctrines sustained by the schools or sects or from the place they inhabited or from the name of their founder. They usually receive the collective name of Hīnayāna. The term 'Hīnayāna': 'Little or inferior Vehicle' was used by the Mahāyānists (those belonging to the 'Great Vehicle') to refer to these sects. They are also referred to as constituting the 'Nikāya Buddhism' or the Shrāvakayāna or 'Vehicle of the Disciples' (who directly listened to the words of the Buddha) or Abhidharma Buddhism, since the diverse opinions of these sects were included in their respective Abhidharma literature. Many of these sects continued existing after the beginning of the Christian Era, and even in the present time the Nikāya tradition is represented in Sri Lanka and Southeast Asia specially by the Theravāda School.

Early Buddhism and Hīnayāna Buddhism in their realistic position maintain that the empirical world is external to the mind, it is really existing independently of the mind that apprehends it, it exists even when it is not apprehended, it can be apprehended by the mind as it really is, it is the same for all the apprehending minds.

The Arising of the Buddhist Idealistic Position

Around the second century of the Christian Era began to appear in a more or less developed way, in several Buddhist texts (*sūtras*), themes that afterwards will constitute the fundamental doctrines of the Yogācāra Buddhist idealistic school such as *cittamātra* (mind only), *ālayavijñāna* (receptacle-consciousness), *trisvabhāva* (three natures), etc. These themes present new ideas, many of which are in clear opposition to the previous realistic approach and show an open idealistic conception of reality, centered around the idea that the empirical world is nothing else than a mental creation (*cittamātra*).

Sūtras of Idealistic Tendency

Among the *Sūtras* that manifest the new tendency of thought there are the following ones :

1. Saṃdhinirmocanasūtra

Chapters V-VII. According to É. Lamotte, p.22 of his edition, the *Chapters V-VII* of this *sūtra* contain an "Outline of the great theses of the idealistic school", and, p.24, "it (=this *sūtra*) is the link between the Prajñāpāramitā literature and the beginnings of the Yogācāra Vijñānavāda school". He considers, p.25, that "the different parts of the *sūtra* have been put together during the second century C.E. and it got its present form at the beginning of the third century C.E.".

The Sanskrit text is not available. Chinese translations : *Taishō* 675, 676, 677, 678, 679. Tibetan translation: *Tōhoku* 106=*Catalogue* 774. Edition of the Tibetan text and French translation from the Tibetan: É. Lamotte, Louvain: Université de Louvain, 1935. German translation from Tibetan of Chapters VI and VII (partial): E. Frauwallner, *Die Philosophie des Buddhismus,* 1969, pp.284-295. Edition of the Tibetan text and English translation from the Tibetan: J. Powers, Berkeley, USA: Dharma Publishing, 1995.

2. Laṅkāvatārasūtra

This *sūtra* is considered to be a not very careful compilation of diverse texts that seems to have taken place during the IIIrd and IVth centuries. In this *sūtra* the idealistic theses are constantly and unsystematically referred to. According to É. Lamotte, *op. cit.*, p.25, "the oldest portions of the *Laṅkāvatāra* are more or less contemporary with the *Saṃdhinirmocanasūtra*".

Sanskrit text: editions by B. Nanjio, Kyoto: Otani University Press, 1923 (reprint 1956); P.L. Vaidya, Darbhanga, India: The Mithila Institute, 1963. Chinese translation: *Taishō* 670, 671, 672. Tibetan translation: *Ṭōhoku* 107=*Catalogue* 775. English translation from the Sanskrit text: D.T. Suzuki, London: Routledge and Kegan Paul, 1968, together with which must be mentioned *Studies in the Laṅkāvatāra Sūtra*, by the same author, London, the same press, 1972. German translation from the Sanskrit text: Karl-Heinz Golzio, München: O.W. Barth Verlag, 1996.

These two *sūtras* constitute the most important authoritative texts for the Yogācāra idealistic school. Besides them we can mention the following *sūtras* which teach also some doctrines proper to that school.

3. Śrīmālādevīsiṃhanādasūtra

This *sūtra* refers to the doctrine of the *ālayavijñāna*, characteristic of the Yogācāra school. The *Śrīmālā* must be contemporary with or previous to the *Laṅkāvatārasūtra* which quotes it.

The Sanskrit text is not available. Chinese translations: *Taishō* 310 (*Ratnakūṭa*, 48) and 353. Tibetan translation: *Tōhoku* 92=*Catalogue* 760 (48). English translation: Alex and Hideko Wayman, *The Lion's Roar of Queen Śrīmālā*, Delhi: Motilal Banarsidass, 1990.

4. Ghanavyūhasūtra

It is a late text. It also refers to the *ālayavijñana*.

The Sanskrit text is not available. Chinese translations: *Taishō* 681 and 682. Tibetan translation: *Tōhoku* 110=*Catalogue* 778.

5. Daśabhūmikasūtra

In this *sūtra* is found the categorical affirmation of the mental character of everything. See note 20 for the commentary of the *Viṃśatikā* of Vasubandhu in this same book. According to É. Lamotte, *op. cit.*, p.25, the *Daśabhūmika* could be considered somewhat anterior to the *Saṃdhinirmocanasūtra*.

Sanskrit text: editions by Ryūkō Kondō, Kyoto: Rinsen Book Co., 1983 (reprint of the 1936 edition); and P.L. Vaidya, Darbhanga, India: The Mithila Institute, 1967. Chinese translations: *Taishō* 285, 286 and 287. It is considered a part of the *[Buddha] avataṃsakasūtra, Taishō* 278 (22) and 279 (26). Tibetan translation in *Buddhāvataṃsakanāmamahāvaipūlyasūtra: Tōhoku* 44=*Catalogue* 761 (31). English translation: in Thomas Cleary, *The Flower Ornament Scripture*, Boston USA: Shambala Publications, 1993 (reissue).

6. Pratyutpanna-buddha-saṃmukhāvasthita-samādhi-sūtra or Bhadrapālasūtra

In this *sūtra* the thesis that the whole world is only mind also occurs. According to L. Schmithausen, "On the problem of the Relation between Spiritual Practice and Philosophical Theory in Buddhism", p.247, "Such a coherent exposition of the idealistic thesis that the world is nothing but mind (*cittamātra*) does not occur in any other of the early Mahāyānasūtras. This fact, in combination with the earliest *terminus ante quem* of our *sūtra* (=the *Bhadrapālasūtra*), suggests that the Bhadrapālasūtra was the first text to enunciate the thesis of the universal idealism and to express this by the term *cittamātra*".

The Sanskrit text is not available. Chinese translations: *Taishō* 416, 417, 418 and 419. Tibetan translation: *Tōhoku* 133=*Catalogue* 801. Edition of the Tibetan text: Paul M. Harrison, Tokyo: The Reiyukai Library, 1978. English translation from the Tibetan text: Paul M. Harrison, *The Samādhi of Direct Encounter with the Buddhas of the Present*, Tokyo: The International Institute for Buddhist Studies, 1990.

The Great Masters of the Idealistic Yogācāra School

The theses such as *cittamātra, ālayavijñāna, trisvabhāva,* etc. contained in the mentioned *sūtras* and which were to constitute important elements of the idealistic doctrine of the Yogācāra school, were developed, systematized and put together in a coherent whole logically constructed, during the third and fourth centuries C.E. by the great Buddhist Masters Maitreyanātha or Maitreya (*circa* 300), Asaṅga (315-390) and Vasubandhu (320-380). To these Masters we must add Dignāga (480-540), the founder of the Buddhist school of logic and epistemology, because of his treatise *Ālambanaparīkṣā* so important for the understanding of the Yogācāra school. In the sixth century are active a series of great commentators of the works of Maitreya, Asaṅga and Vasubandhu; among them we mention Dharmapāla (530-561) and Sthiramati (both middle of the sixth century) and Hiuan-tsang (602-664), who wrote a commentary (*Ch' êng wei shih lun, Vijñaptimātratāsiddhi*) on the *Triṃśikā* of Vasubandhu on the basis of ten Indian commentaries. With this last treatise, written in Chinese by a Chinese Master, comes to an end the great period of the Indian idealistic school of philosophy. It will be followed in India by the brilliant development of the Buddhist school of logic and epistemology, in which Dharmakīrti (600-660), disciple of Īśvarasena (disciple at his turn of Dignāga) and of Dharmapāla, will excel, by the syncretic school of Śāntarakṣita (*circa* 725-788) and Kamalaśīla (*circa* 740-795), and, beyond the boundaries of India, by the great achievements of Tibetan, Chinese and Japanese Masters of Yogācāra inspiration.

We shall now refer only to authors of the great Indian period of the idealistic school.

MAITREYANĀTHA (CIRCA 300)

The Yogācāra school of philosophy was founded by Maitreyanātha. He was the teacher of Asaṅga. According to various ancient texts of India, China and Tibet, Asaṅga ascended to the Tuṣita Heaven, where he received direct instruction from Bodhisattva Maitreya. Maitreya would have transmitted him also several treatises. See for instance the accounts of Buston and Tāranātha. However, the predominant opinion today is that Maitreya, the teacher of Asaṅga, is a historical personage. H. Sastri, "The Northern Buddhism III", in *Indian Historical Quarterly* 1, 1925, pp.464-472, specially pp.465-466; H. Ui, "Maitreya as an Historical Personage", in *Indian Studies in Honor* of *Charles Rockwell Lanman*, Cambridge, Mass.: Harvard University Press, 1929, pp. 95-101 (cf. H. Ui, "On the Author of the Mahāyāna-sūtrālaṅkāra", in *Zeitschrift für die Indologie und Iranistik* 6.2, 1928, pp.215-225, specially pp.223-225); G. Tucci, *On some aspects of the Doctrines of Maitreya (nātha)*, pp.2 ff. (cf. G. Tucci, *Storia della Filosofia Indiana*, p. 82), "Animadversiones Indicae: 1. On Maitreya, The Yogācāra Doctor", in *Opera Minora*, Parte I, Roma: G. Bardi, 1971 (Universitá di Roma, Vol. VI), pp.195-198, etc., have established the historicity of Maitreyanātha. See also T.R.V. Murti, *The Central Philosophy of Buddhism*, p.107 and note 6 of the same page; E. Frauwallner, *Die Philosophie des Buddhismus*, pp.296 and 327.[2]

The principal works attributed to Maitreyanātha are:

1. The Abhisamayālaṅkāra (273 Kārikās)

This treatise expounds in a synthetic, systematic and rigorous way the Path that leads to the realization of Buddhahood according to the *Pañcaviṃśatisāhasrikā Prajñāpāramitāsūtra*. In this work are found, as it is obvious, numerous references to theories of the *Prajñāpāramitā* and the Mādhyamika school and to the conception of all that exists as mere *prajñapti* (nominal concept, conceptual entity, nominal entity, concept). The work ends with an exposition of the doctrine of the Three Bodies.

The Sanskrit text of this treatise has been preserved. It has been edited several times: by Th. Stcherbastky and E. Obermiller, Leningrad:

Bibliotheca Buddhica XXIII. 1929, G. Tucci, Baroda, 1932, and U. Wogihara, Tokyo 1932-935 (reprint 1973, Sankibo Buddhist Bookstore). P.L. Vaidya, Darbhanga, 1960, published the Sanskrit text of the *Abhisamayālaṅkārālokā* of Haribhadra, which is a commentary on *Aṣṭasāhasrikāprajñāpāramitā* and includes Maitreya's *kārikās*. Tibetan translation of Haribhadra's work: *Tōhoku* 3791=*Catalogue* 5189. The Central Institute of Higher Tibetan Studies of Sarnath (Varanasi), in its Bibliotheca-Indo-Tibetica 2, 1977, edited the Sanskrit text of Maitreya's *kārikās* and the Tibetan text of Haribhadra's commentary on them, known as "*Sphuṭārthā Vṛttiḥ*" (with a Sanskrit reconstruction). Tibetan translation of Haribhadra's work: *Tōhoku* 3793=*Catalogue* 5191. Tibetan translation of Maitreya's *kārikās* alone: *Tōhoku* 3786=*Catalogue* 5184. English translation of Maitreya's *kārikās*: E. Conze, *Abhisamayālaṅkāra*, Roma: IsME O, 1954. E. Obermiller has an *Analysis of the Abhisamayālaṅkāra*, London: Luzac and Co. Calcutta Oriental Series 27, three fascicles, 1933, 1936 and 1943 (ends at IV.5.3). Cf. E. Conze, "*Abhisamayālaṅkāra* (1)" and Wang Sen, "*Abhisamayālaṅkāra* (2)", in *Encyclopaedia of Buddhism*, Ceylon, 1961, Vol. 1, fasc. 1, pp.114-118.

2. Dharmadharmatāvibhāga or Dharmadharmatāvibhaṅga-kārikā

This treatise studies the elements which constitute the phenomenic world (*dharmas*) and their ultimate essence (*dharmatā*). The *dharmas* are characterized by the subject-object duality and they, being multiple, are mere modifications of the unique and indifferentiated true reality, which is their essence: consciousness. They give the impression of an independently existing external world, but when they are known in their essence, their false and impure aspect disappear and the way to Nirvāṇa is free from obstacles.

Preserved in two Tibetan translations: *Tōhoku* 4022 (in prose) and 4023 (in verses)=*Catalogue* 5523 (in prose) and 5524 (in verses). See second part of this book, Introduction B.2. for the editions and translations of the commentary of this treatise by Vasubandhu, which includes the *kārikās* of Maitreya.

3. Madhyāntavibhāga or Madhyāntavibhaṅga (111 Kārikās)

The most important treatise of Maitreya from the philosophical point of view. In it for the first time is presented in a systematic way the philosophical tenets of the Yogācāra school. The empirical reality is a mere creation of our mind (*citta, vijñāna*) that manifests itself under the duality subject-object, and it exists as such. *Citta* is the only true reality; the empirical reality, the unreal mental creation, is the impure aspect of *citta*. *Citta* is *śūnyatā*, conceived as "the absence of duality". Other names to designate it are *tathatā*, suchness, thus-ness, because of being always such (*nityaṃ tathā eva*); *bhūtakoṭi*, the extreme point of truth, because of being free from error (*aviparyāsārthena*); *animitta*, devoid of all characteristics (*sarvanimittābhāva*); *paramārtha*, supreme reality, because it is the object of the supreme knowledge (*paramajñānaviṣayatvāt*); *dharmadhātu*, the fundamentals of the *dharmas*, because it is the cause of all the noble attributes (*āryadharmahetutvāt*).

The Sanskrit text has been preserved included in Vasubandhu's commentary. On the editions and translations of this commentary see the Second part of this book, Introduction, under B.1. Chinese translation of the *kārikās* alone: *Taishō* 1601. Tibetan translation of the *kārikās* alone: *Tōhoku* 4021=*Catalogue* 5522.

4. Ratnagotravibhāga-Mahāyānottaratantraśāstra or Uttaratantra

This treatise is constituted by 282 *kārikās* and a commentary. According to Takasaki, p. 62 of his translation of this treatise, "most probably" the authorship of the *kārikās* "is to be attributed to Maitreya" and "the author of the commentary of the *Ratna* must be Sāramati". Anyhow, let us remark that according to Tibetan tradition the author of the *kārikās* is Maitreya and the author of the commentary would be Asaṅga (*ibidem*, p. 7). But according to Frauwallner, *Die Philosophie des Buddhismus*, p. 255, and "Amalavijñānam und Ālayavijñānam", in *Kleine Schriften*, pp. 642-643, the author of *Ratnagotravibhāga* (*kārikās* and commentary) is Sāramati (*circa* 250 C.E.), agreeing in this point with the Chinese tradition.

The basic theme of the *Ratnagotravibhāga* is the important *Tathāgatagarbha* theory, according to which the Buddha nature is present in all beings. The treatise describes the Absolute, the *Tathāgatagarbha*, in very positive terms. It is conceived as being pure mind, and designated as *cittaprakṛtivaimalyadhātu*, "Element of purity of the nature of the Mind". "The *Ratna* cannot be regarded as a work of the Vijñānavāda" (Takasaki, quoted work, p.58), since in it "there is no quotation from the *Saṃdhinirmocana*, nor any use of the terms like *trisvabhāva or ālayavijñāna" (ibidem)*, or *cittamātra*.

The Sanskrit text is available and has been edited by E. H. Johnston and T. Chowdhury, Patna: Vihar Research Society, 1950, and by Zuiryū Nakamura, Tokyo: 1967. Chinese translation: *Taishō* 1611 (*kārikās* and commentary). Tibetan translation: *Tōhoku* 4025 (*kārikās)* and 4026 *(kārikās* and commentary)=*Catalogue* 5525 (*kārikās)* and 5526 *(kārikās* and commentary). English translations by E. Obermiller in *Acta Orientalia* IX, parts II, III and IV, 1930, pp. 81-306, under the title of "The Sublime Science of the Great Vehicle to Salvation", and by J. Takasaki, Roma: IsMEO, 1966 under the title *A Study of the Ratnagotravibhāga (Uttaratantra).*

5. Sūtrālaṅkāra or Mahāyānasūtrālaṅkāra

This treatise is composed by 804 *kārikās* and commentary. There is not unanimity in relation to the authorship of the commentary and stanzas. For instance according to the colophon of the Sanskrit text this treatise has been said *(bhāṣita)* by a certain Bodhisattva Vyavadātasamaya, but it is impossible to know to whom this name or epithet refers; according to the *K' ai yuen lu* catalogue (730 A. D.), *Taishō* 2154 and the Sung, Yuen, Ming and Kaoli editions of the Chinese Buddhist Canon, the commentary and the stanzas were composed by Asaṅga; according to Hui chao (died 714 A. D.), disciple of Hiuan tsang, the *kārikās* were composed by Maitreya and the commentary by Vasubandhu; according to the Tibetan tradition the *kārikās* were composed by Maitreya (nātha) and the commentary by Vasubandhu- opinion this one to which we adhere. C f. Hakuju Ui, "On the Author of the Mahāyānasūtrālaṅkāra", and "Maitreya as an historical personage", pp.98-99; D. Seyfort Ruegg, *La théorie du tathāgatagarbha et du gotra,* p. 40; S. Lévi, translation of the *Mahāyānasūtrālaṅkāra*, Paris: H. Champion, 1911, (Tome II), pp.7-9.

The subject matter of this treatise is the ideal of the Bodhisattva; it depicts his career and achievements. It asserts the mental nature of the world and the inexistence of duality in the Absolute, and expounds the theories of the Three Bodies and of the Three Natures.

On the editions and translations of this treatise see Second Part of this book (*Viṃśatikā* of Vasubandhu), Introduction, under *B. Commentaries of Treatises or of commentaries by other authors (4).*

On Maitreya doctrines see: G. Tucci, *On some aspects of the doctrines of Maitreya (nātha)* and *Asaṅga,* San Francisco: Chinese Materials Center, 1975 (reprint of the 1930 edition Calcutta) and E. Frauwallner, *Die Philosophie des Buddhismus,* 1969, pp. 296-326.

ASAṄGA (315-390)

He was a brother of Vasubandhu (see Introduction to the Second Part of this same book), a disciple of Maitreyanātha and the most famous Master of the Yogācāra school. For those who do not accept the historicity of Maitreyanātha, Asaṅga is the founder of the Yogācāra School.

The principal works of Asaṅga are :

1. Abhidharmasamuccaya

It is summary work by Asaṅga. It explains the principal doctrines of the Mahāyāna following the method already employed by the Abhidharma treatises of the Hīnayāna. He analyzes in this way the *dharmas* and their different kinds, the Four Noble Truths, the Nirvāṇa, the Path, the diverse kinds of individuals, the rules of debate, etc. In this treatise there are some references to *cittamātra,* the *ālayavijñāna,* to the three characteristics of being (*parikalpita, paratantra and pariniṣpanna).* The Sanskrit text has been preserved and has been edited by Prahlad Pradhan, Santiniketan: Visva-bharati, 1950. Chinese translation: *Taishō*1605. Tibetan translation: *Tōhoku* 4049=*Catalogue* 5550. French translation from the Sanskrit text: Walpola Rahula, *Le Compendium de la Super-Doctrine (Philosophie) (Abhidharma-samuccaya) d' Asaṅga,* Paris: École Francaise d' Extrême Orient, 1971.

2. Mahāyānasaṃgraha

This treatise is a summary work of the doctrines of the Yogācāra school. In a clear and complete way it deals with the principal themes of this school, giving them their canonical expression: the *ālayavijñāna* (names, characteristics, demonstration, kinds, moral nature); the three natures (definitions, relations, subdivisions), the *vijñaptimātratā* and the inexistence of the external object; the three bodies of the Buddha, etc.

The Sanskrit text is not available. Chinese translations: 1592, 1593, 1594. Tibetan translation: *Tōhoku 4048=Catalogue 5549.* French translation from the Tibetan: É. Lamotte, *La Somme du Grand Véhicule d 'Asaṅga,* Louvain-la-Neuve: Institut Orientaliste, 1973 (includes an edition of the Tibetan text and a reproduction of the Chinese text 1594 from *Taishō).* Amalia Pezzali, *L 'Idealismo Buddhista di Asaṅga,* Bologna: E.M.I., 1984, gives a summary and study of this treatise.

3. Yogācārabhūmiśastra

This treatise is generally considered as the *magnum opus* of Asaṅga, although in some sources it is attributed to Maitreyanātha and even it has been thought (as for instance by E. Frauwallner, *Die Philosophie des Buddhismus,* p. 265, and L. Schmithausen, "Zur Literaturgeschichte der älteren Yogācāra-Schule") that it is a compilation work composed by several Yogācāra authors. It is a voluminous work. It comprises five major divisions of which the first, called *Bahubhūmikavastu,* is the most important one. At its turn this first part contains seventeen sections, which describe the stages *(bhūmi)*, that are to be passed through by the follower of the Mahāyāna in order to reach the ultimate goal, the Nirvāṇa without residue (*nirupādhiśeṣanirvāṇa)* and also the achievements he attains in each stage. The doctrine of the *ālayavijñāna* is mentioned in this treatise.

The Sanskrit text has been preserved but has been only partially edited. See F. Bandurski, "Übersicht über die Göttinger Sammlungen der von Rāhula Sāṅkṛtyāyana in Tibet aufgefundenen buddhistischen Sanskrit-Texte", pp.61-66, for a list of the diverse chapters or sections of the work that have been already edited and/or translated. A very important chapter of the treatise is the *Bodhisattvabhūmi,* which constitutes the fifteenth section of the first major division. The Sanskrit text of the *Bodhisattvabhūmi* has been edited by N. Dutt, Patna: K.P. Jayaswal Research Institute, 1966 and by U. Wogihara, Tokyo: Sankibo Buddhist Book Store, 1971. Chinese translation of the *Yogācārabhūmiśāstra: Taishō* 1579. Tibetan translation: *Tōhoku* 4035-4042=*Catalogue* 5536-5543.

4. Commentary on the Saṃdhinirmocanasūtra

The Sanskrit text has not been preserved. Tibetan translation*: Tōhoku* 3981=*Catalogue* 5481. English translation by John Powers, Lewiston : The Edwin Mellen Press, 1992.

5. Commentary on the Vajracchedikā Prajñāpāramitāsūtra

Sanskrit text: edited by G. Tucci, *Minor Buddhist texts,* Part I, Roma: IsMEO, 1956, pp. 51-128 (Sanskrit Text with Chinese, Tibetan and English translations). Chinese Text: *Taishō* 1514. Tibetan translation: *Tōhoku* missing; *Catalogue* 5864 (Cf. Tucci's quoted edition p.7).

VASUBANDHU (320-380)

See the Introduction of the *Second Part* of this book.

DIGNĀGA (480-540)

See the Introduction of the *First Part* of this book.

DHARMAPĀLA (530-561)

Son of a minister of Kāñcīpura in South India. He became a Buddhist monk and went to Nālandā. He obtained a great renown as scholar. He became the head of the Nālandā University. Had many excellent disciples, among whom was Śīlabhadra who was Hiuan-tsang's teacher. He is considered as one of the great masters of the Yogācāra school. He wrote the following commentaries:

1. On the *Ālambanaparīkṣā* of Dignāga (included in this book). This work is known only in its Chinese (incomplete) translation (*Taishō* 1625)
2. On the *Catuḥśataka* of Āryadeva, not preserved in Sanskrit. Chinese text: *Taishō* 1571.
3. On the *Triṃśikā* of Vasubandhu, not preserved in Sanskrit. Extracts of this commentary were incorporated by Hiuan Tsang in his *Tch' eng wei che louen (Taishō 1585).*
4. On the *Viṃśatikā* of Vasubandhu (included in this book). This commentary is known only in its Chinese translation (*Taishō* 1591).

STHIRAMATI (MIDDLE OF THE SIXTH CENTURY)

Born in South India. He was the most important scholar of Vallabhī University in Kāṭhiāvāḍa, which had been founded by his teacher Guṇamati. He is also considered as one of the great masters of the Yogācāra school. Among his works we mention the following ones:

1. Commentary on the *Abhidharmakośa* of Vasubandhu
This text is known in its Chinese translation *(Taishō* 1561), under the name of *Kiu chö louen che yi chou: Tattvārthaṭīkā* (?), and in its Tibetan translation: *Tōhoku* 4421=*Catalogue* 5875.

2. Commentary on the *Abhidharmasamuccaya* of Asaṅga
The Sanskrit text has been edited by Nathmal Tatia, Patna: K. P. Jayaswal Research Institute, 1976. Chinese translation: *Taishō* 1606, attributing it to Sthiramati. Tibetan translations: *Tōhoku* 4053 and 4054= *Catalogue* 5554 and 5555, attributing it to Rgyal baḥi sras or Jinaputra.

3. Ṭīkā on Vasubandhu's commentary on the *Madhyāntavibhāga* of Maitreya
The Sanskrit text is available. For editions and translations of this *ṭīkā* see Second Part of this Introduction, *Works attributed to Vasubandhu, B. Commentaries of treatises or of commentaries by other authors (1).* Tibetan translation: *Tōhoku* 4032=*Catalogue* 5534.

4. Commentary on the *Mūlamadhyamakakārikā* of Nāgārjuna
The Sanskrit text is not available. Chinese translation: *Taishō* 1567.

5. Commentary on the *Pañcaskandhaprakaraṇa* of Vasubandhu
The Sanskrit text is not available. Chinese translation: *Taishō* 1613. Tibetan translation: *Tōhoku* 4066=*Catalogue* 5567.

6. Tīkā on Vasubandhu's Commentary on the *Sūtrālaṅkāra* of Maitreya

The Sanskrit text is not available. Tibetan translation: *Tōhoku 4034=Catalogue* 5531.

7. Commentary on the *Triṃśikā* of Vasubandhu

The Sanskrit text has been preserved. For editions and translations of this commentary see Second Part of this book. Introduction, *Works attributed to Vasubandhu, A. Treatises (6)*. Extracts of this commentary were also incorporated by Hiuan-tsang in his work *Tch 'eng wei che louen (Taishō* 1585). Tibetan translation: *Tōhoku 4064=Catalogue 5565*.

HIUAN-TSANG OR HSÜAN-TSANG OR HSÜAN-CHUANG (602-664)

He was born in Chin-lu (China). He studied in Lo-yang and Tch'ang-ngan under various teachers. Perplexed by their different opinions he travelled in 629 through Central Asia to India in order to look for the Buddhist texts in the original Sanskrit, and also for the teachings of Indian Buddhist Masters, that he could not find in China. He studied in the Nālandā University Sanskrit and Buddhist philosophy, specially the idealistic Yogācāra system, to which he finally adhered. He worked under Śīlabhadra, the renowned Master of the Yogācāra school. In 645 he returned to China with more than 650 Buddhist texts in Sanskrit, which contained 224 *sūtras,* 192 *śāstras* of the Mahāyāna and works belonging to different Hīnayāna schools. Back to China he retired to a monastery and dedicated the rest of his life to the gigantic task of translating 75 Buddhist texts. The rapidity with which his task of translation was carried on, the rigour of his terminology, the erudition and penetration of this Master, unique in China, and who combined a first-class Chinese culture and a perfect knowledge of Sanskrit and Buddhist thought are really amazing.

In *Rêpertoire du Canon Bouddhique sino-japonais* of the Hōbōgirin, *Index,* p.250 *sub Genjō* (the Japanese name of Hiuan-tsang), and in Bagchi's *Le Canon Bouddhique en China* II, pp. 473- 494, can be found a list of works translated by Hiuan-tsang into Chinese.

Let us mention among Hiuan-tsang's works in a special way his *Tch' eng wei che louen (Taishō 1585) (Vijñaptimātratāsiddhi)* which is the translation into Chinese of the *Thirty Stanzas (Triṃśikā)* of Vasubandhu together with the resumé or extracts from the ten principal commentaries (by Dharmapāla, Sthiramati, etc.) on Vasubandhu's treatise, today lost with the exception of that of Sthiramati. See Second Part of this book, Introduction, *Works attributed to Vasubandhu (13)*. This work is a monumental contribution of Hiuan-tsang to the knowledge of the Yogācāra school.

The Name of the Idealistic School

The Buddhist idealistic school receives several names: *Cittamātra,* Only Mind, as the only existing reality is Mind deprived of duality; *Vijñānamātra,* understanding *vijñāna* in the same exalted sense as *citta; Vijñaptimātra* in that all existing things are only cognition; *Yogācāra,* due to the fact that its first adherents were persons dedicated to the practice (*ācāra)* of meditation *(yoga)* and also due to the great importance meditation has in this school as the means to attain the Supreme Goal. Cf. D.Snellgrove, *Indo-Tibetan Buddhism,* pp.97 and 125, and L. Schmithausen, "*Zur Literaturgeschichte* ", p.811, note 2. The synonymic value given by Vasubandhu in the beginning of the *Viṃśatikā* to the words *citta, manas, vijñāna, vijñapti,* explains the simultaneous use of the above indicated terms as names of the idealistic school of Buddhist philosophy.

Principal Philosophical Tenets of the Yogācāra School

We give now a brief survey of the principal doctrines of the Yogācāra school, fundamentally those of a philosophical character, and putting special emphasis on the doctrines that are dealt with in the three treatises included in this book. As a matter of course the Yogācāra school accepts many other doctrines proper of Buddhism in general and Mahāyāna in particular. Those that are surveyed below are those that give this school its essential identity. More information will be given in the *Introductions* of each treatise included in this book.

Cittamātra : "Only Mind"

All that exists is only ideas, representations, images, imaginations, creations of the mind, to which no real object existing outside the mind corresponds. These ideas are the only object of any cognition. The whole universe is a mental universe. It is similar to a dream, a mirage, a magical illusion, where what we perceive are only products of our mind, without a real external existence. Thus only mind (*cittamātra*), only consciousness *(vijñānamātra),* only cognition (*vijñaptimātra)* in the meaning of *only ideas* is the basic ontological and epistemological tenet of the school. The assertion of only mind opens Vasubandhu's fundamental treatise, the *Viṃśatikā*.

Arguments in Favour of "Only Mind"

The great Masters of the Yogācāra school endeavoured to give a rational foundation to the thesis of only mind sustained by their school.

First of all they affirmed the possibility of the existence of representations without an external object and having notwithstanding the characteristics of the representations with an external object as conceived by the realist. These characteristics are: determination or non-arbitrariness in regard to place and time, indetermination or non-exclusiveness in regard to a sole individual, and efficiency in regard to their specific function (*Viṃśatikā*, Section II). Examples of representations without an object, that possess these characteristics, are: all dreams for determination or non-arbitrariness in regard to place and time; some kind of dreams (erotic dreams) for efficiency; the vision by *pretas* of a river of pus and excrements, where there is only water, for the indetermination or non-exclusiveness in regard to a sole individual; and the experiences of beings condemned to hell for the four characteristics.

The main argument adduced by the Yogācāra in order to found the only mind thesis is the impossibility of the existence of an external object. This argument is developed by Vasubandhu in his *Viṃśatikā* (Sections XVII-XXVII) against Buddhist realists, and by Dignāga in the first part (Sections I-VIII) of his *Ālambanaparīkṣā* against the atomists (Hindu or Buddhist).

Other arguments are given in *Trisvabhāva, kārikās* 35-36, which are inspired in Buddhist traditional religious beliefs. See our commentary thereon. These arguments are: 1. one and the same thing appears differently to beings that are in different states of existence (*pretas*, men and gods); 2. the hability of the bodhisattvas and *dhyāyins* (practitioners of meditation) who have attained the power over thinking (*cetovaśitā)* to visualize objects at will; the capacity of the *yogins* who have obtained serenity of mind *(śamatha)* and practice the analysis of the *dharmas (dharmavipaśyanā)* to perceive things at the very moment of the concentration of mind (*manasikāra)* with their essential characteristics of impermanence, suffering, etc.; and the power of those who have attained intuitive knowledge (*nirvikalpakajñāna)* and remain in it, which enables them not to perceive things at all-these facts of experience show that the objects do not exist really outside the mind, that their appearance or non appearance and the form of their appearance depend on the mind, and that they consequently are a product of it; and 3. if things really exist and we know them as they really are, then our common knowledge would be a true knowledge and no special training would be necessary to reach reality, to have the supreme intuitive knowledge and to attain liberation.

And finally the word of the Buddha expressed in the *sūtras* is adduced as an authority which grants validity to the thesis of only mind. The *Viṃśatikā* starts quoting the *Daśabhūmikasūtra (or Bhadrapālasūtra).* Hiuan-tsang in *Tch' eng wei che louen* 1585, p.39 a=L. de la Vallée Poussin's translation, pp.419-423, cites several *sūtras* which affirm the *vijñaptimātratā*.

The Structure of the Mind.
The Explanation of Cognition without an External Object

If there is no external object, if only mind exists, how do the representations arise in it? To answer this question it is necessary to take into account the conception of the mind proper of the Yogācāra school.

Mind (*citta, vijñāna, manas, vijñapti*. On their synonymous value see our commentary on *Viṃśatikā,* Section I). Mind is conceived as a result of the philosophical analysis as having eight functions (" aspects" or "parts"): the six kinds of cognitive activities through the sense-organs, the ego-consciousness, and the *ālayavijñāna*.

According to the Buddhist conception, mind is not a substantial permanent entity (as the soul or the *ātman* are conceived); it is only a *series* of consciousnesses, cognitions, acts of knowledge, momentary, instantaneous, which as soon as they arise, vanish and are replaced by other consciousnesses, cognitions, acts of knowledge. This series of consciousnesses comes from a beginningless *(anādi)* eternity flowing like a river which has no source.

The *ālayavijñāna* or "deposit"-consciousness is the subliminal or sub-conscious aspect of mind. In it are "deposited" the *vāsanās* (=Tibetan *nus pa*: "virtuality" in Dignāga) or subliminal impressions left by all the experiences that man has had in all his previous existences. (It would be more precise to say that the *ālayavijñāna* is constituted by the *vāsanās,* that the *vāsanās* are the *ālayavijñāna*). The *ālayavijñāna* shares all the characteristics of mind, but it has the peculiar feature of being in a subliminal latent level.

Given the appropriate conditions imposed by *karman,* the *vāsanās* abandon their subliminal state and, passing to the conscious state, become the representations, the ideas, that are essentially of two kinds: subjective, of an ego who cognizes, and objective, simultaneous with the previous ones, of beings and things that are the objects of our cognitions.

This conception of the mind and the important theory of the *ālayavijñāna* (its nature and its functioning), proper of the Yogācāra school, are at the basis of the explanation of how knowledge without an external object is produced given by Vasubandhu and Dignāga in the three treatises presented in this book.

Although the word *ālayavijñāna* is not mentioned either in the *Viṃśatikā* or in the *Ālambanaparīkṣā,* evidently both treatises presuppose the *ālayavijñāna* theory, since they explain the cognition process on the basis of the *vāsanās*.

Avoidance of Solipsism

If all is only mind, and mind is a series of consciousnesses, and each individual series gives rise to a mere mental world, proper to that series, how to explain that all these mental worlds agree, creating in us the conviction that we live all of us in one and the same world ? How to avoid the solipsism that always threatens the kind of idealism propounded by the Yogācāra school ? The explanation is found in *Viṃśatikā,* Section IV. All living beings see the same world at the same moment because of the identical maturation of their *karmans;* the karmic histories of these beings have similitudes and therefore the consequences are also similar. This fact introduces organization and order where otherwise there would be only arbitrariness and chaos. The result is in a certain sense an *objective* world without external object valid for all that participate in it.

The Three Natures

An important Yogācāra theory is the theory of the Three Natures, explained in Vasubandhu's treatise *Trisvabhāvakārikā or Trisvabhāvanirdeśa* included in this book. The term *trisvabhāva* indicates the three forms of being: the dependent on other (*paratantra*), the imagined (*parikalpita*) and the perfected or absolute (*pariniṣpanna*). The importance of this theory derives from the fact that the *paratantra* and the *parikalpita* nature correspond to the empirical reality and the *pariniṣpanna* nature is the Absolute Reality. Consequently to analyze the Three Natures is to analyze the empirical and the absolute aspects of reality and to know their essence and their mutual relations.

The Three Natures theory is not referred to in the *Viṃśatikā* or the *Ālambanaparīkṣā*. Without any doubt Vasubandhu (on writing the *Viṃśatikā)* and Dignāga knew this theory which was expounded in *sūtras and śāstras* composed before them. Given the monographic nature of both treatises this lack of reference to that theory is not amazing.

The Paratantra and the Parikalpita Nature

The *paratantra* nature is nothing else than the series of conscious mental representations which are produced when the *vāsanās* or subliminal impressions pass from their latent state to their conscious level. The *paratantra* nature is so called because it depends on the *vāsanās*.

The *parikalpita* nature is the attribute of subject-object duality that inexorably accompanies the *paratantra* nature. If the *paratantra* is "what appears", the *parikalpita* is the form under which "what appears" appears, i.e. duality. The *parikalpita* nature is so called (imagined) because duality is only an unreal mental creation.

The Pariniṣpanna Nature

In the *Ālambanaparīkṣā* there is no reference to any notion of the Absolute; this treatise limits itself to analyze the act of cognition and to explain it from the idealistic point of view which affirms that there is no external real object of cognition.

The *Viṃśatikā,* in Section XVI, affirms that the *dharmas* exist with the "indefinable substantiality" (*anabhilāpyenātmanā)* which is the object of the knowledge of the Buddhas (*buddhānāṃ viṣaya iti).* This same idea is applied to consciousness as the only existing entity (*vijñaptimātratā).* In Section XXXIII the *Viṃśatikā* refers to the world-transcending knowledge or supermundane cognition without any mental construction (*lokottaranirvikalpajñāna),* that is the only means to reach the True Reality. Thus, although the *Viṃśatikā* does not explicitly speak of an Absolute, anyhow, when referring to the kind of substantiality proper of the *dharmas,* indescribable and object of Buddhas' cognition, it is alluding to *citta,* the mind in its absolute aspect, devoid of the subject-object duality, conceived as the essence of all that exist-position openly adopted in the *Trisvabhāvakārikā.* And also, when the *Viṃśatikā* speaks of the world-transcending knowledge that leads to the Ultimate Reality, it is presupposing the existence of an Absolute, that is the aim of that special knowledge.

The *Trisvabhāvakārikā* fully develops the notion of an Absolute on dealing with the *pariniṣpanna* nature. In *kārikā* 3 the Absolute nature is defined as the *eternal non-existence with duality of the mind* (or dependent nature). According to *kārikā* 13 the Absolute nature *is only non-existence of duality,* and to *kārikā* 25 it is the *existence of the inexistence of duality*. In other words we could say that the Absolute is the mind devoid of duality i.e. the Pure Mind, since impurity is nothing else that the subject-object duality (*kārikā* 17-21). The Absolute nature is characterized by its full inalterability, since it has always been, is and will always be the same: inexistence of duality (*kārikā* 3). Because of this characteristic the Absolute nature is designated in *kārikā* 30 with the name of *tathatā*: "Suchness", "the fact of being so" (*de bžin ñid* in Tibetan). In *kārikā* 37 the Absolute nature i.e. *citta* devoid of duality is implicitly identified with the *dharmadhātu*, the fundament or ultimate essence of the *dharmas*.

It is necessary to call the attention to the emphasis put on the notions of *existence* and *purity* in the definition of the *parinispanna* nature as the mind deprived of duality, the true Reality. This fact links *Trisvabhāva's* conception of Absolute with the *pabhassaraṃ cittam* (luminous mind) of the *Aṅguttaranikāya* I, 10 and the *viśuddhaṃ cittam* (pure mind) of Sāramati. See E. Frauwallner, "Amalavijñānam und Ālayavijñānam".

Some Other Themes that Appear in the Three Treatises

We mention some other themes of the treatises that show the richness of ideas and approaches which explains their importance for the exposition of the Yogācāra system of Buddhist philosophy.

In the Ālambanaparīkṣā

1. Refutation of the realistic and atomistic theories (Sections I -VIII)
2. Definition of object of cognition (*yul* in Tibetan, *viṣaya* in Sanskrit) and support of cognition (*dmigs pa* in Tibetan, *ālambana* in Sanskrit) (Sections II and III).
3. Conception of the sense-organs as mere aspects of the *vāsanās* and as non material entities, and of the knowable internal form (which is the reactualized *vāsanā*) as the object of cognition. And the theory of perception based on the absence of an external object and on the mentioned conception of the sense-organs and the object (Section XI). Dignāga's explanation of perception in the idealistic context seems to be more elaborated than Vasubandhu's one in the *Viṃśatikā* (See No. 8 under).
4. Conception of causal relation (Section X).
5. *Anāditva* or beginninglessness of the series of *vāsanās* (Section XIII).

In the Viṃśatikā

6. Refutation of the realistic and atomistic theories (Sections II-XXVII).

7. Peculiar conception of the hells and of the hell-guards as a mental creation of the damned (Sections IV-X).
8. Interpretation of the traditional Buddhist conception of 1. the internal *āyatana* (senses) and 2. the external *āyatana* (objects) as merely being 1. the *vāsanā* which reactualizes in a new representation, and 2. the image with which that representation arises. And the idealistic explanation of perception which results from that interpretation (Sections XI-XXVII).
9. The *neyārtha* (concealed meaning to be established) — *nītārtha* (clear and immediate meaning) hermeneutic principle, applied in order to avoid the difficulties that the ancient Buddhist doctrines of realistic inspiration caused to the new idealistic positions (Sections XII-XIII) or in order to eliminate apparent contradictions in the teachings of the Buddha (Section XII).
10. The *pudgalanairātmya* (unsubstantiality of man) and the *dharmanairātmya* (unsubstantiality of the *dharmas)* connected with the idealistic interpretation of the *āyatanas* (Section XIV).
11. The "indefinable substantiality" of the *dharmas* and of the *vijñaptimātratā* (consciousness as the only existing thing) (Section XVI).
12. Refutation of the *avayavin* (Sections XVIII, XXVII).
13. Noteworthy analysis of the mechanism of *pratyakṣa* (perception) in two moments; the *nirvikalpa pratyakṣa* (perception that lacks any mental construction) and the *savikalpapratyakṣa* (perception with mental construction), with the aim to prove that in fact all perception is without an object (Section XXIX). It is interesting to point out that for Dignāga, *Pramāṇasamuccaya, Pratyakṣapariccheda* I, *kārikā* 3 c, perception is defined as "free from mental constructions" *(mṅom sum rtog pa daṅ bral ba)* and for Dharmakīrti, *Nyāyabindu* I, 4 *pratyakṣa* is also "free from mental constructions" and moreover "free from error" (*kalpanāpoḍham abhrāntaṃ pratyakṣam).* The definitions of these two authors correspond, in the analysis of Vasubandhu, to the first moment, i.e. to pure sensation.
14. Explanation of recollection through the mechanism of the *vāsanās* (Section XXXI).
15. The world transcending knowledge as a means to attain True Reality and to become free from the vāsanic sleep (=error consisting in considering objects as real and external) (Section XXXIII).

16. Possibility of a consciousness as determining and influencing another consciousness. Avoidance of isolation of consciousnesses (Section XXXV).
17. Moral responsibility's dependence on the conscious state of mind, which is proper only of the normal waking state (Section XXXVII).
18. Possibility of a mental act to cause an alteration in other series of consciousnesses (Section XXXIX).
19. The use of the word of the Buddha as a means to validate an idealistic thesis (Section XL).
20. Possibility of the knowledge of another mind, although it is a limited knowledge bound to the subject-object duality and unable to grasp the true nature of the mind, as it happens also with one's own mind (Section XLII).
21. Profoundity and richness of the only-mind theory which can be mastered in all its extension and complexity only by the Buddhas, the Enlightened Ones (Section XLIII).

In the Trisvabhāva

22. The analysis of the cognitive process that leads to intuitive knowledge *(sakṣātkriyā)* of True Reality *(kārikās* 31-37).
23. Achievements obtained through knowledge of the ultimate essence of the *dharmas (vibhutva* : sovereignty) and through the *Bodhisattvacaryā* (Course of conduct of Boddhisattvas) (*anuttarā bodhi:* Supreme Enlightenment) (*kārikās* 37-38).
24. The Three Bodies as the essence of Enlightenment (*kārikā* 38).

Factors that Contributed to the Arising of the Idealistic Conception of Cittamātra

The Yogācāra system is composed as it has been seen by a great number of theories. In order to establish the way it was formed, it would be necessary to study when, where and how each one of these theories originated, and also to study when, where and how these diverse theories where assembled giving rise to a new structure of philosophical thought. (The same thing would have to be done *mutatis mutandis* in regard to the origin of the Mahāyāna). The creation of the Yogācāra theories (as those of the Mahāyāna) has been a dynamic process, covering a long period of time, and in which many factors have participated. To these circumstances, that make difficult a study of the origin of the Buddhist idealistic philosophy, are to be added other facts that render that study more difficult still: the texts that must be used for this study are in most cases anonymous; their relative chronology is difficult or impossible to establish; great part of Buddhist literature is lost; many important texts are known to us only in their Chinese and Tibetan translations, which often present problems of interpretation.

We shall point out some factors, that seem to have contributed to a great extent to the formation of the fundamental Yogācāra doctrine, *cittamātra*. Similarly, factors, that participated in the formation of the other theories of the Yogācāra school, could also be traced.

The Importance of Citta (mind)

Since its beginnings Buddhism has given to mind (*citta, cetas, manas, viññāṇa or vijñāna)* a great importance, attributing to it fundamental functions. Mind is the determining condition for the arising of the individual existence (*nāmarūpa)* in the twelve members of the Dependent Origination (*paṭiccasamuppāda* or *pratītyasamutpāda)*. Human conduct depends on mind. Mind is the cause of purity or impurity. Man is directed by mind. *Karman* gets its moral qualification according to the mental state or disposition with which it has been carried out. Individual destiny and world destiny depend on *karman* and therefore indirectly on mind. Many of the moral qualities propounded by Buddhist ethics belong to the realm of mind (*sati or smṛti, appamāda* or *apramāda*, etc.) The two pillars of the Buddhist Path are knowledge (*ñāṇa* or *jñāna, paññā* or *prajñā*) and compassion (*karuṇā*), and knowledge is gained through the activity and development of mind. In the way to Liberation meditation (*jhāna* or *dhyāna)* and concentration of mind (*samādhi)* play an important role. Through a well-trained and purified mind the Supreme Enlightenment (*bodhi*), the ultimate goal of Buddhist effort, is reached.

In many texts this special importance of mind is extolled as for instance: *Saṃyuttanikāya* I, p.39 PTS; *Aṅguttaranikāya* II, p.177 PTS; *Dhammapāda* I, 1-2; *Vimalakīrtinirdeśa* III, paragraph 34; *Āryaratnamegha* quoted in Śantideva's *Śikṣasamuccaya*, pp.121-122 ed. Bendall. See Lamotte's translation of *Vimalakīrtinirdeśa*, Introduction, pp.51-53, for other references.

The pre-eminent position that *citta* has in the Yogācāra is thus coherent with the importance it always has had in Buddhism. Yogācāra carried one fundamental trend of Buddhist thought to its extreme point, making mind the only existing entity and deriving everything from it.

"Nominalism"

Buddhist philosophy distinguished between things existing *dravyasat* and things existing *prajñaptisat*. *Dravyasat* points to something that exists as a substance, as a real entity; *prajñaptisat* on the contrary points to something that has only a nominal existence, the existence of a mere concept, that is conventionally assumed to exist but has no objective reality. *Dravyasat* exists in *re*, *prajñaptisat* exists in *mente*.

In *Milindapañho* II, pp. 25-28, in the celebrated dialogue between the king Milinda and the Venerable Nāgasena, it is declared (in the context of the negation of an *ātman)* that 'Nāgasena' exists only "as a denotation (*saṅkhā*), appellation (*samaññā)*, designation (*paññatti)*, as a current usage (*vohāro)*, merely as a name (*nāmamattam)*" (Horner's translation). And a stanza of *Saṃyuttanikāya* (I, p.135 PTS) is quoted where it is said that "Just as when the parts are rightly set the word 'chariot' is spoken, so when there are the *kandhas (=skandhas)*, it is the convention (*sammuti*) to say that there is 'an individual' (*satto)*".

The attribution of a *prajñaptisat* existence, nominal existence, to diverse kinds of things is frequently met with in the Hīnayāna literature. We give some examples, which show how spread this opinion was.

The Vātsīputrīya (Thesis 1, Vasumitra) maintained that the "pudgala" (person, individual) is a mere denomination (*prajñapti)* established in relation to the *skandhas, the āyatanas and dhātus*. Cf. *Mahāyānasūtrālaṅkāra* XVIII, 92: *prajñaptyastitayā vācyaḥ pudgalo dravyato na tu* and commentary *ad locum: prajñaptito'stīti vaktavyo dravyato nāstīti vaktavyaḥ*.

The Prajñaptivāda school (Thesis 3, Vasumitra) taught that all the *saṃskāras or saṃskṛtas* (all composed or conditioned things) are *prajñaptisat*.

According to a text of Paramārtha's commentary on Vasumitra's treatise on the sects (*Samayabhedoparacanacakra,* quoted by Chūgan (*Chōzen* in Japanese) in his *San louen hiuan yi (Taishō* 2300, p.459 b 29-c 2, the sect of the Ekavyāvahārikas held that all the mundane (*laukika)* and supra-mundane (*lokottara) dharmas* have only a nominal existence.

The Bahuśrutīyas also declared that the Four Great Elements that constitute matter are only nominally existent (*prajñaptisat)*, according to the *Satyasiddhiśāstra* of Harivarman (middle of the third century C.E.) who expresses the point of view of that school (*Taishō* 1646, p.261 a, Section 37 and b-c, Section 38 (Sanskrit "reconstruction" and

English translation by N.Aiyaswami Sastri, Baroda: Oriental Institute, 1975 -1978), and that the *dharmas* are not real and consequently are only name (*nāmamātra)*, conventional denomination (*Taishō* 1646, p. 327 a, beginning of Section 141).

The Sautrāntikas or Saṅkrāntivādins or Dārṣṭāntikas fully adhered to the nominalist conception of reality. They considered *prajñaptisat* many entities that for the Sarvastivādins, in their realistic inspiration, were really existent. According to them form (*saṃsthāna)* does not exist as a *dravya* (substance, thing) (Vasubandhu, *Abhidharmakośa* IV 3b, p.573, Bauddha Bharati ed., 1971) and according to the context it exists only *prajñaptitaḥ* (nominally, conventionally). In the Sarvāstivādin classification of *dharmas, prāpti* was an important *cittaviprayukta dharma (a dharma* non-associated with mind), whose function was to connect any acquired object with the individual who possessed it, specially to connect the accomplished act with the series of consciousnesses of the individual who had accomplished it. *Prāpti* allowed the Sarvāstivādins to explain the mechanism of the ċasual retribution of actions. The Sautrāntikas attributed to *prāpti* a nominal existence (*prajñaptitaḥ)* (Vasubandhu, *Abhidharmakośa* II ad 36 c-d at the end, pp.217-218 of Bauddha Bharati ed.,1971), contrarily to the Sarvāstivādins who considered *prāpti* as having a real existence *(dravyataḥ)*. Another *dharma,* to which the Sarvāstivādins attributed a real existence, was the *avijñapti*. Any volition (*cetanā)*, which is of a mere mental nature, may externally manifest itself through a corporal or vocal act. The gesture or words are *vijñapti*, " information", because they make known the will of the person. But, at the same time, the volition gives rise to an invisible act, which continues to exist and is the receptacle of the moral responsibility derived from that act. This invisible act is the *avijñapti,* "non-information", because, as it does not appear, it does not give any information. For the Sautrāntikas *avijñapti* existed also *prajñaptitaḥ,* as a nominal entity.

Even the Sarvāstivādins, who represented an extreme realistic position, maintained that all beings had a nominal existence grounded on the series (*santāti)* that constitute them (Thesis 33,Vasumitra).

In the treatise *Bhavasaṅkrāntiparikathā* attributed to Nāgārjuna, *kārikā* 11 a expresses: *ḥdi dag thams cad miṅ tsam ste/ḥdu śes tsam la rab tu gnas/rjod par byed las tha dad paḥi/brjod par bya ba yod ma yin* (all things are only name *(nāmamātra*), they dwell only in thought; separate from the word, what it designates does not exist).

Many other examples of the attribution of a nominal existence to diverse entities can be found in the theses maintained by the Hīnayānist sects. In fact, the nominalist conception agrees with the non-substantialist position adopted by Buddhism since its very beginning. This "nominalism", which pervades the thought of the Abhidharmic period, does not mean the negation of the existence of beings and things, it affects the kind of existence that beings and things possess. But anyhow it undermined the consistency of existence, paving the way for the future conception of Voidness and Only-Mind, in the Mahāyāna period.

Perception without External Objects

Dreams *(svapna)*, magical creations *(nirmāṇa)*, illusions *(māyā)*, mirages *(marīci)*, eye disorders *(timira)*, the whirling firebrand *(alātacakra)*, the moon reflected in water *(udakacandra)*, and other similar phenomena interested Buddhist thinkers. They saw in them cases of cognitive experiences in which non existing objects appeared to the mind as if they were really existing. Thus these perceptions were used as comparisons (*upamāna)* or examples (*dṛṣṭānta)* for the unreality of the empirical world, as for instance by Nāgārjuna in *Mūlamadhyamakakārikā* VII, 34:*yathā māyā yathā svapno gandharvanagaraṃ yathā/tathotpādas tathā sthānaṃ tathā bhaṅga udāhṛtam.* Cf. *Ta tche tou louen (Mahāprajñāpāramitopadeśa* or *Mahāprajñāpāramitāśāstra), Taishō* 1509, pp.101 c and ff., for a detailed enumeration and explanation of these *upamānas,* and Lamotte's translation, pp.357 ff., for more references.

In several sūtras magical creations are employed as *upāya,* means to obtain some beneficial effects, as for instance *Bhadramāyākāravyākaraṇa, Vimalakīrtinirdeśa-sūtra* (See E. Hamlin, "Magical *Upāya* in the Vimalakīrtinirdeśasūtra", in *The Journal of the International Association of Buddhist Studies,* Vol. 11, No. 1, 1988, pp. 89-121), *Saddharmapuṇḍarīkasūtra,* Chapter VII, pp. 187-188 and pp. 195-197, Kern-Nanjio edition.

Moreover, these peculiar cases of perception showed the possibility of the existence of acts of perceptual cognition which do not comply with the conditions required by the common notion of normal perception: a sense organ and a real external object corresponding to that sense organ. The Sautrāntikas accepted the existence of cognitions without an external object against the opinion of the Sarvāstivādins who argued that all congnition necessarily has a real entity as its object. Cf. Colette Cox, "On the Possibility of a Non-existent Object of Consciousness: Sarvāstivādin and Dārṣṭāntika Theories", in *The*

Journal of the International Association of Buddhist Studies, Vol. 11, No. 1, 1988, pp.31-87.

In *Viṃśatikā*, Sections I-III, the cases of *taimirikas*, persons who have their visual sense organ afflicted by ophthalmic disorders, of dreams and mirages are mentioned as examples of representations without object, and in *Trisvabhāva*, Section K, the magical creation of an elephant by the power of the *mantras* is presented as a case of representations without object.

The acceptance of representations without a real external object is the *conditio sine qua non* for the arising, development and establishment of an idealistic explanation of reality. If the possibility of cognitions without an object did not exist (as it was maintained by the Sarvāstivādins), an idealistic conception has no place.

Meditation

The *Pratyutpanna-buddha-saṃmukhāvasthita-samādhi-sūtra* or *Bhadrapālasūtra* offers as instances of cognitions without really existing external object, dreams (3 H,Harrison's edition), *aśubhabhāvanā* or meditation on the repulsive practised by the Bhikṣu (3J,*ibidem)*, images reflected in a mirror (3 K,*ibidem)*, and compare to them the visualizations of Tathāgatas that occur in the meditative concentration of the Bodhisattvas. The *Saṃdhinirmocanasūtra* VIII, paragraph 7 (Lamotte's edition and translation=pp.152-155 Power's edition and translation) expresses the same idea in relation to images seen in meditation: *gzugs brñam de rnam par rig pa tsam du zad paḥi phyir te.*

In *Trisvabhāvakārikā*, Section M, reference is made tó the "three knowledges " thanks to which Bodhisattvas, *dhyāyins* and wise people have also the experience of cognitions without external object.

An important difference between the cases of cognitions without object given in the previous section and those occuring in meditation is that these latter take place as a result of the practitioner's voluntary resolve and the application of a yogic technique.

The experience of meditation could contribute in another way to the constitution of the *cittamātra* theory. Meditation, as a yogic process, has as its effect to allow the meditator to get diverse attainments and also to void his mind, to liberate it from its psychological and intellectual contents, passing through the diverse stages of the meditative process, in which the experience becomes gradually deeper. At the end of the process the external world and the internal world (sensations, notions) have disappeared for the meditator, who "enters in a state of calm and cessation similar to *nirvāṇa" (Ta tche tou louen, Taishō* 1509, p.216 a, lines 2-3).

A complete description of the meditative process is found in the just quoted *Ta tche tou louen,* pp.206a -217a= Lamotte's translation III, pp. 1216-1309. Lamotte gives in the notes to his translation a detailed account of references concerning meditation. In *Mahāvyutpatti* Nos. 1477-1540 there is a complete enumeration of *dhyānas, samāpattis, apramāṇas, vimokṣas, abhibhvāyatanas* and *kṛtsnāyatanas,* which constitute the elements of the meditation path, in Sanskrit, Tibetan and Chinese.

The meditative process shows that the mind, *citta,* can remain alone and isolated in itself, that it can subsist without the presence of an object, freeing itself from the subject-object duality, getting rid of the empirical reality, and manifesting itself as the transcendent supreme reality.

The Instantaneity of the Dharmas

Buddhism has a dynamic conception of reality. This manifests itself in the peculiar doctrine of the *dharmas.* The *dharmas* are the elements, the constituent factors of all that exists. All that is 'material', as human body, is constituted by material *dharmas.* The mental phenomena as perceptions, sensations, volitions, acts of consciousness are nothing but *dharmas.* And man is only a psycho-physical aggregate of material *dharmas* and of mental *dharmas.* Reality, in its integrity, is likewise nothing else that *dharmas*—isolated or accumulated. *Dharmas* are unsubstantial *(anātman),* because (using the Western terminology) they do not exist in *se et per se* or (using the Buddhist terminology) they do not exist *svabhāvena,* i.e. they do not possess an own being; they are dependent, produced by causes and conditions. And, besides that, since the first period of Buddhist thought, *dharmas* were conceived as impermanent *(anitya).* For Early Buddhism and for the Hīnayānist schools *dharmas,* although unsubstantial and impermanent, were real. But in the Hīnayāna several sects added to the transitory *dharmas* the attribute of instantaneity: *dharmas* not only are impermanent, but also they disappear as soon as they arise, and are replaced by other *dharmas* of the same species as long as the causes that provoked the appearance of the replaced *dharma* continue to exist. Thus reality is an accumulation of series of *dharmas,* in a process of accelerate constant replacement. The result is that, as D. N. Shastri, *The Philosophy of Nyāya,* p.189, says: "the reality, according to the Buddhist, is not static, it is dynamic. it is not being; it is becoming".

Among the Hīnayānist sects that maintained the instantaneity of the *dharmas* were the Sarvāstivādins, the Vātsīputrīyas, the Mahīśāsakas, and the Kāśyapīyas, and the sects derived from them, according to Vasumitra's *I pu tsung lun lun, Taishō* 2031, pp.16 c, line 2; 16 c, lines 15-16; 17 a, lines 13-14; and 17b, line 1 (=A. Bareau, "Trois Traités sur les Sectes Bouddhiques attribués á Vasumitra, Bhāvya et Vinītadeva", in *Journal Asiatique*, 1954, pp.255, 257, 262 and 265, and J. Masuda, "Origin and Doctrines of Early Indian Buddhist Schools", in *Asia Major*, II, 1925, pp.50, 54, 62 and 65). The Pubbaseliyas and the Aparaseliyas, both derived from the Mahāsaṃghikas affirmed also the instantaneity of the *dharmas*, according to Buddhaghosa's commentary of *Kathāvatthu* (XXII, p. 620 PTS edition). Vasubandhu in *Abhidharmakośa* IV, 2 d, pp.568-569 emphatically declares that "what is conditioned (-and all is-) is momentary" (*saṃskṛtaṃ kṣāṇikam)*, and *bhāṣya ad locum: ko yaṃ kṣaṇo nāma? ātmalābho 'nantaravināśī, so 'syāstīti kṣanikaḥ*. Yaśomitra commentary *ad Abhidharmakośa* II, 46 b, p.262, line 26, refers to the Vaibhāṣikas with the term *kṣaṇikavādin*. On the contrary the Theravādins, according to the quoted text of the *Kathāvatthu*, did not accept the momentariness of the *dharmas*, and this explains why they remained attached to the realistic conception of the world.[3]

The new attribute of instantaneity produced an enormous effect in the Buddhist theory of knowledge: if *dharmas* are not only impermanent but also instantaneous—and *dharmas* constitute the whole reality—and we do not perceive that momentariness of the *dharmas* but only compact things that seem to be there as the objects of cognition, then we do not see reality as it truly is.

Nāgārjuna's Conception of Reality

One of the principal tasks of Nāgārjuna is to establish the logical impossibility of the existence of elements, manifestations, categories of the empirical reality, as for instance: birth and destruction, causality, movement, time, sensorial activity, the elements that constitute man, passion and its subject, action and its agent, suffering, *karman, saṃsāra,* etc. This impossibility derives from the fact that all is conditioned, related, dependent, contingent, and as such lacks an own being, a *svabhāva*, an existence in *se et per se*. Everything is *śūnya*, "void", *svabhāvaśūnya*, "void of an own being". The abolishing analysis, to which Nāgārjuna submits the whole reality, leaves a great void, *Śūnyatā*, Voidness, in which nothing belonging to the empirical reality which appears before us remains. But normal knowledge does not reach the true reality of *Śūnyatā,* which is covered, concealed by an apparitional reality, the empirical reality, beyond which normal knowledge cannot go. We do not perceive what really exists (*paramārthasatya,* Supreme Truth or Reality); we only perceive something that is inexistent, false, illusory (*saṃvṛtisatya,* concealing truth or reality=Relative Truth or Reality), as the dreams, mirages, magical creations etc. to which Nāgārjuna's school so frequently compares the world in which we live. The situation in the case of Nāgārjuna is similar to that of the theory of the *dharmas* as maintained in the Hīnayāna: we perceive something different from what really exists, things are not as they appear.

It seems that the theory of the instantaneity of the *dharmas* and Nāgārjuna's conception of reality, which stress the separation between what is outside our mind and our mental representations, are the two more important factors for the forthcoming of the idealistic theory that there is nothing apart from the creations of our mind.

The Philosophical Inference

Given the preceding historical, philosophical conceptions—the importance of the mind conceived as the determining principle of human conduct and of man's and world's destiny; nominalism which transforms the reality in which we exist in a collection of names and labels and undermines the consistency of beings and things; the awareness of the existence of many cognitions being cases of representations without a real external object; the experience of meditation which has both powers: to visualize objects at will and to suppress the surrounding reality and the contents of the mind, leaving the mind empty and isolated ; the instantaneity of the *dharmas,* the constituent factors of what exists, the sole existing true reality that remains concealed to our normal knowledge limited to perceive something that is not there and unable to perceive what is really there; and Nāgārjuna's conception of reality which dissolves all that exists into a Void, depriving beings and things of real existence, making cognition an instrument condemned to grasp only illusions and falseties, and positing the impossibility for normal knowledge to reach reality- given these conceptions, it was not difficult for philosophically very well trained minds, as were Buddhist thinkers, to ask themselves : if what we perceive is not outside (the realm of the object), wherefrom does it come? and to answer: from the mind (the realm of the subject). Thus they rounded an inference whose premises originated in the beginnings of Buddhism. *Only Mind* was the logically valid conclusion for a reasoning that had lasted for centuries.

The Importance of the Yogācāra School of Philosophy

The Yogācāra is one of the great philosophical schools of Mahāyāna Buddhism. It had strong influence not only in Buddhist circles[4] but also in Brahmanical currents of thought.[5] It was introduced in China, Tibet, Korea and Japan; its doctrines were cultivated and developed there. Many persons adhered to its philosophical points of view. The Yogācāra produced many first class philosophers, of deep and subtle insight, systematization hability, bold inspiration, logical rigour, who raised a great, all encompassing philosophical construction of well defined lines and firm structure. It gave rise to a huge literature, many of whose works can be considered, according to universal criteria, as philosophical masterpieces, as for instance the three treatises that this volume contains. The Yogācāra showed a great capacity for change and self-enrichment, constantly adding new tenets to the ancient ones, refining the traditional concepts, giving more subtlety to their arguments, introducing more coherence in their classifications. A major glory of the Yogācāra is that it gave rise to one of the most brilliant products of Indian genius: the Buddhist school of logic and epistemology.

Besides its philosophical activity, the Yogācāra had also a religious interest centered around the notion of Bodhisattva, the ideal of perfected man, the moral and intellectual Path he must follow, the stages he must pass through, the goals he must reach. And in this respect the Yogācāra revealed the same masterly qualities that it showed in the accomplishment of its philosophical labours.

Notes for the General Introduction

1. There are great divergencies among the different Buddhist traditions, and among modern scholars in relation to the date of birth of Buddha. Following É. Lamotte, *Histoire du Bouddhisme Indien,* Louvain: Institut Orientaliste, 1958, we have adopted the year 486 B.C.. for the *Parinirvāṇa* of Buddha and consequently the year 566 B.C. for his birth. The modern tendency is to shorten the interval between Buddha and the reign of Buddhist Emperor Aśoka (*circa* 268-233 B.C.), as shown by the papers presented in the *Symposium* on Buddha's date held in Göttingen, April 1988. On the problem of the date of Buddha's *Parinirvāṇa* and the different opinions and theories regarding it see the proceedings of that Symposium: *The Dating of the Historical Buddha, Die Datierung des historischen*

Buddha (three volumes), edited by Heinz Bechert, Göttingen: Vandenhoeck und Ruprecht, 1991-1997, and F. Tola and C.Dragonetti, "Fecha del Parinirvāṇa de Buda", in *Revista de Estudios Budistas* (México-Buenos Aires), No. 7, pp.89-106.

2. The historicity of Maitreyanātha, the teacher of Asaṅga, is not accepted by P. Démiéville, "Le Yogācārabhūmi de Saṅgharakṣa", in *Bulletin de l 'École Francaise d'Extrême Orient XLIV,* 2, 1954, pp.376-387 and 434, note 9, specially note 4 of p. 381; L. de la Vallée Poussin, *L'Abhidharmakośa,* Bruxelles: 1971, Institut Belge des Hautes Études Chinoises, Vol. 1, pp.XXV-XXVI; É. Lamotte, "Mañjuśrī", in *T 'oung Pao* 48, 1960, pp. 8-9 ; D. S. Ruegg, *La Théorie du Tathāgatagarbha et du Gotra,* Paris: Adrien Maisonneuve, 1969, pp. 50-55. The same Tucci in *Minor Buddhist Text I,* Roma: Is. M. E. O., 1956, p. 14 note 1, changes his opinion and adheres to the non-historicity, expressed by Démiéville in his quoted article.
3. For the momentariness of the *dharmas* in Mahāyāna see the *Second Part* of this book, note 59 (to the translation of the *Viṃśatikā).*
4. As it is the case of the Yogācāra-Madhyamaka school, founded by Śāntarakṣita (VIIIth century). Cf.D.Seyfort Ruegg, *The Literature of the Madhyamaka School of Philosophy,* pp.87-100.
5. For instance in the great Hindu philosopher Gauḍapāda. See V. Bhattacharya, *The Āgamaśāstra of Gauḍapāda,* Calcutta: University of Calcutta, 1943, and L. Schmithausen, "Zur Literaturgeschichte der älteren Yogācāra-Schule", p.811, note 3.

Part I

DMIGS PA BRTAG PAḤI ḤGREL PA OF PHYOGS KYI GLAṄ PO (*ĀLAMBANAPARĪKṢĀVṚTTI* OF DIGNĀGA)

To Akira Yuyama

... whereas sand can never be numbered, and who could ever count up all the joys that he hath given to others ?

Pindar, *Olympian Ode* II 98 -100,
Trans. by J. Sandys
(The Loeb Classical Library, 1915)

INTRODUCTION

Life of Dignāga[1]

Dignāga was the founder of Buddhist logic and one of the most prominent figures not only of the *Yogācāra* School, but also of Buddhist philosophy in general.[2] With Dignāga the philosophical research of the *Yogācāra* School centers itself specially in logic and theory of knowledge.

He is supposed to have lived around the years 480-540 A.D. He was born in a brahman family in South India, near Kāncī, in the present Madras Estate. He was converted to Buddhism, belonging first to the *Vātsīputrīya* School of Hīnayāna Buddhism, and then to Mahāyāna Buddhism. He was well versed in the Theravāda *Tipiṭaka*. In the Buddhist University of Nālandā (North-east India), he followed the teachings of Vasubandhu, under whose direction he studied the Hīnayāna and Mahāyāna systems, specially that of the *Yogācāra* School or *Vijñānavāda*, to which he adhered, and logic (*Nyāya*), field in which he excelled. He was the teacher of Īśvarasena, who at his turn had as his dissciple Dharmakīrti, another of the great Indian logicians. He often travelled throughout India engaging in philosophical debates with his opponents specially with brahmanic masters whom he is said to have defeated because of his mastery of logic. He was a person of very great erudition.

Works of Dignāga

To Dignāga are attributed by tradition numerous works, most part of which dealt with logic. The original Sanskrit text of many of them has not been preserved, so they are known only through Tibetan and Chinese translations. Let us indicate the most important ones with a brief bibliographical information.[3]

1. *Abhidharmamarmapradīpa*, a summary of the *Abhidharmakośa* the principal work of Vasubandhu. It is available only in its Tibetan translation (*Tōhoku* 4095=*Catalogue* 5596). Outlined *by* Hajime Sakurabe in "Jinna ni kiserareta Kusharon no

ichikōyōsho" ("An Abridgment of the Abhidhamakośa ascribed to Dignāga"), *Tōkai Bukkyō* ("Journal of the Tōkai Association of Indian and Buddhist Studies"), Nagoya, 2, 1956, pp. 33-36.

2. *Ālambanaparīkṣā*. *Cf. infra* the principal ancient and modern editions and translations of this work.
3. The hymn *Āryamañjughoṣastotra (Tōhoku* 2712=*Catalogue* 3536).
4. *Guṇāparyantastotraṭīkā (Tōhoku* 1156 and 4560=*Catalogue* 2045 and 5474), a commentary on the *Guṇāparyantastotra* of Ratnadāsa; *Guṇāparyantastotrapadakārikā or Guṇāparyantastotrārthakārikā or Guṇāparyantastotravastukārikā* (*Tōhoku* 1157 and 4561=*Catalogue* 2046 and 5475), stanzas on the above mentioned *stotra*.
5. *Hastavālanāmaprakaraṇa,* a work that has the aim of demonstrating the non-existence of empirical reality as it appears. It is ascribed to Dignāga, and also to Āryadeva.The Sanskrit original text of this work is not preserved; it is known through its Tibetan translations (the stanzas: *Tōhoku* 3844 and 3848=*Catalogue* 5244 and 5248;the commentary: *Tōhoku* 3845 and3849=*Catalogue* 5245 and 5249), and through its Chinese translations (*Taishō* 1620 and 1621). F.W. Thomas and Hakuju Ui, "The Hand Treatise", a work of Āryadeva", *Journal Of the Royal Asiatic Society,* 1918,vols. 1-2, pp. 267-310, edited a Tibetan text of this work, eclectically established on the basis of the preserved Tibetan and Chinese texts, a Sanskrit reconstruction and an English translation. J. Nagasawa in *Chizan Gakuhō* 4, 1955, pp. 46-56, published the two Chinese translations and a Japanese translation of the Tibetan translation 3849. Hakuju Ui, in *Jinna chosaku no kenkyū* ("Studies of Dignāga's Works"), 1958, pp.133-165, has a Japanese translation of the two Chinese translations. E. Frauwallner, "Dignāga, sein Werk und seine Entwicklung", 1959, pp.152-156 (=*Kleine Schriften,* pp. 828-833), edited the Tibetan text. M. Hattori also has a Japanese translation form Tibetan in "Dignāga ni okeru kashō to jitsuzai" ("Dignāga's views of saṃvṛti-sat and paramārtha-sat"), *F.A.S. Zen Institute,* 50, Kyōto, 1961, pp. 16-28. F. Tola and C. Dragonetti published in *Revista Latinoamericana de Filosofia,* Vol. III, No 2, Buenos Aires, Julio 1977, pp. 159-175 (= *Budismo Mahāyāna,* Buenos Aires: Kier, 1980, pp. 75-101) a Spanish translation from Tibetan of this work, and in *The Journal of Religious Studies,* Patiala,

Vol. VIII, 1980, No 1, pp. 18-31, and in the *Boletin de la Asociación Española de Orientalistas,* Madrid, 1985, pp. 137-156, the Tibetan text and, respectively, an English and a revised Spanish translation. Finally, they published in *Nihilismo Budista,* Mexico: Premiá, 1990, pp. 47-60, a new revised Spanish translation, and in *On Voidness. A Study on Buddhist Nihilism,* Delhi: Motilal Banarsidass, 1995, pp. 1-17, the revised Tibetan text and a new English translation of this work.

6. *Hetucakraḍamaru,* the first work on logic written by Dignāga. It is only known through its Tibetan translation (*Tōhoku* 4209= *Catalogue* 5708). The Tibetan translation has been edited by S.C. Vidyabhusana, "Hetucakrahamaru, or Dignāga's Wheel of Reasons, recovered from Labrang in Sikkim", *Journal of the Royal Asiatic Society of Bengal* 3, 1907, pp. 627 -632, by D.C. Chatterjee, "Hetucakranirṇaya", *Indian Historical Quarterly* IX, 1933, pp.266-272 and 511-514, with a Sanskrit reconstruction, and by E. Frauwallner, "Dignāga, sein Werk und seine Entwicklung", 1959, pp. 161-164 (=*Kleine Schriften,* pp. 837- 840). S. Takemura, in *Bukkyōgaku Kenkyū* ("Studies in Buddhism"), Kyōto, Vol. 8, No 9, 1953, pp. 100-110, gives a Japanese translation. R.S.Y. Chi, in *Buddhist Formal Logic,* Delhi: Motilal Banarsidass, 1984, reprint of the *Royal Asiatic Society of Great Britain's* edition of 1969, pp. XI-XII, and 2-3, has an English translation of this brief treatise.
7. *Miśrakastotra,* the 'Mixed' Hymn of Praise preserved only in Tibetan (*Tōhoku* 1150=*Catalogue* 2041). D.R. Shackleton Bailey edited the Tibetan text in *The Śatapañcāśatka of Mātṛceṭa,* Cambridge: Cambridge University Press, 1951, Appendix II, pp. 182-198. I tsing, *Nan hai ki kouei nei fa tchouan, Taishō* 2125, p. 227c 7-12 (=*A Record of the Buddhist Religion,* J. Takakusu's translation, Delhi: Munshiram Manoharlal, 1966, p. 158) refers to this poem as composed by Bodhisattva Dignāga.
8. *Nyāyamukha, Nyāyadvāra; Nyāyadvāratarkaśāstra?*, a treatise of logic, preserved only in two Chinese translations *(Taishō* 1628 and 1629). There is a Japanese translation of Hakuju Ui in *Indo tetsugaku kenkyū* (" Studies in Indian Philosophy"), V, pp. 505-694. G. Tucci published an English translation, *The Nyāyamukha of Dignāga,* Heidelberg: 1930 (Materialien zur Kunde des Buddhismus), reprint in San Francisco (U.S.A.), 1976, by Chinese Materials Center.

9. *Nyāyapraveśa*, a treatise of logic, preserved in Sanskrit, in its Chinese translation (*Taishō* 1630), and in its Tibetan translation (*Tōhoku* 4208 [translated from the Chinese version]=*Catalogue* 5707 [translated from the Chinese version] and 5706 [translated from the Sanskrit original]). The Sanskrit text was edited by A.B. Dhruva, Baroda: Oriental Institute, 1968 (2d. ed.; 1st. ed.: 1930), and reprint in Delhi: Sri Satguru, 1987, and by N.D. Mironov, "Nyāyapraveśa, I. Sanskrit text. Edited and Reconstructed", *T 'oung Pao* XXVIII, 1931, pp. 1-24. Vidhushekara Bhattacharya edited the Tibetan text in the Gaekwad's Oriental Series of Baroda under the title of *Nyāyapraveśa of Ācārya Diṅnāga,* 1927. M. Tachikawa, "A Sixth Century Manual of Indian Logic", *Journal of Indian Philosophy* 1, 1970-72, pp. 111-145, gives an English translation of this treatise. The Sanskrit text and the Tibetan translation were edited by Sempa Dorje, in Varanasi: Kendriya Ucca Tibbati Siksha Samsthana, 1983.
10. *Prajñāpāramitāpiṇḍārthasaṃgraha,* enumerates the principal subjects dealt with in the *Aṣṭasāhasrikāprajñāpāramitā,* as for instance the diverse types of "voidness" (*śūnyatā).* The Sanskrit text is preserved. There are a Tibetan translation (*Tōhoku* 3809=*Catalogue* 5207) and a Chinese translation (*Taishō* 1518). The Sanskrit text was edited by G. Tucci, in *Journal of the Royal Asiatic Society* 1947, pp. 53-75 (= *Opera Minora,* Parte II, Roma: G. Bardi, 1971, pp. 429-452) together with an English translation. In his work Tucci included the text of the Tibetan translation. E. Frauwallner edited also the Sanskrit text in "Dignāga, sein Werk und seine Entwicklung", 1959, pp. 140-144 (=*Kleine Schriften,* 1982, pp. 816-821). It was translated into Japanese by Hakuju Ui, *Jinna chosaku no kenkyū* ("Studies of Dignāga's Works"), 1958, pp. 233-329, and by M. Hattori, "Dignāga no Hannyakyō Kaishaku" ("Dignāga's interpretation of the Prajñāpāramitāsūtra"), in *Ōsaka Furitsu Daigaku Kiyō* ("Bulletin of the University of Ōsaka Prefecture"), series C. 9, 1961, pp. 119-136.
11. *Pramāṇasamuccaya,* a systematic exposition of epistemology, logic and semantics, which gathers in an unitarian whole the researches carried out by Dignāga in previous works. It contains stanzas and a commentary (*vṛtti)* by Dignāga himself. It is preserved only in its Tibetan translations (stanzas: *Tōhoku*

4203=*Catalogue* 5700; commentary: *Tōhoku* 4204=*Catalogue* 5701 and 5702). H.R. Iyengar restored into Sanskrit the first chapter: *Pramāṇasamuccaya, Chapter I, edited and restored into Sanskrit,* Mysore, 1930. Muni Jambūvijayī, in *Vaiśeṣikasūtra of Kaṇāda, with the Commentary of Candrānanda,* Baroda: Gaekwad's Oriental Series 136, 1961 (reprint 1982), pp. 169-219, restored into Sanskrit the parts of the treatise related to Vaiśeṣika and Nyāya systems, and in his edition of Mallavādin's *Dvādaśāraṃ Nayacakram,* Bhāvnagar: Śrī Jain Ātmānand Sabhā, 1966 (Part I, pp. 97-140), 1976 (Part II, pp. 607-608, 629-633, 638-640, 650-651, 728-729 [note]) restored into Sanskrit many passages of the whole treatise. H. Kitagawa, in *Indo koten ronrigaku no kenkyū-Jinna no taikei-*, 1965, edited and translated into Japanese a great part of this work (Chapters II, III, IV and VI). M. Hattori, in *Dignāga, On Perception,* Cambridge Mass.: Harvard University Press, 1968, edited and translated Chapter I of this work with an excellent commentary, and, in *The Pramāṇasamuccayavṛtti of Dignāga, with Jinendrabuddhi's Commentary. Chapter Five: Anyāpoha-parīkṣā. Tibetan Text with Sanskrit Fragments,* Kyōto: Kyōto University, No 21, 1982 (Memoirs of The Faculty of Letters), edited also Chapter V (in its two Tibetan versions) with the commentary of Jinendrabuddhi. R.P. Hayes, "Diṅnāga's Views on Reasoning *(Svārthānumāna)", Journal of Indian Philosophy,* Vol. 8,No 3, 1980, pp. 219-277, has a study on reasoning in Dignāga, and a translation of the first 25 stanzas of Chapter II, *On inference,* and in *Dignāga on the interpretation of signs,* Dordrecht-Boston: D. Reidel, 1988, includes the English translation of Chapter II and Chapter V of *Pramāṇasamuccaya.*

12. *Samantabhadracaryāpraṇidhānārthasaṃgraha (Tōhoku* 4012= *Catalogue* 5513), a commentary on the *Samantabhadracaryā-praṇidhāna,* the last chapter of the *Gaṇḍavyūhasūtra.*
13. *Sāmānyalakṣaṇaparīkṣā* (or *Sarvalakṣaṇadhyānaśāstrakārikā, Nanjio* 1229), a short and difficult treatise on logic preserved only in an incomplete Chinese translation *(Taishō* 1623). I tsing, *Nan hai ki kouei nei fa tchouan, Taishō* 2125, note of I tsing in the beginning of p.230 a (=*A Record of the Buddhist Religion,* p. 186), mentions it among the eight treatises on logic by Dignāga.

14. *Traikālyaparīkṣā* or *Trikālaparīkṣā*, deals with some aspects of the theory of knowledge. This work has 33 stanzas. It has been preserved in its Tibetan translation (*Tōhoku* 4207= *Catalogue* 5705). It constitutes an imitation of the verses 53-87 of the chapter *Saṃbandhasamuddeśa* of Bhartṛhari's *Vākyapadīya* (W. Rau ed., Wiesbaden: F. Steiner, 1977, pp. 122-126. Cf. Frauwallner's edition of Dignāga's text for the correspondence between both works.

The differences between the work of Bhartṛhari and that of Dignāga are not many. Among the principal ones let us mention that Dignāga adds, as a first stanza, a stanza in which he affirms the non-existence of the three times; he leaves aside the stanzas 64 (63), 74-75 (72-73), 87 (85) of Bhartṛhari; he adds at the end two stanzas, that are the imitation of other two stanzas that can also be attributed to Bhartṛhari, probably taken from another work of this same author, the lost *Śabdadhātusamīkṣā,* and cited by the same Bhartṛihari at the end of his *vṛtti* to the first *kārikā* of the first chapter of his *Vākyapadīya* (M. Biardeau's edition, Paris: Publications de l' Institut de Civilisation Indienne, 1964, pp. 26 and 28, and E. Frauwallner, "Dignāga und anderes", in *Festschrift für Moriz Winternitz,* Leipzig, 1933, p.237=*Kleine Schriften* of Frauwallner, p.484); and, finally, he puts *vijñāna* (consciousness) in the place of (Bhartṛhari's) *Brahman* in stanza 33, the last one of his treatise. Frauwallner, in "Dignāga, sein Werk und seine Entwicklung", pp. 145-152 (=*Kleine Schriften,* pp. 821-828), gives the text of the Tibetan translation, together with the correspondent stanzas of Bhartṛhari. M. Hattori, "Dignāga oyobi sono shūhen no nendai" ("The Date of Dignāga and his milieu"), in *Tsukamoto Hakushi Shōju Kinen Bukkyō Shigaku Ronshū* ("Essays on the History of Buddhism presented to Professor Zenryu Tsukamoto on his retirement from The Research Institute for Humanistic Studies"), Kyōto: Kyōto University, 1961, pp. 79-96, translates this work into Japanese (pp. 13-18).

15. *Upādāyaprajñaptiprakaraṇa* or *Prajñaptihetusaṃgrahaśāstra,* develops the thesis that things only exist as mere conventional denominations (*prajñaptisat),* but not with a real existence. It is preserved only in a Chinese translation (*Taishō* 1622). H. Kitagawa, "A Study of a short philosophical treatise ascribed

to Dignāga", in *Indo Koten ronrigaku no kenkyū, Jinna no taikei* ("A Study of Classical Indian Logic. The System of Dignāga"), 1965, appendix A. II (first published in *Sino-Indian Studies,* Vol. 5, 1957, Nos. 3-4, pp. 126-138, has an abridged English translation of this work. Hakuju Ui, *Jinna chosaku no kenkyū,* pp. 167-231, has a Japanese translation. I tsing, *Nan hai ki kouei nei fa tchouan, Taishō* 2125, note of I tsing in the beginning of p. 230 a, mentions it among the eight treatises of Dignāga that should be studied by the priest who: "wishes to distinguish himself in the study of logic".

16. *Yogāvatāra,* a small treatise on the practice of Yoga from an idealistic perspective. The Sanskrit text is available. There is a Tibetan translation (*Tōhoku* 4074 and 4539=*Catalogue* 5453 and 5575). The Sanskrit text has been edited by Vidhushekara Bhattacharya, *Indian Historical Quarterly* IV, 1928, pp.775-778. It was also edited by Frauwallner, "Dignāga, sein Werk und seine Entwicklung", pp. 144-145 (=*Kleine Schriften,* pp.820-821). It was translated into Japanese by M. Hattori in "Dignāga no Hannyakyō kaishaku", pp. 135-136. This work of Dignāga is included in the *Yogāvatāropadeśa* of Dharmendra of which only the Tibetan translation is available (*Tōhoku* 4075 and 4544=*Catalogue* 5458 and 5576). D. Chatterji, "The Yogāvatāropadeśa, A Mahāyāna treatise on yoga by Dharmendra", published the Tibetan translation of this work together with a Sanskrit restoration of the same and an English translation in *Journal and Proceedings, Asiatic Society of Bengal, new series,* Vol. XXIII, 1927, pp. 249-259.

Authenticity of the works attributed to Dignāga

In regard to the authenticity of the works attributed to Dignāga by tradition, it seems to us that this tradition must be accepted as valid, as long as sound arguments against the attribution are not adduced. According to this criterion we think that the *Hastavālanāmaprakaraṇa* must be eliminated from the list of works written by Dignāga taking into account the reasons we have expressed in the introduction to our mentioned editions of the treatise. Likewise the same must to be done in regard to *Nyāyapraveśa* considering the arguments adduced by Dhruva in his edition of the work. The learned editor of this text considers that this treatise was not composed by Dignāga but by Śaṅkarasvāmin.

The Ālambanaparīkṣā

The *Ālambanaparīkṣā* is one of the most important texts not only of Dignāga but of the Yogācāra School of Buddhism in general. This work together with Vasubandhu's *Viṃśatikā* and *Triṃśikā* are fundamental texts of the Yogācāra School; in them we find expounded the principal philosophical tenets of the school, centered around the thesis of the sole existence of consciousness, the thesis of "being as consciousness".

In relation to the *Ālambanaparīkṣā*, its authenticity affirmed by tradition can be accepted as there are no reasons to deny it.

Editions and/or Translations of *Ālambanaparīkṣā* and of its Commentaries

The small treatise *Ālambanaparīkṣā,* which contains 8 *kārikās* and their *vṛtti,* both composed by Dignāga, has not been preserved in Sanskrit. There is a Tibetan translation of the *kārikās* and another of the *vṛtti: Tōhoku* 4205 (*kārikās*) and 4206 (*vṛtti*)=*Catalogue* 5703 and 5704. There are also two Chinese translations of the *kārikās* with the *vṛtti: Taishō* 1619 and 1624 (cf. Nanjio 1172 and 1173, *Répertoire,* p.137).

Besides Dignāga's own commentary two more commentaries have been preserved: one by Dharmapāla, incomplete and only in its Chinese version: *Taishō* 1625 (cf. Nanjio 1174, *Répertoire,* pp.137-138), and another by Vinītadeva, complete and only in its Tibetan version: *Tōhoku* 4241=*Catalogue* 5739.

There are several modern editions and translations of this treatise and its commentaries. We mention some of them:

S. Yamaguchi, "Dignāga, Examen de l' objet de la connaissance. (*Ālambanaparīkṣā*) Textes Tibétain et Chinois et traduction des stances et du commentaire. Eclaircissements et notes d 'aprés le commentaire tibétain de Vinītadeva (en collaboration avec Henriette Meyer)", in *Journal Asiatique,* Janvier-Mars 1929, pp. 1-65.

E. Frauwallner, "Dignāgas Ālambanaparīkṣā. Text, Ubersetzung und Erläuterungen", *Wiener Zeitschrift für die Kunde Morgenlandes* 37, 1930, pp.174-194 (=*Kleine Schriften,* pp.340-360). It includes the Tibetan text of the treatise together with a German translation and an exposition of its contents.

M. Schott, *Sein als Bewusstsein. Ein Beitrag zur Mahāyāna-Philosophie,* Heidelberg: Carl Winters Universitätsbuchhandlung (Materialien zur Kunde des Buddhismus, 20. Heft), 1935. In its second part: B. *Ālambanaparīkṣāśāstravyākhyā,* it contains a German translation of the incomplete Chinese version of Dharmapāla's commentary, in which there are included the *kārikās* of Dignāga's treatise. The title of M. Schott's book inspired us for the title of this book.

N. Aiyaswami Sastri, *Ālambanaparīkṣā and Vṛtti by Diṅnāga. With the Commentary of Dharmapāla. Restored into Sanskrit from the Tibetan and Chinese Versions and edited with English Translations and Notes and with copious extracts from Vinītadeva's Commentary,* Adyar-Madras: The Adyar Library, 1942. It contains also the romanized Tibetan version of the text.

S. Yamaguchi and J. Nozawa, *Seshin Yuishiki no genten kaimei* ("Textual Studies of Vasubandhu's Treatise on Vijñaptimātratā"), Kyōto: Hōzōkan, 1953, pp. 409-484. It includes the Japanese translation of the treatise (*kārikās* and *vṛtti),* and of Vinītadeva's commentary, and, as an appendix, the Tibetan text and a reconstruction of the Sanskrit original text.

H. Ui, *Jinna chosaku no kenkyū* ("Studies on Dignāga's works"), Tōkyō, 1958, pp. 23-132. It includes the annotated Japanese translation of the two Chinese versions of Dignāga's *kārikās* and of Dharmapāla's commentary, together with an extensive study.

E. Frauwallner, "Dignāga, sein Werk und seine Entwicklung", *Wiener Zeitschrift für die Kunde Süd-und Ost-Asiens 3,* 1959, pp. 157-161 (=*Kleine Schriften,* pp. 833-837), contains the Tibetan text with some Sanskrit fragments of the *kārikās and vṛtti* of Dignāga.

A. K. Chatterjee, *Readings on Yogācāra Buddhism,* Varanasi: Banaras Hindu University, 1971, pp. 40-42. It has a Sanskrit translation of the *Ālambanaparīkṣā.*

A. Wayman, "Yogācāra and the Buddhist Logicians", *The Journal of the International Association of Buddhist Studies,* Vol. 2, No. 1, 1979, pp. 65-78. It has an English translation of the *kārikās.*

F. Tola and C. Dragonetti, "Ālambanaparīkṣā. Investigación sobre el 'Punto de apoyo' del conocimiento (Estrofas y Comentario) de Dignāga", in *Boletīn de la Asociación Española de Orientalistas,* XVI, Madrid, 1980, pp. 91-126 (=*El Idealismo Budista,* México: Premiá, 1989, pp. 21-55, a revised version of the previous article without the Tibetan text); and "Dignāga's Ālambanaparīkṣāvṛtti", in *Journal of Indian Philosophy* 10, 1982, pp. 105-134. The articles of 1980 and 1982 contain an edition of the Tibetan text and, respectively, a Spanish and an English translation of the Treatise.

Now in this book they offer a completely revised, corrected and augmented version of their work on *Ālambanaparīkṣāvṛtti* of Dignāga.

Some Fragments of the *Ālambanaparīkṣā* Preserved in Sanskrit, in Quotations by Other Authors

Kārikā 1 *a-d.* Kamalaśīla, *ad Tattvasaṅgraha* 2081-2083, II, p. 711 (ed. Bauddha Bharati Series-2, Varanasi, 1968), with a small variant (*grāhyāṃśaḥ*: "a part of the object", instead of *phra. rab. rdul. dag*: "the atoms"):

yady apīndriyavijñapter grāhyāṃśaḥ karaṇaṃ bhavet/
atadābhatayā tasyā nākṣavad viṣayaḥ sa tu//

Kārikā 6 *a-d.* Kamalaśīla, *ad Tattvasaṅgraha, ibidem*, II, p. 710 (quoted ed.):

yad antarjñeyarūpaṃ tu bahirvad avabhāsate /
so 'rtho vijñānarūpatvāt tatpratyayatayāpi ca //

Kārikā 6 *a-b.* Śaṅkara, *Bhāṣya* of the *Brahmasūtras*, p.548, line 9 (ed. Nirṇaya Sāgar Press, Bombay, 1938):

yad antarjñeyarūpaṃ tad bahirvad avabhāsate /

Vṛtti (partial) of kārikā 7b. Kamalaśīla, *ibidem*, II, p.710 (quoted ed.):

atha vā śaktyarpaṇāt krameṇāpi so 'rthāvabhāsaḥ svānurūpakāryotpattaye śaktiṃ vijñānācāraṃ karotīty avirodhaḥ.

Adopted Text

For our work we have adopted the text of the Tibetan translation of the *Sde-dge* edition of the *Tibetan Buddhist Canon: Bstan-ḥgyur, Tshad-ma*, Ce. 86 a[5]-87 b[2] (*Tōhoku* 4206). In some places, that we indicate in notes, we have for clearness sake preferred either the readings of the *Peking* edition: *Bstan-ḥgyur*, Vol. 130, *Mdo-ḥgrel (Tshad-ma)* XCV, 73-2-5 up to 73-5-4, pp. 177 b[5]-179 a[3] (*Catalogue* 5704) or the readings of Vinītadeva's commentary, according to the *Sde-dge* edition: *Bstan-ḥgyur, Tshad-ma*, She. 175 a[3]-187 b[5] (*Tōhoku* 4241) and/or *Peking* edition: *Bstan-ḥgyur*, Vol. 138, *Mdo-ḥgrel* (*Tshad-ma*) CXII, 45-5-7 up to 51-4-7, pp. 183 a[7]-197 b[7] (*Catalogue* 5739).

The Tibetan title of the work is *Dmigs pa brtag paḥi ḥgrel pa* which corresponds exactly to the Sanskrit *Ālambanaparīkṣāvṛtti*.

The translation into Tibetan was done by the pandit Śāntākaragupta and the lotsava Tshul-khrims rgyal-mtshan according to the *Sde-dge* edition. The Tibetan translation is excellent because of its clearness and conciseness; we perceive, by its mere reading, that it is an extremely faithful version of the lost Sanskrit text; this impression is corroborated by the comparison of the fragments preserved in Sanskrit with the corresponding parts of it.

We have divided the text into sections with subtitles. And we have adopted the same procedure in the translation and in our commentary on the text.

DOCTRINARY COMMENTARY OF *ĀLAMBANAPARĪKṢĀVṚTTI*

Previous Remarks

Let us begin indicating that Dignāga himself gives in paragraph 2 the definition of the "object of cognition" (*yul* in Tibetan, *viṣaya* in Sanskrit), term that appears in *kārikā I c;* and that he gives in paragraph 5 the definition of "support of cognition" (*dmigs-pa* in Tibetan, *ālambana* in Sanskrit), term that appears in the first paragraph.

The definition of "object of cognition" is the following one: something is object of the cognition when 1. its own being[4] is grasped with certainty by the cognition, 2. because the cognition comes forth appearing under the form[5] of that own being.

The definition of "support of cognition" is the following one: something is support of the cognition when 1. that thing produces a cognition, 2. which appears under the form of that thing. In this way that thing is the determining condition of the cognition.

Both terms indicate very similar concepts. In both definitions we find the agreement between the *thing* (to which the cognition refers) and the *representation* (which is produced in the mind).

Any thing, whose own being is not grasped, as it happens with the atoms (see *Section II, kārikā I a-d,* and paragraphs 2 and 3, in the translation and in our commentary), cannot be object of a cognition.

And whatever cannot be the object of a cognition, it cannot be its support—as it happens with the atoms, because there is no agreement between the *thing* (of atomic size) and any *representation* in the mind (of not atomic size).

Any inexistent thing, to which cannot be attributed an own being that could be grasped and which as such cannot be the cause of anything, as it happens with the second moon (see *Section III, kārikā II b,* and paragraph 7), cannot be support of the cognition.

And whatever cannot be the support of a cognition, cannot be its object—as it happens with the second moon, because it is not possible that there be an agreement between any *representation* in the mind and an *inexistent thing,* and also because an inexistent thing cannot be a cause of knowledge. See paragraphs 3 and 7 of the treatise and our commentary thereon, where the relation between "support" and "object" of cognition is indicated.

Section I: Paragraph 1

Paragraph 1 expresses the realistic position of the atomists, Hindus or Buddhists[6]: there are external objects which act as support for the sensorial cognition. According to this realistic position the support must be either the atoms or the conglomerates or aggregates formed by those atoms.

Section II: kārikā I a-d and paragraphs 2-3

This section refers to the first alternative.

Paragraph 2 contains the definition of the object of cognition, which we have given in the *Previous remarks* of our commentary.

Dignāga accepts, in *kārikā I a-b* and in paragraph 3, that the atoms could be the cause of the sensorial cognition, considering that a cognitive act or process originates in the mind of a person only because the atoms are in front of him. If in front of that person there were no atoms, there could not be things, that are objects of knowledge, and no knowledge could be produced. The atoms are in this way a determining condition of that cognition, in the same way as the sense organs are, the sense organs without which there could not be a cognitive act or process. But the atoms are not the object of the cognition because of the reasons that are formulated in *kārikā I c-d* and in paragraph 3.

Kārikā I c-d expresses that the atoms are not the object of cognition, because the representation that is produced in the mind does not correspond to the own being of the atoms. The atoms are not perceived, they are not the object of knowledge, although this one is originated through the concealed presence (we can say) of the atoms. They collaborate as a cause in the arising of cognition, in the same way as the sense organs, which nevertheless are not the objects of cognition.

Paragraph 3 expresses that the atoms do not agree with the definition of object of knowledge ("they are not thus"), of course because of the fact indicated in *kārikā I c-d* referred to in the previous paragraph.

Paragraph 3 ends indicating that the atoms cannot be the cognition's support. And this is right, because something that cannot be the object of a cognition cannot be the support of the same, as we have already said in the *Previous remarks* of this commentary.

Section III: Kārikā II a-b and Paragraphs 4-7
In paragraphs 4-7 and in *kārikā II a-b* Dignāga examines the second alternative which considers the conglomerates or aggregates of atoms as the cognition's support.

Dignāga gives in paragraph 5 the definition of support of cognition, to which we have referred in the *Previous remarks* of this commentary.

The conglomerate fulfills only the second of the two requirements of the definition, since, in the conglomerate's case, the cognition appears under the form of, i.e. bears the representation of a conglomerate (paragraph 4 and *kārikā* II at the end), but does not comply with the first requirement. In fact, the cognition of a conglomerate does not proceed from a conglomerate (*kārikā II a*); a conglomerate is not the cause of the conglomerate's cognition (paragraph 7 at the end), simply because a conglomerate does not exist (*kārikā II b* and paragraph 7 at the end)[7] and we must understand that something that is inexistent cannot be the cause of anything else.

In *kārikā II b* and in paragraph 7 Dignāga presents, as a case similar to the conglomerate's one, the case of the second moon which is perceived, instead of a single moon, owing to a defect of the eyes, and he explains that it cannot be the object of the cognition. Although the present section centers on the notion of *"support of cognition"*, nevertheless Dignāga concludes that the second moon cannot be the *object* of the cognition. We have also here the relation of both concepts. And, as we have already indicated in the *Previous remarks* of this commentary, the second moon cannot be the cognition's support, not only because it is not the object of the cognition (since it has not an own being that can be grasped), but also because something inexistent, as it is, cannot be the cause of anything else.

Another example will help to a better understanding of Dignāga's thought. We see a compact and dark mass, a forest, because our vision has not sufficient power to penetrate up to the trees, trunks, branches and leaves, which are the only (relatively) real thing in this case, and which are what we perceive under the appearance of a compact and dark mass. The compact and dark mass does not exist as such; we perceive it only owing to a deficiency, a weakness of our vision. The same thing happens with the conglomerate formed by atoms. The real thing in this case are the atoms; the conglomerate is only a construction of our mind, something unreal, due to the deficiency, the weakness of our sight, which cannot reach up to the atoms.

See in *Section VI* some other examples that illustrate the non-existence of the conglomerate as such.

Section IV: kārikā II c-d and paragraph 8

This section presents the conclusion that has been reached up to now: nothing external can be the object of the perception; neither the atoms nor the conglomerate can be *support* of the cognition, because they do not fulfill the two requirements indicated by the definitions of the terms "object" and "support"; each one fulfills only one of the two requirements. The atom can be the cognition's remote cause, but the cognition does not bear the representation of an atom; and as to the conglomerate, although in the mind a conglomerate's image is formed, nevertheless a conglomerate is not the cause of that cognition, because it does not exist.

Section V: kārikās III a-d and IV a-b and paragraphs 9-12

In *kārikā III a-d* and in paragraphs 9-11 a new thesis is presented from a realistic position in order to save the conglomerate as the cognition's object. This thesis affirms that the atoms possess the "nature of cause", that is to say: the capacity to produce a cognition that "appears under the form [not of themselves, but] of a conglomerate" (paragraph 10). Since the only thing that really exists are the atoms and the existence of conglomerates formed by them is not accepted, the capacity to give rise to a cognition that bears the representation of a conglomerate is attributed not to the conglomerates (because they are inexistent) but to the atoms that exist. Consequently we must understand that, when *kārikā III a-b* refers to "the forms of conglomerate", presenting them as the efficient cause of a conglomerate's cognition, it is referring to the conglomerate's forms that belong to the atom.

Those who hold the thesis that the atom possesses the indicated capacity, argue that all the objects, including of course the atom itself, possess several forms, several aspects under which they present themselves to us (paragraph 9). We grasp one or another of those forms. For instance, the solidity of something, even if it exists, is not an object of the visual perception (paragraph 11), which on the contrary grasps other forms or aspects of that thing. Consequently, there is no contradiction between the fact that the conglomerate's form that the atom possesses, and under which it can manifest itself, is grasped, and the fact that its atomicity (i.e., its infinitely small spheric form) is not grasped. When *kārikā III c-d* refers to the form of the atoms, it is referring to the atomicity of the atoms, as we see by paragraph 11.

According to Dignāga's opponent the atom would have among its forms, first, its "atomicity", its infinitely small spheric form, and secondly its conglomerate's form, which allows it to produce a conglomerate's representation in the mind. The atom in itself, isolated, cannot be grasped because of its infinitely small size; in other words, its " atomicity" which is one of its aspects, is not perceptible, even if it exists; in other conditions, as for instance if we had a more powerful sight, the atom could be an object of visual perception. Something similar happens with the conglomerate's form of the atom, which is another of its aspects of manifestation: normally, when the atom is isolated, this conglomerate's form is not perceived; in order that it be, it is necessary some special conditions: the atoms must be united, connected and then, and only then, the atom appears under its conglomerate's form and produces in the mind a conglomerate's representation.

We can therefore think according to the indicated arguments that the atom is the cognition's support, because it is something which produces a cognition that bears the representation of one of its forms, of one of the aspects under which it can present itself to us.

In *kārikā IV a -b* and in paragraph 12 Dignāga refutes the previous thesis. He only says that, even if the atoms have really the capacity to produce a conglomerate's representation in the mind, nevertheless there could not be different representations as, for instance, a representation of a cup and another representation of a vessel. Since the atoms notwithstanding their number are all identical, they would produce in all the cases the representation of the same conglomerate, without the specific differences, as those which distinguish a vessel from a cup. It could be said that atoms would produce the representation of *conglomerate* and nothing else, i.e., of an abstract unspecified conglomerate, which is something that does not exist.

Section VI: kārikās IV c-d and V a-b and paragraphs 13-15

In *kārikā IV c*, completed by paragraph 13, we have a new position in defence of realism. According to this position there is a difference in the perceptions of a vessel, of a cup, etc., because among the vessel, the cup, etc. there is a difference, which originates in the differences of the respective forms of each part of the vessel, the cup, etc., as the neck, the basis, etc. In other words the differences of the parts produce the differences of the things to which they belong, and the differences of the perceptions of the parts produce the differences of the perceptions of the things.

With this position the opponent tries to eliminate the objection of Dignāga that the images of all the conglomerates, produced by the conglomerate form possessed by the atoms (as maintained by the opponent in the previous section), would be all identical.

Dignāga, in the last line of paragraph 13, in *kārikās IV d* and *V a-b,* and in paragraphs 14-15, refutes the opponent's position expressing that it is possible to admit that the differences among the vessel, the cup, etc., produced (as the opponent thinks) by the differences of their parts, exist; but nevertheless these differences do not exist in the atoms, which are the only real thing and the last part of every thing (according to the atomistic thesis), because all atoms are spheric and there is not diversity among them; these differences among the vessel, the cup, etc. exist therefore only in the vessel, in the cup, etc., which exist only by human convention.

The right, curved or wavy surface or line, etc., which distinguish the parts of the vessel, the cup, etc., are not found in the atoms, since they have all the same form, even if they are made of different matter (earth, fire, etc.); they are found in the objects themselves which are unreal, which exist only by convention, as Dignāga will explain in the next paragraph.

Some examples may illustrate the previous explanations. With identical and square bricks we can build walls that have right, curved or wavy surfaces or lines; these surfaces or lines are not in the bricks but in the walls built with them.

Let us mark in a white sheet of paper black points, forming squares, rectangles, etc. Each black point will produce in our mind the image of a black point and nothing else. The images produced by each black point will be all of them identical among themselves. The squares, rectangles, etc. we see are not in the atoms, they are only in our mind owing to the special nature of our senses. If our senses were stronger, we could see the atoms in themselves, and the squares, rectangles, etc. would disappear-in the same way as the compact and dark mass, the forest, disappears, as we come nearer to it.

We can approach Dignāga's thought from another point of view. The realist opponent has argued that the differences among the parts produce the differences of the things. We may ask now: What produces the differences among the parts (which must be considered as wholes in relation to their sub-parts)?, and the answer of the opponent would have to be: The differences of the sub-parts (parts of the parts) produce the differences of the parts, and, at their turn, the differences of the parts of the sub-parts produce the differences of the sub-parts, and so, successively and gradually, we reach the atoms which constitute the last part of all.

But atoms are all identical among themselves, all of them are of infinitely small size and of spherical form, there is not among them any difference. Then the atoms, which do not possess any difference among them, cannot produce real differences among the sub-parts that they produce by their union; and, at their turn, these sub-parts, which as a consequence of what has been said have not real differences among them, cannot either produce real differences among the parts that they produce by their union. And thus, successively and gradually, following in an inverse direction the path we have done, we reach the total and last conglomerate, which cannot show any difference in relation to other conglomerates, to which the same reasoning can be applied. The atoms, which by their union produce all the conglomerates, are devoid of specific differences, of really existing differences which the atoms could transmit to the entities they produce by their union.

Consequently, the differences we perceive among the conglomerates or things cannot really exist, as they do not exist in the only really existing entities which are the atoms (according to the atomist opponent); thus they must be mere creations of our subjectivity, of our senses, of our mind, and we attribute them, as really existing, to those things.

When Dignāga says that the differences among things are only in the things that have a conventional existence, he is asserting the illusory, mental, unreal nature of those things.

Section VII: kārikā V c-d and paragraphs 16-17

Kārikā V c -d and paragraph 17 explain why the vessel, the cup, etc. exist only by convention: if we eliminate the atoms whose union gives rise to the vessel, the cup, etc., the cognition of the vessel, the cup, etc. comes to an end. What is conventional (as for instance the conglomerate) depends on its parts, is conditioned by them, does not exist without them. On the contrary, says paragraph 17, the cognition of something really existent does not end, even if we eliminate anything that is connected with it[8], for instance the color etc., in other words even if we eliminate all attributes, qualities, etc. that inhere in it.

The idea of Dignāga is that a really existent thing is a thing that exists independently of anything as, for instance, parts (in other words a really existing thing is *one*) and whatever is connected with it; and a conventionally existent thing is a thing that does not exist independently of its parts and of all that is connected with it, and consequently ceases to be when these parts, etc. disappear.

Section VIII: paragraph 18

Dignāga concludes expressing in paragraph 18 that thus the objects of sensorial perception do not exist outside the subject of cognition, since the two only forms of existence for an external thing: atoms and conglomerates, have been discarded as objects of cognition.

In this way ends the first part of the treatise, which aims at refuting realism, showing the impossibility that something external be the cognition's object. Dignāga's approach is an epistemological one: he is interested in the nature of the *object of knowledge*.

In *kārikās VI, VII* and *VIII* and their respective commentaries (paragraphs 19 -28), Dignāga will explain his own idealist thesis, will show how cognition is produced with absolute absence of an external object, only by the internal dynamism of consciousness, and will establish the nature of the object of cognition. Dignāga's explanation fills the void left by the rejection of the realist thesis.

Section IX: kārikā VI a-d and paragraphs 19-20

Kārikā VI a-d and paragraphs 19-20 expound the mechanism of the cognitive act according to Dignāga. We have in our mind representations, ideas, images of a world that appears to us as external and that we consider as real. These representations include visual sensations (images: form and colour), taste, smell, acustic and tact sensations. What Dignāga, in *kārikā VI a-d,* calls "knowable internal form"[9] are these representations.

Let us reflect upon what happens during the sleep: we have oniric representations or dreams (visual sensations, etc.) to which nothing corresponds outside. These oniric representations are also " knowable internal forms". For Dignāga the representations that occur during the wakeful state are of the same nature and characteristics as those produced during the sleep: they lack a corresponding external object.

In *Section XIII* we shall see which is the mechanism that produces in our mind those knowable internal forms which appear during our wakeful hours, even if there is not an external object corresponding to them. For the moment let us say that the knowable internal forms, constituted by the representations, come forth in the mind during the wakeful state due, not to the fact that there is an external object that impresses the mind, but to the reactualization of the "marks" (*vāsanā)* that all experience leaves in the mind, in the same way as the knowable internal forms, constituted by dreams, come forth in the mind due to the reactualization of impressions that one had during the wakeful state.

This knowable internal form is the object (*don)* of the cognition (*kārikā* VI *a-c*). The commentary (paragraph 19), expresses that it is the *dmigs paḥi rkyen*, "(that) determining condition which is the support of the cognition". A cognition requires the existence of several determining conditions; one of these is the support of the cognition. The knowable internal form is the support of the cognition, because it fulfills the two requirements indicated by the definition of "support of cognition" given in paragraph 5: the cognition comes forth having as its contents that knowable internal form, bearing its representation (*kārikā VI c-d* and paragraph 20), and comes forth having it as its cause. What precedes becomes clear if we examine what happens with the oniric representations or dreams, which are also, as already said, "knowable internal forms". An oniric representation or dream occurs in the mind due to the reactualization of an impression one has had before during the wakeful state. That representation has no corresponding external object. That oniric representation is the cause of the oniric cognition: one "sees" that oniric representation, because it comes forth in the mind due to some psychological causes, if these psychological causes did not exist, the oniric representation would not occur and one would not have the corresponding oniric cognition. And the oniric representation (produced by the mentioned psychological causes) and the oniric cognition exactly correspond each other: what one cognizes is nothing else than the oniric representation that comes forth in the mind. All these remarks apply to the mechanism of cognition during the wakeful state.

Section X: kārikā VII a-b and paragraphs 21-23

Paragraph 21 adduces an objection attributed to a realist opponent: the knowable internal form (produced by the reactualization of the marks *(vāsanā)* left in the mind by previous impressions) cannot be the determining condition of the cognition, since it is a part of that cognition, a part which does not exist before the cognition is produced, and which comes forth together with the cognition. For the opponent the cognition depends on an object that pre-exists the cognition itself, that exists apart from the cognition, that impresses the mind giving rise to a mental representation which agrees with the form or own being of the object. In this way such an object can be the determining condition of the cognition.

Kārikā VII a-b and paragraphs 22-23 refute this objection adopting two alternatives: the first one considers the *simultaneous* arising of the knowable internal form and of the cognition; the second one considers the *consecutive* arising firstly of the knowable internal form and secondly of the cognition.

With reference to the first alternative, Dignāga (*kārikā VII a* and paragraph 22) says that there is no difficulty to accept that the knowable internal form (which is the determining condition of the cognition) be born together with that cognition, since, according to logicians, the characteristic of the relation cause-effect is "the concomitance of being and not-being"[10] even if the cause comes forth in the first place and the effect in the second place (as it is the case with the second alternative which will be dealt with afterwards). The meaning of this expression is the following one: if the cause exists, the effect also exists; if the cause does not exist, the effect does not exist. We find this necessary dependence even in our present case: if the knowable internal form exists, there is cognition; if the knowable internal form does not exist, there is not cognition.

Then Dignāga, in *kārikā VII b* and in paragraph 23, deals with the second alternative: the consecutive arising firstly of the knowable internal form, which is the cause, and then of the cognition which is the effect. Dignāga expresses that in this case also there is no difficulty, because the representation of any object leaves in the consciousness a virtuality, a "seed", which produces (as cause) the arising of another similar representation (as effect).

To understand paragraph 23 it is necessary to make a reference to the theory of the *vāsanās* (this term literally means: "impregnation by a scent") or of the *bījas* ("seeds")[11]. According to this theory (which is accepted both by Buddhists and Hindus and which reminds us of the modern theory of subconsciousness) every experience, as for instance a cognition, leaves after itself in the consciousness (in the subconsciousness) a trace, a mark, in other words a *virtuality* as Dignāga says. This virtuality, when the appropriate conditions are given, actualizes itself giving rise to a new similar representation.

Let us add to this explanation that the object of the cognition has not to be necessarily an external object, an object really existent. It can be (and for the *Yogācāras* it always is) an internal object, an illusory object that is a mere mental creation. The cognition or representation of this illusory object leaves also in the mind a virtuality from which comes forth a new representation similar to the previous one. It is not necessary that the object of the representations in the series representation-virtuality-representation, etc. be real external objects; they may also be (and for Dignāga they actually are) internal mental creations. For the *Yogācāras* the only thing that has existed are representations of unreal, internal, mental objects (as in dreams, hallucinations, etc.) which left virtualities that at their turn gave birth to new representations of unreal, internal, mental objects. And this process comes from a beginningless eternity. See *Section M*.

When the text speaks of the consecutive arising, we must understand, as it is seen by the preceding explanation, that it is referring to the consecutive arising, at a first time, of the virtuality (left by a previous cognitive experience, and which contains in itself, in a latent, potential state, the knowable internal form, that will be the contents of the new cognition which will come forth when the virtuality is reactualized) and, at a second time, of the cognition (which is the effect of the actualization of that virtuality). It is possible to say that the knowable internal form, which exists in a virtual state in the consciousness from the moment that the previous representation is produced, precedes the cognition whose object it (= the knowable internal form) is. But, we must have in mind that if the *creation* of the virtuality in the mind *precedes* the cognition, the *reactualization* of that virtuality is simultaneous with the cognition, to which it gives rise.

We have said before that Dignāga conceives the knowable internal forms as having the nature of dream images. Let us add now (using the same analogy of the dream) that in the same form as many dream images originate in the dreamer's mind owing to the reactivation of impressions which he had during his wakeful hours, so also the knowable internal forms come forth as an actualization of the marks (which Dignāga calls "virtualities") impressed in the consciousness by previous experiences. The only difference between both processes is that the impressions that are reactualized would have, for Western thought, as their limit *a quo* one own's birth, while the virtualities referred to by Dignāga come from the previous lives, according to the Indian postulate of the reincarnation.

Section XI: kārikā VII c-d and paragraphs 24-25

In paragraph 24 Dignāga presents the following objection that could be raised from the traditional Buddhist theory of perception: if only the (knowable) internal form-colour[12] is the determining condition, the support of cognition, how would it be possible that visual cognition (or any other sensorial cognition) be born depending only on the internal form (visual sensations, etc.) and on the eye (or on any other sense-organ) ? The Buddhist theory of knowledge taught that visual cognition, etc. are produced depending on the object, on the eye, etc[13]. If there is *only* the knowable internal form, which can be grasped solely by mind, the consequence is that the eye, etc. have no function to fulfill in the cognition process. The Buddhist theory referred to before, generally accepted, is thus left aside.

Dignāga answers this objection in *kārikā VII c-d* and in paragraph 25 manifesting that the senses are only collaborating faculties; that from their effect it can be concluded that they are the form of the virtuality, and that they are not composed by material elements.

We must understand these affirmations of Dignāga in the following way. The senses are not material entities, but only powers, faculties which collaborate, together with the cognition's object, in the production of the cognitive act. From the effect produced by the senses, i.e., from the sensorial cognition, we cannot infer necessarily that the senses are something made up of material elements. The only thing that we can conclude is that they are the from of the virtuality. As we have said, every representation leaves in consciousness a virtuality which produces a new representation similar to the previous one. These virtualities must have different forms, they must belong to different classes. The virtuality left by a representation produced by a visual perception will be different from the virtuality produced by an auditive perception, and so on in the other cases related to any one of the other senses. From a generic point of view all will be virtualities; from a specific point of view one virtuality will be visual virtuality, another will be auditive virtuality, and so on. The visual virtuality will actualize itself producing a visual cognition, the auditive virtuality will actualize itself producing an auditive cognition, and so on.

If all the representations leave only *in abstracto, in genere* virtualities, then, when they are reactualized, they would produce only *in abstracto, in genere* cognitions, nothing else, without the visual, auditive, etc. specification. But when a cognitive act is produced, it presents itself as visual, auditive, etc. and never *in abstracto*. If we do not accept the division of virtualities into visual virtualities, etc., we could not explain how from identical virtualities we have different cognitions. But if we accept that the virtualities left by previous representations are visual, auditive, etc., then we understand that the cognitions, which they produce, are visual, auditive, etc.

For Dignāga, according to what has been said, the senses are nothing else than the forms assumed by the virtualities when they are reactualized, and become acts of cognition.

Section XII: kārikā VIII a and paragraph 26

In ***kārikā VIII a*** and in paragraph 26 Dignāga expresses that the virtuality left by a previous representation can dwell, i.e., subsist in a latent form, either in the consciousness or in its own indefinable form,[14] but that in any case there would not be difference in relation to the effect produced by the virtuality.[15] That virtuality, subsisting either in the consciousness or in its own form, produces, reactualizing itself, a new act of cognition. Wherever it dwells, the effect will be the same.

Dignāga does not say anything else about the "place" where the virtuality is kept, because in this treatise his sole interest is to demonstrate that the cognition's process is produced without the intervention of something external, that the act of cognition comes forth from absolutely internal elements.

Section XIII: kārikā VIII b-d and paragraphs 27-28

In ***kārikā VIII b-d*** and in paragraph 27 Dignāga indicates the relation between the form of the object and the virtuality.

The commentary begins expressing that the cognition is produced depending on the virtuality called "eye" and on the internal form.

With the expression "virtuality called 'eye'" Dignāga refers to the visual form under which the virtuality left by a previous representation actualizes itself. Dignāga employs the expression "virtuality called 'eye'", because (as it has been said in paragraphs 24-25) the virtuality actualizes itself *only* under the form of any one of the sensorial cognitions. What he says about the eye must be applied to the other sense organs. (See note 12). This is the first requirement on which depends the arising of the cognition.

The second requirement is the knowable internal form, which in ***kārikā VIII b-d*** is designated with the words "the form of the object" (*yul gyi ṅo bo*), and in the beginning of his commentary ***ad locum*** with the expression "internal form-colour" (***naṅ gi gzugs***). As it has been said previously (see *Section IX* and *X* of this commentary) the knowable internal form is the (unavoidable) object of the act of cognition - the cognition into which is transformed the (visual, auditive, etc.) virtuality left by a previous representation.

So we have 1. a virtuality that actualizes itself as a cognition; 2. this cognition can be visual, auditive, etc. (this is the element equivalent to the senses); 3. this cognition has necessarily an object; and 4. this object is the knowable internal form (this is the element equivalent to the external object). The knowable internal form is a part of the cognition's act, it comes forth necessarily with the cognition's act, and it is also its cause.

The cognition, which comes forth depending on the visual, auditive, etc. aspects of the virtuality and on the object that for Dignāga is nothing else than the "knowable internal form", arises under the appearance of that object, having that object as its contents, essentially identified with that object.

Dignāga says moreover that the cognition arises "not divided"[16] by the support. Cognition remains always *one*, the presence of the support does not imply, does not introduce any division in it, because the support of the cognition is something mental, internal, of the nature of knowledge, and also because cognition arises assuming the form of the support, having that form. Knowledge and knowable are essentially of the same nature: the nature of consciousness. The knowable is nothing else than the form of knowledge.

The virtuality (visual, etc.) and the form of the knowable internal object (the two causes of the production of knowledge) are mutually caused, and are beginningless[17] (*karikā VIII b-d* and the second and third sentences of paragraph 27). As we have already said (*Section X*) the representation of an object (which is nothing else than a simple mental creation) leaves in consciousness (or wherever it may be) a virtuality, and owing to this virtuality, when it is reactualized, there comes forth a new representation of a similar object. So there is a series representation-virtuality-representation, etc. which has not had a temporal beginning. If the series had begun with a representation, the question "how has been produced that representation?" would remain without answer, since the existence of a real external object, that could produce it, is not accepted. If the series had begun with a virtuality, the question "how has been produced that virtuality?" would similarly remain without answer, since the existence of a previous representation is not posited.

The virtuality and the internal form (the object) can be considered as different or as not different from the cognition according to the point of view one adopts. From the point of view of the philosophical analysis, in which Dignāga places himself, we can distinguish the different elements that constitute the cognition's process: a virtuality left by a previous representation, the cognition's act that comes forth from that virtuality and the cognition's object, similar to the object of the previous representation. But rigorously there is no difference among these three factors: the cognition is nothing else than the reactualized virtuality (it could be said that virtuality and cognition are the same at different moments), and the knowable interior form is nothing else than the manner under which the virtuality manifests itself. These three factors are only aspects, forms, parts (individualized only in theory through the conceptual analysis) of one indivisible, undivided entity: cognition, consciousness.

Dignāga concludes the treatise expressing that the *internal support* is the *object of cognition*, that is to say that the *knowable internal form, which produces the cognition and under whose appearance the cognition comes forth* (complying in this way with the two requirements of the definitions of 'object' and 'support' of cognition given in paragraphs 2 and 5), *is the object of cognition*.

TIBETAN TEXT

DMIGS PA BRTAG PAḤI ḤGREL PA

rgya gar skad du/ālambanaparīkṣābṛtti/
bod skad du/dmigs pa brtag paḥi ḥgrel pa/

saṅs rgyas daṅ byaṅ chub sems dpaḥ thams cad la phyag ḥtshal lo/

[Section I: paragraph 1]

1. gaṅ dag mig la sogs paḥi rnam par śes paḥi dmigs pa phyi rol gyi don yin par ḥdod pa de dag ni deḥi rgyu yin paḥi phyir rdul phra rab dag yin pa ḥam der snaṅ baḥi śes pa skye baḥi phyir de ḥdus pa yin par rtog graṅ na/

[Section II: kārikā I a-d and paragraphs 2-3]

de la re źig

dbaṅ po rnam par rig paḥi rgyu/
phra rab rdul dag yin mod kyi/
der mi snaṅ phyir deḥi yul[18] ni/
rdul phran ma yin dbaṅ po bźin//1//

2. yul źes bya ba ni śes pas[19] raṅ gi ṅo bo ṅes par ḥdsin pa yin te deḥi rnam par skye baḥi phyir ro/
3. rdul phra mo dag ni[20] deḥi rgyu ñid yin du zin kyaṅ de lta ma yin te dbaṅ po bźin no/ de ltar na re źig rdul phra mo dag dmigs pa ma yin no/

[Section III: kārikā II a-b and paragraphs 4-7]

4. ḥdus pa ni der snaṅ ba ñid yin du zin kyaṅ/

gaṅ ltar snaṅ de de las min/

5. don gaṅ źig raṅ snaṅ baḥi rnam par rig pa bskyed pa de ni dmigs pa yin par rigs te/ḥdi ltar de ni skye[21] baḥi rkyen ñid du bśad pas so/
6. ḥdus pa ni de lta yaṅ ma yin te/

rdsas su med phyir zla gñis bźin/

7. dbaṅ po ma tshaṅ baḥi phyir zla ba gñis mthoṅ ba ni der snaṅ ba ñid yin du zin kyaṅ deḥi yul ma yin no/de bźin du rdsas su yod pa ma yin pa ñid kyis rgyu ma yin paḥi phyir ḥdus pa dmigs pa ma yin no/

[Section IV: kārikā II c-d and paragraph 8]

de ltar phyi rol gñis kar yaṅ/
blo yi yul du mi ruṅ ṅo //2//

8. yan lag gcig ma tshaṅ baḥi phyir phyi rol gyi rdul phra mo daṅ tshogs pa źes bya baḥi don ni dmigs pa ma yin no/

[Section V: kārikās III a-d and IV a-b and paragraphs 9-12]
ḥdi la ni/

kha cig ḥdus paḥi rnam pa dag/
sgrub pa yin par ḥdod par byed/

9. don thams cad ni rnam pa du ma can yin pas de la rnam pa ḥgaḥ źig gis mṅon sum ñid du ḥdod do/
10. rdul phra rab rnams la yaṅ ḥdus par snaṅ baḥi śes pa skyed paḥi rgyuḥi dṅos po[22] yod do/

rdul phran rnam pa rnam rig gi/
don min sra ñid la sogs bźin //3//

11. ji ltar sra ñid la sogs pa ni yod bźin du yaṅ mig gi bloḥi yul ma yin pa ltar rdul phra mo ñid kyaṅ de daṅ ḥdraḥo/

de dag ltar na bum pa daṅ/[23]
kham phor sogs blo mtshuṅs par ḥgyur/

12. bum pa daṅ kham phor la sogs paḥi rdul phra mo rnams la ni maṅ du zin kyaṅ khyad par ḥgaḥ yaṅ med do/

[Section VI: kārikās IV c-d and V a-b and paragraphs 13-15]

gal te rnam paḥi dbye bas dbye/

13. gal te ḥdi sñam du mgrin pa la sogs paḥi rnam paḥi khyad par las gaṅ gis ni bloḥi khyad par du ḥgyur baḥi khyad par yod do sñam du sems na khyad par ḥdi ni bum pa la sogs pa la yod kyi/

de ni rdul phran rdsas yod la //4//

med de tshad dbye med phyir ro/

14. rdul phra rab rnams ni rdsas gźan yin du zin kyaṅ zlum po la ni dbye ba med do/

de phyir de rdsas med la yod/

15. rnam paḥi dbye ba ni kun rdsob tu yod pa dag kho na la yod kyi rdul phra mo rnams la ma yin no/

[Section VII: kārikā V c-d and paragraphs 16-17]

16. bum pa la sogs pa ni kun rdsob tu yod pa ñid do/

rdul phran yoṅs su bsal na ni/
der snaṅ śes pa ñams ḥgyur phyir //5//

17. rdsas su yod pa rnams la ni ḥbrel pa can bsal du zin kyaṅ kha dog la sogs pa bźin du raṅ gi blo ḥdor pa med do[24]/

[Section VIII: paragraph 18]

18. de lta bas na dbaṅ poḥi blo rnams kyi yul ni phyi rol na ma yin par ḥthad do/

[Section IX: kārikā VI a-d and paragraphs 19-20]

naṅ gi śes byaḥi ṅo bo ni/
phyi rol ltar snaṅ gaṅ yin de/
don yin

19. phyi rol gyi don med bźin du phyi rol lta bur snaṅ ba naṅ na yod pa kho na dmigs paḥi rkyen yin no/

rnam śes ṅo boḥi phyir/
de rkyen ñid kyaṅ yin phyir ro //6//

20. naṅ gi rnam par śes pa ni don du snaṅ ba daṅ/de las skyes pa yin pas/chos ñid gñis daṅ ldan paḥi phyir naṅ na yod pa kho na dmigs paḥi rkyen yin no/

[Section X: kārikā VII a-b and paragraphs 21-23]

21. re źig de ltar snaṅ ba ñid yin la ni rag la/deḥi phyogs gcig po lhan cig skyes pa go ji ltar rkyen yin źe na/

gcig na ḥaṅ mi ḥkhrul phyir na rkyen/

22. lhan cig par gyur du zin kyaṅ ḥkhrul pa med paḥi phyir gźan las skye baḥi rkyen du ḥgyur te/ḥdi ltar gtan tshigs dag ni yod pa daṅ med pa dag gi de daṅ ldan pa ñid ni[25] rgyu daṅ rgyu daṅ ldan pa[26] rim gyis skye ba dag gi yaṅ mtshan ñid yin par smraḥo/yaṅ na/

nus pa ḥjog phyir rim gyis yin/

23. rim gyis kyaṅ yin te/don du snaṅ ba[27] de ni raṅ snaṅ ba daṅ

mthun paḥi ḥbras bu skyed par byed paḥi[28] nus pa/ rnam par śes paḥi rten can byed pas mi ḥgal lo/

[Section XI: kārikā VII c-d and paragraphs 24-25]

24. gal te ḥo na ni naṅ gi gzugs kho na dmigs paḥi rkyen yin na/ ji ltar de daṅ mig la brten nas[29] mig gi rnam par śes pa skye źe na /

lhan cig byed dbaṅ nus pa yi/
ṅo bo gaṅ yin dbaṅ po ḥaṅ yin //7//

25. dbaṅ po ni raṅ gi ḥbras bu las nus paḥi ṅo bo ñid du rjes su dpag gi ḥbyuṅ ba las gyur pa ñid du ni ma yin no/

[Section XII: kārikā VIII a and paragraph 26]

de yaṅ rnam rig la mi ḥgal/

26. nus pa ni[30] rnam par śes pa la yod kyaṅ ruṅ/bstan du med paḥi raṅ gi ṅo bo la yod kyaṅ ruṅ ste/ḥbras bu skyed pa la khyad par med do/

[Section XIII: kārikā VIII b-d and paragraphs 27-28]

de ltar yul gyi ṅo bo daṅ/
nus pa phan tshun rgyu can daṅ/
thog ma med dus[31] ḥjug pa yin //8//

27. mig ces bya baḥi nus pa daṅ/naṅ gi gzugs la brten nas rnam par śes pa don du snaṅ ba dmigs kyis ma phye ba[32] skyeḥo/ ḥdi gñis kyaṅ phan tshun gyi rgyu can daṅ/thog ma med paḥi dus can yin te/res ḥgaḥ ni[33] nus pa yoṅs su smin pa las rnam par śes pa[34] yul gyi rnam pa ñid du[35] ḥbyuṅ la res ḥgaḥ ni deḥi rnam pa las[36] nus paḥo/rnam par śes pa las de gñis gźan ñid daṅ gźan ma yin pa ñid du ci dgar brjod par byaḥo/

28. de ltar naṅ gi dmigs pa ni chos ñid gñis daṅ ldan paḥi phyir yul ñid du ḥthad do[37]/

dmigs pa brtags paḥi ḥgrel pa slob dpon phyogs kyi glaṅ pos mdsad pa rdsogs so[38]/

TRANSLATION

INVESTIGATION ABOUT THE SUPPORT OF THE COGNITION

Stanzas and Commentary
by Dignāga

In Sanskrit: ***Ālambanaparīkṣāvṛtti;***
In Tibetan: ***Dmigs pa brtag paḥi ḥgrel pa.***

I pay homage to all the Buddhas and Bodhisattvas.

Section I: paragraph 1

1. Those who postulate that the support of the cognition through the eye, etc. is an external thing, consider that either the atoms are (the cognition's support), because they are its cause, or that a conglomerate of those (atoms) is (the cognition's support), because there arises a cognition which appears under the form of that (conglomerate).

Section II: kārikā I a-d and paragraphs 2-3

Concerning that (the author says):

I *a-d* *Even if the atoms are*
the cause of the cognition through the senses,
since (the cognition) does not appear
under the form of those (atoms),
the atoms are not the object of that (cognition),
in the same way as the sense-organs (are not).

2. (Something is) "object of cognition", because its own being is grasped with certainty by the cognition, and (so) (the cognition) arises under the form of that (own being).
3. Concerning the atoms, although they are the cause of that (=the cognition), they are not thus (as an object of cognition must be according to the definition given in paragraph 2), and (so) they are as the sense-organs.
Therefore no, atom is the support of the cognition.

Section III: kārikā II a-b and paragraphs 4-7

4. Concerning the conglomerate, although (the cognition) appears under the form of it (=a conglomerate),

II a *that (cognition of a conglomerate)*
does not arise from that
under whose form it appears
(i. e. does not arise from a conglomerate).

5. It is right (to consider) that any thing, which produces a cognition which appears under its own form (i.e. the form of that thing), is, just it, the support of cognition, because it has been taught that in this way it is the determining condition of the arising (of the cognition).
6. Concerning the conglomerate neither it is thus (as the cognition's support must be, according to paragraph 5),

II b *because (the conglomerate) does not exist*
as something real,
in the same way as a second moon
(does not exist as something real).

7. As regards the vision of a second moon because of a defect in the senses, even if (the cognition) appears under its form (i. e. the form of a second moon), (the second moon) is not the object of that (cognition). In the same way an aggregate is not the support of the cognition, because it is not the cause (of the cognition), since it does not exist as something real.

Section IV: kārikā II c-d and paragraph 8

II c-d *Thus, in both cases,*
(something) external cannot be
the object of perception.

8. The external things that are called "atoms" and "conglomerate" are not the support of the cognition, because of the absence of one part (of the requirements necessary to be support of the cognition).

Section V: kārikā III a-d and IV a-b and paragraphs 9-12

Concerning this,

III a-b *some (masters) hold*
that the forms of conglomerate
are the efficient (cause of the cognition).

9. (They) hold that all things, because of being possessed of several forms, are perceptible under one form thereamong.
10. There exists also in the atoms the nature of being a cause productive of a cognition which appears under the form of a conglomerate.

III c-d *The form of the atom is not an object*
of the (visual) cognition,
in the same way as the solidity, etc. (are not).

11. Just as the solidity, etc., although existing, are not an object of the perception of the eye, so also the atomicity is like them (i. e., like the solidity, etc. because, although the atomicity exists, it is not an object of the visual perception).

IVa-b *According to them (it would happen that)*
the perceptions of a pot, a cup, etc.
would be all the same.

12. Among the atoms of a pot, a cup, etc., although they are very numerous, there is not any difference.

Section VI: kārikās IV c-d and V a-b and paragraphs 13-15

IV c *If (it is held that)*
the diversity (among the pot, the cup, etc.)
exists owing to the diversity of the forms
(which they possess),

13. If somebody thinks that, (even) being so, (the diversity still exists) because, owing to the difference of the forms of the neck, etc. (of the pot, the cup, etc.), there exists a difference (among the pot and the cup, etc. as wholes) which comes forth as a difference of the perception, (then, we must answer that) although the difference (of the pot, the cup, etc. as wholes) exists in the pot, etc.

IV d-Va *it (i. e. the difference)*
does not exist in the atoms
which (according to the opponent) are
(the only thing that is)
(really) existent matter,
because there is not (in them)
any diversity of measure.

14. Even if atoms are (of) different matter, there is no difference (among them), being they (all) spherical.

V b *Therefore it (i.e. the difference*
among the pot, the cup, etc.,
and in general among things) exists (only)
in (those things which are)
not (really existing) matter,

15. The diversity of the forms does not exist in the atoms, even if it exists in things existing only by (human) convention.

Section VII : kārikā V c-d and paragraphs 16-17

16. The pot, etc. exist only by (human) convention,

V *c-d because, if the atoms are eliminated,*
the cognition which appears under their form
(i.e. the form of the pot,etc.), ceases.

17. In relation to (really) existent things, even if one eliminates what is connected (with them), as colour, etc. the very perception of them is not eliminated.

Section VIII : paragraph 18

18. Therefore, it is logically admissible that the object of the perceptions through the senses does not exist externally.

Section IX: kārikā VI a-d and paragraphs 19-20

VI *a-c The knowable internal form,*
which appears as external,
is the object (of the cognition),

19. (The knowable internal form), which appears as external although an external object does not exist, (and) which exists only internally, is (that) determining condition (of the cognitive process), which is the support of the cognition.

VI *c-d because it (=the knowable internal form)*
is the form of the cognition
and because it is also its determining condition.

20. (The knowable internal form), which exists only internally, is that determining condition (of the cognitive process), which is the support of the cognition, because it is provided with the two characteristics (indicated in paragraph 5), since the internal cognition appears under the form of the object (i.e. the knowable internal form) and comes forth through it.

Section X: kārikā VII a-b and paragraphs 21-23

21. If somebody asks : As (the internal cognition) is dependent on something that appears (in the mind) in the indicated way (i.e. under the form of the object, being there agreement between the thing and the representation in the mind), how can it be understood that (this knowable internal form-the object according to you [Dignāga]-which is only) a part of that (internal

cognition and) which comes forth together (with that internal cognition) could be the determining condition (of that internal cognition)?, (we answer:)

VII a *Even if (the knowable internal form*
comes forth) together
(with the internal cognition),
it is the determining condition
because of the necessary relation
(between the knowable internal form
and the internal cognition).

22. Even if (the knowable internal form) arises together (with the internal cognition), it happens to be the determining condition of what comes forth out of another, because there exists a necessary relation (between both), (since) to this effect the logicians say that "the concomitance of being and not being is the essential characteristic of cause and effect, even if they come forth successively". Moreover:

VII *b* *(Even if the knowable internal form*
and the cognition come forth) successively
(the knowable internal form)
is (the determining condition of the cognition),
because it leaves a virtuality.

23. Even if (the knowable internal form and the internal cognition) come forth successively, there is not contradiction (between this fact and the fact of the knowable internal form being the determining condition of the cognition), because that (cognition A) which appears under the form of an object gives rise to a virtuality, which (at its own turn) produces an effect (i.e., a new cognition B which appears under the form of an object) similar to that same (cognition A) which appeared (under the form of that object), and which has its abode in the consciousness.

Section XI: kārikā VII c-d and paragraphs 24-25

24. Now if it is asked: If only the (knowable) internal form-colour is that determining condition, which is the support of the cognition, how can the eye's cognition (i.e., the cognition through the eye) be born depending on that (knowable internal form-colour) and on the eye ? (-we answer:)

VII *c-d* *Senses are the form (or aspect)*
of the virtuality,
(and) a collaborating force.

25. Senses, from their own effect, are inferred to be the form (or aspect) of the virtuality, but they do not exist as something constituted by elements.

Section XII: kārikā VIII a and paragraph 26

VIII *a Neither it is contradictory*
that this (virtuality lie) in the consciousness.

26. The virtuality either exists in the consciousness or exists in its own indefinable form; (in both cases) there is no difference in relation to the production of the effect.

Section XIII: kārikā VIII b-d and paragraphs 27-28

VIII *b-d So the form of the object*
and the virtuality function
mutually caused
and since a beginningless time.

27. The cognition, depending on the virtuality (that is) called 'eye' and on the (knowable) internal form-colour, comes forth appearing under the form of the object, not divided by the support. These two (i.e., the form of the object or knowable internal form, and the virtuality) are mutually caused and have no beginning in time. And the cognition arises from the virtuality fully matured under the form of an object, and at its turn the virtuality (arises) from that form. Both (i.e., the form of the object or knowable internal form, and the virtuality) must be considered, according to one's own will, either as different or as not different from the cognition.
28. So it can be admitted that an internal support is the object (of the cognition), because it is endowed with the two characteristics (indicated in paragraphs 2 and 5).

The *Investigation about the support of the cognition* composed by Ācārya Dignāga is finished.

NOTES FOR THE FIRST PART

1. On Dignāga and his works see: E. Frauwallner, "Dignāga, sein Werk und seine Entwicklung", in *Wiener Zeitschrift für die Kunde Süd-und Ost-Asiens,* 3, 1959, pp. 83-164 (=*Kleine Schriften,* Wiesbaden, F. Steiner, 1982, pp. 759-841); "Landmarks in the History of Indian Logic", *ibidem,* 5, 1961, pp. 125-148 (=*Kleine Schriften,* pp. 847 -870); *Die Philosophie des Buddhismus,* Berlin: Akademie-Verlag, 1969, pp. 390-392; M. Hattori, Dignāga, On Perception, Cambridge (Mass.): Harvard University Press, 1968; A.G.S.K (ariyawasam), "Dinnāga", in *Encyclopaedia of Buddhism,* Sri Lanka, 1989, Vol. IV, 4, pp. 617-625; A. B. Keith, *Buddhist Philosophy in India and Ceylon,* Varanasi: Chowkhamba, 1963 (First edition: Oxford, 1923); H. Kitagawa, *Indo koten ronrigaku no kenkyū-Jinna no taikei-* ("Study of Indian Classical Logic-Dignāga's system"), Tokyo: Suzuki Research Foundation, 1965; D.N. Shastri, *The Philosophy of Nyāya-Vaiśeṣika and its Conflict with The Buddhist Dignāga School (Critique of Indian Realism),* Delhi: Bharatiya Vidya Prakashan, 1976; M. Schott, *Sein als Bewusstsein,* Heidelberg: Carl Winters Universitätsbuchhandlung, 1935; Ts. Stcherbatsky, "Dignāga's Theory of Perception", in *Taishō Daigaku Gakuhō* ("Journal of the Taishō University"), 1930, pp. 89 -130; *Buddhist Logic,* Vol. I, New York: Dover Publications, s.d. (First edition : Leningrad, 1927); S. Ch. Vidyabhusana, *A History of Indian Logic,* Delhi: Motilal Banarsidass, 1971, pp. 270-301.
2 On Dignāga's relevant position in the history of Indian philosophy, we refer to the following opinions:
S. Ch. Vidyabhusana, Professor in the University of Calcutta, *A History of Indian Logic* (quoted in note 1), p. 270: *"Dignāga is justly regarded as the Father of Mediaeval Logic. Both in matter and in manner his works marked a distinct departure from those of his predecessors. The keenness of his insight*

and the soundness of his critical acumen combined to stamp him with an individuality all his own. No praise seems too high for him".

Ts. Stcherbastky, Professor in the University of Leningrad, "Dignāga's Theory of Perception" (quoted in note 1), pp. 89-90: "*The name of Dignāga marks a boundary in the history of Buddhist philosophy. Before him Buddhist philosophy may be characterized as a system of Radical Pluralism engaged in finding out the ultimate elements of existence (dharmapravicaya). These elements (dharma) were regarded as real in Hīnayāna, as relative, and therefore unreal, in Mahāyāna. With Dignāga Buddhism forsakes the field of metaphysics and devotes all its attention to problems of logic and epistemology. He thus occupies in the history of Buddhist philosophy a position analogous to the position of Aristoteles in the Greek philosophy and of Kant in modern European philosophy. These three great men mark an analogous turning point in the history of the development of philosophic ideas in mankind. When all the works of Dignāga have been critically studied, edited and translated in an intelligible way, the time will come to appreciate the Indian Kant and to compare him with the European one, and since the logic of Dignāga is the logic of the Eastern part of humanity, just as the logic of Aristoteles is the logic of its Western part, the time will then come to pronounce a judgment upon their comparative value. At present we must be satisfied to collect every piece of evidence which is likely to elucidate the thoughts, and make intelligible to us the logical system of the great man whose fate it was to be for the East at once its Aristoteles and its Kant.*"

M. Winternitz, Professor in the University of Prague, *A History of Indian Literature, Vol. II, Buddhist Literature and Jaina Literature,* 1972 (First published : University of Calcutta, 1933; translation from the original German, 1905 ff.), p. 363: "*The greatest and most independent thinker among the successors of Vasubandhu is Dignāga, the founder of Buddhist logic, and one of the foremost figures in the history of Indian Philosophy.*"

E. Frauwallner, Professor in the University of Vienna, "Dignāga, sein Werk und seine Entwicklung" (quoted in note 1), pp. 136-137 (=pp. 812-813): "*And now he (Dignāga) gathered all that he had worked out, in a great treatise, the Pramāṇasamuccayaḥ. It was no more dialectics, what he offered here, but theory of knowledge, organized according to the two great realms of perception and inference...With this, Dignāga concluded the work of his life. But, at the same time, with this work, a huge complete doctrinary system was created and the Buddhist school of logic and theory of knowledge was founded...Whoever knows the last works of Dignāga, stands in front of something new and great, that is beyond all that had been written before and that seems to arise suddenly out of nothing. Our research has taught us to understand this original creation. We come to know the sources from which Dignāga drew his incentives and we can follow how he gradually put together, piece by piece, the stones for his great building. It is seen that there much has been taken from ancient traditions. But in his mind he has given new form to and has made use of all that he had inherited from the past. And, even if it is admitted that he has utilized a great amount of ancient materials, what he has created remains, as a whole, new and great. And thus it is established anew that the Buddhist school of epistemology and logic is essentially the creation of only one man: Dignāga*" [our translation from the German original].

3 *Tōhoku, Index*, p. 96, under the name *Phyos-kyi glaṅ po* (=Dignāga) registers eighteen works translated into Tibetan, and *Répertoire*, p. 259, under the name *Jinna (Tch 'en na)* (=Dignāga in Japanese and Chinese respectively) registers ten works translated into Chinese. Cf. E. Steinkellner und M.T. Much, *Texte der erkenntnistheoretischen Schule des Buddhismus*, Göttingen: Vandenhoeck und Ruprecht, 1995, pp.1-15, who give detailed information on Dignāga's works on logic and epistemology (editions and translations).

4. *Own being: raṅ gi ṅo bo* in Tibetan: *svarūpa, svabhāva* in Sanskrit. These words indicate the way of being of a thing, (which is proper to it and individualizes it, distinguishing it from others), its essential nature.

5. *Rnam pa* in Tibetan corresponds to Sanskrit *ākāra,* which means "form", "figure", "appearance", "external aspect". We have translated it by "form"; we must understand by this word

the appearance under which the thing, which is the object of knowledge, presents itself before the mind.

6. The atomic theory was the explanation of the world generally accepted in India in Dignāga's epoch. On Indian atomism see: the relevant sections of the histories of Indian philosophy; and also: B. Faddegon, *The Vaiśeṣika-System, described with the help of the oldest texts,* Wiesbaden: M. Sändig, 1969 (first published: 1918); M.K. Gaṇgopadhyaya, *Indian Atomism: History and Sources,* Calcutta: Bagchi Indological Series, 1, 1980; W. Halbfass, *On Being and What There Is. Classical Vaiśeṣika and the History of Indian Ontology,* Albany: State University of New York, 1992; H. Jacobi, "Atomic theory" (Indian), in J. Hastings, *Encyclopaedia of Religion and Ethics,* Edinburg: T. & T. Clark, 1964, 2, pp. 199 -202 (first published: 1909); A.B. Keith, *Indian Logic and Atomism. An exposition of the Nyāya and Vaiśeṣika Systems,* New York: Greenwood Press, 1968 (first published: 1921); V. Lyssenko, " La doctrine des atomes (*aṇu, paramāṇu)* chez Kaṇāda et Praśastapāda", in *Journal Asiatique,* 284, 1996, 1, pp. 137-158; P. Masson-Oursel, "L 'atomisme indien", in *Revue Philosophique (de la France et de l 'étranger), 99,* Paris, 1925, pp. 342-368; K. H. Potter, *Encyclopedia of Indian Philosophies. Indian Metaphysics and Epistemology: The Tradition of Nyāya-Vaiśeṣika up to Gaṅgeśa,* Delhi: Motilal Banarsidass, 1977; H. Ui, *The Vaiśeshika Philosophy according to the Daśapadārtha-Śāstra. Chinese text with Introduction, translation and notes,* Varanasi: Chowkhamba, 1962 (first published: 1917). See *Viṃśatikā* in this book, Commentary on Section XVIII, and note 55.

7. One of the most discussed questions in Indian philosophy was that referring to the whole (*avayavin)* and the parts (*avayava*). It opposed specially, on one side, the Hindu *Nyāya* and the *Vaiśeṣika* schools and, on the other, the Buddhist *Yogācāra* school. The *Nyāya* and the *Vaiśeṣika* affirmed that the whole exists and is one, real and different from its parts. The Buddhist on their side affirmed that the whole does not exist, that it has no reality, and that it is only a conventional denomitation.

   The first Hindu text that treats this subject is Gotama, *Nyāyasūtra* II, 1, 31-36 and II, 2, 4-25. In this text Gotama analyzes in first place, in order to refute it, the thesis of some authors who maintain that the perception is only an inference, since from grasping only a part we infer either the other parts or the other parts and the whole. Then Gotama in the remaining *sūtras* defends the real existence of the whole against the Buddhist thesis which admits the (relatively) real existence of the parts. Other Hindu texts that defend the existence of the whole are the sections of the *Bhāṣya* of Vātsyāyana, of the *Nyāyavārttika* of Uddyotakara, and of the *Nyāyavārttikatātparyaṭīkā* of Vācaspati Miśra, referring to Gotama's *sūtras;* Bhāsarvajña, *Nyāyabhūṣana*, pp. 104-115 and 121-129, Varanasi: Ṣaḍdarśana Prakāṣana Pratiṣṭhānam, 1968; Śrīdhara Bhaṭṭa, *Nyāyakandalī*, pp. 105-109, Varanasi: Gaṅgānāthajhā-Granthamālā, 1977; Vyomaśiva, commentary *ṭīkā* on the *Padārthadharmasaṃgraha* of Praśastapāda, pp. 44-46, Benares: Chowkhamba, 1983; Vallabhācārya, *Nyāyalīlāvatī*, pp.125-131, Benares: Chowkhamba, 1927; Udayana, *Ātmatattvaviveka*, pp. 258-280, Benares: Chowkhamba, 1940.

On the Buddhist side, in the *Milindapañha*, pp. 26-28, London: PTS, 1962, Nāgasena explains to the Greek King Menander that the whole does not truly exist and that the only thing *relatively* real are the parts, employing the celebrated analogy of the car: the axle, the wheels, the helm really exist; 'car' is only a conventional denomination to which nothing real corresponds. As H. Oldenberg, *Buddha. Sein Leben, Seine Lehre, Seine Gemeinde*, München: Wilhelm Goldmann, 1961 (first published: 1881), p.241, comments, Nāgasena's thesis agrees with the most ancient Buddha's teaching, because the verses quoted by Nāgasena, which synthesize his views are from *Saṃyutta Nikāya* I, p. 135 (PTS edition). Cf. Buddhaghosa, *Visuddhimagga* XVIII, paragraphs 25-28, pp.508-509, Cambridge Mass.: Harvard Oriental Series, 1950. The position that is maintained by the verses of the *Saṃyutta Nikāya* and by Nāgasena is followed by the other later Buddhist authors, and is severely criticised by the Hindu authors.

Arguments against the existence of the whole have been dealt with by several Buddhist authors, as for instance: Dharmakīrti, *Pramāṇavārttika, Pramāṇasiddhiḥ* 86-87; Dharmakīrti, *Pramāṇaviniścaya, Pratyakṣam*, T. Vetter ed., Wien, 1966, pp. 84-87; Dharmottara, commentary on Dharmakīrti, *Pramāṇaviniścaya, Sde-dge* ed., Tokyo, 1983, ff. 143 b^3-146 a^1; Śāntarakṣita, *Tattvasaṅgraha* 592-593, and 601, and Kamalaśīla *ad locum;* (Nāgārjuna), *Ta chih tu lun, Taishō* XXV, 1509, p. 206 b^{17}-c^{1}, and p.287 a^{18}-b^{13} (=É. Lamotte, *Le Traité de la Grande Vertu de Sagesse,* Louvain: Institut Orientaliste, 1966, pp.1217-1218, and pp.2058-2059). In *Vaidalyaprakaraṇa* (Sections XXXIII-XL: On *avayavas),* attributed to Nāgārjuna, the non-existence of the whole is used in order to establish the impossibility of the syllogism, and with arguments related to the whole and the parts discussion. See F. Tola and C. Dragonetti's edition and translation, Delhi: Motilal Banarsidass, 1995. *Avayavinirākaraṇa* of Paṇḍita Aśoka is the only monograph on this important subject matter of Indian philosophy that has been preserved. See F. Tola and C. Dragonetti's edition and translation of this valuable Buddhist treatise.

One can find in the indicated authors a broad argumentation employed in favour or against both thesis. The arguments developed by Dignāga in this treatise against the existence of the conglomerate (i.e. against a really existing whole besides the parts that compose it) are only a fragment of that argumentation.

We have said that for Buddhists the only thing *relatively* real are the parts. Actually the existence, which corresponds to the parts, is not an absolute one, but only a relative one, since the parts on their turn can be analysed into their respective parts and these into their constituting elements, and so on in an analytical abolishing process which has no end, since Buddhists do not accept the atom's existence. This is the position developed by the *Hastavālanāmaprakaraṇa's* author (Āryadeva or Dignāga). See F. Tola and C. Dragonetti, "Nāgārjuna's conception of 'voidness' (śūnyatā)", in *Journal of Indian Philosophy* 9, 3, 1981,pp. 273-282, and "The Hastavālanāmaprakaraṇavṛtti", in *The Journal of Religious Studies,* Patiala, VIII, 1, 1980, pp.18-31, included in *On Voidness,* Delhi: Motilal Banarsidass, 1995, by the same authors. This position agrees with the non acceptance of the whole as something real.

The refusal of the real existence of the whole is a logical consequence of the Mahāyāna principle according to which anything that is conditioned (dependent, relative or composed) does not really exist.

On the question of the whole and the parts, cf. S. Bhaduri,

Studies in Nyāya-Vaiśeṣika Metaphysics, Poona: Bhandarkar Oriental Research Institute, 1947, *Chapter XI: Whole and part,* pp. 229-270; S. Chatterjee, *The Nyāya theory of knowledge. A critical study of some problems of Logic and Metaphysics,* Calcutta: University of Calcutta, 1965 (first published: 1939) pp. 156-159; B. Faddegon, *The Vaiçeṣika system,* pp. 50-51, 371-375 (translation of the relevant text of the *Nyāyakandalī*); Y. Kajiyama, "The Avayavinirākaraṇa of Paṇḍita Aśoka", in *Indogaku Bukkyōgaku Kenkyū* ("Journal of Indian and Buddhist Studies"), Tokyo, 9, 1961, pp. 371-366; A. B. Keith, *Indian Logic and Atomism,* pp. 16, 23, 70, 183, 225; M. Müller, *The Six Systems of Indian Philosophy,* Varanasi: Chowkhamba, New impression of the 1919 edition (first published : 1899), p. 393; K. Potter (ed.), *The Encyclopedia of Indian Philosophies* Vol. II, *Indian Metaphysics and Epistemology: The Tradition of Nyāya-Vaiśeṣika up to Gaṅgeśa,* 1977, pp. 74-79; S. Radhakrishnan, *Indian Philosophy,* Vol, II, New York-London: Macmillan-Allen & Unwin, 1962, pp. 187-188 (first published: 1923); B. K. Matilal, *Epistemology, Logic and Grammar in Indian Philosophical Analysis,* The Hague: Mouton, 1971, pp. 52-55; T.R. Sundararaman, "Refutation of the Buddhist doctrine of aggregates", in *Philosophical Quarterly,* Amalner, 16, 1940-1941, pp. 164-171; J. Sinha, *A History of Indian Philosophy,* Vol. I, Calcutta: Sinha Publishing House, 1956, pp. 313-314; D. N. Shastri, *The Philosophy of Nyāya-Vaiśeṣika and its Conflict with The Buddhist Dignāga School,* pp. 248-261.

On the problem of the whole and the parts in Western philosophy see J. Ritter (ed.), *Historisches Wörterbuch der Philosophie,* Vol.III, sub *Ganzes/Teil,* Darmstadt: Wissenschaftliche Buchgesellschaft, 1974.

8. It must be remarked that Dignāga says that the perception of what really exists does not cease even if we eliminate from it anything that is *connected* with it. He does not speak of parts, since, as we have already said, if something real exists, it cannot have parts.
9. The text has *naṅ gi śes byaḥi ṅo bo*. The Tibetan word *ṅo bo* has two fundamental values: 1. "thing" (=*vastu* in Sanskrit), and 2. "form" (=*rūpa* in Sanskrit). We have translated it by the word "form", as Frauwallner does. By this word we must understand the representations to which we have referred in the commentary. It is obvious that, when the representation

occurs in the mind, the object or the thing itself is not inside the mind, but only a "form", i.e. a mental "image" of that object or thing.

10. For Dignāga, among the characteristics which define the cause-effect relation, the most important is the coincidence between the existence and non existence of the cause and the effect. It must be of course a necessary and obligatory coincidence: if A exists, necessarily B is produced; if A does not exist, necessarily B does not come into existence. For Dignāga both cause and effect can be simultaneous, as in the case of the knowable internal form and the cognition that it produces.

The coincidence of being and not being of cause and effect is mentioned by several logicians when they deal with the cause. Keśava Miśra, *Tarkabhāṣā,* p. 2, Poona: Oriental Book Agency, 1953, after giving the definition of the cause according to the Nyāya school (to which he belongs), indicates that several authors wrongly define the cause as: yat tu kaścid āha kāryānukṛtānvayavyatireki kāraṇam iti, tad ayuktam (" *'that whose presence and absence are imitated by the presence and absence of the effect'-that is not logical").* Keśava Miśra does not accept this definition. Dharmottara, on commenting Dharmakīrti's *Nyāyabindu* II, 17, p. 28, Banaras : Chowkhamba, 1954, indicates that: kāryakāraṇabhāvo loke pratyakṣānupalambhanibandhanaḥ pratīta iti ("*causality is a conception familiar in common life. It is known to be derived from experience [of the presence of the cause wherever there is an effect present], and from the negative experience [of the absence of the effect when the cause is deficient]").* (F.Th. Stcherbatsky's translation, in *Buddhist Logic,* Vol. II, p. 67). Cf. Vasubandhu, *Abhidharmakośa,* II, pp. 84 line 20-85 line 1, P. Pradhan's edition, Patna: K.P. Jayaswal Research Institute, 1967: saṃpradhāryaṃ tāvad etat "kiṃ prabhāyāḥ pradīpo hetur āhosvit pūrvotpannaiva sāmagrī saprabhasya pradīpasya sacchāyasyāṅkurasyotpattau hetur" iti/ itas tarhi bhāvābhāvayos tadvattvāt-etad dhi hetuhetumato lakṣaṇam ācakṣate haitukāḥ/"yasya bhāvābhāvayoḥ yasya bhāvābhāvau niyamataḥ, sa hetur itaro hetumān" iti/-sahabhuvāṃ ca dharmāṇām ekasya bhāve sarveṣāṃ bhāva ekasyābhāve sarveṣām abhāva iti yukto hetuphalabhāvaḥ. (*"[The Sautrāntika :] It is necessary to determine first whether the lamp is the cause of the light or the totality [of causes and conditions] arisen before is the cause for the production of the lamp with its light, and of the sprout with its shade. [The Sarvāstivādin:] In regard to these two alternatives then owing to the conformity [=concomitance] of being and non-being-since logicians teach that this is the definition of cause and effect: 'If, given the being or non-being of a thing, the being or non-being of another thing is necessarily produced, the first one is the cause, the second one is the effect'-a logical causal relation would be: 'given the being of one of the dharmas that arise together, the being of all [the other dharmas that arise together] is produced; given the non-being of one [of them], the non-being of all [of them] is produced'"*). *Cf.* Vijaya Rani, *The Buddhist philosophy as presented in Mīmāṃsā-Śloka-Varttika*, Delhi: Parimal Publications, 1982, pp. 116-118, for the Mīmāṃsā's opinion on this point. On the problem of the simultaneity of cause and effect see also Gauḍapāda, *Āgamaśāstra* IV, 16, Bhattacharya ed., 1943, and texts of Nāgarjuna and Candrakīrti quoted there. The notion of coincidence between being and not being has also an important function in theories of induction as its fundament and as a criterion to classify the different types of inference. Cf. A.B. Keith, *Indian Logic and Atomism*, pp. 111-122; S. Chatterjee, *The Nyāya theory of knowledge*, pp. 247-250 (quoted in note 7).

It is interesting to compare the Indian reasoning about the simultaneity of the cause and the effect with the following text of Saint Thomas of Aquinas from " De aeternitate mundi contra murmurantes" (Opusculum XXIII, Sancti Thomae Aquinatis, *Opera Omnia*, Tomus XVI, New York: Musargia Publishers, pp. 318-319). In this tract Saint Thomas defends the possibility of the eternity of the world, notwithstanding its having been created by God.

....*Primo ergo ostendendum, quod non est necesse ut causa agens, scilicet Deus, praecedat duratione suum causatum, si ipse voluisset.*

Primo sic. Nulla causa producens effectum suum subito, necessario praecedit effectum suum duratione. Sed Deus est causa producens effectum suum non per motum, sed subito. Ergo non est necessarium quod duratione praecedat effectum suum. Primum patet per inductionem in omnibus mutationibus subitis, sicut est illuminatio et hujusmodi. Nihilominus potest probari per rationem sic. In quocumque instanti ponitur res esse, potest poni principium actionis ejus, ut patet in omnibus generabilibus: quia in illo instanti in quo incipit ignis, incipit esse calefactio. Sed in operatione subita, simul, immo idem est principium et finis ejus, sicut in omnibus indivisibilibus. Ergo in quocumque instanti ponitur agens producens effectum suum subito, potest poni terminus actionis suae. Sed terminus actionis est simul cum ipso facto. Ergo non repugnat intellectui, si ponatur causa producens effectum suum subito, non praecedere duratione causatum suum. Repugnaret autem in causis producentibus effectus suos per motum: quia oportet quod principium motus praecedat finem ejus. Et quia homines consueti sunt considerare hujusmodi factiones quae sunt per motum; ideo non facile capiunt quod causa agens duratione effectus suum non praecedat. Et inde est quod multorum inexperti ad pauca respicientes enuntiant facile.

"...Firstly then it must be shown that it is not necessary that the efficient cause, i.e., God, precede in time [chronologically] His effect [=the world that is postulated to be eternal], if He would have desired so [=to create it]. In the first place [this thesis is demonstrated] thus. No cause which *suddenly* produces its effect necessarily precedes in time its effect. God is a cause producing His effect not through a motion, but suddenly. Then it is not necessary that He precede in time His effect. In the first place, [that] is evident, through induction, in all sudden changes, as it happens in the illumination and [other] similar [processes]. Moreover, [that] can be proved by deductive reasoning in this way. In whatever moment a thing is posited to be, [just in that moment] the beginning of its action can be posited, as it is evident in all things that are produced, because [for instance] in the same moment in which fire begins, warming begins. But, in a sudden operation its beginning and its end are simultaneous, still more: they are the same—as it happens in regard to all the things that cannot be separated. Consequently in whatever moment an agent suddenly producing its effect is posited, [in that same moment] the conclusion of its action can be posited. But the conclusion of the action is simultaneous with what has been made [i.e., the effect]. Consequently, it is not contrary to reason if it is posited that a cause, which suddenly produces its effect, does not precede in time its effect. It would be contrary [to reason] in those causes which produce their effects through motion, because the beginning of the motion must precede its end. And since men are accustomed to take into account such productions that exist through motion, it is not easy that they understand that an efficient cause does not precede in time its effect. And so it happens that those who are inexpert in a great number of things, taking into account [only] few things, easily make [such] affirmations."

11. Among the most important presuppositions of Indian thought we have the *saṃsāra* (see F. Tola and C. Dragonetti, "Saṃsāra, anāditva y nirvāṇa", *Boletin de la Asociación Española de Orientalistas,* Madrid, 1979, pp. 95-114), the *anāditva* (see F. Tola and C. Dragonetti, "*Anāditva* or beginninglessness in Indian Philosophy", *Annals of the Bhandarkar Oriental Research Institute,* Poona, 1980, pp. 1-20), and the *bījas (saṃskāras, vāsanās)* (see note 10 in *Trisvabhāvakārikā* in this book). Cf. F. Tola, "Principios fundamentales de la Filosofía de la India", in *Revista Venezolana de Filosofía* No. 19, Caracas (Venezuela), 1985, pp. 89-101.

12. In Tibetan we have the word *gzugs* which corresponds to Sanskrit *rūpa. Gzugs, rūpa,* indicate the object of visual cognition, fundamentally the form and the colour under which things appear before us. We have translated *gzugs* by "form-colour". *Gzugs* is to be differentiated from *ṅo bo* (see note 9): *ṅo bo* applies to any mental representation (visual, auditive, etc.) in general; *gzugs* applies only to visual representations. "Internal form-colour" signifies in this passage the visual representations that arise as the actualization of (visual) virtualities (that is to say, one of the classes of knowable internal forms which produce the cognition). But we must understand that what Dignāga says in relation to the visual internal form must be applied also to the other knowable internal forms, like taste-sensations, etc., and that what he says in relation to the eye must be applied also to the other sense-organs like the ear, etc.

13. According to the oldest Buddhist teaching the cognition's act comes forth depending on several factors. So *Śalistambasūtra* says: tadyathā pañcabhiḥ kāraṇaiś cakṣurvijñānam utpadyate. Katamaiḥ pañcabhiḥ ? yad uta cakṣuḥ pratītya rūpaṃ cālokaṃ cākaśaṃ ca tajjamanasikāraṃ ca pratītyotpadyate cakṣurvijñānam ... asatsveṣu pratyayeṣu cakṣurvijñānaṃ notpadyate (*"In this way the eye-consciousness (cakṣurvijñāna) comes forth through five causes. Which five? Through the eye, the form, the light, the space and the attention produced by*

the former ones, the eye-consciousness comes forth", p.85 in L. de la Vallée Poussin, *Bouddhisme. Études et Matériaux. Théorie des Douze Causes*, Gand: Université de Gand, 1913=p.15 in *Śālistamba Sūtra,* N. A. Sastri ed., Adyar: Adyar Library, 1950. See Section 11 of our commentary on *Viṃśatikā*. Dignāga maintains also that for the production of the cognition several factors are necessary, but in his opinion these factors are only two: The (visual, etc.) *virtuality* and the *internal form*. The eye is nothing else than the visual virtuality or, in other words, "eye" is a specific form of the virtuality as the other sense-organs also are.

14. Dignāga deals very briefly with the problem of the "place" in which remains the virtuality which is actualized into a cognition. We must relate this passage with the discussion, raised in the different Buddhist schools, in reference to the place in which the *bījas,* seeds, virtualities, left by all human act, are preserved. See L. de la Vallée Poussin, *La morale bouddhique,* Paris: Nouvelle Librairie Nationale, 1927, pp.196-200, "Note sur l' Ālayavijñāna", *Mēlanges Chinois et Bouddhiques,* Bruxelles, 1934, 3, pp. 145-168; É. Lamotte, "Le traité de l' acte de Vasubandhu", *Mēlanges Chinois et Bouddhiques,* Bruxelles, 1936, 4, Introduction. L. Schmithausen, "Sautrāntika-Voraussetzungen in Viṃśatikā und Triṃśikā", in *Wiener Zeitschrift für die kunde Süd-und Ost-Asiens,* 1967, pp. 113-114, and *Ālayavijñāna. On the Origin and the Early Development of a Central Concept of Yogācāra Philosophy,* Tokyo: The International Institute for Buddhist Studies, 1987, specially pp. 26-27, 42-43, 111-112, 179, and notes 288, 1165. Dignāga indicates two alternatives : the virtualities remain either in the consciousness (cf. Hiuan Tsang, *Tch 'eng wei che louen, Vijñaptimātratāsiddhi, Taishō* XXXI, 1585, p. 8, a^{11-12}=L. de la Vallée Poussin, *La Siddhi de Hiuan Tsang,* Paris: Geuthner, 1928 -29, p. 101), more properly in that aspect of consciousness that was called "*ālayavijñāna*"(that is to be compared in some way with the concept of subconsciousness in modern psychology) or in "its own indefinable form". We must understand this expression with the meaning of: "in itself".

Dignāga says that the own form (or essential nature) of the virtuality is "indefinable" (*bstan du med pa* in Tibetan, *anirdeśya* in Sanskrit), that is to say, that, although we cannot doubt about the existence, activities and effects of the virtuality, we cannot say anything about its nature.

15. The important thing for the arising of a cognition is that the virtuality be actualized into the form of a visual cognition, etc.; the place where the virtuality remains does not affect the process of knowledge.
16. *Dmigs kyis ma phye ba* in the original. Sastri translates: *undifferentiated from the perceivable object* in his English translation (p. 54), and *ālambanād avibhaktam* in his Sanskrit reconstruction (p. 7). Yamaguchi: *mais encore non discerné* (avivṛta) *par l 'objet percevable* (ālambana), and Frauwallner: *durch einen Anhaltspunkt* (ālambana) *nicht bestimmt.*
17. On *anāditva* see the article of F. Tola and C. Dragonetti quoted in note 11.
18. deḥi yul: *Peking. Sde-dge* : de yul.
19. śes pas: *Peking. Sde-dge* : śes pas gaṅ gis.
20. rdul phra mo dag ni: *Peking. Sde-dge*: rdul phra mo dag gi ni.
21. skye: *Peking. Sde-dge* : skya.
22. rgyuḥi dṅos po: *Peking. Sde-dge* : rgyu.
23. tshad: *Peking. Sde-dge: deest.*
24. ḥdor pa med do: *Peking. Sde-dge* : ḥdor bar byed do.
25. ḥdi ltar gtan tshigs dag ni yod pa daṅ med pa dag gi de daṅ ldan pa ñid ni : *Peking. Sde-dge:* ḥdi ltar gtan tshigs yod pa daṅ med pa dag ni yod pa daṅ med pa dag gi de daṅ ldan pa ñid na.
26. rgyu daṅ rgyu daṅ ldan pa: Vinītadeva, *Sde-dge* and *Peking. Sde-dge*: rgyu daṅ ldan pa.
27. snaṅ ba: *Peking. Sde-dge :* snaṅ bas.
28. byed paḥi: *Peking. Sde-dge* : byed par.
29. brten nas: *Peking. Sde-dge* : brten na.
30. nus pa ni: Vinītadeva, *Sde-dge* and *Peking. Sde-dge* : nus paḥi.
31. dus: according to Dignāga's own Commentary, *Sde-dge* and *Peking,* the *Ālambanaparīkṣākārikā, Sde-dge* (4205) and *Peking* (5703), and Vinītadeva, *Sde-dge* and *Peking. Sde-dge*:du.
32. ma phye ba: *Peking. Sde-dge* : ma bstan pa.
33. ni: *Peking. Sde-dge* : na.
34. rnam par śes pa: Vinītadeva, *Peking. Sde-dge :* rnam par śes pas.
35. rnam pa ñid du: *Peking. Sde-dge* : rnam pa ñid.
36. rnam pa las: Vinītadeva, *Sde-dge* and *Peking. Sde-dge* : rnam pa la.
37. yul ñid du ḥthad do: *Peking. Sde-dge* : yul du mthoṅ ṅo.
38. mdsad pa rdsogs so: *Peking. Sde-dge* : mdsad paḥo.

Part II

THE *VIṂŚATIKĀ VIJÑAPTIMĀTRATĀSIDDHIḤ* OF VASUBANDHU

To Susana Chamas and Mito Bronfman
whose friendship is for us "a joy for ever"

INTRODUCTION

Vasubandhu

According to tradition[1] Vasubandhu was born in Puruṣapura, the capital of Gāndhāra (the modern Peshawar in Western Pakistan); he lived during the IVth or Vth century A.D., being under discussion the exact dates of his birth and death[2]. His father was a brāhmaṇa whose name was Kauśika. Vasubandhu had two brothers, Asaṅga and Viriñcivatsa. Buddhamitra was one of his masters. In his youth he belonged to the Hīnayānist Sarvāstivāda-Vaibhāṣika[3] sect and wrote the important treatise *Abhidharmakośa*, in which he exposes the doctrines of that sect, although many times he favours the opinion of the Sautrāntikas[4]. He wrote also the *Paramārthasaptatikā* against Vindhyavastu or Vindhyavāsin,[5] a master of the Hindu Sāṃkhya school, who had defeated his master Buddhamitra in a philosophical discussion.[6] King Skandagupta Vikramāditya, of the Gupta dynasty, who reigned *circa* 455-467 A.D. rewarded him for his victory. After Vikramāditya's death, Vasubandhu was invited to go to the royal court at Ayodhyā (the modern Oude) by Bālāditya, successor of Vikramāditya and whose preceptor Vasubandhu had been. Bālāditya must have reigned *circa* 467-473 A.D. Vasubandhu carried on a discussion with the grammarian Vasurāta and the Buddhist monk Saṃghabhadra who belonged to the Vaibhāṣika[7] orthodoxy. Besides the mentioned works, Vasubandhu wrote in this period of his life numerous works of Hīnayānist inspiration.[8] Invited by his brother Asaṅga, Vasubandhu comes back to Puruṣapura. He is converted by his brother Asaṅga to Mahāyāna, and composes then many works of Mahāyānist inspiration.[9] He dies at the age of 80 years in Ayodhyā.

The Two Vasubandhus

E. Frauwallner in his scholarly study *On the date of the Buddhist Master of the Law Vasubandhu,* Roma: IsMEO, 1951, reaches the conclusion, that is accepted by many scholars in Buddhism,[10] that in fact there were two Vasubandhus, one the brother of Asaṅga, who lived in the IVth century A.D. and another who lived in Vth century A.D. As it will be seen in the following paragraphs, the events attributed to the life of the only Vasubandhu that tradition knows are distributed by Frauwallner between the lives of the two Vasubandhus that according to him have existed. If Frauwallner's theory is admitted, then the works that are attributed by tradition to Vasubandhu are also to be distributed between both Vasubandhus, what is not an easy task.

Vasubandhu the Old

According to Frauwallner, cited work pp. 54-55, Vasubandhu the Old was born around 320 A.D. in Puruṣapura. His father, the brāhmaṇa Kauśika, was a teacher. He had two brothers, Asaṅga and Viriñcivatsa. In his youth he belonged to the Sarvāstivāda sect and wrote many works of Hīnayānist inspiration, which have been lost. Under the influence of his brother Asaṅga he converted to Mahāyāna and wrote also numerous works of Mahāyānist inspiration. Vasubandhu died before his brother Asaṅga, probably around 380A.D.

Vasubandhu the Young

Likewise according to Frauwallner, pp. 55-56, Vasubandhu the Young was born around 400 A.D. Nothing is known about the place of his birth and about his family. He belonged to the Sarvāstivāda sect but gradually he became more attached to the Sautrāntika's doctrines. One of his Masters was Buddhamitra. He was protected by King Skandagupta Vikramāditya of the Gupta dynasty (reigned *circa* 455-467A.D.). He was invited to the royal court in Ayodhyā by Bālāditya (reigned *circa* 467-473 A.D.). Vasubandhu had been preceptor of Bālāditya and received from him many honours. The first work he composed and which made Vasubandhu famous was the *Paramārthasaptatikā*, which contains a refutation of Master Vindhyavāsin of the Sāṃkhya school, who had defeated in a discussion his Master Buddhamitra. His principal work was the *Abhidharmakośa*, in which he exposed the doctrines of the Sarvāstivāda school to which he gave their definitive form. But in the commentary, which he wrote on that treatise, he manifests his preference for the doctrines of the Sautrāntika sect. After the composition of the *Abhidharmakośa* he successfully defended his ideas against the attack of the grammarian Vasurāta, but he refused on account of his old age to discuss the critics of Saṃghabhadra of the Hīnayānist Vaibhāṣika sect. Saṃghabhadra attacked the *Abhidharmakośa*'s commentary from a strict Vaibhāṣika point of view. Vasubandhu the Young died in Ayodhyā at the age of 80 years.

Works Attributted to Vasubandhu

Under the name "Vasubandhu" are mentioned numerous works.[11] We refer to the principal of them in what follows, indicating some of their editions and translations.

A. Treatises

1. *Abhidharmakośa*. Until 1935 only the Tibetan translations (*Tōhoku* 4089 [*kārikās*] and 4090 [*bhāṣya*] =*Catalogue* 5590 [*kārikās*] and 5591 [*bhāṣya*]) and the Chinese translations (*Taishō* 1558, 1559, and 1560 [*kārikās*]) of this work were known. In that year Rāhula Sāṅkrityāyana[12] discovered the Sanskrit text of this treatise in the Tibetan Monastery of Ṅor. Considering the importance of the *Abhidharmakośa*, this discovery was a most notorious event. The treatise contains 600 *kārikās* and a commentary by Vasubandhu. It is divided in 9 books. It is a large exposition of the Buddhist Hīnayānist doctrines as they were taught by the Sarvāstivāda-Vaibhāṣika sect.But, as it has already been said, in many points Vasubandhu's opinion differs from the orthodox opinion of that sect.
   The Sanskrit text was published for the first time by P. Pradhan in 1967 in the *Tibetan Sanskrit Works Series*, Vol. VIII of the *Kashi Prasad Jayaswal Research Institute* of Patna. It has been reedited by Swami Dwarikadas Shastri in 1970 in the *Bauddha Bharati Series*, 5, Varanasi.
   Between the years 1923 and 1931 Louis de la Vallée Poussin published the French translation of the *Abhidharmakośa* on the basis of the Tibetan and Chinese versions. The translation of the *Abhidharmakośa* of the great Belgian scholar has become a classic. It has been reprinted in 1971 by the *Institut Belge des Hautes Études Chinoises* of Brussels. There is an English translation of L. de la Vallée Poussin's French translation by Leo Marvel Pruden, *Abhidharmakośabhāṣyam*, five volumes, Berkeley: Asian Humanities Press, 1988-1990.
2. *Bodhicittotpādanaśāstra*. It deals with the means to attain *bodhicitta*, mind of Enlightenment. It has been preserved only in its Chinese translation (*Taishō* 1659). There is a Sanskrit translation of this text published by Bhadanta Santi Bhikshu in

Visva Bharati Annals, Vol. II, 1949, pp.185-243, under the title *"Fa fu t'i hsin ching lun, Bodhicittotpada-sutra-sastra* of Vasubandhu".

3. *Buddhatāśāstra* (?) or *Buddhatvaśāstra*(?) [Hōbōgirin] or *Buddhagotraś' āstra* [Nanjio]. It is a treatise on Buddha's nature. It is preserved only in its Chinese translation (*Taishō* 1610). There is a Japanese translation by Takemura Shōhō, *Busshōron Kenkyū*, Kyōto, Hyakkaen, Shōwa 52 (1977).
4. *Gāthāsaṃgrahaśāstra*. It is a collection of moral maxims with a commentary by Vasubandhu. It has been preserved only in one Tibetan translation (*Tōhoku* 4102 [stanzas] and 4103 [stanzas with commentary]=*Catalogue* 5603 [stanzas] and 5604 [stanzas with commentary]). The stanzas have been edited with a German translation, and a study of the commentary by A. Schiefner in, "Uber Vasubandhu's Gāthāsaṁgraha", *Mélanges Asiatiques,* VIII, Saint Petersburg, 1878, pp.559-593.
5. *Karmasiddhiprakaraṇa*. It deals with the theory of action (*karman*). It has come to us in one Tibetan translation (*Tōhoku* 4062=*Catalogue* 5563) and two Chinese translations (*Taishō* 1608 and 1609). É. Lamotte published the Tibetan translation, one of the Chinese translations (*Taishō* 1609), a French translation, and an erudite introduction in *Mélanges Chinois* et *Bouddhiques* IV, 1936, pp. 151-264 (English translation of Lamotte's work by L. M. Pruden, Berkeley: Asian Humanities Press, 1988). There is an English translation in S.Anacker, *Seven Works of Vasubandhu, the Buddhist Psychological Doctor,* pp. 83-156, Delhi: Motilal Banarsidass, 1984. S. Yamaguchi published the Tibetan translation of the treatise, a Japanese translation of the treatise and of its commentary by Sumatiśīla (*Tōhoku* 4071=*Catalogue* 5572), under the title *Sheshin no Jōgōron*, Kyōto: Hōzōkan, Shōwa 26 (1951); reprint 1975. Mitsuo Sato, *Daijō jōgō ron*, Tōkyō: Daizo Shuppan, 1978, published the Chinese text of the treatise with a Japanese translation.
6. *Pañcaskandhaprakaraṇa*. This treatise has as its central theme the theory of *dharmas*. According to E. Frauwallner, *Studies in Abhidharma Literature*, Albany: University of New York Press, 1995, p. 144, this work is "nothing more than a free adaptation" of the first chapter of the *Abhidharmasamuccaya* of Asaṅga. It has been preserved only in a Tibetan translation

(*Tōhoku* 4059=*Catalogue* 5560) and in a Chinese translation (*Taishō* 1612). Shanti Bhikshu Shastri published a Sanskrit "reconstruction" of this treatise from its Tibetan version, "Pañcaskandhaprakaraṇa of Vasubandhu", *Indian Historical Quarterly* 32, 1956, pp. 368-385. This "reconstruction" was also published in *Sārasvatī Suṣamā*, X, 1-4, Varanasi, Saṃvat 2012. There is a Japanese translation from the Tibetan version by Shimokawabe Kiyoshi and Takayama Hiroshi, "Gounron kenkyū" ("A Study of the Pañcaskandhaprakaraṇa"), in *Bukkyō Gaku Ronshū* ("Buddhist Studies"). Risshō University, XII, 1976, pp. 1-29. S. Anacker, *Seven Works*, 1984, pp.49-82, has an English translation of this text. V.V.Gokhale in "Pañcaskandhaka by Vasubandhu and its commentary by Sthiramati", *Annals of the Bhandarkar Oriental Research Institute*, Vol. XVIII, 1937, pp. 276-286, has a synopsis of this treatise.

7. *Paramārthasaptatikā or Paramārthasaptati.* It is a refutation of the Sāṃkhya doctrine. The Sanskrit original is not available and there are not either Chinese or Tibetan translations of it.[13]
8. *Śamathavipaśyanā (or-vidarśana)-dvāra-śāstra-kārikā* [Nanjio]. A metrical treatise on meditation. It consists of 77 verses. It is preserved only in its Chinese translation (*Taishō* 1655). There is a Japanese translation by Tsusho Byōdō in *Kokuyaku Issaikyō,* Ronshū-bu, Vol. 6, Tōkyō: Daitō Suppansha.
9. *Śatadharmavidyādvāraśāstra [Nanjio1213] or Mahāyānaśata dharmaprakāśaśāstra [Hōbōgirin] or Śatadharmavidyāmukha* [Sastri N. A.] (?). It is an enumeration of the principal (hundred) *dharmas,* selected from those enumerated in Asaṅga's *Yogācārabhūmi.* It is preserved only in its Tibetan translation (*Tōhoku* 4063=*Catalogue* 5564) and in its Chinese translation (*Taishō* 1614). There is a Sanskrit "reconstruction" from the Chinese version by N. A. Sastri, as an *Appendix* to his article on "Pañcavastukaśāstra and Vibhāṣa", *Visva-Bharati Annals* Vol. X, Santiniketan, 1961. It has been translated from Chinese into English, with a commentary of Master Hsüan Hua, by the Buddhist Text Translation Society, Talmage (California), 1983, and by A. Hirakawa, *Index to the Abhidharmakośabhāṣya,* pp.XX-XXII.
10. *Śīlaparikathā.* It is a collection of eleven stanzas, which develops the thesis that the moral discipline is more effective than liberality. Only two Tibetan translations of this text have

been preserved (*Tōhoku* 4164 and 4508=*Catalogue* 5421 and 5664). The Tibetan text of this work has been published by Anathnath Basu in *Indian Historical Quarterly* 7, 1931, pp. 28-33, with a "reconstruction" into Sanskrit and an English translation.

11. *Sukhāvatīvyūhopadeśa.* It is known only through its Chinese translation (*Taishō* 1524). There is a Japanese translation from the Chinese version done by Susumu Yamaguchi, *Sheshin no Jōdoron: Muryōjukyō upadaisha ganshōge no shikai ("A Treatise of Vasubandhu on Pure Land: the Sukhāvatīvyūhopadeśa")*, Kyōto: Hōzōkan, Shōwa 41 (1966), Shōwa 56 (1981), pp.189-206. Minoru Kiyota in his "Buddhist Devotional Meditation: A Study of the Sukhāvatīvyūhopadeśa" (in Minoru Kiyota [Ed.] *Mahāyāna Buddhist Meditation: Theory and Practice,* Honolulu: University Press of Hawaii. 1978, pp. 249-296) includes an English translation of this treatise in pp. 274-290. On this text see Luis O. Gómez, *The Land of Bliss*, Honolulu: University of Hawai'i Press, 1996, pp. 115, 120-122, 135.
12. *Tarkaśāstra* (?). It is a treatise on logic. It has been preserved only in a Chinese translation (*Taishō* 1633). G. Tucci has done a Sanskrit "retranslation" of this treatise, included in *Pre-Diṅnāga Buddhist Texts on Logic,* Baroda: Oriental Institute, 1929, reprint in San Francisco: Chinese Materials Center, 1976, pp. 3-40.
13. *Triṃśikā*. The Sanskrit text of this most important treatise with Sthiramati's commentary was discovered by S. Lévi in Nepal in 1922 thanks to the help of Hemrāj Śarman, The Rāj-Guru of the Mahārāja Chandra Shamsher Jang of Nepal. Before Lévi's discovery it was known only in its Tibetan translation (*Tōhoku* 4055=*Catalogue* 5556) and in its Chinese translation (*Taishō* 1586). S. Lévi edited this work, together with the *Viṃśatikā* (that he had also found in Nepal), under the title *Vijñaptimātratāsiddhi. Deux Traités de Vasubandhu, Viṃśatikā (La Vingtaine), accompagnée d' une explication en prose et Triṃśikā (La Trentaine) avec le Commentaire de Sthiramati, originel sanscrit publié pour la première fois d' aprés des manuscrits rapportés du Nepal, as the 245th fascicle of the Bibliothèque de l' École des Hautes Études*. Afterwards S. Lévi published the translation of both treatises under the title *Matériaux pour l'Etude du Systéme Vijñaptimātra,* Paris, 1932, as the 260th fascicle of the same *Bibliothèque*.

Katsumi Mimaki, Musashi Tachikawa and Akira Yuyama, in *Three Works of Vasubandhu in Sanskrit Manuscript. The Trisvabhāvanirdeśa, the Viṃśatikā with its Vṛtti, and the Triṃśikā with Sthiramati's Commentary*, Tokyo: The Centre for East Asian Cultural Studies, 1989 (Bibliotheca Codicum Asiaticorum 1), edited in facsimile 2 manuscripts of the *kārikās of the Triṃśikā* (designated as A and J) and 6 manuscripts of the *kārikās* together with the Commentary of Sthiramati (designated as C, D, E, F, G, and H). The manuscript discovered by Lévi is a copy of the manuscript designated as C, which is in palm-leaf, and now is located in the *National Archives of Kathmandu,* Nepal, and come from the famous *Durbar Library,* the Royal Library of that country.

After that first edition, the *Triṃśikā* of Vasubandhu has been edited numerous times reproducing Lévi's edition. Let us indicate some editions and translations of the *Triṃśikā*: Thubtan Chogdub, Śāstrī and Rāmaśaṅkara Tripāṭhi, *Vijñaptimātratāsiddhiḥ,* Varanasi: Gaṅgānāthajhā-Granthamālā, 1972, edition of the *Triṃśikā* with Sthiramati's commentary (and of the *Viṃśatikā* and the *Trisvabhāvanirdeśa),* with a Hindi translation and commentary. H. Jacobi, *Triṃśikāvijñapti des Vasubandhu mit Bhāṣya des Ācārya Sthiramati,* Stuttgart : W. Kohlhammer, 1932, in the series *Beiträge zur indischen Sprachwissenschaft und Religionsgeschichte,* German translation of Vasubandhu's treatise and Sthiramati's commentary. E.Frauwallner, *Die Philosophie des Buddhismus,* Berlin: Akademie Verlag, 1969, pp. 383-390, German translation of the *Triṃśikā* (stanzas alone). Enga Teramoto, *Bonzōkanwa shiyakutaishō Anne zō Yuishikisanjūron So ("Vijñaptimātratriṃśikā*. Sanskrit,Tibetan and Chinese texts, and a Japanese translation of Sthiramati's commentary"), Kyōto: Ōtani University Press, 1933. Unrai Wogihara, in *Wogihara Unrai Bunshū* ("Collection of Wogihara Unrai's Works"), Tōkyō: Taishō University, 1938 reprint Tōkyō, 1972, pp. 628-677, Japanese translation of the *Triṃśikā* and its commentary by Sthiramati. Hakuju Ui, *Anne Gohō Yuishiki sanjūju shakuron* ("Commentaries by Sthiramati and Dharmapāla on the kārikās of Vijñaptimātratriṃśikā"), Tōkyō: Iwanami Shoten, 1952, Sanskrit and Chinese texts with the Japanese translation of the commentaries by Sthiramati and Dharmapāla on Vasubandhu's *Triṃśikā*. Susumu Yamaguchi and Jōshō Nozawa, *Sheshin Yuishiki no genten kaimei* ("Textual Studies of Vasubandhu's Treatise on Vijñaptimātratā"), Kyōto: Hōzōkan, 1953, Japanese translation of the *Triṃśikā* with the Commentary by Sthiramati and *ṭīkā* by Vinītadeva. Noritoshi Aramaki, in the series *Daijō Butten,* Volume 15, Tōkyō, Shōwa 62 (1988), pp. 31-190. K.N. Chatterjee, *Vasubandhu's Vijñaptimatratā-siddhi (With Sthiramati's Commentary),*Varanasi: Kishor Vidya Niketan, 1980, pp. 33-133, Sanskrit text with English translation. Th. A. Kochumuttom, *A Buddhist Doctrine of Experience,* Delhi: Motilal Banarsidass, 1982, pp.128-160 and pp.254- 259, English translation of the stanzas alone. S.Anacker, *Seven works,* 1984, pp. 186-189, English translation of the stanzas alone, pp. 422-423, Sanskrit text of the stanzas[14].

The *Triṃśikā* contains thirty *kārikās* and is an exposition of some of the most fundamental themes of the Yogācāra school. This treatise is the nucleus of the important work composed by Hiuan tsang (or Hsüan tsang) *Ch' eng wei shih lun (Vijñaptimātratāsiddhi) (Taishō* 1585). In this work Hiuan tsang gives the Chinese translation of the *Triṃśikā* with translations or resumes of the ten principal commentaries written on it. All these Sanskrit commentaries have been lost with exception of Sthiramati's one. The work of Hiuan tsang was translated from Chinese into French by Louis de la Vallée Poussin under the title *La Siddhi de Hiuan-Tsang. Vijñaptimātratāsiddhi,* Paris: Paul Geuthner,Volume I,1928, Volume II,1929, in the series *Buddhica, Documents et Travaux pour l'Étude du Bouddhisme*. This translation became also a classic as L. de la Vallée Poussin's translation of the *Abhidharmakośa* of Vasubandhu. In 1948 L. de la Vallée Poussin published a useful *Index* of his translation, Paris: Paul Geuthner. There is an English translation of Hiuan tsang's work under the title *Ch'eng wei shih lun, The Doctrine of mere-consciousness by Hsüan Tsang,* done by Wei Tat, Hong Kong: Ch'eng Wei-Shih Lun Publication Committee, 1973. It contains also the Sanskrit text of the *Triṃśikā* and its commentary, and the Chinese text of Hiuan tsang.

14. *Trisvabhāvanirdeśa* or *Trisvabhāvakārikā*. It deals with three forms of being, imaginary, dependent and absolute. This work of Vasubandhu is included in this book.

15. *Vādavidhi*. The subject matter of this treatise is the rules of debate. The Sanskrit text has not been preserved and there are not Chinese or Tibetan translations of it, but a great number of fragments are known thanks to quotations by other authors as Uddyotakara and specially Dignāga. E.Frauwallner, "Vasubandhu's Vādavidhiḥ", *Wiener Zeitschrift für die Kunde Süd-und Ost-Asiens*, 1, 1957, pp. 104-146 (= *Kleine Schriften*, pp. 716-758) has collected all these fragments (*Appendix* I) and given their translation (*Kleine Schriften*, pp. 730-740). Cf. E. Frauwallner, "Zu den Fragmenten buddhistischer Logiker im Nyāyavārttikam", *Wiener Zeitschrift für die Kunde Morgenlandes*, 40, 1933, pp. 281-304 (= *Kleine Schriften*, pp. 460-483 in especial pp. 461, 475-478 and 482. Anacker, *Seven Works of Vasubandhu*, pp. 38-47 gives an English translation of the *Vādavidhi*'s fragments.
16. *Vādavidhāna*, a work similar to *Vādaviddhi*. The Sanskrit text has been lost and there exist no Chinese or Tibetan translation. It is known only by fragments that have been collected by E. Frauwallner, in pp. 479- 481 of his article "Zu den Fragmenten buddhistischen Logiker in Nyāyavārttikam", 1933, pp. 300-302 (=*Kleine Schriften* pp.479-481).
17. *Vimśatikā*. This work contains twenty two stanzas and a commentary by Vasubandhu himself, and is like the *Trimśikā* an exposition of several important doctrines of the Yogācāra school. We shall refer to this work with more details later on.
18. *Vyākhyāyukti*. It is a treatise that teaches how to interpret and explain the content of a *sūtra*. It is preserved only in its Tibetan translation (*Tōhoku* 4061=*Catalogue* 5562). On this text see the article of Susumu Yamaguchi in *Nippon Bukkyō Gakukai Nenpō* (" The Journal of the Japan Buddhist Research Association"), 25, 1959, pp. 35-68, and *Tōhō Gakkai Commemoration Volume*, Tōkyo, 1962, pp. 369-391.

B. Commentaries of treatises or of commentaries by other authors

1. Commentary of the *Madhyāntavibhāga* or *Madhyāntavibhaṅga (kārikās)* of Maitreya. The Sanskrit text of this commentary has been preserved. It was discovered by Rāhula Sāṅkṛtyāyana in Tibet in 1934.[15] Before this discovery, the commentary by Vasubandhu was only known in its Tibetan translation (*Tōhoku* 4027=*Catalogue* 5528) and in its Chinese translations (*Taishō* 1599 and 1600). It was edited for the first time by G. M. Nagao,

in his book *Madhyāntavibhāga-bhāṣya. A Buddhist Philosophical Treatise edited for the first time from a Sanskrit manuscript,* Tokyo: Suzuki Research Foundation, 1964, and afterwards by Nathmal Tatia and Anantalal Thakur, *Madhyānta-Vibhāga-Bhāṣya,* Patna : K. P. Jayaswal Research Institute, 1967; by R.C.Pandeya, under the title of *Madhyānta-Vibhāga-Śāstra,* Delhi: Motilal Banarsidass, 1971, with the important sub-commentary (*ṭīkā*) of Sthiramati; and by Swami Dwarikadas Shastri, under the same title, and also with Sthiramati's commentary and with a Hindi translation, Varanasi: Bauddha Bharati Series, 1994. There are an English translation of the first book, done by Th. Stcherbatsky, *Discourse on Discrimination between middle and extremes,* 1936, reprinted in Calcutta, 1971, in the series *Indian Studies: Past and Present;* and an English translation of the third book by P.W.O' Brien, "A Chapter on Reality from the *Madhyānta-vibhāga-śāstra*", in *Monumenta Nipponica,* Tōkyō: Sophia University, 1953, Vol. IX, pp. 277-303, and 1954, Vol. X, pp. 227-269. These translations contain also the translation of the *kārikās* of Maitreya and of the sub-commentary by Sthiramati. In the series *Daijō Butten,* Volume 15, Tōkyō, 1977, pp. 215-358, G.M.Nagao published a Japanese translation from the original Sanskrit text of the complete commentary of Vasubandhu. S. Anacker, *Seven Works,* 1984, pp. 211-273, published an English translation of the commentary by Vasubandhu and the Sanskrit text of this work, pp. 424-463. Th. A. Kochumuttom, *A Buddhist Doctrine of Experience,* 1982, in pp. 27-89 has an interpretation of the first chapter of Vasubandhu's commentary. S.Yamaguchi, *Sthiramati Madhyāntavibhāgaṭīkā. Exposition Systématique du Yogācāravijñaptivāda,* Nagoya: Librairie Hajinkaku, 1934, reprint Tōkyō: Suzuki Research Foundation, 1966, 3 Vols., edited the Sanskrit text of the sub-commentary of Sthiramati (Vol. I), and accompanied it with the Tibetan and Chinese translation of the commentary of Vasubandhu (Vol. III).

2. Commentary of the *Dharmadharmatāvibhaṅgakārikā* or *Dharmadharmatāvibhāgakārikā* of Maitreya. It has been preserved only in its Tibetan version (*Tōhoku* 4028=*Catalogue* 5529). Sylvain Lévi, *Asaṅga. Mahāyāna-Sūtrālaṃkāra. Exposé de la Doctrine du Grand Véhicule selon le Système Yogācāra,* Tome I.-Texte, Paris: Honoré Champion, 1907, pp. 190-191:

Appendices, has a fragment in Sanskrit, which later on was identified as belonging to the *Dharmadharmatāvibhāga* by Hideo Kawai, and critically edited by Susumu Yamaguchi, "*Hohosshōfunbetsuron no bonbun ampen*" ("Fragments of the Sanskrit text of the *Dharmadharmatāvibhāgaśāstra"), Ōtani Gakuhō*: Ōtani University, Vol. 17, No.4, 1936, pp. 40-47, reprint Tōkyō, 1972, pp. 201-211. Jōshō Nozawa, "The *Dharmadharmatāvibhaṅga* and the *Dharmadharmatāvibhaṅga-vṛtti*", *Studies in Indology and Buddhology Presented in honour of Professor Susumu Yamaguchi,* Kyōto: Hōzōkan, 1955, pp. 9-49, published the Tibetan translations (pp. 9-18) of this work (Peking and Sde-dge ed.) with the Sanskrit fragments (pp. 46-49). The Tibetan version of this commentary has been edited with a Sanskrit "reconstruction" by Chulathima Phunachoga, Sarnath; Kendriya Ucca Tibbati- Śikṣā-Saṃsthāna, 1990. Klaus -Dieter Mathes, *Unterscheidung der Gegebenheiten von ihrem wahren Wesen,* Swisttal- Odendorf: Indica et Tibetica Verlag, 1996, has given a most complete edition of this treatise.

3. Commentary of the *Mahāyānasaṃ (pari) grahaśāstra* or *Mahāyānasaṃgrahabhāṣya* of Asaṅga (or Maitreya). It has come to us only in its Tibetan translation (*Tōhoku* 4050=*Catalogue* 5551) and in three Chinese translations (*Taishō* 1595, 1596 and 1597). There are Japanese translations by Etō Sokuō of Hiuan Tsang's (1597) and Paramārtha's (1595) Chinese versions of Vasubandhu's commentary in *Kokuyaku Issaikyō,* Yuga-bu, Tōkyō: Daitō Shuppansha, Vol. 8, 1935, reprint Tōkyō, 1977, pp. 1-207, and Vol. 9, Tōkyō, 1935, reprint Tōkyō, 1977. É. Lamotte in his translation of Asaṅga's *Mahāyāna-saṃgraha* has given in notes the translation into French of numerous extracts from Vasubandhu's commentary.
4. Commentary (prose) of the 100 stanzas (*kārikās)* of the *Mahāyānasūtrālaṅkāra.* The commentary and the stanzas have been transmitted together as forming a single work. The Sanskrit text has been preserved, and edited and translated into French by S. Lévi, Paris: H. Champion, 1907 (Tome I. Texte), Paris: H. Champion, 1911 (Tome II. Traduction). The Sanskrit text was reprinted in Tōkyō: Rinsen Sanskrit Text Series, 1983. S. Bagchi, *Mahāyāna-Sūtrālaṅkāra of Asaṅga,* Darbhanga: The Mithila Institute, 1970, edited the Sanskrit text on the basis of Lévi's edition with *corrigenda* in pp. 289-328. Surekha Vijay

Limaye, edited the Sanskrit text and translated it into English, Delhi: Indian Book Centre, 1992. There is a Chinese translation (*Taishō* 1604, *kārikās* and commentary) and a Tibetan translation (*kārikās: Tōhoku* 4020=*Catalogue* 5521; *commentary: Tōhoku* 4026=*Catalogue* 5527) of this work.

5. Commentary of the *Śataśāstra* or *Śata [ka] śāstra* (?) [Hōbōgirin] of Āryadeva, preserved in a Chinese translation (*Taishō* 1569). G. Tucci translated this work from the Chinese first into Italian, *Le cento strofe (Śataśāstra), testo buddhistico mahāyāna tradotto dal cinese, con introduzione e note, in Studi e Materiali di Storia delle Religioni,* Vol. I., Roma, 1925, pp. 66-128, 161-189, and afterwards also into English in *Pre-Diṅnāga Buddhist Texts on Logic from Chinese Sources,* Gaekwad's Oriental Series 49, 1929, reprint 1976, pp. 1-89. L. de la Vallée Poussin, "Le Nirvāṇa d'aprés Āryadeva", *Mélanges Chinois et Bouddhiques, Premier volume:* 1931-1932. Bruxelles: Marcel Istas, Juillet 1932, pp. 128-130, has the French translation of a fragment of this work concerning *nirvāṇa* (=pp. 80-82 of G. Tucci's English translation). H. Ui in *Kokuyaku Daizō-kyō,* Ron-bu, Tōkyō: Kokumin Bunko Kankō-kai, 1921, Vol. 5, reprint 1975, pp. 481-608, published a Japanese translation of this commentary. The Chinese tradition attributes this work to Vasu who has been identified with Vasubandhu. Cf. Noël Péri, "A propos de la date de Vasubandhu", 1911, pp. 361-368; Richard Gard, "On the Authenticity of the *Pai-lun* and *Shih-erh-mên-lun", Journal of Indian and Buddhist Studies,* Vol. II, No. 2, Tokyo: Japanese Association of Indian and Buddhist Studies, 1954, pp. 751-742; and E. Frauwallner, *On the date,* 1951, pp. 36-37.

6. Sub-commentary on the *Vajracchedikāprajñāpāramitāśāstra* of Asaṅga *(Taishō* 1514), preserved in two Chinese translations (*Taishō* 1511 and 1513). An analysis of this text is given by G. Tucci, in *Minor Buddhist Texts,* Roma: IsMEO, 1956. Hakuju Ui, translated it into Japanese in *Daijō Butten no Kenkyū,*: Tokyo: Iwanami Shoten, 1962.

C. Commentaries of Sūtras

1. Commentary of the *Daśabhūmikasūtra,* (entitled: *Ārya-daśabhūmi-vyākhyana)* known only in its Chinese translation (*Taishō* 1522) and in its Tibetan translation (*Tōhoku* 3993= *Catalogue* 5494). Johannes Rahder, in "*Daśabhūmika-sūtra,*

Seventh Stage", *Acta Orientalia,* Vol. 4, 1925, pp. 214-256, includes the English tranlsation of the corresponding part of Vasubandhu's commentary. There is a Japanese translation from the Chinese version of Vasubandhu's commentary done by Kyōdō Ishii in *Kokuyaku Issaikyō,* Tokyo.

2. Commentary of the *Pratityasamutpādasūtra,* which has been preserved in a complete form in one Tibetan translation (*Tōhoku* 3995=*Catalogue* 5496). G. Tucci found in Nepal a manuscript containing part of the original Sanskrit text of this work. It was edited by him in "A Fragment from *Pratītya-samutpāda-vyākhyā* of Vasubandhu", *Journal of the Royal Asiatic Society,* 1930, pp. 611-623 (=*Opera Minora,* Parte I, Roma: G. Bardi, 1971, in the series *Studi Orientali* of the University of Rome, pp. 239-248). E. Frauwallner, *Die Philosophie des Buddhismus,* pp. 43-48, translated into German from Sanskrit the chapter on *Tṛṣṇā.* The Tibetan text of two chapters *(Saṃskāra* and *Vijñānavibhaṅga)* of this work has been edited with a German translation by Yoshihito G. Muroji, *Vasubandhus Interpretation des Pratītyasamutpāda,* Stuttgart: F. Steiner, 1993. In Muroji's book can be found other references to translations of other sections of Vasubandhu's commentary into Japanese.
3. Commentary of the *Saddharmapuṇḍarīkasūtra,* preserved only in its Chinese translations (*Taishō* 1519 and 1520). On this commentary cf. Terry Rae Abbott, *Vasubandhu's commentary to the Saddharmapuṇḍarīkasūtra, a Study of its History and Significance* (Ph. D. Thesis) University of California, Berkeley, Dec. 1985. Ryōzan Shimizu translated this work into Japanese in *Kokuyaku Daizō-kyō,* Ron-bu, Tōkyō: Kakumin Bunko Kankōkai, 1921, reprint 1975, Vol. 5, pp. 741-766.
4. Commentary of the *Vajracchedikāprajñāpāramitāsūtra,* preserved in its Tibetan translation (*Tōhoku* 3816=*Catalogue* 5864). The Tibetan translation gives to this text the name of *Āryabhagavatīprajñāpāramitāvajracchedikāyāḥ saptārthaṭīkā* and attributes it to Vasubandhu (Sde-dge ed.); or *Vajra cchedikāyāḥ prajñāpāramitāyā vyākhyānopanibandhana-kārikā* without mention of the author of the work (Peking ed.). In the Chinese Buddhist Canon *(Taishō* 1510) this commentary is attributed to Asaṅga. *Répertoire,* p. 128 (1510), considers that it must be rather attributed to Vasubandhu. According also

to G. Tucci, *Minor Buddhist Texts,* Roma: IsMEO, 1956 (reprinted in Delhi: Motilal Banarsidass, 1986), Volume I, pp.14-18, this commentary was not composed by Asaṅga, but rather by Vasubandhu. An English translation of this commentary is included by Tucci, *ibidem,* pp. 51-128.

5. Commentary on the *Dharmacakrapravartanasūtra,* existing only in its Chinese version (*Taishō* 1533, Nanjio 1205). There is a Japanese translation by Hōkei Idzumi in *Kokuyaku Issaikyō,* Shakukyōron-bu 8.
6. *Nirvāṇaśāstra,* a brief commentary of the *Mahāparinirvāṇasūtra,* existing only in its Chinese version (*Taishō* 1527, Nanjio 1206). There is a Japanese translation by Kogaku Fuse in *Kokuyaku Issaikyō,* Shakukyōron-bu 8.
7. Commentary of a verse of the *Mahāparinirvāṇasūtra* on the state of being formerly existing and then extinct, existing only in its Chinese version (*Taishō* 1528, Nanjio 1207). There is a Japanese translation by Kogaku Fuse in *Kokugaku Issaikyō,* Shakukyōron-bu 8.
8. Commentary of the *Ratnacūḍaparipṛcchā,* existing only in its Chinese version (*Taishō* 1526, Nanjio 1241). The *Ratnacūḍaparipṛcchā* belongs to the *Ratnakūṭasūtra (Taishō* 310-47, *Tōhoku* 91 =*Catalogue* 760-47). There is a Japanese translation by Hōkei Idzumi in *Kokuyaku Issaikyō,* Shakukyōron-bu 8.
9. Commentary of the *Viśeṣacintābrahmaparipṛcchāsūtra,* existing only in its Chinese version (*Taisho* 1532, Nanjio 1193).

Distribution of the Works Attributed to Vasubandhu

I. The tradition that there existed only one Vasubandhu considers that the works of Hīnayānist inspiration attributed to him were written by him in the epoch in which he belonged to the Hīnayāna Buddhism, and that the works of Mahāyānist inspiration were written by him after his conversion to Mahāyāna.

Among the works we have enumerated could be considered of Hīnayāna inspiration the following ones:

Abhidharmakośa (A.1)
Gāthāsaṃgraha (A.4)
Pañcaskandhaprakaraṇa (A. 6)
Śīlaparikathā (A.10)

Could be considered of Mahāyānist inspiration the following ones:

A. Treatises:

Bodhicittotpādaśāstra (A.2)

Buddhatāśāstra (?) (A.3)
Karmasiddhiprakaraṇa (A.5)
Śatadharmavidyādvāra (?) (A.9)
Sukhāvatīvyūhopadeśa (A.11)
Triṃśikā (A.13)
Trisvabhāva-kārikā (or *°nirdeśa)* (A.14)
Viṃśatikā (A. 17)
Vyākhyāyukti (A.18)

B. Commentaries of treatises or of commentaries by other authors
of the *Madhyāntavibhāga of Maitreya* (B. 1)
of the *Dharmadharmatāvibhaṅga* of Maitreya (B. 2)
of the *Mahāyānasaṃ (pari) graha* of Asaṅga (B. 3)
of the *Mahāyānasūtrālaṅkāra* of Maitreya or Asaṅga (B. 4)
of the *Śataśāstra* of Āryadeva (B.5)
of the *commentary* of the *Vajracchedikāprajñāpāramitāsūtra* attributed to Asaṅga but more probably of Vasubandhu (B. 6)

C. Commentaries of Sūtras:
of the *Daśabhūmikasūtra* (C.1)
of the *Pratītyasamutpādasūtra* (C.2)
of the *Saddharmapuṇḍarīkasūtra* (C.3)
of the *Vajracchedikāprajñāpāramitāsūtra* (C.4)
of the *Dharmacakrapravartanasūtra* (C. 5)
of the *Mahāparinirvāṇasūtra* (C.6)
of a verse of the *Mahāparinirvāṇasūtra* (C.7)
of the *Ratnacūḍaparipṛcchā* (C.8)
of the *Viśeṣacintābrahmaparipṛcchāsūtra* (C.9)

Are of a technical character and therefore impossible to be discriminated as Hīnayānist or as Mahāyānist the following ones :
Paramārthasaptati (against the Sāṃkhya) (A. 7)
Tarkaśāstra (Logic) (A. 12)
Vādavidhi (Debate) (A. 15)
Vādavidhāna (Debate) (A. 16)

II. If Frauwallner's thesis about the two Vasubandhus is admitted, the situation becomes more complex, because any work could have been composed by one or the other of the two Vasubandhus, since, in the case of Vasubandhu the Old, he belonged—according to Frauwallner—firstly to the Hīnayāna sect and then to the Mahāyāna, and thus he could have composed works adhering to any one of the two tendencies; and, in the case of Vasubandhu the Young, nothing hinders that, besides the Hīnayānist works he composed, he wrote also works exposing Mahāyānist doctrines, even if he did not adhere to any Mahāyānist sect.

According to what Frauwallner expresses in his quoted book on the date of Vasubandhu it is possible to think that Vasubandhu the Old composed the *Bodhicittotpādaśāstra* (A. 2) and the commentaries on the *Madhyāntavibhāga* of Maitreya (B.1), the *Śataśāstra* of Āryadeva (B. 5), the *Daśabhūmikasūtra* (C.1), the *Saddharmapuṇḍarīkasūtra* (C.3), and the sub-commentary on the commentary of Asaṅga on the *Vajracchedikāprajñāpāramitāsūtra* (B.6).

To Vasubandhu the Young could be attributed—according to Frauwallner—the *Paramārthasaptati* (A.7) and the *Abhidharmakośa* (A.1).

In relation to the other works that are considered by tradition to have been composed by Vasubandhu, Frauwallner, in his quoted work p. 56, does not emit an opinion as there are no sufficient elements that allow a decision. In *Die Philosophie des Buddhismus,* p.351, and in "Landmarks in the history of Indian Logic", published in *Wiener Zeitschrift für die Kunde Süd-und Ost-Asiens,* 5, 1961, p. 132 (= *Kleine Schriften,* Wiesbaden: F. Steiner, 1982, p. 854), Frauwallner thinks that the *Viṃśatikā* and the *Triṃśikā* are of the junior Vasubandhu, but without entering into details and without giving any support to his opinion.

III. It is interesting to refer to L. Schmithausen's opinion in regard to the distribution of the works attributed by tradition to Vasubandhu, as expressed in his work on *Ālayavijñāna,* 1987, Part II, pp. 262-263. According to Schmithausen, "there are good reasons for taking the author of *"Abhidharmakośabhāṣya, Vyākyāyukti, Karmasiddhi, Pratītyasamutpādavyākhyā, Pañcaskandhaka, Viṃśatikā* and *Triṃśikā* to be one and the same person". Then he adds, p.262-263: "On the other hand... I prefer to treat the Vasubandhu commentaries on *Madhyāntavibhāga, Dharmadharmatāvibhāga, Mahāyānasaṃgraha* and *Mahāyānasūtrālaṃkāra* (the commentary of the latter being, sometimes, even ascribed to Asaṅga) as well as the *Trisvabhāvanirdeśa* (the authorship of which may at any rate need reconsideration) as a separate group, because in these certain central doctrinal peculiarities of the comparable parts of the first group seem to be lacking (or at best marginal)".

Authenticity of the Works

A problem different from that of the distribution of the works is that of their authenticity. This problem is to be formulated in diverse ways if one accepts the tradition of only one Vasubandhu or if one admits Frauwallner's thesis of two Vasubandhus: are all the works that tradition attributes to the only Vasubandhu that it accepts really his ?, and are all the works attributed to Vasubandhu the Old and those attributed to Vasubandhu the Young really theirs ?

We cannot answer these questions in this book. They require a research in relation to each of the works attributed to Vasubandhu. We shall limit ourselves to say something in the following paragraph in relation to the *Viṃśatikā*.

It is obvious that the problems of the existence of one or two Vasubandhus, and of the authenticity of the works attributed to him or them are of utmost importance.

As in regard to the problem of the authenticity of the works attributed to Dignāga, our criterion concerning the works attributed to Vasubandhu by tradition is to accept that attribution as long as founded arguments are not adduced against it.

Authenticity of the *Viṃśatikā*

The tradition that asserts the existence of only one Vasubandhu does not doubt about the authenticity of the *Viṃśatikā*. The Sanskrit manuscript found by S. Lévi in Nepal (= the Sanskṛit manuscript edited by Mimaki, Tachikawa and Yuyama), the colophons of the Tibetan translations (*Tōhoku* 4056 and 4057=*Catalogue* 5557 and 5558) and of the Chinese translations (*Taishō* 1588, 1589 and 1590) attribute this work to Vasubandhu. Paramārtha, Life of Vasubandhu (*Taishō* 2049, p.191 c, line 8), enumerates among the works of Vasubandhu the *Vijñaptimātratāsiddhi* which includes the *Viṃśatikā* and the *Triṃśikā*; cf. J. Takakusu, " The Life of Vasubandhu", in *T 'oung Pao Archives Series* II, Vol. 4-5, 1904, p. 292. Buston, *History of Buddhism (Chos-ḥbyung)*, I. Part, Heidelberg: Otto Harrassovitz, 1931, E. Obermiller's translation, pp. 56-57, mentions the *Viṃśatikā* among the works of Vasubandhu. In general modern scholars accept the authenticity of the *Viṃśatikā*, as for instance M. Winternitz, *History of Indian Literature*, II, New Delhi: Oriental Books Reprint Corporation, 1972, p. 360; A.K. Chatterjee, *The Yogācāra Idealism*, Delhi: Motilal Banarsidass, 1975, p. 38; A. K. Warder, *Indian Buddhism*, Delhi: Motilal Banarsidass, 1970, p. 445; A. Bareau, *Die Religionen Indiens* III, Stuttgart: W. Kohlhammer, 1964, p. 141; H. Nakamura, *Indian Buddhism*, Delhi: Motilal Banarsidass, 1987, pp. 268-269.

Discovery of the *Viṃśatikā*[16]

The manuscript of this work, *kārikās* and commentary, was found in Kathmandu, Nepal, by Hemrāj Śarman, *Rāj-Guru* of the Mahārāja of Nepal Chandra Shamsher Jang. Hemrāj Śarman informed Sylvain Lévi about this discovery in a personal letter of the 24th February 1924, and soon after he sent him a copy of the manuscript. We designate this manuscript *MS1*. In this manuscript the two first *kārikās* and the beginning of the commentary are missing. See the second note to the Sanskrit text of the *Viṃśatikā* in this book. Before that date the *Vimśatikā* was known only in its Tibetan and Chinese translations, to which we shall refer in a following paragraph. Soon afterwards two other manuscripts were found in Kathmandu containing the Sanskrit text of the (complete) *kārikās* of the *Viṃśatikā*, and of those of the *Triṃśikā* respectively. We designate the second manuscript of the complete *kārikās* alone *MS2*. In 1925 S. Lévi published the Sanskrit text of the *Viṃśatikā* together with that of the *Triṃśikā* under the title *Vijñapti mātratā siddhi*. See *supra A. Treatises* 13. In 1932 S. Lévi published a translation of both treatises in his book *Matériaux pour l' étude du système Vijñaptimātra* (see *ibidem*). In pp.175-179 of this book he reproduced the Sanskrit text of the two first *kārikās* that are in the second discovered manuscript, but that lack in the first discovered manuscript, as already said. He corrected also some mistakes of his edition of the *Viṃśatikā*.

Mimaki, Tachikawa and Yuyama, in their edition of *Three Works of Vasubandhu in Sanskrit Manuscript*, published in facsimile a Sanskrit manuscript of the *kārikās* of the *Viṃśatikā* (designated as *A* in their book), and a manuscript of the *kārikās* with commentary (designated as *B* in their book), both in palm-leaf, both at present in possession of the *National Archives* of Kathmandu, and both coming from the *Durbar Library*. We designate these manuscripts *MTY-A* and *MTY-B*. Taking into account that Lévi got copies of his two manuscripts (one of the *kārikās* and commentary, and another of the *kārikās* alone) from the *rājaguru* of the Mahārāja of Nepal, the owner of the *Durbar Library*, that his manuscript containing *kārikās* and commentary lack the first page as it also happens with the corresponding manuscript *(B)* edited by these three Japanese scholars, and that the beginning of the leaves of Lévi's manuscript (sent to him in copy by the Rāj-Guru of Nepal) agrees almost in all the cases with the beginning of the leaves of the manuscript edited by the three Japanese scholars, it is possible to conclude that Lévi's manuscripts *MS1* and *MS2* are copies of the referred two manuscripts *MTY-A* and *MTY-B*.

Importance of the *Viṃśatikā*

The *Viṃśatikā* is one of the most important texts of Vasubandhu and of the Yogācāra school. In it is exposed the fundamental thesis of that school: the inexistence of the external object of knowledge/the existence of sole consciousness. Besides that, this work deals in a more or less detailed way and in clear terms with other themes of the school: the world as a mere mental creation, the theory of *vāsanās* or subliminal impressions, the theory of the *dharmas* or factors or elements of existence, the criticism of the atomist theory, the method to interpret Buddha's teachings, the Buddhist conception of the whole and the parts, the perception with and without *vikalpas* (mental elements that accompany the cognitive process), the problems to which gives rise the inexistence of an external object of knowledge in relation to memory, moral responsibility, etc. The value of the *Viṃśatikā* is enhanced by the fact that the original Sanskrit text has been preserved as well as the Sanskrit text of the commentary by Vasubandhu himself.

Vasubandhu's Opponents in *Viṃśatikā*

The word of the Buddha (*āgama*) could be used by Buddhist thinkers as an "argument" only in a discussion with other Buddhists, but not in a discussion with non-Buddhists (Hindus, Jainas). In this last case it was necessary to have recourse only to rational arguments. On their turn, Hindus and Jainas could not adduce against Buddhists the texts that were sacred for them. This circumstance forced Buddhists, Hindus and Jains to carry on their doctrinary discussions in a philosophical, rational level, without offering as a proof the authority of their respective canonical texts. This circumstance favoured the development of logic and dialectics in Indian philosophy from very early times.

As in the *Viṃśatikā* Vasubandhu appeals several times to texts that contain "the word of the Buddha"(*sūtras*), and to doctrines that are specifically Buddhist (see for an example note 34), we have to consider that this treatise has been composed by him having in mind Buddhist realist opponents. His intention was to expound the idealistic doctrine in a Buddhist context and besides that to convince other Buddhists of obvious realistic philosophical tendency.

Some Editions and Translations of the *Viṃśatikā*

We indicate some editions and translations of this work out of the numerous ones that exist:

I. Old Editions and Translations

Translations into Chinese by Paramārtha (*Taishō* 1589).

Translation into Chinese by Gautama Prajñāruci (*Taishō* 1588)

Translation into Chinese by Hiuan tsang (*Taishō* 1590). This translation is much superior to the other two.

All these Chinese translations are of the *kārikās* and their commentary.

Translation into Tibetan of the *kārikās* by Jinamitra, Śīlendrabodhi and Ye-śes sde, according to Sde-dge edition (*Tōhoku* 4056); according to Peking edition (*Catalogue* 5557) by Jinamitra, Śīlendrabodhi, Dānaśīla and Ye-śes sde.

Translation into Tibetan of the *kārikās* and the commentary by Jinamitra, Śīlendrabodhi and Ye-śes sde, according to Sde-dge edition (*Tōhoku* 4057); and Peking edition (*Catalogue* 5558).

II. Modern Editions and Translations

L. de la Vallée Poussin, "Vasubandhu, Viṃśakakārikāprakaraṇa. Traité des vingt ślokas avec le commentaire de l' auteur", in *Le Muséon,* Nouvelle Série, Vol. XIII, No. 1, Louvain: J. -B., Istas, 1912, pp. 53-90, edited the Tibetan text according to the red Narthang edition with variant readings of the black Narthang edition, and with a French translation.

Sasaki Genjun, *Yuishiki Nijūron no taiyaku kenkyū* (A comparative Study of the *Viṃśatikā* of the Vijñāna school), Kyotō: Heirakuji Shoten, 1940, reprint of the 1923 edition, published the Chinese and the Tibetan versions of the treatise (*kārikās* and commentary) with a Japanese translation.

S. Lévi, *Vijñaptimātratāsiddhi, Deux traités de Vasubandhu,* 1925, pp. 1-14, edited the Sanskrit text of the *Viṃśatikā (kārikās* and commentary).

S. Lévi, *Matériaux pour l' étude du système Vijñaptimātra,* 1932, pp. 43-59, published a French translation of the *Viṃśatikā (kārikās* and commentary)

More references on the last two works have been given before in *A. Treatises 13.*

Junyu Kitayama, *Metaphysik des Buddhismus,* San Francisco (USA), Chinese Materials Center, 1976, reprint of the 1934 edition, pp.234- 268, offers a German translation with analysis and notes of the *kārikās* only.

Unrai Wogihara, *Wogihara Unrai Bunshū* (Collected Works of Unrai Wogihara, Tōkyō: Taishō University, 1938, pp. 343-423, published the Sanskrit text of the treatise (*kārikās* and commentary) together with a Japanese translation and the Chinese versions of Hiuan Tsang (*Taishō* 1590) and Paramārtha (*Taishō* 1589). In pp. 679-680 he gives a list with explanations of the *errata* of Lévi's edition with the respective corrections and suggestions.

C.H. Hamilton, *Wei shih er shih lun or The treatise in twenty stanzas on representation-only by Vasubandhu, translated from the Chinese version of Hsüan Tsang, Tripiṭaka Master of the T'ang dinasty,* New Haven: American Oriental Society, 1938, reprint New York, 1967, gives the Chinese text with English translation of the *kārikās* and the commentary.[17]

Susumu Yamaguchi, in collaboration with Nozawa Jōshō, *Sheshin Yuishiki no genten kaimei* ("Textual Studies of Vasubandhu's Treatise that deals with the Vijñaptimātra"), Kyōto: Hōzōkan, Shōwa 28 (1953), offers a Japanese translation with notes of the *kārikās* and the commentary.

Hakuju Ui, *Shiyaku taishō yuishiki Nijūron kenkyū* ("Study of the *Viṃśatikā* of the Vijñaptimātra School with a comparison of the four translations"), Tōkyō: Iwanami Shoten, 1990, reprint of 1953 edition, published the Chinese versions with a Japanese translation (*kārikās* and commentary).

S.S. Bagchi, "Vijñaptimātratāsiddhi, Viṃśatikā of Vasubandhu", in *Nava-Nālandā-Mahāvihāra Research Publication* I, 1957, pp. 367-389, offers an English translation of the Sanskrit text (*kārikās* and commentary) and as an appendix, pp. 1-12, gives the Sanskrit text.

M.Tiwary, *Vijñaptimātratāsiddhi,* Varanasi: Chowkhamba Vidyābhavan, 1967, published the edition and a Hindi translation of the *Viṃśatikā* (*kārikās* and commentary).

Erich Frauwallner, *Die Philosophie des Buddhismus,* Berlin: Akademie-Verlag, 1969, pp. 356-383, offers an analysis (in his Introduction) and a German translation of the *kārikās.*

Thubtan Chogdub, Śāstrī and Rāmaśaṅkara Tripāṭhī, *Vijñaptimātratāsiddhiḥ,* Varanasi: Sanskrit University, Gaṅgānāthajhā-granthamālā Vol. V, 1972, pp. 7-77, edited the Sanskrit text together with a Hindi translation and a commentary of their own of *kārikās* and commentary.

Yuichi Kajiyama, *Daijō Butten,* Tōkyō, Shōwa 62 (1988), reprint of the 1977 and 1982 editions, Vol. 15 (Vasubandhu's works), pp.5-30, gives a Japanese translation of *kārikās* and commentary.

K.N. Chatterjee, *Vasubandhu's Vijñaptimātratāsiddhi, with*

Sthiramati commentary, Varanasi: Kishor Vidyā Niketan, 1980, edited the Sanskrit text with an English translation.

Th. A. Kochumuttom, *A Buddhist Doctrine of Experience,* Delhi: Motilal Banarsidass, 1982, has in Appendix IV, pp. 260-275, an English translation of both *kārikās* and commentary.

S. Anacker, *Seven Works of Vasubandhu,* Delhi: Motilal Banarsidass, 1984, gives in pp. 161-175 the English translation of *kārikās* and commentary, and in pp. 413-421 *(Appendix)* the Sanskrit text.

Rāmaśaṅkara Tripāthī and Sempa Dorje, *Vijñaptimātratāsiddhiḥ prakaraṇadvayam,* Leha (Ladakha): Kendriya-Bauddha Vidyāsaṃsthānam, 1984, published the Sanskrit text, the Tibetan version, and a Hindi translation of the *Viṃśatikā* (*kārikās* and commentary).

Katsumi Mimaki, Musashi Tachikawa and Akira Yuyama, *Three works of Vasubandhu,* Tokyo: The Centre for East Asian Cultural Studies, 1989, presented the facsimile edition of one manuscript of the *kārikās* of the *Viṃśatikā,* and of two manuscripts of the *kārikās* and commentary. We have already referred to this important work in *A. Treatises* 13.

Th. E. Wood, *Mind only: a philosophical and doctrinal analysis of the Vijñānavāda,* Honolulu: University of Hawaii Press, 1991, pp. 97-102, published an English translation of the *Viṃśatikā (kārikās).*

T.R. Sharma, *Vijñaptimātratāsiddhi (Viṃśatikā),* Delhi: Eastern Book Linkers, 1993, edited the Sanskrit text (*kārikās* and commentary) with introduction and a commentary of his own.

Adopted Text

We reproduce the Sanskrit text of the *Viṃśatikā* as edited by Sylvain Lévi (Paris,1925), which we consider as a copy of the manuscript *B* edited by Mimaki, Tachikawa and Yuyama, but we have introduced in it some changes: 1. we have corrected some misprints or orthographic errors; 2. we have adopted some variant readings taken from *MS2* and *MTY-A* and/or *MTY-B;* and 3. we suggest some other readings (minor changes). We have indicated in the notes of the Sanskrit text these corrections, variant readings, and changes.

As the first page of the Sanskrit manuscript has been lost, we have replaced it (as it is the usual practice) by the Sanskrit "reconstruction" done by S. Lévi on the basis of the corresponding part of the Tibetan and Chinese translations. In the second note to the Sanskrit text we give the corresponding part of the Tibetan translation (reproducing the text of the Nyingma edition), as well as the corresponding part of the Chinese translation of Hiuan tsang as it appears in *Taishō* 1590.

We have divided the text into sections with sub-titles. We have adopted the same procedure in the translation and in our commentary on the text.

Sigla

MTY-A: the original of *MS1*.

MTY-B: the original of *MS2*.

MS1: copy of the manuscript of *kārikās* and commentary, sent from Nepal, known to us through S. Lévi's edition.

MS2: copy of the manuscript of *kārikās*, sent from Nepal, known to us through S. Lévi's edition.

S. Lévi: edition of *MS1*.

S. Lévi *(Matériaux)* : edition of *MS2*.

DOCTRINARY COMMENTARY OF *VIMŚATIKĀ*

Section I: The thesis of the author: all is mere mental creations; only the mind exists

In this Section Vasubandhu states in first place the fundamental thesis of the Yogācāra school of the Mahāyāna Buddhism,[18] to which he belongs as one of its great Masters: All is only mind, consciousness; there exist only representations, mental creations, ideas to which no external object corresponds. This is the idealistic position proper of the school.[19]

Vasubandhu gives as the immediate fundament of the Yogācāra's thesis that all is only consciousness the text that according to S. Lévi (*Matériaux*, p. 43 note 1) comes from the *Daśabhūmikasūtra*:[20] "Only mind (*citta*), O sons of the Victorious, are the three worlds".[21] Afterwards, in the course of the treatise, all Vasubandhu's effort is directed, starting from that text, to demonstrate the validity of the propounded thesis by means of logical reasoning and also by means of the logical refutation of the objections that are raised against this Yogācāra's thesis. Thus we have as a first fundament of the Yogācāra thesis an assertion by the Buddha himself, rationally demonstrated in the Buddhist context in the further course of the treatise.

Those representations without object, those mere mental creations, those ideas without an objective counterpart—to which is reduced the whole reality, the realm of human experience—are similar (the stanza 1 says) to the visions of the *taimirikas*,[22] those persons who, owing to a defect in their eyes, see black shadows under the form of hairs, etc. In this case the object perceived by the *taimirikas* (the hairs, etc.) does not exist; there is only a representation, a mental creation, an idea. Other examples to which those representations could be compared, and which will be mentioned afterwards, are the oniric visions[23] and the mirages: in both cases there are images in our mind without anything existing in the external reality which corresponds to them.

In this Section Vasubandhu indicates also that the words (he is going to use in the treatise) *citta (sems,* in Tibetan), *manas (yid,* in Tibetan), *vijñāna* (*rnam par śes pa,* in Tibetan), *vijñapti (rnam par rig pa,* in Tibetan) are synonyms.[24] We have translated *citta* and *manas* by "mind", and *vijñāna* and *vijñapti* by "consciousness"and " knowledge". It is necessary to have always present the synonymous value of the four Sanskrit terms and their indicated translation, taking into account that it is the author himself who, before starting his demonstration of the Yogācāra thesis of the sole existence of mind, points out their equivalence and, in the course of the exposition of his treatise, uses them indistinctly.[25]

Section II: Objections derived from the characteristics of the mental creations

Section II exposes the objections against Vasubandhu's idealistic thesis propoused by a realistic adversary, for whom the external world really exists independently from our mind. This external real world is the object of our representations, of the images created in our minds; it is their cause; our representations, our images have thus an external, independent counterpart. This realistic position was characteristic of Hīnayāna Buddhism and, in the Hindu context, of the Pūrva Mīmāṃsā, the Nyāya-Vaiśeṣika, the Sāṃkhya, Madhva's Vedānta,[26] etc. One of the most important aspects of Indian Philosophy, since the beginning of the Christian Era, and for several centuries, is the conflict which opposed the propounders of the realistic position and the propounders of the idealistic one.[27]

The objections of Vasubandhu's realistic opponent can be summarized in the following terms.

The mere mental creations, which lack an external objective counterpart, as the *taimirika*'s vision, the oniric visions, etc., have the following characteristics:

1.and 2.: *they are arbitrary in relation to place and time,* i.e. they are not connected to a determinate place and to a determinate moment, since mind can create them in any place, at any moment. The same thing does not happen with the representations to which corresponds a real object, which produces them: these representations do not arise in any place, at any moment, since for their coming forth they depend on an object and they can arise in the mind of a person only when that object is in front of that person, in a determinate place at a determinate moment. The representation of an object can arise necessarily only where the object is, when it is there. The above mentioned characteristic of the cognitions with (external) object is called in the *karika 3 determination (niyama) in regard to place and time.*

3. *they are exclusive of one sole series of consciousnesses* (of a single person). The vision of hairs, etc. by the *taimirika,* which is a mere representation without corresponding external real object, takes place only for him; the oniric vision, which is likewise a mere mental creation without corresponding real counterpart, exists only for the sleeping and dreaming person. The situation is different from that of the representations provoked by an external object which really exists: this kind of representations occurs in the series of consciousnesses of all the persons that are in the place where the object is and when it is there. But the mere mental creation belongs to only one person (solipsism); the representations with an external autonomous support are common to many persons. This characteristic of the cognitions with (external) object, is called in *kārikā 3 indetermination (aniyama) in regard to the series of consciousnesses.*

In *kārikā* 2 Vasubandhu, on referring to the indetermination in relation to place and time, which affects the mere mental creations, uses the word *saṃtāna* which means *series, succession,* and to which we have added "of consciousnesses". It is interesting to remark that Paramārtha in his *Viṃśatikā*'s translation renders *saṃtāna* by the Chinese character meaning "man" and, according to K'uei Chi, Hiuan Tsang understood *saṃtāna* as "sentient being" (Hamilton, *Wei Shih Er Shih lun,* p. 21, note 10). Let us remember that for Buddhism there is not in man an *ātman,* and Ego, a Self, a consciousness, a soul, one, eternal, not conditioned to anything, not dependent on anything, unalterable, always identical to itself, the witness of human psychological processes, experiences, life.[28] For Buddhism man, the individual, the person is only a series, a succession of consciousnesses, of conscious states related among themselves. We must understand the word "consciousness" in the meaning of "acts of cognition", of "cognitions".[29] These consciousnesses as soon as they arise, disappear; they are instantaneous. No consciousness is the same as the preceding or the following one, they are different phenomena. No one of these consciousnesses, which follow one another and which constitute the individual, is *pure* consciousness, they always are *consciousnesses* (or cognitions) *of* something, of something that is their object, the "contents" of the cognition. Without an object, without such a contents, these consciousnesses could not arise to the instantaneous existence which characterizes them.

4. *they are inefficient,* as far as the objects, which are mere mental creations, mere illusions, do not carry out the specific function which these objects (when they are real) possess: a sword, for instance, when seen in a dream, does not cut. Contrarily, the objects of the representations with a real counterpart fulfill their specific function: the really existing sword fulfills its proper function of cutting. Efficiency (*arthakriyāsamarthya, arthakriyākaritva*) is the criterion of truth for Buddhists.[30]

Now, the representations, the ideas, the images that we *normally* have of the world in which we exist, do not have the enumerated characteristics which are proper to the mere mental creations which lack a real counterpart. The normal representations are not arbitrary in regard to place and time, neither are they exclusive of a single series of consciousness (of that series in which they arise) nor are they ineffective. These normal representations are just all the contrary: they have determination (certainty) in regard to place and time, they are common to several series of consciousnesses (to several persons), and the represented objects fulfill their specific function. So we must conclude that the normal representations we have of the world are different from the representations without a corresponding object that occur in our minds in special situations (in a dream for instance). And the difference consists in the normal representations having an object which provokes them. These characteristic marks of these normal representations would be inexplicable, inadmissible, would not be logical, if our representations were mere mental creations, if they were not roused out of external objects, existing with absolute independence from our minds.

Thus—the realist opponent concludes-the thesis maintained by Vasubandhu *(in Section I)* that only the mind exists, that only mere mental creations, ideas, images without corresponding objects exist, cannot be accepted.

Section III: Refutation of the objections one by one. The characteristics indicated in Section II are not proper to all mental creations.

In *Section III* Vasubandhu refutes one after the other all the objections put forward in the previous Section. He asserts that the determination in regard to place and time (i. e. the certainty, the inexistence of arbitrariness), the indetermination in regard to the stream of consciousness (i.e. they are not exclusive of only one series of consciousness, of only one person, what implies solipsism), and the efficacy in relation to the accomplishment of the specific function are possible in the case of mere mental creations without an external, real counterpart. In other words Vasubandhu maintains that the four characteristics enumerated by the realistic opponent in the previous Section do not affect all the mere mental creations.

In fact, he says, the determination (certainty) in regard to place and time exists in relation to dreams. The oniric visions do not arise in any place and at any moment, but in a certain place and at a certain moment. In other words the dreams impose themselves upon the person who dreams; this person cannot arbitrarily provoke an oniric vision, according to his or her will and whims. Thus there are mental creations which are not indeterminate, uncertain, arbitrary in regard to place and time.

Moreover, there are mental creations which are not exclusive of only one series of consciousnesses (indetermination or exclusiveness in regard to that series). For instance the *pretas* or dead condemned to an existence of suffering see all of them, and simultaneously, a river of pus, etc., that does not really exist, that is only a simple idea created by their mind owing to their same bad *karman*. See next Section and Section XIII, and note 37 of the Third Part of this book.

And, finally, with the example of the nocturnal pollution as the effect of an erotic dream without sexual union, Vasubandhu proves that a mere mental creation can be efficacious for the accomplishment of its specific function.

Section IV: Refutation (similar to that of Section III) of the objections of Section II, but all together

In this Section Vasubandhu comes back to the case of the condemned to hell,[31] in order to refute as a whole the objections presented by his realist opponent. He manifests that in hell (i. e. in the same place) the condemned see all of them and not only one of them, and at the same time, the infernal torturers and their diverse instruments of torture, with determination or certainty as regards place and time, since these torturers and their instruments of torture do not appear and disappear according to the will and whim of the condemned. Moreover the condemned experience pain and suffering through the tortures inflicted on them by the torturers (and their instruments of torture), which fulfill in this manner in an efficacious way their own function. And Vasubandhu adds the most important remark that these torturers (and their instruments of torture) do not really exist, i. e. they are nothing else than simple mental creations, mere illusions or hallucinations created by the mind of the condemned to hell, as he will demonstrate in *Sections V-X*. So we have in the case of the condemned to hell a kind of mere mental creations which are neither arbitrary nor exclusive of a single series of consciousnesses (=of a single person) nor ineffective; they are mental creations that possess determination (certainty, lack of arbitrariness) in regard to place and time, indetermination (unexclusiveness) in regard to the current of consciousness, and accomplishment of the specific function.

In this Section Vasubandhu also expounds why the condemned to hell see all of them at the same time the same infernal spectacle. That simultaneous vision is due to the power of the identical maturation of the *karman* of the condemned. This explanation is related of course to the doctrines of *saṃsāra* (reincarnations) and of *karman* (past actions, moral retribution of actions through the appropriate form of reincarnation)—fundamental principles of Indian philosophies. The condemned have accomplished in their previous existences actions which have as their "fruit", as their differred effect, that they imagine to be in the hell seeing the torturers and the instruments of torture, and experiencing suffering and pain as punishment for the bad actions they have performed. The coincidences in their visions, the identity of what they separately see, are due to the fact that in the series of actions that they performed in past lives there are coincidences, similitudes; and, owing to these coincidences and similitudes, coincident and similar effects had to be produced. In other words, the *karmic* histories of the condemned had similitudes, and therefore their consequences were also similar-as the referred one of imagining the same hell in which they suffer the same punishments. It is as if several mentally sick persons had similar clinical histories which would produce in all of them the same hallucinations at the same moment.

The mechanism, thanks to which there arises in the consciousness (in the mind) of the condemned the vision of hell is clearly explained by the action of the *vāsanās* or subliminal impressions. Vasubandhu will refer to the *vāsanās* in *Section X.*

If there were not coincidences and similitudes among the *karmic* series of the condemned and as an effect of them coincident or similar "fruits"or consequences, we would incur in the most absolute solipsism: each condemned would have his own idea, his own hallucination of his hell, independently of the hells imagined, mentally created by other condemned.[32] Vasubandhu overcomes this solipsist consequences by means of the theory of the identical "maturation"of actions. He has recourse in this way to the doctrines of *saṃsāra* and *karman.*[33]

Vasubandhu concludes this Section expressing that the determination (certainty, lack of arbitrariness) in regard to place and time, the indetermination (the act of cognition is not exclusive for one single series of consciousness, for one single person) and the accomplishment of the specific function, which are observed in the case of the condemned to hell—all these characteristics must be accepted in relation to *all* the other situations, i.e. in relation to all the other mental creations that constitute our normal experience during the wakeful state. This last proposition of Vasubandhu will be established in the remaining Sections of the treatise, according to the reasoning that we present now in its general lines.

Till now we have the following situation. The opponent has affirmed two propositions: A. all our (normal) representations have a real, external object or counterpart (that provokes them), and B. all our (normal) representations (as it is proved by common experience) have the four characteristics that he has mentioned in *kārikā* 2: local and temporal determination, non-exclusiveness in regard to the person that has the representation, and efficiency. Vasubandhu *denies* proposition A asserting that all our representations lack a real, external object, but *does not deny* proposition B: he implicitly accepts that all our (normal) representations have the four mentioned characteristics, but adds something new: there are *several* representations (as those of the damned in hells) which, although lacking a real, external object, nevertheless have the four mentioned characteristics. Now Vasubandhu will demonstrate in *Sections XVIII-XXV* (reaching the same conclusion as Dignāga in the *Ālambanaparīkṣā*) that *all* our representations lack a real, external object. Then we must conclude that all our representations, although lacking a real, external object and being only mere mental creations, imaginations, illusions, nevertheless have the four characteristics mentioned in *kārikā* 2, since the proposition B (all the representations have the four characteristics), asserted by the opponent and not denied and implicitly accepted by Vasubandhu applies to them.

Section V: Opponent's objection against the inexistence (previously adduced by Vasubandhu) of the hell-guards

In this Section the realist opponent puts forward the obvious question: Why is it to be thought that the hell-guards and the instruments of torture do not really exist?[34] This is a most important point in Vasubandhu's demonstration, since, if he is unable to prove that the hell-guards do not really exist and that they are a mere illusory creation, then his assertion (of *Section III* as well as of *Section IV*) that there exist mental creations which are neither arbitrary nor exclusive of a single consciousness nor inefficient would fall down by lack of logical fundament. The demonstration that the hell-guards in charge of the torture of the condemned cannot really exist is given by Vasubandhu in *Sections VII* to *X*.

Section VI: Vasubandhu's answer to the previous objection

Vasubandhu expresses that the existence of infernal hell-guards in charge of the torture of the condemned to hell is logically impossible. He presents two alternatives: 1. If the hell-guards do not experience the suffering that is proper to and characteristic of the infernal world, then they would not be beings condemned to hell. And how can not-condemned beings be born and dwell in hells? (Cf. our commentary of *Section VIII*). 2. If the hell-guards experience the suffering that is proper to and characteristic of the infernal world, then a) they would be condemned beings and it would not be possible to divide all the inhabitants of the hells into "condemned" and "guards", since all would be condemned; and b) if all of them are equal and if they mutually torture one another, it would be impossible that some of them inspire the others with the fear necessary to carry out their function of torturers; and c) if all the inhabitants of the hells suffer the torture of the infernal fire, could some of them have the force and will to torture others?[35]

Section VII: Solution proposed by the opponent asserting the birth in the hells of not condemned beings acting as hell-guards

The realist opponent makes in this Section a suggestion in order to make possible the existence in hell of guards and torturers. His idea is that some animal and *pretas* could be born in hell to accomplish the function of torturers, in the same way as some animals are born in heaven to accomplish certain functions, as for instance to serve as mounts for the Gods.[36]

Section VIII: Refutation of the previous solution
Vasubandhu discards the previous suggestion expressing that the animals that are born in heaven, due to the merits of the good actions they have done in past lives, experience the happiness that is proper to and characteristic of heavens, while the animals and *pretas,* who could be sent to hells to act as guards and torturers, would not experience the suffering that is proper to and characteristic of hells, because, if they experience it, they would be unable to carry out their torturer function, as it has been explained in *Section VI.* They are two completely different situations, and this lack of similarity deprives the suggestion of *Section VII* of all its force.

In this Section as in *Section VI* appears a fundamental element of the Buddhist as well as the Hindu conception of hell and heaven. The being who is reborn in hell as a condemned is reborn there as a consequence of the evil actions that he or she accomplished in previous lives, and is reborn there to be punished and to suffer; the being that is reborn in heaven is reborn there as a consequence of the good actions that he or she accomplished in previous lives. Therefore it cannot be admitted that someone can be reborn in hell or heaven without his actions demanding such a thing, and with a purpose different from the specific purpose of hell and heaven as the seat of punishment or reward. This idea agrees with the conception of *karman* as a means to accomplish the just retribution of actions: all beings must receive as punishment or reward the kind of reincarnation required by his or her acts; nobody must get a reincarnation that is not adequate to the good or bad actions he has done in past lives.

Section IX: New suggestion on the part of the opponent affirming that in the hells there arise conglomerates of elements adopting the form of hell-guards and acting as such
In this Section the opponent puts forward the following suggestion in order to save the real existence of hell-guards : the actions performed by the condemned in previous existences have as a consequence that there arise in the hells with a real, objective and autonomous existence a number of material elements with certain characteristics, and these elements transform themselves and assume the appearance of infernal instruments of torture and of infernal guards.

Section X: Refutation of the previous suggestion: Why not to admit that the hell-guards, etc. are a mental product of the transformation of the vāsanās, and that the vāsanās and their effect are both in the mind ?

Vasubandhu in order to discard the previous suggestion asks two questions to his opponent. Before indicating the contents of both questions, let us briefly remember the theory of the *vāsanās* (to which we have already referred in relation to Dignāga's *Ālambanaparīkṣā*, see our commentary on Section X and note 11, and to which we shall refer in relation to the *Trisvabhāva* of Vasubandhu (see note 10 of the Third Part of this Book). According to this theory, accepted by Buddhists and Hindus, the actions or better said the cognitive, volitive, emotive mental processes, which accompany the actions, leave in the series of consciousnesses,[37] that constitute the individual, a *vāsanā*, literally: a scent, metaphorically: a trace, a mark, an impression, a virtuality. Synonymous with the word *vāsanā* are the terms *bīja*: seed; *śakti*: power, capacity, virtuality; *saṃskāra*: (literally): putting together, (technically) predisposition (s), conditioning (s). The *vāsanās* can be conceived as subliminal impressions left by experiences, waiting for the moment to re-appear in the conscious level, to manifest themselves anew in the conscious level. It can be said that the series of consciousnesses (in a way about which there are different opinions)[38] carries with itself all the *vāsanās* left by all the experiences that the individual has had in all his/her previous lives. In certain circumstances these *vāsanās* are reactualized and produce a "fruit" or effect similar to the cause that gave rise to the *vāsanā*. As we shall see in the following paragraphs the discrepancy between Vasubandhu and his opponent is only in relation to the nature of that "fruit" or effect.

The first question that Vasubandhu asks is: Instead of affirming the arising in the hells of real material elements which assume the form of instruments of torture and of hell-guards, all this by the force of the past actions of the condemned, why is it not admitted that by the effect of the *vāsanās* a transformation of the consciousness (*vijñānapariṇāma*)[39] takes place and produces the illusion, the hallucination, the mental creations of the hell-guards and of the torture instruments ? According to the opponent the past actions of the condemned do that real elements arise in the hells and adopt certain forms and functions; according to Vasubandhu these actions through the mechanism of the *vāsanās* give rise to a transformation of conscious, to a mental process of illusory fearful visions and of illusory terrible pains.

On putting the second questions, Vasubandhu adduces an argument against the alternative adopted by his opponent and in favour of his own alternative. The *vāsanās*, left by previous actions or better said by the mental processes that accompany these actions, are *in* the series of consciousnesses, are only consciousness, mental phenomena. Why not to admit that the effects of the *vāsanās* are also in the series of consciousnesses, are only consciousness, mere mental phenomena, simple illusory visions and pains ? There is no reason to think that the *vāsanās* are in the series of consciousnesses, are only consciousness, mental phenomena, and that nevertheless their effects are not in the series of consciousnesses, but outside the consciousness, in an external world. According to the opponent the *vāsanās* are in the series of consciousnesses and their effects are outside; according to Vasubandhu the *vāsanās* and also their "fruits" or effects are in the series of consciousnesses.

The opposition between the idealistic position adopted by Vasubandhu and the realistic position adopted by the adversary in regard to the hells and what happens in them is of great importance, since the position that one elects will be applied not only to the condemned to hell (which is a mere example for the demonstration's sake), but to the whole empirical reality in which we exist. For the idealistic position the world we perceive and all that exists or happens in it are mere mental creations, mere mental phenomena, produced by the reactualization of the *vāsanās*; for the realistic position the world and all it contains have real existence, apart and independent from the consciousness or mind that grasps it; they are created by the force of the actions of the beings who have to live in it and to experience the good or bad effects of their past actions.

Section XI: Fundamentation of the opponent's thesis that the "fruit" of actions in not where the vāsanā is

In this Section is given the reason why according to the propounder of realism, on one side, it is necessary to discard the thesis maintained by Vasubandhu that where the *vāsanā* is (i. e. in consciousness), there also is its effect (in other terms, that all is *vāsanās* in their potential or in their actual state, that all consequently is a mere manifestation of consciousness, a mere mental creation) and, on the other side, it is contrarily necessary to accept the thesis (put forward by the propounder of realism) that where the *vāsanā* is (i.e. in consciousness), there is not its effect, but in another place, in the external reality (or, in other terms, that the external objects really exist).

The reason in favour of the realistic thesis is the following one: according to Buddhism in order that an act of cognition be produced, in order that a sensorial cognition arise, it is necessary among other factors or elements the existence of an exterior *āyatana* (basis) (*bāhirāni āyatanāni*), either form-colour or any other sensorial object, and an internal *āyatana (ajjhattikāni āyatanāni)* located in the individual, either the eye or any other sense.[40] The Buddha would not have affirmed the existence of the *āyatanas* form-colour, etc., if there were not external objects, if there were only processes in the interior of consciousness, if there existed only internal illusory visions of form-colour, etc., produced by consciousness, by the mind in itself, in its own interior.[41] The thesis of the only existence of mind (*cittamātra*: "only mind") sustained by Vasubandhu leaves aside the teaching of the Buddha regarding the necessity of exterior (objects) and interior (senses) *āyatanas*, and accepted by Buddhist theory of sensorial cognition, by Buddhist theory of perception.[42]

Section XII: Refutation of the previous fundamentation

Vasubandhu does not deny that the Buddha has affirmed the existence of the *āyatanas* form-colour, etc., but he remarks that that affirmation is a *neyārtha* affirmation.

To understand Vasubandhu's argumentation it is necessary to remember something about the history and evolution of Buddhism.

The initial philosophical position of the Buddha and of Early and Hīnayāna Buddhism was a realistic one: the world has a real existence. This position is present in the whole of the Pali *Suttapiṭaka* which contains the oldest form of Buddhist teaching, and is the one maintained nowadays by the Theravāda tradition of Sri Lanka and South-East Asia. But in the beginning of Christian Era, more or less 500 years after the Buddha's *Parinirvāṇa*, there appears a series of texts, considered by tradition as being composed by the Buddha himself, the so called Mahāyānist Sūtras in which is found a philosophical position which denies the real existence of the world and considers it a mere mental creation. This is the position of the Mahāyāna schools, specially the Yogācāra one, which consider these texts as the ultimate and definitive teaching of the Buddha.

One of the difficulties which the Masters of the Mahāyāna had to confront was how to explain the old Buddhist texts that maintained a realistic position, in order to discard the opinions that the Buddha has changed his teachings passing from one position to the other, or that the teachings of the Mahāyāna texts, so different to those of the Hīnayāna, were not the Buddha's teachings but fake creations of some of his followers[43] and so on, with all the serious consequences that these opinions carried with themselves. The Mahāyānist Masters had recourse to a very simple and clever explanation. They maintained that the texts which contained the word of the Buddha had to be divided in two classes: 1. those that express a clear and immediate meaning *(nītārtha)*, i. e. that are to be understood with the sense that their words directly transmit. The Mahāyāna Sūtras are of this class. These *sūtras* were delivered by the Buddha to those of his disciples who thanks to their training were already prepared to receive the true definitive doctrines of the Buddha which these sūtras transmit and which many times are contrary to preexistent traditions; and 2. those texts that are called *neyārtha*. These texts have two meanings, on one side,a *prima facie* meaning, the meaning that is directly, immediately conveyed by the words of the text; and, on the other side, a concealed meaning that (as the word *neyārtha* literally expresses) is to be looked for, is to be deduced, is to be established, it to be discovered. These texts were delivered by the Buddha to those of his disciples who had not the necessary preparation and who could grasp and accept only the *prima facie* meaning and be content with it; this *prima facie* meaning does not scare them away; they remain near the Buddha; they are instructed gradually by him; are slowly prepared to receive his true teachings; and, when they are ready to receive the true teaching, the Buddha will reveal it to them, and at that moment they will understand the *neyārtha* texts, not in their provisional, *prima facie* meaning, but in their concealed, true definitive meaning. The *neyārtha* meaning, the true meaning of many of the first assertions of the Buddha, is thus a more profound, more subtle meaning, which can be grasped only by those persons duly prepared and trained.[44]

In the commentary to *kārikā* 8 the Buddha's words that are of the *neyārtha* kind are designated with the word *ābhiprāyika* that we have translated by "intentional". This word is derived from *abhiprāya* which is also used in *kārikā* 8 and in its commentary and which means "intention", "purpose", "wish". An *ābhiprāyika* word (or sentence) said by the Buddha is a word (or sentence) that the Buddha says with the intention either that it convey a meaning different from the meaning that this word (or this sentence) usually and normally conveys or that together with its usual and normal meaning it express also something else. The disciple who hears that word (or sentence), if he is not yet duly trained, will grasp the usual and normal meaning of that word (or sentence); if he is duly trained, he will grasp the "intentional" meaning of that word (or that sentence) i. e. what the Buddha *intended* it to express. The expression *abhiprāyavaśāt* used in *kārikā* 8 and its commentary must be accordingly understood.

What Vasubandhu does in this Section is simply to indicate that the texts in which the Buddha affirmed the existence of the *āyatanas* are texts of the second *neyārtha* category. The way in which the Buddha's words concerning the *āyatanas* must be understood will be explained in the next Section; in *Sections XVII-XXVII* will be given the arguments to support the thesis, that these words of the Buddha are to be understood in that way.

In this Section Vasubandhu gives another example of the teaching of the Buddha "with a determinate, certain purpose" i.e. another example of a *neyārtha* teaching. This second case are the words of the Buddha which say that "there are *upapāduka* (spontaneous) beings".[45] The spontaneous beings are those that are born as infernal beings, as Gods, or as the beings which arise between a reincarnation and the following one, all of them without the cooperation of a father and a mother.[46]

The affirmation of the Buddha that "there are spontaneous beings" cannot be taken in the meaning that it seems to have *prima facie*, in a first moment, in a first approach. A "spontaneous being", a being born without causes, by *spontaneous generation*, would be in contradiction with two fundamental theories of Buddhism: the first one is the doctrine according to which there is not an eternal and inalterable being, but only *dharmas*, factors, elements that constitute all that exists; [47] the second one is that theory according to which all beings exist owing to a series of causes for their existence.[48] These theories are the basis of the words of the Buddha that Vasubandhu quotes: "There is not a Being, an *ātman*, but (only) *dharmas* which have causes".[49]

What the Buddha intended to say with the affirmation "there are spontaneous beings"is nothing else that "the series of consciousnesses in not interrupted." In this affirmation of the Buddha: "There are spontaneous beings", the existence of such beings is the *prima facie* provisional meaning; the non-interruption of the series of consciousnesses is the concealed definitive meaning. This affirmation of the Buddha is a *neyārtha* affirmation, one whose true meaning must be searched for and discovered, what is possible only for a trained person well instructed in the Buddhist teachings and well prepared to receive them. Vasubandhu says that the real concealed meaning of the words of the Buddha about spontaneous beings is that the series of consciousnesses is not interrupted.

And in fact that is what happens with the three kinds of spontaneous beings we have previously mentioned: the infernal beings, the Gods, and the beings that arise between one reincarnation and the following one. Each individual is a series of consciousnesses that since a beginningless eternity has passed through an incalculable number of reincarnations. This series can be divided in segments marked by a moment that is called "birth" and a moment that is called "death";[50] each one of these segments is an individual. If this series thanks to its *karman* has to reincarnate as a human being, it gets a human body produced by the union of a father and a mother; but, if it has to reincarnate as an infernal being, it does not get a body from a father and a mother since infernal beings do not have sexual intercourse; it gets a body directly produced by the force of its own *karman,* that-so to say—is waiting for that series of consciousnesses in order that the new individual in that "spontaneous" body may suffer the deserved punishment. If the series of consciousnesses has to incarnate as a God, the same mechanism takes place: the incarnation occurs in a divine body directly produced by the *karman* and not by the sexual union of a celestial father and a celestial mother, since the new God arises as a completely formed celestial being and not as a celestial child that will gradually grow into a celestial adult. And, during the lapse that separates a reincarnation from the following one (*antarābhava),* the indescriptible being, under whose form the series of consciousnesses subsists during that period of time, does not arise from the union of a man and a woman. In the three cases the series of consciousnesses is not interrupted, and there is birth, arising, existence without the intervention of a couple. In this way the series of consciousnesses, to which the future infernal being and God and the intermediate being belong, is not interrupted by the absence of a father and a mother.

Section XIII: Which is the true meaning of the words of the Buddha that affirm the existence of āyatanas ?

In this Section Vasubandhu explains how it is necessary to understand the assertion of the Buddha that there exist the *āyatanas* form-colour, etc., giving in *Sections XVIII-XXVII* the reasons that support his interpretation.

We have said in *Section X* that the mental processes of cognition, volition, emotion etc. that accompany any action leave in the series of consciousnesses which constitute the individual a *vāsanā*, i.e. a mark, a trace, a subliminal impression, a "seed" (*bīja*), which remains as a virtuality and which on certain circumstances is reactualized producing a new "fruit"or effect. For instance a mental representation which one has had leaves in the series of consciousnesses a *vāsanā*, a subliminal impression, a virtuality, a "seed", which at a certain moment, when certain circumstances are there, actualizes itself, "matures", producing a representation. The representation produced by the *vāsanā*, being a cognition, has a contents, an object, as it happens with any cognition.

According to Vasubandhu that *vāsanā*, virtuality, "seed" and its unavoidable object (with whose image the representation arises) are the two *āyatanas* (basis) of the cognitions, of the consciousnesses, of the mental acts which constitute the individual: the virtuality as such is for Vasubandhu the *āyatana* (basis) eye or any other sense, the contents or object of that representation is the *āyatana* (basis) form-colour or any other object of the senses.

It is interesting to compare with Vasubandhu's explanation the similar one given by Dignāga in the *Ālambanaparīkṣā (Section XI,* in this book). There is a difference between both: for Dignāga the *vāsanā* reactualizes itself in a visual, olfatory, tactile, etc,. cognition or representation; the visuality, olfatority, tactibility, etc., of the reactualized cognition would be the *āyatana* sense (eye, etc.); the contents or object of the cognition or representation would be the *āyatana* object.

So the texts in which the Buddha affirms that "there are two *āyatanas*" (basis necessary for the cognition: the *āyatana*-eye and the *āyatana*-form-colour) are interpreted in two ways. On one side, there is the realistic interpretation of the Early and the Hīnayāna Buddhism, according to which the *āyatanas* are the sense organs and their corresponding objects, being both really existing and external to the mind, which knows the objects by means of the sense organs. On the other side, there is the idealistic interpretation of the Mahāyāna Buddhism, according to which both *āyatanas* are constituted by the *vāsanā*, the virtuality, and by the object of the representation that comes forth when the *vāsanā* is reactualized.

Section XIV: Good results obtained through the Buddha's teaching understood in this way

Vasubandhu points out in this Section the two advantages that are produced by the interpretation he has just given of the Buddha's words relative to the *āyatanas*. Of course they are advantages from his own idealistic position.

In the first place, this interpretation allows the entry into the doctrine of the *unsubstantiality of man*, of the individual, of the person. Thanks to this interpretation one knows that each consciousness, each act of cognition, each mental moment of the series of consciousnesses, cognitions, mental processes, which constitute man, is produced *only* through the actualization of the *vāsanās* or virtualities lying in consciousness in a latent, subliminal condition; and one also knows that it is *only* the mechanism of the *vāsanā* or virtuality that gives rise at the same time to the sense organ and to the object, being both of mental nature. Nothing else is necessary for the arising, for the existence of consciousness. This knowledge is thus an introduction into the doctrine of the unsubstantiality of man, an introduction into the doctrine that in man there is not an *ātman*, a soul, eternal and existing by itself and in itself. It is one of the oldest theories of Buddhism, the so called *nairātmya* (negation of an *ātman) or pudgalanairātmya*-as Vasubandhu calls it in this treatise. Cf. note 28.

In the second place, Vasubandhu's interpretation can be taught in another way, from another point of view: as the doctrine of "only mind", of the sole existence of consciousness. This interpretation allows us to know that it is only consciousness what arises under the appearance of the *dharmas* form-colour, etc. just in the moment in which a *vāsanā*, a virtuality, actualizes itself under a certain representation, and that consequently there is not any real *dharma* form-colour etc. This knowledge is an "introduction into", an *understanding* of the doctrine that the dharmas do not substantially exist either as autonomous, objective entities. This is the so called *dharmanairātmya*.[51]

Section XV: Objection: Does the inexistence of dharmas not imply the inexistence of consciousness ?

The objection put forward in this Section is very simple and coherent: if *dharmas* do not exist, then consciousness-which is a *dharma*[52] —does not exist either. It is consequently absurd to say, as Vasubandhu says in the previous Section, that "consciousness arises under the image, etc."

Section XVI: Refutation of the previous objection. How the affirmation that the dharmas do not exist is to be understood

Vasubandhu answers the previous objection saying in the first sentence of this Section that it is erroneous to think that to affirm the unsubstantiality of the *dharmas (dharmanairātmya)* means that the *dharmas* (elements of existence) do not exist in an absolute way; to affirm the unsubstantiality of the *dharmas* means that they do not exist with the substantiality imagined (*kalpita*) by the ignorant. This assertion means that they do not exist with a substantiality conceived as an own being in the realm of the subject-object duality. Being *substantial* means for the ignorant being possessed of *an own being connected with the subject-object duality*; that is their wrong idea of substantiality; Vasubandhu denies that the *dharmas* possess such substantiality. Therefore he affirms the unsubstantiality of the *dharmas*. We must think that the word *ādi* ("etc.") which Vasubandhu adds to the words "subject"(*grāhaka*) and "object" (*grāhya*) includes also the mental categories of being (existence), space, time, etc. Ignorants not only attribute to the *dharmas* substantiality (as it has been just described) through intellectual acts, but also live and act with the conscious or unconscious conviction that *dharmas* possess such substantiality. The *dharmas* exist with the indefinable substantiality which is the object *only* of the knowledge that belongs to the Buddhas, i.e. to those beings that have reached the highest development of intelligence and consciousness. Vasubandhu has denied that the *dharmas* exist with the substantiality as conceived by the ignorant, but he accepts that they exist with a kind of substantiality that is indescribable and that is the object of Buddhas' cognition.

The first sentence of this Section asserts that the kind of substantiality (form of existence) attributed to *dharmas* by the ignorant is to be rejected; but it admits that the Buddhas know the specific kind of substantiality (form of existence) possessed by *dharmas*. What has been said in relation to the *dharmas* can be applied to *vijñaptimātratā* (i. e. to consciousness as the only existing thing): it exists with an indefinable substantiality (form of existence) which only the Buddhas know.

After the first sentence Vasubandhu adds a new idea. This new idea will help to understand by analogy what is meant by saying that the *dharmas* are unsubstantial. The understanding of the unsubstantiality of all the *dharmas* is produced when one postulates the *vijñaptimātratā*, affirming that the *vijñaptimātratā* is unsubstantial in the sense that it is *not* provided with an essence (*ātman*) that is imagined by another consciousness. But the fact of lacking an essence as imagined by the ignorant does not imply that the *vijñaptimātratā* lacks that indefinable substantiality (form of being) that is attributed to the *dharmas*. The reason why it is not possible to attribute to the *vijñaptimātratā* an essence imagined by another consciousness is that, if the possibility that a consciousness (that is posited as the only one that exists) be imagined by another is admitted, the *imagined* consciousness would become something different from the *imagining* consciousness, would become its object. And, owing to the duality that occurs, it would be no more possible to speak of *vijñaptimātratā* either in relation to the imagined consciousness (that would be an object) or in relation to the imagining consciousness (that would be a subject). The hypothesis of *vijñaptimātratā* requires the absolute isolation of consciousness.

The second paragraph is centered in the idea that *vijñaptimātratā* cannot be the object of a normal act of cognition of another consciousness. But we must have in mind that *vijñaptimātratā* can be the object of an act of cognition of the Buddhas, who can know it by means of their superior kind of knowledge, which is by essence outside the range of duality, and is not liable to nullify the absolute oneness of the *vijñaptimātratā*.

Before trying to explain what is the indefinable substantiality of the *dharmas* and by extension, of the *vijñaptimātratā*, it is convenient to make a brief reference to the stages or degrees of knowledge within a Buddhist perspective,[53] since that indefinable substantiality is the object of one of those stages or degrees of knowledge, the knowledge of the Buddhas.

We can consider that for Buddhism as well as for Hinduism there are three stages or degrees of knowledge from a philosophical point of view of any doctrine or theory. In first place there is a literal knowledge of the text in which that doctrine is expounded (the monk learns by heart the text). Of course this kind of knowledge does not give a profound contact with the contents of that doctrine or theory. In second place we have the proper philosophical knowledge which allows to penetrate more deeply into the meaning of that doctrine or theory, submitting it to a rigorous criticism, examining the arguments that are adduced to support it and those that are adduced to criticize it, in order to reach a conviction, a certainty firmly founded from an intellectual, a rational, a logical point of view, of the validity of that doctrine or theory. (The *Mūlamādhyamikakārikā* is an example of this activity). This second stage or degree of knowledge constitutes an entirely rational task in which one proceeds with the means offered by conceptual analysis, logical argumentation, rational criticism. Finally we have the yogic (meditative or mystic or trascendental) knowledge (the *Śamathavipaśyanā* practices). In India Yoga was always considered to be the means to obtain an extra-ordinary knowledge which gives the exact and perfect knowledge of its object, whatever this object may be: Brahman, *Śūnyatā*, God, etc. In order that this knowledge be produced it is necessary to have recourse to a special training that requires first to master the theories about that object, then to submit oneself to a moral and ascetic discipline, and finally to carry on technical bodily and mental practices, that are taught by Yoga, under the guidance of an expert and wise Master. When one is duly prepared, that extra-ordinary knowledge, exclusive of Yoga, may be produced. Of course, it is very difficult or even impossible to have a clear insight of what really is that supreme yogic experience. It is an *experience* difficult or even impossible to communicate to others and to make others understand it.

This third stage or degree of knowledge, product of study, discipline and yogic practices is something proper to the Buddhas, and by means of it they can reach the true knowledge of the "indefinable substantiality" of the *dharmas* and of the *vijñaptimātratā*.

This "indefinable substantiality", the true form of being of the *dharmas* and of the *vijñaptimātratā,* is (according to what will be said below taking into account the *Trisvabhāva*) the inexistence or absolute absence of the subject-object duality and of all mental categories to which reference has been made. And, *just* because of being in an absolute way beyond the categories of subject and object, that substantiality proper to the *dharmas* and to the *vijñaptimātratā* is indefinable, impossible to be expressed or thought, something completely heterogeneous to man but within the reach only of the Buddhas.

Vasubandhu in this Section deals with the kind of unsubstantiality or the form of existence of the *dharmas* and of the *vijñaptimātratā* in a very brief way, even without giving a definition of that unsubstantiality. He says only what is necessary in order to discard the objection of the opponent, who adduces the non existence of the *dharmas* with the intention of making impossible the existence of *vijñaptimātratā*.

It is in the treatise *Trisvabhāvanirdeśa (or Trisvabhāvakārikā)* included in this volume that he will deal with that question in a more detailed way. Summarizing, it can be said that the *dharmas* constitute the *paratantra* (dependent) and the *(pari) kalpita* (imaginary) natures of that treatise. These two natures constitute the empirical reality marked by duality. But the ultimate essence of the *dharmas* or of empirical reality is the *pariniṣpanna* (perfect, absolute) nature marked by the complete absence of subject-object duality and defined by

Vasubandhu as "the eternal non-existence with duality of the dependent nature" (*kārikā* 3), "existence with non-duality" (*kārikā* 13) and "existence of the non-existence of duality" (*kārikā* 25). This is the True Reality, the Absolute, the Supreme Principle, the *Vijñaptimātratā*.[54] The *dharmas* or the *paratantra* and (*pari*) *kalpita* natures or the empirical reality is the object of knowledge of the ignorant; the *pariniṣpanna* nature or True Reality is the object only of the Buddhas' knowledge.

Section XVII: Opponent's question: Why is it necessary to accept the non-existence of the external āyatanas that are the objects of cognition ?

The opponent asks in this Section an utmost important question: Why must we accept in relation to the texts, where the Buddha refers to the *āyatanas* (basis) form-colour, etc. (see *Section XI*), Vasubandhu's interpretation according to which these texts have to be taken with a "determined meaning" (see *Section XII*), and that as a consequence of that the *āyatana* eye, etc. and the *āyatana* form-colour, etc. are nothing else than the virtuality and the represented object, with whose image that virtuality is reactualized and comes forth? Why must we discard the traditional realistic interpretation which maintains that in these texts the *āyatana* eye, etc. and the *āyatana* form-colour, etc. are the eye, etc. and the form-colour, etc. as they are commonly understood to be: really existing and external to the mind ?

Here we have again, clearly expressed, the opposition between the idealistic thesis maintained by the Mahāyāna and the realistic one maintained by Early Buddhism and Hīnayāna Buddhism.

Section XVIII : Vasubandhu's answer: It is impossible that external āyatanas exist

Vasubandhu's answer is very simple: we must accept the idealistic interpretation as presented by him, because external *āyatanas* form-colour, etc. do not exist, i. e. external objects of cognition do not exist. That existence is logically impossible.

Vasubandhu's demonstration is the following one: if according to the realistic thesis there were an *āyatana* form-colour, etc., external to the mind and acting as an object of cognition, then this *āyatana* would have to be:

1. either *one* in the way the Nyāya-Vaiśeṣikas conceive the whole (*avayavin*): as something constituted by parts (*avayava*) but being one, different from the parts that compose it, and having a real existence apart from the existence of the parts. The

problem of the whole and the parts was one of the most important of Indian philosophy and we have referred to it with some detail in note 7 of *Ālambanaparīkṣā* where bibliography can be found. Paṇḍita Aśoka's monography *The Avayavinirākaraṇa* (F. Tola and C. Dragonetti's edition, Tokyo: The International Institute for Buddhist Studies, 1994) contains a careful demonstration of the impossibility of the existence of the whole as conceived by the Vaiśeṣika system of philosophy;

2. or the *āyatana* would have to be multiple atoms, i.e. it would have to be a number or a group of atoms coexisting one besides the other, but without forming a conglomerate provided with mutual cohesion between the atoms;
3. or the *āyatana* would have to be atoms grouped together, massed together, united among themselves with a tight cohesion.

These are the three only possible forms of existence that can be accepted for the supposed *āyatanas* form-colour, etc., when imagined as external and functioning as objects of cognition. Of these three possibilities the first one points to the *unity* of the *āyatana* form-colour, etc. conceived as the whole, and the second and third ones point to the *multiplicity* of the *āyatana* (loose atoms, conglomerated atoms).

According to Vasubandhu no one of these three alternatives can be accepted. In fact the *āyatana* conceived as a whole, one, etc. does not exist. In this Section Vasubandhu limits himself to say that nowhere such a whole is grasped. In *Sections XXVI and XXVII* Vasubandhu will adduce arguments against the existence of an external *āyatana*, the *datum* form-colour, etc., conceived as one. The arguments developed by Vasubandhu in *Section XXVII* could be adduced against the existence of the whole (*avayavin)*, because when the unity is proved not to exist, then the whole is not anymore possible, since unity is an essential attribute of the whole, as indivisibility is of the atom. This is in fact the method employed by Paṇḍita Aśoka in his treatise *Avayavinirākaraṇa* for his refutation of the whole. Neither is there an *āyatana* constituted by a multitude of loose atoms, since we do not perceive the atoms one by one. Arguments against the possibility of the existence of the indivisible atom will be adduced in *Sections XXIII-XXV*. Finally, neither can there be atoms cohesively conglomerated, because, if atoms could get such a cohesion, then it could not be anymore accepted that they are indivisible particles of matter. The arguments for this last alternative are found in *Sections XIX- XXII.*

We think, as expressed in the last paragraph, that the reason why it cannot be accepted that the atoms be cohesively conglomerated is that, in that case, the consequence would be that *atoms could not anymore be considered as indivisible,* which is the fundamental assertion of the atomists. We interpret accordingly the sentences *yasmāt paramāṇur na sidhyati* in *kārikā* 11, and *yasmāt paramāṇur ekaṃ dravyaṃ na sidhyati.* Several translators interpret these two sentences as meaning that the reason why it cannot be accepted that the atoms conglomerate is that *the atom has not been proved to exist.* We consider that this last interpretation is erroneous. If Vasubandhu had wanted to adduce in the present reasoning the non existence of the atom as an argument against the possibility of an external *āyatana,* he would have adduced it also in relation to alternative 2., which has to do with the isolated atoms. All the argumentation of Vasubandhu in *Section XIX* is not based on the idea that the agglomeration of the atoms is to be discarded because atoms have not been proved to exist, but on the idea that, if that agglomeration is admitted, the thesis of the indivisibility of the atoms is to be discarded because the concept of 'atom' itself becomes not logically possible.

Let us remark that, when Vasubandhu says that the whole as unity or the isolated loose atoms are not *perceived,* we must understand that he is referring not only to the *sensorial* perception (we do not perceive through our senses either the whole or the isolated atoms), but also to the *rational* "perception" (reasoning reaches the conclusion that owing to a logical impossibility neither the whole nor the isolated atoms can exist).

Since in this Section and in the following ones Vasubandhu refers in his argumentation to the atom, it is convenient to say something about the atomist theory in Buddhism.[55] For the Vaiśeṣika school of philosophy,[56] which developed in India the atomist theory, the atom is an infinitely small particle of matter, indivisible, eternal, of spherical form. The union of atoms gives rise to the things and beings of the empirical reality. Several of these characteristics were adopted by the Buddhist atomic conception. In the oldest Buddhist texts, those included in the Pali Canon, no mention is found of the atomist theory as a theory adopted by Buddhism.[57] Probably it was the Sarvāstivāda school or sect which introduced that theory into Buddhism. The *Mahāvibhāṣa,* a canonical treatise of that school, is the first Buddhist text which has frequent references to atomism.

O. Rosenberg, *Die Probleme der buddhistischen Philosophie*, pp.150 and 152, considers that the atomist theory is in Buddhism one of the most difficult, and points out that the speculations about the atoms are filled with contradictions and that this theory was for the Buddhists a source of polemics. We think that these difficulties, contradictions and polemics are due to the fact that the relation between the atom and the *dharmas* (elements of existence) and specially with the *rūpa dharma* is not clear at all, besides the natural difficulties which offer the ancient atomist theories.

The *rūpa dharma* is considered as matter, and it is thus generally translated, but it would be more correct and more in agreement with the Buddhist conceptions to understand by *rūpa* the attributes or qualities which distinguish things, which stimulate our senses, as form, colour, hardness, roughness, etc., but these attributes or qualities are not a matter nor a substance, and they are not inherent in a matter or in a substance different from and independent of them.

Vasubandhu in *Abhidharmakośabhāṣya ad* I, 22 (I, p. 180 Bauddha Bharati edition= L. de la Vallée Poussin's translation I, p. 144) defines the atom (*paramāṇu*) as "the subtlest (=smallest) aggregate of *rūpa* (*sarvasūkṣmo hi rūpasaṃghātaḥ paramāṇur iti*). Yaśomitra in his commentary *ad locum* remarks that Vasubandhu is referring to the *saṃghataparamāṇu* or aggregate-atom and not to the *dravyaparamāṇu* or matter-atom which does not possess either a fore part or a back part, and is consequently indivisible.

Of these two kinds of atoms it is the *dravyaparamāṇu* which corresponds to the atom of matter as conceived by the Vaiśeṣikas. The *dravyaparamāṇu* mentioned by Yaśomitra has in common with the Vaiśeṣika atom the infinitely small size and the indivisibility, but it differs from it, on one side, in the fact that it is not eternal but impermanent (which is a general characteristic of all *dharmas*) and, on other side, in the fact that it is not a particle of matter but an attribute or quality.

Section XIX: Arguments which hinder to admit that a conglomeration of atoms (as conceived by the Vaiśeṣikas) could be the external āyatana, object of cognition

Vasubandhu begins dealing with the third alternative referred to in previous Section. His argumentation is in reference to the atom as something indivisible as conceived by the Hindu and Buddhist atomism.

Vasubandhu develops his argumentation examining what happens when six atoms coming from the six different directions of space, join another atom (that we can call the "central" one). Vasubandhu considers two possible situations.

1. First situation (first half of the *kārikā*): The six adventitious atoms join the (central) atom in six different places. *Ipso facto* the (central) atom would have six parts, corresponding to the six places (or faces) in which the six adventitious atoms join the (central) atom—merely touching it, without being superimposed on it. Consequently the divisibility of the atom is evident.
2. Second situation (second half of the *kārikā)*: To avoid the consequence of the first situation, which implies the existence of six places in the (central) atom, what means its division into six parts, it can be supposed that the six adventitious atoms join the (central) atom not in six places but just in one and the same place (*samānadeśa).* The idea of this second situation is that the six adventitious atoms join the (central) atom being superimposed in it and without any one of the seven atoms jutting out. If any atom juts out, then it would be divided in parts: one part would be the jutting out, another would be the not jutting out. With this second situation it could be argued that, being all the atoms joined in one and the same place, then no division into parts occurs. But this argument concerning the second situation carries with itself a most unwanted consequence : if all the atoms are united in one and the same place and no one juts out in relation to the others, the mass formed by all the atoms would have the size of a single atom, and so nothing in the world would be perceived, since, as the atom due to its infinitely small size is imperceptible, so would be the mass formed by numerous atoms occupying one and the same place in the indicated conditions.

There is in Vasubandhu's *Abhidharmakośabhāṣya ad* I, 43 (= I, 121 Bauddha Bharati edition=L. de la Vallée Poussin's translation I, p. 89) a passage which expresses in a succinct way Vasubandhu's reasoning in this section: *yadi tāvat sarvātmanā* [the atoms] *spṛśeyur miśrībhaveyur dravyāṇi/athaikadeśena sāvayavāḥ prasajyeran/ niravayavāś ca paramāṇavaḥ* ("If atoms touch themselves with the whole of their mass, things would get confounded; if they touch themselves in one single place, atoms would happen to have parts, and atoms are without parts"). Vasubandhu in *Abhidharmakośabhāṣya, ad* I, 43 (=I, p. 122 quoted edition), considers another hypothesis that he attributes to Vasumitra: the atoms, on one side, do not touch one another although they give the false impression of touching one another (so there is no place for their divisibility), but, on the other side, there is no gap or interval among them (so there is no place for the isolation of the second alternative) (*na spṛśanti, nirantare tu spṛṣṭasaṃjñeti*). Paṇḍita Aśoka has an interesting opinion on this matter: what separates the atoms is not an interval, but the "absence of the form of another" (F. Tola's and C. Dragonetti's edition, Section III, p. 4, second paragraph, and note 28).

In this way is discarded the third alternative of *Section XVIII*: the possibility of the existence of an external *āyatana*, an external object of cognition, formed by a conglomeration of atoms-indivisible, infinitely small elements.

Section XX: Explanation of the Vaibhāṣikas of Kashmir: the molecules (groups of seven atoms) can be connected among themselves

In this Section Vasubandhu presents a theory of the Buddhist school of the Vaibhāṣikas of Kashmir, whose purpose is to save the indivisibility of the atoms and at the same time, to make possible its agglomeration. They maintain that atoms, when individually considered, cannot conglomerate, since they are indivisible by nature, accepting in this way Vasubandhu's argumentation. But the Vaibhāṣikas of Kashmir maintained also that the atoms do not present themselves isolated, but forming cohesive groups of seven atoms each. These groups (molecules) constitute the smallest atomic unity. In these groups one atom occupies the center and the others are joined to it "coming" from the six directions of space. These groups of seven atoms can be connected among themselves, since they possess parts. And in fact these groups connect themselves in more or less great number to build up the things that constitute the external world.

This explanation of the Vaibhāṣikas is expressed in *Abhidharmakośabhāṣya ad* I, 43 (I, p. 121 Bauddha Bharati edition= L. de la Vallée Poussin's translation, I, p. 90): *api khalu saṃghātāḥ sāvayavatvāt spṛśanti*: "certainly the conglomerates touch (themselves mutually), since they have parts".

Section XXI: Refutation of the previous explanation of the Vaibhāṣikas: the molecules cannot be connected among themselves either

Vasubandhu answers saying that the conglomerate of seven atoms is not different from the atoms that constitute it. In *Abhidharmakośa* I, 43 (I,p. 122 Bauddha Bharati edition=L. de la Vallée Poussin's translation, I, p. 92) is expressed the same idea: *na ca paramāṇubhyo 'nye saṃghātā iti:* "the conglomerates are not different from the atoms".

Buddhism does not accept the existence of a whole (*avayavin)* as something real, independent from the parts and different from them. (See commentary on *Section XVIII* point 1, and note 7 of *Ālambanaparīkṣā*). The conglomerate of seven atoms is nothing else than seven atoms located in a certain order. If the atoms cannot connect themselves without losing their indivisibility (i.e. without abandoning their own nature, without ceasing to exist as such), then neither the molecule, that *is* those seven atoms, can be connected with other molecules, without the atoms that constitute it losing their indivisibility. Besides that, how can each of the seven atoms, that constitute the molecule be connected with the others without losing their indivisibility? A connection is not possible for the conglomerate if it is not possible for the atom. Thus the question asked by Vasubandhu in the first part of the *kārika* 13 must be answered: "of nobody"- neither of the atoms which constitute the molecule nor of the molecule constituted by them owing to the fact that the molecule is not different from its atoms.

Section XXII: Refutation of the Vaibhāṣikas' assertion that the atoms cannot be connected, because they do not possess parts

In *Section XX* the Vaibhāṣikas have said that they admit that the atoms do not connect among themselves, *because* they do not possess parts, asserting that on the contrary the conglomerates do. Vasubandhu remarks in this Section that in *Section XXI* it has been shown that the molecules of seven atoms cannot agglomerate, notwithstanding their having parts, since there is no difference between the molecules and the atoms that build them up. Consequently it is not possible to say that it is the absence of parts, the indivisibility, what hinders the connection. A thing may have parts, as the molecule (which has as parts its atoms), and nevertheless be unable to conglomerate with other things, if the parts it has are indivisible (as those atoms are). Only things composed of elements that are not posited as indivisible can be united among themselves in order to form the greater units that constitute our empirical reality. This is not possible with the atomist theory; it is only possible with the Buddhist doctrine that considers that every thing is constituted by parts and these parts by subparts, and so on without an end.

Vasubandhu finishes this Section saying that: "Therefore it is not admitted that the atom be a thing provided of unity (=indivisibility)". In fact the arguments developed in *Sections XVIII-XXI* have discarded the possibility for the atoms to conglomerate and to become in this way the external *āyatana* that is necessary as an object for an act of cognition. This is the principal result of the argumentation carried on up to this moment. This argumentation refers to the third alternative of *Section XVIII.*

But this argumentation has another consequence: it is impossible to admit the existence of indivisible atoms, since they could not cohesively agglomerate in order to build up greater units; and so there would not be the possibility for the existence of the things and the beings of this world, which according to the realist position really exist as external and material things and beings.

Section XXIII: Arguments against the unity (indivisibility) of the atom, individually considered (leaving aside the question of its being connected or not with other atoms)

In *Section XVIII* (second alternative) Vasubandhu has declared that it is not possible to admit an external *āyatana* composed of isolated and not agglomerated atoms, since we do not grasp the atoms one by one. This is a remark of epistemological nature. At the end of the previous Section, Vasubandhu passed to the ontological field asserting that the atom as such cannot exist by virtue of his argumentation aimed at discarding an external *āyatana* constituted by agglomerated atoms. Now, developing an ontological thesis, he will demonstrate that the atom as something indivisible (as it was conceived by Indian atomists) cannot exist; the indivisibility of the atom is a logical impossibility, with or without connection.

The first argument of Vasubandhu is the following one: the atom is in the space, consequently the same divisions or parts that are in the space are in the atom-an eastern part, a western part, etc. It is not possible to assert that something that has parts is indivisible. Vasubandhu, in *Abhidharmakośabhāṣya ad* I, 43 (I, p. 122 Bauddha Bharati edition=L. de la Vallée Poussin's translation, I, p. 92) develops a similar argument: *yadi ca paramāṇor digbhāgabhedaḥ kalpyate spṛṣṭasyāspṛṣṭasya vā sāvayavatvaprasaṅgaḥ* ("if it is assumed that the atom has a division according to the regions of space, the atoms would have parts, being in connection or not being in connection with other atoms"). Cf. *Hastavālanāmaprakaraṇa* 3 a-b and commentary (F. Tola's and C. Dragonetti's edition and translation in *On Voidness*, 1995, p. 7 for the text, p. 11 for the translation).

The second argument expresses that, if the atom is indivisible, then when it is exposed to the sun's light, the whole of it would be illuminated. Not having parts, the atom could not have an illuminated part (that exposed to the sun) and a non illuminated part (that not exposed to the sun); no shadow would be possible for it; and consequently the objects of our empirical reality, being formed by atoms completely illuminated on all sides, would never exhibit a shadow in any of its surfaces.

The third argument offered by Vasubandhu is that, if the atom lacks parts, it would not have any extreme face, any external side or limit; and consequently it would be unable to obstruct, to stop other atoms coming towards it; and, being the atoms unable to mutually obstruct, to stop others, all the atoms would occupy the same place, would be confounded in one, would constitute a mass of the size of an atom. There would not be possibility of a gross thing, of the gross things of our world.

To sum up: the atom is not an external *āyatana* (object of cognition), since owing to its infinitely small measure it cannot be grasped by us, when it is isolated, and it is impossible for it to be connected to other atoms in order to build up a perceptible agglomeration of atoms; otherwise, it would lose its indivisibility, its essential characteristic according to the atomist. (Besides that, an indivisible atom is a not well founded hypothesis).

Section XXIV: Suggestion of the opponent: The shadow and the capacity to obstruct can belong to the conglomerate of atoms and not to the individual atom

The opponent in order to overcome the previous refuting arguments, argues that it can be considered that the atom, when it is isolated, can be illuminated in its totality and can be unable to obstruct other atoms, but that nevertheless it can be accepted that the shadow and the capacity to obstruct belong to the conglomerate of atoms.

Section XXV: Refutation of the previous suggestion: the conglomerate of atoms and the atoms that compose it are not different

In order to refute the previous suggestion Vasubandhu asks whether the conglomerate of atoms is different from the atoms that build it up. The opponent answers is "not", since he is a Buddhist and according to Buddhist doctrine the whole does not exist as something real, different from its parts, and consequently the whole and its parts are the same. See note 7 of *Ālambanaparīkṣā*. Therefore, if the atom cannot have a zone with shadow nor obstruct other atoms, the conglomerate that is not different from them, can neither have a shadow nor obstruct.

Vasubandhu concludes *Section XXV* affirming that the conglomerate is only an illusion or imagination (*parikalpa*) of conglomerate (*saṃniveśa*). And he is right. In *Section XVIII* he has expressed two possibilities in relation to the *āyatana* or object of cognition: 1. the *āyatana* is a group of isolated atoms or 2. the *āyatana* is a conglomerate of connected atoms. In the first case, Vasubandhu declares, atoms cannot be perceived, since they are infinitely small; and, if we could perceive them, we would perceive only isolated atoms and nothing else. If we perceive an (inexisting) conglomerate instead of isolated atoms, that could be only an illusion of our mind. And, as regard the second possibility, the conglomeration of atoms (that is the only thing that could produce in our mind the representation of a conglomerate) has been declared to be impossible to exist, because it nullifies the basic assumption of the indivisibility of the atoms.

Dignāga in the *Ālambanaparīkṣā*, Section C, follows a similar line of discussion: after discarding the atom as possible object of cognition, he maintains that neither the conglomerate can be the object of cognition simply because it does not exist.

Section XXVI: New proposal of the opponent leaving aside atoms and conglomerates

The new proposal in defence of the existence of external *āyatanas* leaves aside atoms and conglomerates, since according to what has been expounded in *Sections XVIII-XXII* it is necessary to admit that the atoms, if they are isolated, cannot be objects of cognition, and, if it is postulated that they are indivisible, they cannot connect among themselves forming a conglomerate which would be the object of cognition.

But, after discarding atoms and conglomerate, there remains something that is to be examined: what objectively presents itself before our sensorial knowledge, what our senses grasp: form-colour, etc.; it is not necessary to inquire whether what our senses grasp is atoms or a conglomerate constructed by them. What our senses grasp is, according to the realist opponent, the external *āyatana*, essential factor of sensorial cognition.

The same opponent indicates, answering a question formulated by Vasubandhu, that the characteristics of this new *āyatana* (basis or object of knowledge are 1. the fact of being the object of knowledge, of functioning as such, and 2. the fact of being blue, etc., i. e. the fact of having the numerous attributes with which it presents itself before our senses-being its essence what it may be, atoms or conglomerate.

Vasubandhu starts his analysis of the new object of cognition asking whether that blue, etc., which is proposed now as object of cognition, is something multiple (i.e. composed of elements) or one (i.e. possessing unity). In the next Section Vasubandhu will deal with both possibilities, demonstrating that the new *āyatana* that has been proposed cannot exist either, because of its logical impossibility.

Section XXVII: Difficulties to which gives rise the new proposal, which confirm the impossibility of the existence of external āyatanas

In this Section Vasubandhu will show that the *datum* form-colour, etc., adduced as the object of cognition, faces the same difficulties that the atoms and the conglomerate, that have been examined and refuted in the preceding Sections.

Vasubandhu studies here the two alternatives indicated in the previous Section: that the blue, etc., thing or *datum* that is now proposed as the external *āyatana* is either multiple or one (provided with unity).

Vasubandhu expresses that, the logical difficulties which occur in relation to the *first hypothesis* (multiplicity) have been already indicated. He is referring to the second and third alternatives of *Section XVIII*, developed in *Sections XVIII-XXV*.

We think that, by reference to the ideas exposed by Vasubandhu, his reasoning in relation to that blue, etc., which our senses grasp, is the following one. If that *datum* is composed of parts, these parts could in their turn be divided into sub-parts and so on, in a dividing process that reaches the atom. The atoms are the last possible parts of things and thus they are to be taken into account in this hypothesis of multiplicity. And it has already been said that the isolated atoms cannot be perceived owing to their infinitely small size, and the atoms as they are conceived by the atomists cannot be connected among themselves on risk of losing their indivisible essence. Thus, not being there either isolated atoms or aggregates of atoms that could be perceived, what we perceive is not what is there; therefore it must be something that our imagination creates and superimposes on the invisible atoms. This is a case of a mere "imagination or illusion of aggregate"—imagination or illusion constituted by a coloured and extended aggregate, but unreal and inexistent as such.

The following example presents an analogous situation: we look from afar at a marching army; the army is not something real, different from the soldiers that build it up; we do not perceive them because of the distance; the only real thing that is there, the soldiers, are not the object of our cognition; its object is something unreal, created by our mind, the army, another mere "illusion or imagination of aggregate", superimposed on the only real thing, the soldiers.

Thus, a thing, which is constituted by a multiplicity of elements that cannot be perceived, either because of their invisibility (the atoms) or because of the distance (the soldiers), and which can be divided unto those elements—that thing will produce a representation of itself that does not correspond to reality, and cannot be considered as an *āyatana*, which has to produce in our mind a representation that corresponds to its true form of being. Cf. in Dignāga's *Ālambanaparīkṣā* (*Previous remarks* of our commentary) the definitions of "object of cognition" and "support of cognition". In both definitions is found the agreement between the *thing* to which the cognition refers and the *representation* which is produced in the mind.

After discarding the *first hypothesis*, Vasubandhu deals with the *second one*: that thing blue, etc. that we grasp is one, and consequently it is deprived of extension, since, if it had extension, it would have parts. This thing blue, etc. which constitutes the second hypothesis has in common with the whole *(avayavin)* as conceived by the *Vaiśeṣikas* the attribute of oneness.

The difficulties adduced by Vasubandhu against this alternative are the following ones, which can be adduced also against the whole as conceived by the Nyāya-Vaiśeṣika.

1. If that thing blue, etc., which I see, as for instance a piece of land, were *one* and consequently without extension, it could be gone through with a single footstep; it could not be gone through gradually.
2. Any thing, as for instance a table, if it were *one* and consequently deprived of extension, could not be seized by a hand in one of its extremes only and not seized at the same time in another of them. It would be seized by that hand everywhere.
3. If I shut in a park elephants and horses, and that park is *one*, without extension, those elephants and horses could not occupy different places; all of them would occupy the same place; there would be no separation between both kind of animals.

And, if it would be possible to separate on one side the elephants and in another the horses, that park would not be *one* since there would be between them an empty space separating them.

4. Finally, if all things and creatures are *one* and deprived of extension, their diversity would not derive from their size, since being deprived of extension they would have no size; their diversity would derive only from their characteristics. Therefore, if we can see a big fish, there is not reason for our not seeing a small, tiny, minute fish, since the characteristics of both are the same and extension or size does not exist for any of them, being one and therefore without extension, and consequently cannot be adduced as a factor of differentiation to explain why we perceive one and do not perceive the other.

Vasubandhu concludes this Section expressing that it is not possible to admit the unity, the indivisibility of the thing, of the *datum* blue, etc., which objectively comes before our eyes and which has been proposed by the opponent as the external *āyatana* or object of cognition. That thing or *datum* is divisible into atoms, and atoms (as it has been demonstrated in *Sections XIX-XXIII)* are in their turn divisible and do not constitute unities.

Thus our empirical reality is a collection of things and beings constituted by parts, by subparts, by "divisible" atoms. If we analyze the things of our empirical reality, then parts and subparts begin to appear in successive waves. But we can only grasp the parts that manifest themselves in the first levels of our analysis; the parts of deeper levels escape from our vision. These parts, subparts, atoms, to which things are reduced, are the only things that are there. Nevertheless what we perceive are *things,* compact unitary individualized things. We grasp what does not really exist, what is only appearances, phenomena, which can only be explained as creations of our mind, like the *taimirika*'s or the oniric visions. So we reach the conclusion that there are not external *āyatanas* for our cognitions, only mental creations; and that it is *only* the *mind* which creates in itself and by itself what we perceive as external object.

In the remaining part of the treatise Vasubandhu will refute several objections adduced against his idealistic thesis of the inexistence of an external *āyatana* and will develop some thesis and conceptions of his school of philosophy.

Section XXVIII: How to explain perception if there is not an external object ?

Perception is the most important of the means of knowledge (*pramāṇas*) and through it it is established whether a thing exists or not. If no external object exists, how can there be perception ? We have already indicated in note 13 of the *Ālambanaparīkṣā* and in our commentary to *Section XI* that in the realistic Buddhist conception of perception an external *āyatana* (basis), i. e. an external object, was necessary : form-colour or any other sensorial object. This was also the position of the realistic Nyāya-Vaiśeṣika. *Nyāyasūtra* I, 1, 4 requires for the coming forth of perception the contact of the sense-organ with an object (*indriyārthasannikarṣa*).

Section XXIX: Vasubandhu answers describing the mechanism of perception which in fact takes places without an external object

Vasubandhu answers declaring that in fact all the acts of perception lack a corresponding external object, and therefore the idealistic thesis that denies the existence of external *āyatanas* does not produce any difficulty. Vasubandhu's answer has three aspects.

In the first place, in a succinct way he points out that a perception without an external object is possible, as it happens in dreams. In fact nothing real and external corresponds to the oniric vision. Vasubandhu adds: "as it has been said before". He is referring to *Section III* where there is a reference to dreams. It is necessary to take into account what has been explained in *Section XIII*. This last Section explains how the sensorial knowledge is produced, without an external object, by the sole mechanism of the *vāsanās* or subliminal impressions left by previous experiences.

Then Vasubandhu adds that in fact, when a cognition called 'perception' takes place, the object of that cognition is not seen at all. For Vasubandhu a perceptive process proceeds in the following way.[58]

In a first moment the sense comes into contact and is in contact with its object; this is pure sensation; mind has no intervention at all; and consequently that pure sensorial knowledge does not involve any mental association or construction (*vikalpa, kalpanā*) of whatever kind it may be, as for instance name, gender, quality, action, accidental attributes, etc. Because of the absence of all extra-sensorial element, this moment of the perceptive process receives the name of "*nirvikalpa* perception", i.e. a perception that lacks any mental construction (*vikalpa*). This is the type of sensorial knowledge that is proper to the child in the first days of life or to a yogin that has reached a deep level of concentration. Anonymous, "The effects of Marijuana in consciousness", in Ch. T. Tart, *Altered states of consciousness*, New York: Anchor Books, 1972, p. 345, aptly describes this moment of the perceptive process: "There are two states of awareness which relate to these sensory effects. The basic one can be called pure awareness. In this state the person is completely and vividly aware of his experience, but there are no processes of thinking, manipulating, or interpreting going on. The sensations fill the person's attention, which is passive but absorbed in what is occurring, which is usually experienced as intense and immediate. Pure awareness is experiencing without associations to what is there".

In a second moment, which constitutes the perception properly said, the *datum* provided by the sense is enriched with mental associations, as those previously indicated such as name, etc. This moment of the perception process receives the name of "*savikalpa* perception". This constitutes the normal form of perception. Anonymous, *ibidem*, p. 345, describes it as follows: "The other state of awareness is one which can be termed conscious awareness, in which the sensory experience is connected to meanings, plans, functions, decisions, and possible actions. This is our normal way of perceiving and how we usually go about our daily lives. We do not sense the world directly, but with the incorporation of our memories, meanings, and uses. In the state of pure awareness objects are experienced as sensory qualities, without the intrusion of interpretation", and p.346: "Consciousness, conscious awareness, or conscious attention involves a connecting function which observes experience in relation to past experience, memory images, memory recording, expectancies, plans, goals, etc. This type of consciousness may intrude on the awareness state at a low level. However, when awareness fills the attention there is a "becoming lost" in the experience, in which there is often not even a memory of what occurred. This seems to be a state in which consciousness functions are not present, and all experience is at the level of awareness. Consciousness, attention, and memory recording are apparently not active".

Now, according to the previous explanation, Vasubandhu argues that the object known by the mind, the object that is represented in the mind, in the second moment of the perception process (the *savikalpa* perception) is not anymore the object that came into contact with the sense in the first moment of the perception process (the *nirvikalpa*, pure, perception). The object that came into contact with the sense in the first moment of the perception process was devoid of any association, was devoid of any mental construction; but the object known by the mind in the second moment of the perception process has been determined, provided and enriched with the associations constructed by the mind. Owing to that transformation it is possible to say that the object of the first moment of perception, the object of the eye-cognition, of the cognitive activity carried on by the eye, is not anymore before the mind in the second moment of perception. Then, Vasubandhu concludes, it is not possible to maintain that the perceptive cognition has taken place with the presence of an external object, of that object which came into contact with the sense. The perception properly said takes place in the absence of that external object, after its disappearance due to the transformation to which it was submitted through the "constructive" activity of the mind.

Vasubandhu adds—and this is the third aspect of his answer—that the previous argumentation is more decisive in relation to instantaneous objects. And this is what Buddhists maintain: all is in a constant flow, since there is not a permanent and unalterable substance and since all the beings and things of our reality are composed of *dharmas*-unsubstantial, impermanent, which as soon as they arise disappear.[59] Consequently the object that came into contact with the sense has ceased to exist when mind accomplishes its cognitive activity.

In this way Vasubandhu has demonstrated that, contrarily to what is ordinarily believed, perception takes place in fact without the presence of external object.

Section XXX: If there are not external objects, how recollection, which requires the previous experience of an object, is to be explained ?

All recollection is supposed to require the previous experience, the previous cognition of the recollected object. It is impossible to recollect something that has not been known. And that necessary experience or cognition is the perception through the senses of *something*.[60]

Section XXXI : Vasubandhu answers that it is only by virtue of the reactualizing of the vāsanās that recollection comes forth

Vasubandhu answers that it has already been explained—in *Section XII*—that the cognition of something arises by virtue of the reactualization of a *vāsanā* or mark or subliminal impression left by a previous act of cognition, without the intervention of a real external object. That cognition, product of the reactualization of a *vāsanā*, is the origin or source of the new recollective cognition. What is recollected is only the object which was perceived in that previous act of cognition and which did not exist outside the mind. Recollection is only of mental products, not of external objects. Something similar happens with the recollection of things seen in dreams or in the course of a hallucination. For a realist thinker there can be recollection of real external things perceived in normal acts of cognition and also recollection of mere mental products as things seen in an oniric vision or under the effect of a delusion; for Vasubandhu in all the acts of recollection what is recollected is *only* a mental creation produced by a mere mental process-the reactualization of a *vāsanā*.

Let us remember that for Vasubandhu man is only a succession of *vāsanā*-act of cognition-*vāsanā*-act of cognition-*vāsanā*-act of cognition, etc. which comes forth from a beginningless eternity.[61] And this alternative process of *vāsanās* and acts of cognition produced by them takes place in the mental level or realm; there was not a first act of cognition produced by a real external object.

Vasubandhu ends his reasoning saying that from the existence of recollection it cannot be necessarily deduced that there has been a previous cognition of an external real object. That he is right is shown by the adduced examples of dreams and hallucinations.

Section XXXII : How can it happen that man is not aware of the unreality of the objects of his acts of cognition ?

As an argument against the idealistic thesis of Vasubandhu is adduced the fact that people are aware of the things that they see in dreams being unreal, but they consider as real the things that they perceive when they are awake. If these last things were also unreal, there would not be difference in the reactions of people. This argument amounts to saying that against Vasubandhu's opinion there is the common opinion of everybody.

Section XXXIII : Vasubandhu answers that people become aware of the unreality of their oniric vision when they awake, and of the unreality of all they perceive when they are free from error

The man that dreams does not become aware of the unreality of his oniric vision so long as he has not awakened. Only when he awakes he becomes aware of that fact. Man, so long as he has not reached the world-transcending knowledge, is submerged in the "sleep of the *vāsanās*". Only when he, acquiring the world-transcending knowledge, becomes free from the "sleep of the *vāsanās*", he gets aware that the objects he saw in the *vāsanic* sleep were as unreal as the objects he sees in dreams.[62]

The "sleep of the *vāsanās*"is nothing else than the illusory world created by the reactualization of the *vāsanās*. Man lives in that world, enchained to it, considering it as external to him and real, in the same way as, when he dreams, he feels that he is dealing with external real beings and things. In both cases there is only delusion. Man cognizes that illusory world, and that cognition is his normal ordinary knowledge.

In this Section Vasubandhu indicates the characteristics of the world-transcending knowledge, which allows man to awake from the "sleep of the *vāsanās*". This world-transcending knowledge is the opposite to the normal ordinary knowledge. It is nothing else than the *Bodhi*, Enlightenment, the knowledge of what the empirical reality truly is, that the Bodhisattva obtains and which transforms him into a *Buddha*, a Tathāgata.

In normal conditions, i.e. in the natural empirical existence of man, mind (through the mechanism of the *vāsanās*) creates an illusory reality. That illusory reality, a mere mental product, is superimposed on the true reality, covering it, concealing it. The true reality cannot be reached by man, precisely because his mind places in front of it a veil of delusion which covers and conceals it. The normal knowledge cannot reach the true reality, its only object are the creations of the mind, that is to say the illusion to which they give rise; this illusion is the limit of ordinary human knowledge. Human mind is condemned to know only the unreal world which it creates.

With the world-transcending knowledge the situation is completely different. That knowledge has as its object, not illusory mental creations—the covering concealing empirical reality—but the true reality that ordinarily is covered and concealed. When that world-transcending knowledge is obtained, mind gets devoid of its capacity to produce new *vāsanās*, mind is thus "purified". Moreover that world-transcending knowledge has another important consequence: the destruction of the old *vāsanās* which lay in subliminal state in the mind, waiting for the moment to be reactualized. Thus this world-transcending knowledge is the opposite of the "sleep of the *vāsanās*", since it stops their functioning and puts an end to their consequences. The world-transcending knowledge is free from the production of unreal mental creations, since its object is the true reality; and, if there were mental creations, these would hinder the perception of that true reality. Contrarily to normal knowledge which is the ordinary and natural behaviour of mind, the world-transcending knowledge is given only in extraordinary conditions; it is the result of an arduous labour imposed by the intellectual and moral Buddhist discipline, and which has as its crowning, in an act that can be considered of *mystic* or *yogic* experience, the cognitive experience of the true reality.

The man who obtains after long efforts that world-transcending knowledge will have the deep conviction that all that is the object of the normal knowledge is a mere mental creation, a mirage, a phantasmagoria without real existence. And, although he continues living in this world, having necessariiy recourse to the normal ordinary knowledge for his empirical activity, anyhow his normal ordinary knowledge has been purified and has been deprived of all its capacity to originate evil effects, thanks to the world-transcending knowledge he has obtained.[63]

Section XXXIV: Without real objects, how can a consciousness determine another ?

If there were not external object which give rise to cognition, if cognition is produced only by virtue of the transformation of consciousness itself, if all is mere illusion created by mind, then it is impossible to admit that a consciousness may be determined, influenced, for better or for worse, through the contact with good or evil friends or through hearing a good or an evil doctrine, since all is unreal and neither those friends nor those doctrines do exist.

In *Section II* the realist opponent of Vasubandhu adduced as a third objection that, if all is mere mental creation, representations would be proper to each series of consciousnesses, and the most absolute solipsism would occur. Vasubandhu in *Section IV* refutes his opponent and overcomes solipsism explaining that the representations in the diverse consciousnesses are similar owing to the similarity of the karmic histories of those individuals that have them.

The question in this Section aims at isolating a consciousness from all the others. We can admit that all consciousnesses can have the same representations, but anyhow they cannot exert a mutual influence. There is not the possibility that a good teacher influence on his disciple neither that the hearing of the Buddhist Dharma produce a beneficial effect on those who receive it. Each consciousness would be isolated in itself.

Section XXXV: Vasubandhu's answer asserts that the possibility of a consciousness influencing on another exists

In his answer Vasubandhu affirms three things: 1. there is among consciousnesses a reciprocal determination or influence;2. that determination or influence exists because each consciousness is for the other a predominant determining condition (*ādhipatipratyaya)*; and 3. consequently an act of cognition in a series of consciousnesses can arise from an act of cognition of another series of consciousnesses, not necessarily from an external object.

The predominant determining condition (*ādhipatipratyaya*) is the most important determining condition in the collection of conditions that are needed for anything being created; it is the determining condition that specifically aims at the production of some affect.[64]

Vasubandhu does not give any fundamentation for these three statements. We think that Vasubandhu's idea can be explained in the following way. We start from the assertion that all men are nothing else than series of consciousnesses. By virtue of the *vāsanās* that belong to them they imagine a world, where they will experience happiness as a reward or suffering as a punishment, as retribution for their good or evil actions. Due to the similarity of their *karman,* there is agreement among all these worlds, giving the impression that they are only one and the same world; and what happens in one of these worlds agrees with what happens in the others, giving the impression of a strict correspondence among all the events that occur in all these worlds. It could be said that there is a pre-established harmony among all the mental creations up to their most minute details. In a certain sense this fact gives a kind of reality to that world and what happens in it.

Now it can happen that in one of these series of consciousnesses (the master, the *kalyāṇamitra),* due merely to the *karman* and the mechanism of the *vāsanās,* some ideas, norms, ways of acting that can help to attain Liberation are conceived. These ideas, etc. are *dharmas* with all the characteristics possessed by the *dharmas* (see note 29). Nothing theoretically hinders that one of these beneficial *dharmas* (which is the effect of the conjunction of several other *dharmas*) in conjunction on its turn with other *dharmas* be the cause of the production in another series (the disciple, the friend of the *kalyāṇamitra*) of a *dharma* that influences (as a teaching, as a good advice) the course that this second series will take-being all the process ruled by the laws of causality, the force of the *karman,* and the mechanism of the *vāsanās* in the context of universal causality and interdependence.[65] So it is possible to say that a cognition—that of the beneficial ideas—that takes place in one consciousness has an effect in another consciousness.

In *Section XXXIX* Vasubandhu will give several examples of how a series of consciousnesses can influence on another series. The events indicated by Vasubandhu were considered as historical events, that had really taken place. Thus they constitute another empirical proof of the possibility of one mind influencing on another.

Section XXXVI: Why the conduct in the dream state and the conduct in the waking state do not give rise to the same effects as to the retribution of actions ?
Cognition in the dream state lacks a real object. If cognition in the waking state lacks also a corresponding real object, then there is no difference between both cognitions, between both experiences. So we cannot admit any difference in the moral results, in the retribution in a future life of an action done in a dream and an action done in waking time. The murder one commits in the waking state is as unreal as the one committed in a dream: in both cases there is neither victim nor murderous action nor killer. Why the first act will produce an evil fruit (as a reincarnation in bad conditions or condemnation to hell) while the second one will be innocuous ? Logically, in both cases, nothing will be produced. And, not being there retribution for good or evil actions, the basis for the moral system is destroyed.[66] This question, to which this Section refers, brings the discussion to a moral level, which is very important for Buddhism whatever be the philosophical position adopted.

Section XXXVII: Vasubandhu answers that there is a fundamental difference between both situations owing to the diverse states of mind
Vasubandhu solves the objection expressing that there is a difference between the act performed in the waking state and the act performed in a dream, owing to which the consequences of both actions are not the same. In fact, during a dream mind is dominated by torpor,[67] is not aware of what it does; during the waking state it is not the same. Thus it is not the existence or the inexistence of a corresponding external real object what produces the diversity of the fruit, but the different state or condition of the mind: conscious during the waking state, unconscious while dreaming.

We find in this Section a reference to two types of illusion. Normally, man in the waking state lives in the illusion (created by his own mind by virtue of the mechanism of the *vāsanās*) of an external and real world. This world (as has been previously expressed) agrees with the worlds created by the other minds owing to the identity of their karmic histories. Consequently, it is a universal illusion shared with by all men. Man is responsible for the acts he performs so long as he acts in that illusory world created by himself. During a dream, mind produces another illusion, which is exclusively proper to him alone, an illusion *inside* another illusion, which is not shared with by other beings. Man is not responsible for his acts during a dream, since his mind does not control itself.

Section XXXVIII: If there are no bodies, how a murder can be produced ? How the crime of murder can be committed?
If all is consciousness only, mind only, there are no bodies; then no man (a butcher for instance) can really kill another living being (a sheep for instance). And, if that is not possible, how can a man be accused of or blamed for having destroyed life, how can he be charged with the crime of murder?

Section XXXIX: Vasubandhu asserts that a mental act of a person can influence on the series of consciousnesses of another, producing his death, and gives examples of cases in which that happened
Vasubandhu answers that a particular act of cognition (more properly an act of volition, a will, a desire) of a person, acting as the predominant determining condition, can give rise to an alteration in the series of consciousnesses of other persons in the way indicated in our commentary on *Section XXXV*. This alteration hinders the functioning of the organ of life or vital organ or vital force or vitality (*jīvitendriya)* of that person, the victim, causing his death—i.e. the interruption not of the infinite series of consciousnesses which constitute the individual, but the interruption of the segment of the series of consciousnesses that constitute his present life or existence.

The organ of life (*jīvitendriya)* is one of the forces or energies which compose the individual and explain his constitution, his evolution and end; it is the force which determines the length of his life. When this vital force becomes exhausted or is stopped by any factor alien to it (as is the case Vasubandhu deals with in this *Section*), the death of the individual is produced.[68]

In order to prove his assertion Vasubandhu mentions *alterations* as loss of memory, visions of dreams, possession by evil spirits produced in the series of consciousnesses of a person by the force of demons (such as *piśācas)* or beings possessed of extraordinary powers. The belief in extraordinary mental powers was common in India at

Vasubandhu's time. Thus Vasubandhu adduces as an argument for his thesis a belief commonly accepted, not only among Hindus but also among Buddhists.[69]

Vasubandhu gives as examples events transmitted by Buddhist tradition as historical facts to which Vasubandhu ascribes full veracity. The events mentioned by Vasubandhu are the visions of dreams by King Sāraṇa as an effect of a mental act on the part of the Buddhist sage, the Venerable Mahākātyāyana, and the defeat of the King of the Asuras as an effect of mental acts of the forest *ṛṣis*.[70]

Section XL : Vasubandhu gives as a ground for his thesis expounded in the previous Section an implicit approval to it given by the Buddha himself

Vasubandhu expresses in this Section that it is necessary to accept the thesis he has expounded in the previous Section, because the Buddha himself has implicitly given his approval to it. The episode Vasubandhu refers to is narrated in the *Upalisutta* in the *Majjhimanikāya*, Vol. I, p. 378 (PTS edition) (= II, p. 43, I. B. Horner's translation, London: Luzac, 1970).[71] In that occasion the Buddha declares that violence through the mind is to be severely condemned, and to illustrate his point he asks Upali whether he knew the cause of the voidness of several forests.[72] Upali answers that the cause was the anger of several *ṛṣis* (sages) who punished their offenders by merely desiring to harm them. Buddha accepts and approves that answer. So the Scripture corroborates Vasubandhu's opinion: a mere volition, wish or desire to inflict violence on another person (as in the case of the mentioned *ṛṣis*) is able to produce that effect and destroy another person.

Two important elements are present in this Section. On one side, the traditional belief that the anger of the *ṛṣis* is able to produce extraordinary effects, and, on the other side, the acceptation of the word of the Buddha as a norm of authority.

Section XLI: An alternative explanation of the voidness of the mentioned forests is discarded by Vasubandhu

Vasubandhu expresses that it could be thought that the beings of these three forests were destroyed not by the mere anger of the *ṛṣis*, but by true acts of violence carried on against the offenders by non-human beings who also lived in the indicated forests and who respected the *ṛṣis*. This explanation cannot be accepted, since in that case the Buddha would not have said that violence manifested through the mind is a greater sin than the violence through the body or through the word, giving as an example of that the events in which the *ṛṣis* were involved.

Section XLII: If the hypothesis of 'only mind' is accepted, how to explain the knowledge of another's mind or thought ? Vasubandhu admits the possibility that this knowledge exists, but affirms that it does not correspond to reality

Vasubandhu is asked by his interlocutor: If the existence of mind only is accepted, then one may ask whether the "knowers of another's mind" really know it or not. The negative answer to this question is to be discarded, because in that case the "knowers of another's mind" would not be "knowers of another's mind". In Vasubandhu's time it was generally believed that some persons, owing to their great spiritual progress, possessed that capacity.[73] So Vasubandhu cannot deny that these persons possessed a knowledge of others' mind, but afterwards he will make clear which is the sort of knowledge these persons possessed.

Then the affirmative answer must be accepted: there are persons who know another's mind. The interlocutor asks: How (or why) the knowledge of the persons who know another's mind is erroneous, does not corresponds to reality ? Vasubandhu answers: It is erroneous, it does not correspond to reality in the same way as the knowledge of one's own mind is erroneous, does not correspond to reality. Both knowledges are *normal ordinary knowledge,* and as such function within the frame of the subject-object duality, and are consequently unable to grasp the essence of the mind which is pure consciousness, beyond the categories of subject and object. Both knowledges grasp a distorted image of their object. The essence of the mind, its true reality is that indefinable substantiality (see *Section XV),* which is the object only of that world-transcending knowledge that is proper to the Buddhas (see *Section XXXIII).* Only the Buddhas can grasp the truth of the essence of the mind.

Section XLIII: Conclusion

Vasubandhu concludes his treatise with some general remarks. He expresses that the theory of *only mind* or of the *sole existence of consciousness,*which he has expounded, is profound and unfathomable, since it proposes numerous questions which give rise to infinite reasonings and speculations. Ordinary persons (and Vasubandhu includes himself among them) are unable to encompass that theory in its whole totality; they can only have a partial, incomplete vision of it. This theory is the realm of the Buddhas (Enlightened Ones), only they are capable to know it completely, because they have reached Enlightenment and consequently they are omniscient; there is not any obstacle for their knowing it in all its forms and in all its implications. Vasubandhu has explained it according to his "capacity"(*śakti)*.

SANSKRIT TEXT

VIṂŚATIKĀ VIJÑAPTIMĀTRATĀSIDDHIḤ

(Mañjuśrīkumārabhūtāya namaḥ)[74]

[Section I: The thesis of the author: all is mere mental creations; only the mind exists][75]

[mahāyāne traidhātukaṃ vijñaptimātraṃ vyavasthāpyate/ cittamātraṃ bho jinaputrā yad uta traidhātukam iti sūtrāt/cittaṃ mano vijñānaṃ vijñaptiś ceti paryāyāḥ/cittam atra sasaṃprayogam abhipretaṃ/mātram ityarthapratiṣedhārthaṃ/]

vijñaptimātram evedam asadarthāvabhāsanāt/
yadvat taimirikasyāsatkeśoṇḍukādidarśanam[76]*//1//*

[Section II: Objections derived from the characteristics of the mental creations]

[atra codyate/]

na deśakālaniyamaḥ santānāniyamo na ca/
na ca kṛtyakriyā yuktā vijñaptir yadi nārthataḥ //2//

[kim uktaṃ bhavati/yadi vinā rūpādyarthena rūpādivijñaptir utpadyate na rūpādyarthāt/kasmāt kvacid deśa utpadyate na sarvatra/tatraiva ca deśe kadācid utpadyate na sarvadā/ taddeśakālapratiṣṭhitānāṃ sarveṣāṃ saṃtāna utpadyate na kevalaṃ ekasya/yathā taimirikāṇāṃ saṃtāne keśādyābhāso nānyeṣāṃ/ kasmād yat taimirikaiḥ keśabhramarādi dṛśyate tena keśādikriyā na kriyate na ca tadanyair na kriyate/yad annapānavastraviṣāyudhādi svapne dṛśyate tenānnādikriyā na kriyate na ca tadanyair na kriyate/ gandharvanagareṇāsattvān nagarakriyā na kriyate na ca tadanyair na kriyate/tasmād arthābhāve deśakālaniyamaḥ saṃtānāniyamaḥ kṛtyakriyā ca na yujyate/

[Section III: Refutation of the objections one by one. The characteristics indicated in Section II are not proper to all mental creations]

na khalu na yujyate yasmāt/

deśādiniyamaḥ siddhaḥ svapnavat

svapna iva svapnavat/kathaṃ tāvat/ [77] svapne vināpyarthena kva cid eva deśe kiṃ cid bhramarārāmastrīpuruṣādikaṃ dṛśyate na sarvatra/tatraiva ca deśe kadā cid dṛśyate na sarvakālam iti siddho vināpyarthena deśakālaniyamaḥ/

pretavat punaḥ/

saṃtānāniyamaḥ

siddha iti vartate/[78] pretānām iva pretavat/[79] kathaṃ siddhaḥ/[80] samam[81]

sarvaiḥ pūyanadyādidarśane //3//

pūyapūrṇā nadī pūyanadī/ghṛtaghaṭavat/tulyakarmavipākāvasthā hi pretāḥ sarve 'pi pūyapūrṇāṃ nadīṃ paśyanti naika eva/yathā pūyapūrṇām evaṃ mūtrapurīṣādipūrṇāṃ daṇḍāsidharaiś ca puruṣair adhiṣṭhitām ityādigrahaṇena/evaṃ saṃtānāniyamo vijñaptīnām asatyapyarthe siddhaḥ/

svapnopaghātavat kṛtyakriyā

siddheti veditavyaṃ/ yathā svapne dvayasamāpattim antareṇa śukravisargalakṣaṇaḥ svapnopaghātaḥ[82]/evaṃ tāvad anyānyair dṛṣṭāntair deśakālaniyamādicatuṣṭayaṃ siddhaṃ /

[Section IV: Refutation (similar to that of Section III) of the objections of Section II, but all together]

narakavat punaḥ/

sarvaṃ

siddham iti veditavyaṃ/narakeṣviva narakavat/kathaṃ siddhaṃ/

narakapālādidarśane taiś ca bādhane //4//

yathā hi narakeṣu nārakāṇāṃ narakapālādidarśanaṃ deśakālaniyamena siddhaṃ śvavāyasāyasaparvatādyāgamanagamanadarśanaṃ cetyādigrahaṇena sarveṣāṃ[83] ca naikasyaiva taiś ca tadbādhanaṃ siddham asatsvapi narakapālādiṣu samānasvakarmavipākādhipatyāt/ tathānyatrāpi sarvam etad deśakālaniyamādicatuṣṭayaṃ siddham iti veditavyaṃ/

[Section V: Opponent's objection against the inexistence (previously adduced by Vasubandhu) of the hell-guards]
kiṃ[84] punaḥ kāraṇaṃ narakapālās te ca śvāno vāyasāś ca sattvā [85] neṣyante/

[Section VI: Vasubandhu's answer to the previous objection]
ayogāt/na hi te nārakā yujyante/ tathaiva tadduḥkhāpratisaṃvedanāt/

parasparaṃ yātayatām ime nārakā ime narakapālā iti vyavasthāna syāt/tulyākṛtipramāṇabalānāṃ[86] ca parasparaṃ yātayatāṃ[87] na tathā bhayaṃ syāt/dāhaduḥkhaṃ[88] ca pradīptāyām ayomayyāṃ bhūmāvasahamānāḥ kathaṃ tatra parān yātayeyuḥ/anārakāṇāṃ vā narake[89] kutaḥ saṃbhavaḥ/

[Section VII: Solution proposed by the opponent asserting the birth in the hells of not condemned beings acting as hell-guards]
kathaṃ tāvat tiraścāṃ svargasaṃbhavaḥ/evaṃ narakeṣu tiryakpretaviśeṣāṇāṃ narakapālādīnāṃ saṃbhavaḥ syāt/

[Section VIII: Refutation of the previous solution]

tiraścāṃ saṃbhavaḥ[90] svarge yathā ca[91] narake tathā/
na pretānāṃ yatas tajjaṃ duḥkhaṃ[92] nānubhavantite//5//

ye hi tiryañcaḥ svarge saṃbhavanti[93] te tadbhājanalokasukhasaṃvartanīyena karmaṇā[94] tatra saṃbhūtās[95] tajjaṃ sukhaṃ pratyanubhavanti/na caivaṃ[96] narakapālādayo nārakaṃ duḥkhaṃ pratyanubhavanti/[97] tasmān na tiraścāṃ saṃbhavo[98] yukto nāpi pretānāṃ/

[Section IX: New suggestion on the part of the opponent affirming that in the hells there arise conglomerates of elements adopting the form of hell-guards and acting as such]
teṣāṃ[99] tarhi nārakāṇāṃ karmabhis[100] tatra bhūtaviśeṣāḥ saṃbhavanti[101] varṇākṛtipramāṇabalaviśiṣṭā ye[102] narakapālādisaṃjñāṃ pratilabhante/tathā ca pariṇamanti yad vividhāṃ hastavikṣepādikriyāṃ kurvanto dṛśyante bhayotpādanārthaṃ/yathā meṣākṛtayaḥ parvatā āgacchanto[103] gacchanto 'yaḥśālmalīvane[104] ca kaṇṭakā adhomukhībhavanta ūrdhvamukhībhavantas[105] ceti/na te na saṃbhavantyeva[106]/

[Section X: Refutation of the previous suggestion: Why not to admit that the hell-guards, etc. are a mental product of the transformation of the vāsanās, and that the vāsanās and their effect are both in the mind ?]

yadi tatkarmabhis[107] tatra bhūtānāṃ saṃbhavas[108] tathā
ṣyate pariṇāmaś ca kiṃ vijñānasya neṣyate[109]//6//

vijñānasyaiva tatkarmabhis[110] tathā pariṇāmaḥ kasmān neṣyate kiṃ punar bhūtāni kalpyante/api ca/

karmaṇo[111] vāsanānyatra phalam anyatra kalpyate/
tatraiva neṣyate[112] yatra vāsanā kiṃ[113] nu kāraṇaṃ//7/

yena hi karmaṇā[114] nārakāṇāṃ tatra tadṛśo bhūtānāṃ saṃbhavaḥ[115] kalpyate pariṇāmaś ca tasya[116] karmaṇo[117] vāsanā teṣāṃ vijñānasaṃtānasaṃniviṣṭā[118] nānyatra/yatraiva ca vāsanā tatraiva tasyāḥ phalaṃ tādṛśo vijñānapariṇāmaḥ kiṃ[119] neṣyate/yatra vāsanā nāsti tatra tasyāḥ phalaṃ kalpyata iti kim atra kāraṇaṃ/

[Section XI: Fundamentation of the opponent's thesis that the "fruit" of actions is not where the vāsanā is]
āgamaḥ kāraṇaṃ/yadi vijñānam eva rūpādipratibhāsaṃ syān na rūpādiko' rthas tadā rūpādyāyatanāstitvaṃ bhagavatā noktaṃ syāt/

[Section XII: Refutation of the previous fundamentation]
akāraṇam etad[120] yasmāt/

rūpādyāyatanāstitvaṃ tadvineyajanaṃ[121] *prati/*
abhiprāyavaśād uktam upapādukasattvavat[122]*//8//*

yathāsti sattva[123] upapāduka ityuktaṃ bhagavatā/abhiprāyavaśāc cittasaṃtatyanucchedam[124] āyatyām abhipretya/nāstīha sattva[125] ātmā vā dharmās[126] tvete sahetukā[127] iti vacanāt/evaṃ rūpādyāyatanāstitvam apyuktaṃ bhagavatā taddeśanāvineyajanam adhikṛtyetyābhiprāyikaṃ tad vacanaṃ/

[Section XIII: Which is the true meaning of the words of the Buddha that affirm the existence of āyatanas ?]
ko 'trābhiprāyaḥ/

yataḥ svabījād vijñaptir yadābhāsā pravartate/
dvividhāyatanatvena te tasyā munir abravīt //9//

kim uktaṃ[128] bhavati/rūpapratibhāsā vijñaptir yataḥ svabījāt pariṇāmaviśeṣaprāptād utpadyate[129] taç ca bījaṃ yatpratibhāsā ca sā te tasyā vijñapteś cakṣūrūpāyatanatvena yathākramaṃ bhagavān abravīt/evaṃ yāvat spraṣṭavyapratibhāsā vijñaptir yataḥ svabījāt pariṇāmaviśeṣaprāptād[130] utpadyate[131] tac ca bījaṃ yatpratibhāsā ca sā te tasyāḥ [132] kāyaspraṣṭavyāyatanatvena yathākramaṃ bhagavān abravīd ityayam[133] abhiprāyaḥ/

[Section XIV: Good results obtained through the Buddha's teaching understood in this way]
evaṃ[134] punar abhiprāyavaśena deśayitvā ko guṇaḥ/

tathā pudgalanairātmyapraveśo hi[135]

tathā hi deśyamāne pudgalanairātmyaṃ praviśanti/dvayād vijñānaṣaṭkaṃ[136] pravartate/[137] na tu kaś cid eko draṣṭāsti na yāvan mantetyevaṃ viditvā ye pudgalanairātmyadeśanāvineyās te pudgalanairātmyaṃ praviśanti/

anyathā punaḥ/[138]

deśanā[139] *dharmanairātmyapraveśaḥ*[140]

anyatheti vijñaptimātradeśanā/[141] kathaṃ dharmanairātmyapraveśaḥ[142]/ vijñaptimātram idaṃ rūpādidharmapratibhāsam[143] utpadyate na tu rūpādilakṣaṇo dharmaḥ[144] ko 'pyastīti viditvā/

[Section XV: Objection: Does not the inexistence of dharmas imply the inexistence of consciousness ?]
yadi tarhi sarvathā dharmo[145] nāsti tad api vijñaptimātraṃ nāstīti kathaṃ tarhi[146] vyavasthāpyate/

[Section XVI: Refutation of the previous objection. How the affirmation that the dharmas do not exist is to be understood]
na khalu sarvathā dharmo[147] nāstīty evaṃ dharmanairātmyapraveśo[148] bhavati[149] api tu/

kalpitātmana[150] *//10//*

yo bālair dharmāṇāṃ[151] svabhāvo grāhyagrāhakādiḥ parikalpitas tena kalpitenātmanā teṣāṃ nairātmyaṃ na tvanabhilāpyenātmanā yo buddhānāṃ[152] viṣaya iti/evaṃ[153] vijñaptimātrasyāpi[154] vijñaptyantaraparikalpitenātmanā nairātmyapraveśād [155] vijñaptimātravyavasthāpanayā sarvadharmāṇāṃ[156] nairātmyapraveśo bhavati na tu sarvathā[157] tadastitvāpavādāt/itarathā hi vijñapter api vijñaptyantaram arthaḥ syād iti vijñaptimātratvaṃ[158] na sidhyetārthavatītvād vijñaptīnāṃ/

[Section XVII: Opponent question: Why is it necessary to accept the non-existence of the external āyatanas that are the objects of cognition ?]
kathaṃ punar idaṃ pratyetavyam anenābhiprāyeṇa bhagavatā rūpādyāyatanāstitvam uktaṃ na punaḥ santyeva tāni yāni rūpādivijñaptīnāṃ pratyekaṃ viṣayībhavantīti/

[Section XVIII: Vasubandhu's answer: It is impossible that the external āyatanas exist]
yasmāt[159]/

na tad ekaṃ na cānekaṃ viṣayaḥ paramāṇuśaḥ/
na ca te saṃhatā yasmāt paramāṇur na[160] *sidhyati //11//*

iti kim uktaṃ[161] bhavati/yat tad rūpādikam āyatanaṃ rūpādivijñaptīnāṃ pratyekaṃ viṣayaḥ syāt tad ekaṃ vā syād yathāvayavirūpaṃ kalpyate vaiśeṣikaiḥ/anekaṃ vā paramāṇuśaḥ/[162] saṃhatā vā ta eva paramāṇavaḥ/na tāvad ekaṃ viṣayo bhavatyavayavebhyo[163] nyasyāvayavirūpasya kva cid apyagrahaṇāt/ nāpyanekaṃ paramāṇūnāṃ pratyekam agrahaṇāt/nāpi te saṃhatā viṣayībhavanti/yasmāt paramāṇur ekaṃ dravyaṃ na sidhyati/kathaṃ na sidhyati/

[Section XIX: Arguments which hinder to admit that a conglomeration of atoms (as conceived by the Vaiśeṣikas) could be the external āyatana, object of cognition]
yasmāt/

ṣaṭkena yugapadyogāt paramāṇoḥ ṣaḍaṃśatā/[164]

ṣaḍbhyo digbhyaḥ ṣaḍbhiḥ paramāṇubhir yugapadyoge sati paramāṇoḥ ṣaḍaṃśatā prāpnoti ekasya yo deśas tatrānyasyāsaṃbhavāt[165]/

ṣaṇṇāṃ samānadeśatvāt piṇḍaḥ syād aṇumātrakaḥ//12//

atha ya evaikasya paramāṇor deśaḥ sa eva ṣaṇṇāṃ/tena sarveṣāṃ samānadeśatvāt sarvaḥ piṇḍaḥ paramāṇumātraḥ syāt parasparāvyatirekād[166] iti na kaś cit piṇḍo dṛśyaḥ syāt/

[Section XX: Explanation of the Vaibhāṣikas of Kashmir: molecules (groups of seven atoms) can be connected among themselves]
naiva hi paramāṇavaḥ saṃyujyante niravayavatvāt [167]/ mā bhūd eṣa doṣaprasaṅgaḥ/[168] saṃhatās tu parasparaṃ saṃyujyanta iti kāśmīravaibhāṣikāḥ/[169]

[Section XXI: Refutation of the previous explanation of the Vaibhāṣikas: the molecules cannot be connected among themselves either]
ta[170] idaṃ praṣṭavyāḥ/yaḥ paramāṇūnāṃ saṃghāto na sa tebhyo 'rthāntaram iti [171]

paramāṇor asaṃyoge/[172] *tatsaṃghāte*[173] *'sti kasya saḥ/*[174]

saṃyoga iti vartate/

[Section XXII: Refutation of the Vaibhāṣikas' assertion that the atoms cannot be connected, because they do not possess parts]

na cānavayavatvena tatsaṃyogo na sidhyati //13//

atha saṃghātā apyanyoyaṃ na saṃyujyante/ [175] na tarhi paramāṇūnāṃ niravayavatvāt[176] saṃyogo na sidhyatīti vaktavyaṃ/sāvayavasyāpi hi saṃghātasya saṃyogānabhyupagamāt/tasmāt paramāṇur[177] ekaṃ dravyaṃ na sidhyati/

[Section XXIII: Arguments against the unity (indivisibility) of the atom, individually considered (leaving aside the question of its being connected or not with other atoms)]
yadi ca paramāṇoḥ saṃyoga iṣyate yadi vā neṣyate/

digbhāgabhedo[178] *yasyāsti tasyaikatvaṃ*[179] *na yujyate/*

anyo hi paramāṇoḥ pūrvadigbhāgo yāvad[180] adhodigbhāga iti

digbhāgabhede[181] sati kathaṃ tadātmakasya paramāṇor ekatvaṃ yokṣyate/

chāyāvṛtī[182] *kathaṃ vā*[183]

yadyekaikasya paramāṇor digbhāgabhedo na syād ādityodaye katham anyatra chāyā bhavatyanyatrātapaḥ[184]/na hi tasyānyaḥ pradeśo[185] 'sti yatrātapo na syāt/āvaraṇaṃ[186] ca kathaṃ bhavati paramāṇoḥ paramāṇvantareṇa yadi digbhāgabhedo neṣyate/na hi kaś cid api paramāṇoḥ[187] parabhāgo[188] 'sti yatrāgamanād anyenānyasya pratighātaḥ syāt/asati ca pratighāte sarveṣāṃ samānadeśatvāt sarvaṃ saṃghātaḥ paramāṇumātraḥ syād ityuktam/

[Section XXIV: Suggestion of the opponent: The shadow and the capacity to obstruct can belong to the conglomerate of atoms and not to the individual atom]
kim evaṃ[189] neṣyate piṇḍasya te cchāyāvṛtī na paramāṇor iti/

[Section XXV: Refutation of the previous suggestion: The conglomerate of atoms and the atoms of which it is composed are not different]
kiṃ khalu paramāṇubhyo 'nyaḥ piṇḍa iṣyate yasya te syātāṃ[190] netyāha/

anyo na[191] *piṇḍaś cen na tasya te //14//*

yadi nānyaḥ[192] paramāṇubhyaḥ piṇḍa iṣyate na te tasyeti siddhaṃ[193] bhavati/saṃniveśaparikalpa[194] eṣaḥ[195]/

[Section XXVI: New proposal of the opponent leaving aside atoms and conglomerates]
paramāṇuḥ saṃghāta iti vā kim anayā cintayā[196] lakṣaṇaṃ[197] tu rūpādi yadi na[198] pratiṣidhyate/kiṃ[199] punas teṣāṃ lakṣaṇaṃ/[200] cakṣurādiviṣayatvaṃ nīlāditvaṃ[201] ca/ tad evedaṃ saṃpradhāryate[202]/ yat tac cakṣurādīnāṃ viṣayo nīlapītādikam iṣyate kiṃ[203] tad ekaṃ dravyam atha vā tad[204] anekam iti/kiṃ[205] cātaḥ/

[Section XXVII: Difficulties to which gives rise the new proposal, which confirm the impossibility of the existence of external āyatanas]
anekatve doṣa uktaḥ/[206]

ekatve na krameṇetir yugapan na grahāgrahau[207]
vicchinnānekavṛttiś ca sūkṣmānīkṣā ca no bhavet//15 /

yadi yāvad avicchinnaṃ nānekaṃ[208] cakṣuṣo viṣayas tad ekaṃ dravyaṃ kalpyate pṛthivyāṃ krameṇetir na syād/[209] gamanam ityarthaḥ/ sakṛtpādakṣepeṇa[210] sarvasya gatatvāt/arvāgbhāgasya ca grahaṇaṃ parabhāgasya cāgrahaṇaṃ yugapan[211] na syāt/[212] na hi tasyaiva tadānīṃ grahaṇaṃ[213] cāgrahaṇaṃ[214] ca yuktam[215]/vicchinnasya cānekasya hastyaśvādikasyānekatra vṛttir na[216] syād yatraiva hyekaṃ[217] tatraivāparam iti kathaṃ[218] tayor viccheda iṣyate[219]/ kathaṃ[220] vā tad ekaṃ yat prāptaṃ[221] ca tābhyāṃ[222] na ca prāptam antarāle tacchūnyagrahaṇāt/sūkṣmāṇāṃ[223] caudakajantūnāṃ sthūlaiḥ samānarūpāṇām anīkṣaṇaṃ na syāt/yadi lakṣaṇabhedād[224] eva dravyāntaratvaṃ kalpyate nānyathā/tasmād avaśyaṃ paramāṇuśo bhedaḥ kalpayitavyaḥ sa caiko na sidhyati/tasyāsiddhau rūpādīnāṃ cakṣurādiviṣayatvam asiddham iti[225] siddhaṃ vijñaptimātraṃ[226] bhavatīti

[Section XXVIII: How to explain perception if there is not an external object?]
pramāṇavaśād astitvaṃ nāstitvaṃ vā nirdhāryate sarveṣāṃ[227] ca pramāṇānāṃ[228] pratyakṣaṃ[229] pramāṇaṃ gariṣṭham ityasatyarthe katham[230] iyaṃ buddhir[231] bhavati pratyakṣam[232] iti/[233]

[Section XXIX: Vasubandhu answers describing the mechanism of perception which in fact takes place without an external object]

pratyakṣabuddhiḥ[234] *svapnādau yathā*[235]

vināpyartheneti pūrvam eva jñāpitaṃ/

sā ca yadā tadā/

na so[236] *'rtho dṛśyate tasya pratyakṣatvaṃ kathaṃ*[237] *mataṃ //16//*

yadā ca[238] sā pratyakṣabuddhir[239] bhavatīdaṃ[240] me pratyakṣam iti tadā na so[241] 'rtho dṛśyate manovijñānenaiva paricchedāc cakṣurvijñānasya ca tadā niruddhatvād iti/[242] kathaṃ tasya pratyakṣatvam iṣṭaṃ/viśeṣeṇa[243] tu kṣaṇikasya viṣayasya[244]/[245] tadānīṃ niruddham eva tadrūpaṃ rasādikaṃ vā/

[Section XXX: If there are not external objects, how recollection, which requires the previous experience of an object, is to be explained ?]
nānanubhūtaṃ[246] manovijñānena smaryata[247] ityavaśyam arthānubhavena bhavitavyaṃ tac ca darśanam ityevaṃ tadviṣayasya rūpādeḥ pratyakṣatvaṃ mataṃ/

[Section XXXI: Vasubandhu answers that it is only by virtue of the reactualizing of the vāsānas that recollection comes forth]
asiddham idam anubhūtasyārthasya smaraṇaṃ[248] bhavatīti/yasmāt/

uktaṃ yathā tadābhāsā vijñaptiḥ[249]

vināpyarthena yathārthābhāsā cakṣurvijñānādikā vijñaptir utpadyate tathoktam/[250]

smaraṇaṃ[251] *tataḥ/*

tato hi vijñapteḥ smṛtisaṃprayuktā[252] tatpratibhāsaiva rūpādivikalpikā manovijñaptir utpadyata iti na smṛtyutpādād arthānubhavaḥ sidhyati/

[Section XXXII: How can it happen that man is not aware of the unreality of the objects of his acts of cognition?]
yadi yathā svapne vijñaptir abhūtārthaviṣayā tathā jāgrato[253] 'pi syāt tathaiva tadabhāvaṃ lokaḥ svayam avagacchet/[254] na caivaṃ[255] bhavati/[256] tasmān na svapna ivārthopalabdhiḥ sarvā nirarthikā/

[Section XXXIII: Vasubandhu answers that people become aware of the unreality of their oniric vision when they awaken, and of the unreality of all what they perceive when they are free from error]
idam ajñāpakaṃ/yasmāt/

svapne dṛgviṣayābhāvaṃ[257] nāprabuddho[258] vagacchati//17//

evaṃ vitathavikalpābhyāsavāsanānidrayā prasupto lokaḥ svapna ivābhūtam arthaṃ[259] paśyan na prabuddhas tadabhāvaṃ yathāvan nāvagacchati/yadā tu tatpratipakṣalokottaranirvikalpajñānalābhāt prabuddho bhavati tadā tatpṛṣṭhalabdhaśuddhalaukikajñānasaṃmukhībhāvād[260] viṣayābhāvaṃ yathāvad avagacchatīti samānam etat/

[Section XXXIV: Without real objects, how can a consciousness determine another ?]
yadi svasaṃtānapariṇāmaviśeṣād[261] eva sattvānām[262] arthapratibhāsā vijñaptaya utpadyante nārthaviśeṣāt/tadā ya eṣa pāpakalyāṇamitrasaṃparkāt sadasaddharmaśravaṇāc[263] ca vijñaptiniyamaḥ sattvānāṃ[264] sa kathaṃ sidhyati asati sadasatsaṃparke taddeśanāyāṃ[265] ca/

[Section XXXV: Vasubandhu's answer asserts that the possibility of a consciousness influencing on another exists]

anyoyādhipatitvena vijñaptiniyamo mithaḥ[266]/

sarveṣāṃ hi sattvānām[267] anyonyavijñaptyādhipatyena mitho vijñapter niyamo bhavati yathāyogaṃ/mitha iti parasparataḥ/ ataḥ saṃtānāntaravijñaptiviśeṣāt[268] saṃtānāntare[269] vijñaptiviśeṣa utpadyate nārthaviśeṣāt/

[Section XXXVI: Why the conduct in a dream state and the conduct in the waking state do not give rise to the same effects as to the retribution of actions ?]
yadi yathā svapne nirarthikā vijñaptir evaṃ[270] jāgrato[271] 'pi syāt kasmāt kuśalākuśalasamudācāre suptāsuptayos tulyaṃ phalam iṣṭāniṣṭam āyatyāṃ[272] na bhavati/[273]

[Section XXXVII: Vasubandhu answers that there is a fundamental difference between both situations owing to the diverse states of mind]

yasmāt/

middhenopahataṃ[274] *cittaṃ svapne tenāsamaṃ phalaṃ //18//*[275]

idam atra kāraṇaṃ na tvarthasadbhāvaḥ/

[Section XXXVIII: If there are no bodies, how murder can be produced ? How the crime of murder can be committed ?]

yadi vijñaptimātram evedaṃ na kasya cit kāyo[276] 'sti na vāk/[277] katham upakramyamāṇānām[278] aurabhrikādibhir urabhrādīnāṃ maraṇaṃ[279] bhavati/atatkṛte vā tanmaraṇe katham aurabhrikādīnāṃ prāṇātipātāvadyena yogo bhavati/[280]

[Section XXXIX: Vasubandhu asserts that a mental act of a person can influence on the series of consciousnesses of another, producing his death and gives examples of cases in which that happened]

maraṇaṃ[281] *paravijñaptiviśeṣād vikriyā yathā/*
smṛtilopādikānyeṣāṃ piśācādimanovaśāt //19//

yathā hi piśācādimanovaśād anyeṣāṃ smṛtilopasvapnadarśanabhūtagrahāveśavikārā bhavanti ṛddhivanmanovaśāc ca/yathā sāraṇasyāryamahākātyāyanādhiṣṭhānāt svapnadarśanaṃ/ āraṇyakarṣimanaḥpradoṣāc ca vemacitraparājayaḥ[282]/tathā paravijñaptiviśeṣādhipatyāt pareṣāṃ jīvitendriyavirodhinī kā cid vikriyotpadyate yayā sabhāgasaṃtativicchedākhyaṃ[283] maraṇaṃ[284] bhavatīti veditavyaṃ/

[Section XL: Vasubandhu gives as a ground for his thesis expounded in the previous Section an implicit approval to it given by the Buddha himself]

kathaṃ vā daṇḍakāraṇyaśūnyatvam ṛṣikopataḥ[285]/

yadi paravijñaptiviśeṣādhipatyāt sattvānāṃ[286] maraṇaṃ neṣyate/ manodaṇḍasya hi mahāsāvadyatvaṃ sādhayatā bhagavatoPalir gṛhapatiḥ pṛṣṭaḥ/[287] kac cit te gṛhapate śrutaṃ kena tāni daṇḍakāraṇyāni mātaṅgāraṇyāni kaliṅgāraṇyāni śūnyāni medhyibhūtāni/[288] tenoktaṃ/[289] śrutaṃ me bho gautama ṛṣīṇāṃ manaḥpradoṣeṇeti/[290]

[Section XLI: An alternative explanation of the voidness of the mentioned forests is discarded by Vasubandhu]

manodaṇḍo mahāvadyaḥ kathaṃ vā tena siddhyati //20// [291]

yadyevaṃ kalpyate/tadabhiprasannair amānuṣais tadvāsinaḥ sattvā[292] utsāditā na tvṛṣīṇāṃ manaḥpradoṣān mṛtā ityevaṃ sati kathaṃ tena karmaṇā[293] manodaṇḍaḥ kāyavāgdaṇḍābhyāṃ[294] mahāvadyatamaḥ siddho bhavati/[295] tanmanaḥpradoṣamātreṇa tāvatāṃ sattvānāṃ[296] maraṇāt sidhyati/

[Section XLII: If the hypothesis of 'only mind' is accepted, how to explain the knowledge of another's mind or thought? Vasubandhu admits the possibility that this knowledge exists, but affirms that it does not correspond to reality]

yadi vijñaptimātram evedaṃ paracittavidaḥ kiṃ paracittaṃ jānantyatha na/kiṃ[297] cātaḥ/yadi na jānanti kathaṃ paracittavido bhavanti/atha jānanti/[298]

> *paracittavidāṃ[299] jñānam ayathārthaṃ kathaṃ yathā/*
> *svacittajñānaṃ[300]*

tad api katham ayathārthaṃ/

> *ajñānād yathā buddhasya gocaraḥ//21//*

yathā tan nirabhilāpyenātmanā buddhānāṃ[301] gocaraḥ tathā tadajñānāt tad ubhayaṃ na yathārthaṃ vitathapratibhāsatayā grāhyagrāhakavikalpasyāprahīṇatvāt[302]/

[Section XLIII: Conclusion]

anantaviniścayaprabhedāgādhagāmbhīryāyāṃ vijñaptimātratāyāṃ[303]

> *vijñaptimātratāsiddhiḥ svaśaktisadṛśī mayā/*
> *kṛteyaṃ sarvathā sā tu na cintyā[304]*

sarvaprakārā tu sā mādṛśaiś cintayituṃ na śakyate/tarkāviṣayatvāt[305]/ kasya punaḥ sā sarvathā gocara ityāha/

> *buddhagocaraḥ //22//[306]*

buddhānāṃ hi sā bhagavatāṃ sarvaprakāraṃ gocaraḥ sarvākārasarvajñeyajñānāvighātād iti/

viṃśatikā vijñaptimātratāsiddhiḥ/[307]
kṛtir iyam ācāryavasubandhoḥ/[308]

TRANSLATION

THE TWENTY STANZAS

The Demonstration of The Only Existence Of Consciousness (Stanzas and Commentary) by Vasubandhu

Section I: Thesis of the author: all is mere mental creations; only the mind exists

In the Mahāyāna the three worlds are established to be only consciousness (*vijñapti*), according to the *sūtra* that affirms: "O sons of the Victorious, the three worlds are only mind (*citta*)." *Citta, manas, vijñāna* and *vijñapti* are synonyms. There (i. e. in the quotation) (the word) *citta* ("mind") is understood as (the mind) together with what is connected with it (*saṃprayoga=caitta*).[309] (The word) *mātra* ("only") is (used) with the purpose of denying (the existence of external) objects.

1. *(All) this is indeed only consciousness,*
   because of the appearance (in it)
   of non existing objects,
   as the vision by the taimirika
   of an inexisting net of hairs, etc.

Section II: Objections derived from the characteristics of the mental creations

Thereupon the following objection is raised:

2. *Neither the determination (certainty)*
   in regard to place and time
   nor the indetermination (unexclusiveness)
   in regard to the series (of consciousnesses)
   nor the performance of the (specific) function
   are logically possible,
   if consciousness (does) not (arise)
   out from an object.

What has been said (in the *kārikā*)? (Its meaning is:) If consciousness (=cognition) of form-colour, etc. arises without (external) objects (constituted by) form-colour, etc., (i.e.) not from (external) objects (constituted by) form-colour, etc., (then) why does it (=consciousness) arise in a (determinate, certain) place, not everywhere? And moreover (why) does it arise in that very place at a (determinate, certain) moment, not always? (And why) does it arise in the series (of consciousnesses) of all those who are present in that place at that moment, not (in the series of consciousnesses) of only one (person) -as (is the case with) the appearance of hairs, etc. only in the series (of consciousnesses) of the *taimirikas,* not (in the series of consciousnesses) of others? Why the hairs, bees, etc., which are seen by the *taimirikas*, do not perform the (specific) function of hairs, etc., but others (=hairs, bees, etc.) different from them do perform it? The food, drink, clothes, poison, weapons, etc., which are seen in a dream, do not perform the (specific) function of food, etc., but others (= food, etc.) different from them do perform it. The (imaginary, illusive) City of the Gandharvas[310] does not perform the (specific) function of a city, because of its inexistence, but others (=cities) different from it do perform it (=the function of a city). Therefore, given the inexistence of objects, neither the determination (certainty) in regard to place and time nor the indetermination (unexclusiveness) in regard to the series (of consciousnesses) nor the performance of the (specific) function are logically possible.

Section III: Refutation of the objections one by one. The characteristics indicated in Section II are not proper to all the mental creations

They are indeed logically possible, since

3. *The determination (certainty)*
in regard to place, etc.,
has to be admitted
as in dreams,

Svapnavat: as in dreams=*svapna iva:* as in dreams[311]

How is it? In a dream, even without an object, something, bees, a garden, a woman, a man, etc. are seen in a (determinate) place, not everywhere, and just in that place (those things) are seen at a (determinate) moment, not at any moment. Therefore, even without an object the determination (certainty, lack of arbitrariness) in regard to place and time has to be admitted.

> *and also, as in the case of the* pretas,
> *the indetermination (non-exclusiveness)*

is to be admitted—so is to be understood.

Pretavat: as (in the case of) the *pretas=pretānām iva*=as in the case of the *pretas*.

Why (that determination) is to be admitted ? (Because) at the same time

> *there is the vision of the river of pus, etc. by all (the* pretas).

Pūnyanadī: river of pus=*pūyapūrṇa nadī:* river full of pus, as a pot of butter.

Because the *pretas*, who are in the situation of having the same maturation of their *karman*, see all of them not only one (of them) the river full of pus. Owing to the word "etc." (=*ādi* employed in the *kārikā*), (the river has to be understood) full of urines, excrements, etc. as well as full of pus and guarded by men holding sticks and swords.

Thus, even given the inexistence of an object, the indetermination (no-exclusiveness) in regard to the series (of consciousnesses) has to be admitted for the acts of cognition (*vijñapti*).

> 4. *As in the case of the (nocturnal) pollution,*
> *the performance of the (specific) function*

is to be admitted-so it must be known. As in a dream, even without the union of the couple, (there occurs) the pollution consisting in the emission of semen.

In this way, by various examples, the set of four, determination in regard to place and time, etc., has to be admitted.

Section IV: Refutation (similar to that of Section III) of the objections of Section II, but all together

> *Moreover, as (it happens) in hells,*
> *all (=the set of four)*

is to be admitted (in any situation)—so it must be known.

Narakavat: as (what happens) in hells=*narakeṣviva*: as (what happens) in hells.

Why (all the set of four) has to be admitted (in any situation)?

> *(because) there is the vision*
> *of the hell-guards, etc.*
> *and the torture (inflicted) by them.*

Because, in the same way as in hells the vision of the hell-guards, etc., with determination in regard to place and time, by all the condemned, not by only one (of them) has to be admitted; and also as the vision of dogs and crows and the coming and going of iron mountains, etc. owing to the word "etc." (=*ādi* in the *kārikā)* (has to be admitted); and also as the torture of these (=the condemned) by those (=the hell-guards) has to be admitted even if the hell-guards, etc. do not exist—(since all this happens) by virtue of the (sole and exclusive) power of the equal maturation of their actions—so in the same manner it must known that all this set of four, determination in regard to place and time, etc., has to be admitted also in other situations.

Section V: The opponent asks the reason for the inexistence (previously adduced by Vasubandhu) of the hell-guards

But which is the reason why the hell-guards and those dogs and crows are not considered as (really) existing beings ?

Section VI: Vasubandhu's answer to the previous question

Because of a logical impossibility. For it is not logically possible that these (=the hell-guards) be condemned beings, since they do not experience the suffering of them (=the condemned beings) in the same way (as these last do). (And, if the hell-guards experience the suffering of the condemned beings in the same way, i.e. being at their turn tortured by others, then) there could not be, among those who torture one another, a division such as: "These are condemned beings" and "These are hell-guards". Neither there could be (a feeling of) fear (in ones in regard to others) among those who torture each other (being all of them) of equal form, size and strength. And (finally) being unable to tolerate the suffering produced by burning in an ablaze ground made of iron, how could they (=the hell-guards) torture the others there (=in hell) ? Or how could it be the birth in hell of not condemned to hell ?

Section VII: Solution proposed by the opponent asserting the birth in the hells of not condemned beings acting as hell-guards

Then, how is it that there is birth in heaven of animals ? In the same way there could be birth in the hells of hell-guards, etc., having as distinguishing trait the being animals and *pretas.*

Section VIII: Refutation of the previous solution

5. *And as the birth of animals*
(is possible) in heaven,

so (the birth) of pretas in hell
is not (possible)
because they (=animals and pretas)
do not undergo the suffering
produced there (=in the hells).

For those animals which are born in heaven—being born there owing to (their) *karman* leading to the happiness of that world of experience [312] —enjoy the happiness produced there (=in heaven), but the hell-guards, etc. do not undergo in the same way the infernal suffering (in the hypothesis which has been discarded). Consequently the birth (in the hells) of animals or of *pretas* (to act as hell-guards and torturers) is not logically possible.

Section IX: New suggestion on the part of the opponent affirming that in hell there arise conglomerates of elements adopting the form of hell-guards and acting as such

In that case, by virtue of the actions of the condemned, there are born there (certain) kinds of elements characterized by their colour, their form, their size and their strength, which get the designation of hell-guards, etc. And they (=the elements) are changed in such a way that they are seen doing the various actions of moving the hands, etc. with the purpose of giving rise to (feelings of) fear, (or are seen) as mountains with the form of rams, coming and going, (or as) thorns in a forest of *śālmalīs* or of iron, (thorns) located in a downward direction and located in a upward direction. (So) it is not impossible that those (hell-guards, etc.) exist (in the hells).

Section X: Refutation of the previous suggestion: Why not to admit that the hell-guards, etc. are a mental product of the transformation of the vāsanās, and that the vāsanās and their effect are both in the mind ?

6. *If the birth of the elements*
is postulated in this way
there (=in the hells) by virtue of the actions
of those (condemned beings),
and (also their) transformation,
why (such a transformation)
is not admitted for consciousness ?

Why such a transformation of consciousness alone by virtue of the actions of those (condemned beings) is not admitted ? Why instead of that the elements are imagined (as really arising and changing in the way previously described)?

And moreover (according to the opponent's hypothesis),

7. *The* vāsanā *of the action* (karman)
is imagined (to be) in one place,
the effect (of it) in another place.
Which is the reason why
(the effect) is not admitted (to be)
there where the vāsanā *is ?*

The *vāsanā* of the action (*karman*) of the condemned beings, by virtue of which action (*karman*) such a birth of elements is imagined (by you to take place) there (=in the hells), as well as their transformation—(that *vāsanā*) is located in the series of consciousnesses of those (condemned beings), not in another place. Why is it not admitted that, where the *vāsanā* is, just there is its effect, (i.e.) such a transformation of consciousness ? Which is the reason for this (thesis of yours) that where the *vāsanā* is not, there its effect is imagined (to be) ?

Section XI: Fundamentation of the opponent's thesis that the "fruit" of actions is not where the vāsanās are

The reason is the Canonical Texts. If consciousness manifests itself as form-colour, etc. and the (external) object (of cognition), form-colour, etc., does not exist, then the existence of the *āyatanas* (basis) form-colour, etc. would not have been affirmed by the Bhagavant.

Section XII: Refutation by Vasubandhu of the previous fundamentation

This is not a (valid) reason because

8. *The existence of the* āyatanas *form-colour, etc.*
has been affirmed (by the Bhagavant)
with a determined intention in view,
for the sake of people
that were to be instructed in this (doctrine),
as the existence of spontaneous beings.

In the same way as it has been said by the Bhagavant: "There exists the spontaneous being", *abhiprāyavaśāt:*[313] with a determined (particular) intention in view, (i.e.) intending (to affirm) the non-interruption of the series of consciousnesses in the future—(as it is clear) from the (Bhagavant's) assertion: "In this world there is not a being nor an *ātman* (soul) but (only) *dharmas*, (all of them) produced by causes "-in the same way also the existence of the *āyatanas* form-colour, etc. has been affirmed by the Bhagavant having in mind people that were to be instructed in this doctrine. Thus that assertion (of the Bhagavant) is (an) intentional (assertion).

Section XIII: Which is the true meaning of the words of the Buddha that affirm the existence of āyatanas?
Which is in this case the determined intention ? (It is the following one:)

9. *That seed of its own*[314]
from which cognition comes forth
(and that object)
with whose representation
(cognition comes forth) -
the Muni has declared both
to be the twofold āyatana *of that (cognition).*

What has been said (in this *kārikā*) ? (What follows:) That seed of its own, that has reached a particular (stage of) transformation, from which the cognition with the representation of form-colour arises, and (that object) whose representation it (=the cognition) is (or bears)— the Bhagavant has declared both to be respectively the *āyatana* eye and the *āyatana* form-colour of that cognition. (And so) in the same way up to:[315] that seed of its own that has reached a particular (stage of) transformation, from which the cognition with the representation of a tangible (object) arises, and (that object) whose representation it (=the cognition) is (or bears)-the Bhagavant has declared both to be respectively the *āyatana* body[316] and the *āyatana* tangible (object). Thus this is the determined intention (the Bhagavant had in view).

Section XIV: Good results obtained through the Buddha's teaching understood in this way
Now, which is the advantage (of His) having taught in this way with a determined intention in view?

10. *Because in this way (is produced)*
the understanding of the (doctrine
of the) unsubstantiality of man.

Because, having (the doctrine) been taught (by the Bhagavant) in this way, they (=the disciples) understand the (doctrine of the) unsubstantiality of man. Knowing that the set of the six cognitions comes forth from the two (=the "seed" or virtuality and the object with whose representation the six cognitions arise), but that (in fact) there is not anybody characterized by unity who sees nor... up to : (anybody characterized by unity) who thinks, those who are to be instructed in the teaching of the unsubstantiality of man understand the (doctrine of the) unsubstantiality of man.

(And) again, (when taught) in another way,
(such a) teaching (constitutes)
the understanding of the (doctrine
of the) unsubstantiality of the dharmas.

(Taught) "*in another way*" =(taught as) the teaching of "*Only consciousness*". How (does that teaching constitute) the understanding of the (doctrine of the) unsubstantiality of the *dharmas*? By knowing that this sole consciousness arises with the representation of the *dharmas* form-colour, etc., but that a *dharma* with the characteristics of form-colour, etc. does not (externally) exist.

Section XV: Objection: Does the inexistence of dharmas not imply the inexistence of consciousness?
If then a (ny) *dharma* does not exist at all, then the sole consciousness does not exist either—consequently how then is it proved to exist?

Section XVI: Refutation of the previous objection. How the affirmation that the dharmas do not exist is to be understood
(In this way:) The understanding of the (doctrine of the) unsubstantiality of the *dharmas* is not produced by thinking that no *dharma* exists at all. But (it is produced by thinking that no *dharma* exists)

with an imagined essence.

The unsubstantiality of the *dharmas* is (possible to be asserted only when they are conceived as provided) with that imagined essence which is an own being consisting of a subject and of an object, etc., as it is imagined by the ignorant, but (that unsubstantiality) is not (possible to be asserted when the *dharmas* are conceived as provided) with the indescribable essence that is the object of (the knowledge of) the Buddhas.

Thus, the (correct) understanding of the unsubstantiality of all the *dharmas* is produced by means of the establishment of the sole (existence of) consciousness (only when one starts), from the understanding of the unsubstantiality even of the sole consciousness (if it is conceived as provided) with an essence imagined by another consciousness; but (that correct understanding is) not (produced when one starts) from the (absolute) negation of the existence of it (=of the sole consciousness). For, otherwise, owing to the fact that another consciousness would be the object of a consciousness, the fact of the existence of the sole consciousness would not be established, because of consciousnesses being provided with an object.

Section XVII: Opponent's question: Why is it necessary to accept the non-existence of the external āyatanas that are the object of cognition?

How is it to be admitted that by the Bhagavant the existence of the *āyatana* form-colour, etc. has been declared with that determined intention (referred to in *Section XIII*) and that (consequently) those *āyatanas,* which are the objects respectively[317] of the cognitions of form-colour, etc., do not exist (as external *āyatanas*)?

Section XVIII: Vasubandhu's answer: It is impossible that the external āyatanas exist

(The *āyatanas* form-colour, etc. cannot exist as external *āyatanas)* because

11. (*An external* āyatana) *cannot be*
the object of a cognition
either as one
or as multiple in (isolated) atoms;
neither can these (atoms),
(when they are) conglomerated,
(be object of cognition),
because (in this case) the atom
cannot be proved to exist.

What has been said (in this *kārikā*)? Whatever (external) *āyatana,* form-colour, etc. would happen to be object respectively of the cognitions of form-colour, etc., that (*āyatana)* would either be *one,* as the form of the whole is conceived by the Vaiśeṣikas, or (would be) *multiple* in (isolated) atoms or (it would be) merely those atoms being *conglomerated.* (The *āyatana*) as *one* cannot be object of cognition, because there is no perception anywhere of the form of a whole different from its parts; not can it be *multiple,* because there is no perception of the atoms individually; nor can they (=the atoms), being *conglomerated,* be the object of cognition, since the atom (in this case) cannot be proved to exist as a thing one (=indivisible). Why it cannot be proved to exist ?

Section XIX: Arguments which hinder to admit that a conglomeration of atoms (as conceived by the Vaiśeṣikas) could be the external āyatana, object of cognition

Because

12. *Owing to its simultaneous connection*
with a set of six (other atoms),
the atom would have six parts,

If there is a simultaneous connection (of an atom) with (other) six atoms (coming) from the six directions of space, the atom would have six parts, because in that place, which is (the place) of one (atom), there another (atom) cannot be.

(because),
if the six (atoms) had the same place
(than the atom to which they are connected),
(then), there would be a mass
of the size of an atom.

In fact, if the place of one atom were (the place) of the six (atoms which come to be connected with it), then since the place of all (= the seven atoms) is the same, the whole mass (constituted by the seven atoms) would be of the size of a single atom, because no (atom) would jut out in relation to the others. Consequently there would be no visible mass.

Section XX: Explanation of the Vaibhāṣikas of Kashmir: molecules (groups of seven atoms) can be connected among themselves

The Vaibhāṣikas of Kashmir (argue): "(We accept that) the atoms indeed do not become connected, because they do not have parts- (so) let it not be (attributed to us) the absurd consequence of that logical defect-but on being conglomerated (the atoms) become connected among themselves".

Section XXI: Refutation of the previous explanation of the Vaibhāṣikas: the molecules cannot be connected among themselves either

They must be asked this question: "The conglomeration of the atoms is not something different from them (=the atoms); in consequence,

13. *not being connection for the atom,*
 in the conglomeration of those (atoms)
 whose is that?"

'connection'—has to be understood (for that).

Section XXII: Refutation of the Vaibhāṣikas 'assertion that the atoms cannot be connected, because they do not possess parts

And (it is) not
owing to the fact of being without parts
(that) the connection of those (atoms)
cannot be accomplished.

If even the conglomerates (of atoms) are not connected among themselves, then it cannot be said that the connection of the atoms is not accomplished owing to the fact of their being without parts, since even the connection of a conglomerate provided with parts (with another conglomerate) is not possible.

Therefore it is not admitted that the atom is a thing one.

Section XXIII: Arguments against the unity (indivisibility) of the atom, individually considered (leaving aside the question of its being connected or not with other atoms)

Whether the connection of one atom (with others) is accepted, whether it is not accepted,

14. *the unity of that (atom)*
 in which there is a division
 according to the sections of the space,
 is not logically possible.

Since there is (in the atom) a division according to the sections of the space-because one is the Eastern section of the atom and *so up to*: (another is) the nadir section[318]—how would it be logically possible the unity of an atom constituted by those (sections)?

Or how the shadow and the obstruction
(could be possible)?

If there were not for each atom a division according to the sections of the space, (then) when the sun rises, how could it be shadow in one place (of the atom) (and) light in another? For there would not be in it (=the atom) a place in which there would not be light.

And how could occur the obstruction of an atom by another atom, if it is not accepted the division (of the atom) according to the sections of the space ? For there would not be any extreme part of the atom, where, on arriving (to it another atom), the mutual obstruction of one by another would be produced. And, not being there obstruction (of one atom by another atom), owing to the fact that the place of all (the atoms) would be (necessarily) the same, all would be a conglomerate of the size of (one single) atom—(as) it has been (already) said.[319]

Section XXIV: Suggestion of the opponent: The shadow and the capacity to obstruct can belong to the conglomerate of atoms and not to the individual atom

Why not to accept that the shadow and the obstruction belong both of them to the mass (of atoms), not to the (isolated) atom

Section XXV: Refutation of the previous suggestion: The conglomerate of atoms and the atoms of which it is composed are not different

Is it accepted that there is different from the atoms a mass (of atoms) to which both (=the shadow and the obstruction) would belong?

(The opponent answers :) "No".

If the mass (of atoms) is not different
(from the atoms of which it is composed),
(then) they (=the shadow and the obstruction)
cannot belong to it (=the mass).

If it is accepted that the mass (of atoms) is not different from the atoms (of which it is composed and which do not admit either shadow or obstruction), (then) it is (also) established that both of them (=the shadow and the obstruction) do not belong to it (=the mass). This (mass) is a (mere) imagination of aggregate.

Section XXVI: New proposal of the opponent leaving aside atoms and conglomerates

(The opponent asks:) Why (to have recourse to) the idea of 'atom' or 'conglomerate' (in order to discard the existence of external *āyatanas*), if (their) essential characteristic as form—colour, etc., has not been negated?

(Vasubandhu asks:) Which is the essential characteristic of those (external *āyatanas*) ?

(The opponent answers :) The fact of being object of (the cognition through) the eye, etc., and the fact of being blue, etc.

(Vasubandhu says:) This is examined (now). (And then he asks:) Is that blue, yellow, etc., which is accepted as object of (the cognition through) the eye, etc., a thing one or is it multiple?

(The opponent asks:) And what (is deduced) from there ?

Section XXVII: Difficulties to which gives rise the new proposal, which confirm the impossibility of the existence of external āyatanas

(Vasubandhu says:) The logical defect in relation to multiplicity (of the *āyatana*) has already been declared.

15. *In (the hypothesis of) the unity*
(of the āyatana*)*
neither going gradually
nor grasping and not grasping at the same time
nor the existence (of beings and things)
separated and multiple
nor the non-vision of minute
(beings and things)
would be possible.

If that (presumed) thing *one* is imagined as undivided, non-multiple, (and, being such,) as object of (the cognition through) the eye, (then)

going (*iti*) gradually on the earth would not be possible—the meaning of *iti* ("going") is *gamana* ("moving")—since with only one step all (distance) would be covered;

there would not be at the same time the grasping of the front part and the not-grasping of the rear part, because the grasping and the not-grasping at the (same) time (of the same unitary thing) are not logically possible;

there would not be the existence in different places of separated (and) multiple elephants, horses and the like, since where one thing is, there the other would (also) be-and thus, how the separation of both (things) could be accepted? Or how could that (thing) be one, (that thing) which is occupied (=by elephants and horses) and which is not occupied (in the totality of its surface) by both of them, since in the midst (of them) (a separating) empty (space) is perceived ?;

there would not be the non-vision of minute animals living in water that are of the same form as the big ones, if it is supposed that only from the diversity of the characteristics the differentiation of things (is produced), not otherwise.

Consequently, the division into atoms (of that presumed thing one, blue, yellow, etc., that is present before us) has to be necessarily assumed; and it (=the atom) is not established as being one

(= indivisible). And, if (the atom) is not admitted (to be one), (then) it is not admitted that the form—colour, etc. (as things external to mind) be the object of (the cognition through) the eye, and therefore *only consciousness* is admitted (to exist).

Section XXVIII: How to explain perception if there is not an external object?

Existence or non-existence (of things) is ascertained by the means of knowledge (*pramāṇa*) and of all the means of knowledge perception (*pratyakṣa*) is the most important means of knowledge—consequently, if any (external) object does not exist, (then) how does this cognition take place: "(This object) is present before (my) eyes".

Section XXIX: Vasubandhu answers describing the mechanism of perception which in fact takes place without an external object

16. *The cognition (called) perception*
(takes place)
as in a dream, etc.,

even without an (external) object—thus has been stated before.

And when that (cognition called perception)
(takes place),
then that (external) object
is not (longer) seen.
How the presence before the eyes
of that (object)
can be assumed ?

And when that cognition (called) perception takes place (expressed in these words:) "This (object) is present before my eyes," then that object is not (longer) seen, owing to the accurate determination effected by the mind—consciousness and owing to the cessation at that time of the eye—consciousness—therefore how the presence before the eyes of that (object) is postulated ? And specially (in the case) of an instantaneous object. Then (=in the moment of the intervention of mind-consciousness) that form-colour or taste, etc., have already ceased (to be).

Section XXX: If there are not external objects, how recollection, which requires the previous existence of an object, is to be explained?

Anything that has not been (previously) experienced (=known) is not remembered by the mind-consciousness—therefore (given the existence of recollection) there must inevitably be the (previous) experience (= knowledge) of an object, and that is "vision" (or any other of the sensorial cognitions); thus the presence before the eyes can be assumed for the form-colour, etc., object of that vision (etc.).

Section XXXI: Vasubandhu answers that it is only by virtue of the reactualizing of the vāsanās that recollection comes forth
This is not admitted, that the act of remembering be of an (external real) object previously experienced (=known), since

17. *it has already been explained*
how cognition (arises)
(provided) with the representation
of that (object).

It has already been explained (in *Section XII*) how even without an object the cognition constituted by the eye-consciousness arises with the representation of an object.

(And) the act of remembering
(comes forth) from that.

From that cognition arises a mind-consciousness, associated with recollection, (provided) with the representation of that (object), creating the illusion of form-colour, etc.—therefore it is not admitted that the experience (=knowledge) of an (external real) object (is proved) by virtue of the coming forth of recollection.

Section XXXII: How can it happen that man is not aware of the unreality of the objects of his acts of cognition?
If, in the same way as cognition in a dream has as its objects unreal things, so also (the cognition) of the awakened (person) (had as its objects unreal things), then people would recognize by themselves the inexistence of those things (of the waking state), but it is not so. Consequently, *all* perception of a thing is not as in a dream deprived of an (external real) object.

Section XXXIII: Vasubandhu answers that people become aware of the unreality of their oniric visions when they awake, and of the unreality of all they perceive when they are free from error
That means nothing, since

the person who has not (yet) awakened
does not recognize the inexistence
of the objects of his vision in a dream.

Likewise, people, submerged in the sleep of the *vāsanās* with their reiteration of false mental creations, on seeing an unreal object, as (it occurs) in a dream, do not recognize as it should be the inexistence of that object, so long as they have not awaked (from the sleep of the *vāsanās*). But, when they have awakened (from the sleep of the *vāsanās*) by virtue of the obtention of that world-transcending knowledge that lacks any mental construction and that is the opposite of that (sleep of the *vāsanās*), then they recognize as it should be the inexistence of the objects, because (now) (the inexistence of the objects) stands in front of (their) purified mundane knowledge acquired (by them) after that (world-transcending knowledge)—thus it is the same (in both cases: that of the knowledge in a dream and that of the knowledge in the normal ordinary knowledge).

Section XXXIV: Without real objects, how can a consciousness determine another?

If the acts of cognition of the (sentient) beings, (provided) with the representation of the object, arise only from a particular transformation of the series (of consciousnesses) proper to each (of those beings) (and) not from a particular (external real) object, then how is it admitted for (those sentient) beings a determination of (their) consciousness through the contact with good or evil friends or through hearing true or false doctrines, since good or evil contact or the teaching of those (true or false doctrines) do not exist ?

Section XXXV: Vasubandhu's answer asserts that the possibility of a consciousness influencing on another exists

(It must be answered:)

18. *There is reciprocally*
determination of consciousnesses
owing to the fact of being
one for the other
the predominant determining condition

Because, for all beings, there reciprocally is a determination of consciousness owing to the fact of one consciousness being for the other the predominant determining condition. (In the *kārikā* the word) *mithaḥ* ("reciprocally") (means): *parasparataḥ* ("one another's"). Therefore, a particular act of cognition arises in a series (of consciousnesses) from a particular act of cognition proper to another series (of consciousnesses), not from a particular (external real)object

Section XXXVI: Why the conduct in the dream state and the conduct in the waking state do not give rise to the same effects as to the retribution of actions?

If as in a dream cognition is without an (external real) object, so also the cognition of the awakened person were (without an external real object), (then) why, when there is a good or bad behaviour (on the part of one who is sleeping and one who is awake), the same consequence, pleasant or unpleasant, does not occur in a later time for the one who is sleeping and for the one who is awake?

Section XXXVII: Vasubandhu answers that there is a fundamental difference between both situations owing to the diverse states of mind

(It is not so,) because

> *mind in a dream is affected*
> *by the torpor (of sleep);*
> *therefore the consequence*
> *is not the same.*

In this case this is the cause (of the difference) but not the real existence of an object.

Section XXXVIII: If there are no bodies, how a murder can be produced ? How the crime of murder can be committed?

If (all) this is only mind and none has a body or voice, how is it that the death of sheep and other animals takes place when violence is done to them by the mutton-butchers, etc.? Or, if the death of those (animals) is not (really) accomplished by those (men), how is there association of the mutton-butchers, etc. with the blame of taking life?

Section XXXIX: Vasubandhu asserts that a mental act of a person can influence on the series of consciousnesses of another producing his death, and gives examples of cases in which that happened

> 19. *Death (is produced)*
> *by virtue of a particular*
> *act of cognition of another,*
> *in the same way as alterations*
> *such as loss of memory, etc.*
> *(are produced) in others*
> *by the power of the mind of* piśācas, *etc.*

For in the same way as alterations such as loss of memory, visions in dreams, possession by demons and evil spirits are produced in others by the power of the mind of *piśācas*, etc. and by the power of the mind of persons endowed with supernatural powers, as for instance the vision of dreams by Sāraṇa by resolution of Ārya Mahākātyāyana or as the defeat of Vemacitra due to the wickedness of mind of the forest *ṛṣis*, so also a certain alteration obstructing the organ of life arises in others due to the predominant determining condition constituted by a particular act of cognition of another, (alteration) by means of which death called 'interruption of the series (of consciousnesses) corresponding (to one and the same individual)'[320]—so it must be known.

Section XL: Vasubandhu gives as a ground for his thesis expounded in the previous Section an implicit approval to it given by the Buddha himself

20. *How (could be explained)*
the voidness of the Daṇḍaka forest
by virtue of the anger of the ṛṣis,

if it is not accepted that the death of beings is (possible) due to the predominant determining condition constituted by a particular act of cognition of another? (It must be accepted,) because the Bhagavant, in order to demonstrate that violence through the mind is liable to great blame, asked the householder Upali: "O householder, have you ever heard why the Daṇḍaka forests, the Mātaṅga forests, the Kaliṅga forests became empty, were cleaned out?" He answered: "O Gautama, I have heard (that it was) due to the wickedness of mind of the forest *ṛṣis*."

Section XLI: An alternative explanation of the voidness of the mentioned forests is discarded by Vasubandhu

Or (if it is not accepted
that the wickedness of mind
of the ṛṣis of the forests
was the cause of the voidness of the forests,)
(then) how does this (event)
prove that the violence of the mind
is greatly to be blamed ?

If it is imagined that the beings who dwelt in those (forests) were destroyed by non-human beings favorably disposed towards those (*ṛṣis*), and that (in fact) they did not die due to the wickedness of mind of the *ṛṣis*—being so, how is it proved by that action (of emptying and cleaning out the forests) that violence through the mind is much more to be blamed than violence through the body and the speech? (Without any doubt, with this latter explanation that cannot be explained, but that) is proved by the death of so many beings only due to the wickedness of mind of those (*ṛṣis*).

Section XLII: If the hypothesis of 'only mind' is accepted, how to explain the knowledge of another's mind or thought? Vasubandhu admits the possibility that this knowledge exists, but affirms that it does not correspond to reality

(The interlocutor asks :) If (all) that is only mind, do the knowers of another's mind know another's mind or not ?

(Vasubandhu asks :) And what (is deduced) from there ?

(The interlocutor says :) If they do not know, how are they knowers of another's mind ? Or they know (,and in this case,)

21. *how the knowledge*
of the knowers of another's mind
is erroneous?
(Vasubandhu says:)
(It is erroneous) as the knowledge
of one's own mind.

(The interlocutor asks:) (And) how is this (latter knowledge) also erroneous?

(Vasubandhu answers:)
Because of ignorance,
as it is the object (of cognition)
of the Buddha.

In the same way as that (mind of another), because of its indefinable nature, is the object of (cognition) of (only) the Buddhas, so also, because of the ignorance of that (indefinable nature of one's own mind and of another's mind), both (cognitions: that of one's own mind and that of another's mind) are not true, owing to the fact that the mental creation of subject and object has not been eliminated (as it should have been done) due to their being erroneous representations.

Section XLIII: Conclusion

Being the (theory of) Only-mind profound and unfathomable, due to the variety of the infinite philosophical disquisitions (to which it gives rise),

22. *this demonstration of the theory*
of Only-mind has been done by me
according to my own capacity;
but it cannot be comprehended
in its totality by thought.

This (theory) cannot be comprehended by thought in all its aspects by persons like me, because it is not an object of (normal) philosophical reasoning. Whose realm then is this (theory) in its totality? (The author) says:

(This theory is)
the realm of the Buddhas.

For this (theory) in all its aspects is the realm of the Buddhas Bhagavants, because there is not obstacle for (their) knowledge of all that is to be known in all its aspects.

The demonstration of Only-mind in Twenty Stanzas,
a work of Vasubandhu

NOTES FOR THE SECOND PART

1. See Paramārtha's *Life of Vasubandhu, Taishō* 2049; J. Takakusu, "The life of Vasubandhu by Paramārtha (A. D. 499-569)", in *T 'oung Pao Archives Series II,* Vol. 4-5, 1904, pp. 269-296, and "A Study of Paramārtha's life of Vasubandhu", in *Journal of the Royal Asiatic Society,* London, 1905, pp. 33-53; *Tāranāthae de Doctrinae Buddhicae in India Propagatione Narratio,* A. Schiefner's edition, Tokyo: Suzuki Research Foundation, Reprint Series, Shōwa 40 (1966), pp. 92, line19-98, line 19=Tāranātha, *Geschichte des Buddhismus in Indien,* A. Schiefner's translation, Tokyo: Suzuki Research Foundation, Shōwa 40 (1966), pp. 118-126; *The Collected Works of Bu-ston,* Part 24 (Ya), edited by Lokesh Chandra, New Delhi: International Academy of Indian Culture, 1971, 842, line 2-845, line 6=Buston, *History of Buddhism (Chos-ḥbyung),*E. Obermiller's translation, Part II, pp. 142-147; Unrai Wogihara, "Vasubandhu", in J. Hastings (ed.), *Encyclopaedia of Religion and Ethics,* Edinburg: T. and T. Clark, 1964, Vol.12, pp. 595-596; Amalia Pezzali,Il *Tesoro della metafisica secondo il maestro buddhista Vasubandhu,* Bologna, EMI della Cooperativa SERMIS, 1987, pp. 30-43; José Pereira and Francis Tiso, "The Life of Vasubandhu according to Recent Research", in *East and West,* Roma, IsMEO, Vol. 37, Nos. 1-4, 1987, pp. 451-454.
2. J. Takakusu, "The Date of Vasubandhu, the Great Buddhist Philosopher", in *Indian Studies in honor of Charles Rockwell Lanman,* Cambridge Mass.: Harvard University Press, 1929, pp. 79-88, and Taiken Kimura, "The Date of Vasubandhu seen from the Abhidharma-Kośa", *ibidem,* pp. 89-92, fix the date of Vasubandhu between 420 and 500 A.D.; Genmyo Ono, "The Date of Vasubandhu seen from the History of Buddhistic Philosophy", *ibidem,* pp. 93-94, sets that date in the middle of Vth century A.D.; N. Péri, "A propos de la date de Vasubandhu",

in *Bulletin de l' École Francaise d' Extrême Orient,* 11, 1911, pp. 339-390, thinks Vasubandhu lived in the IVth century A.D.. and must have died in 350 A.D. Takakusu indicates in his article the opinions of other Japanese scholars in relation to this point: S. Funabashi: IVth century A.D., before Kumārajīva; E. Mayeda: after Kumārajīva who was in China from 383 to 414 A.D..; S. Mochizuki: between 433-533 A.D. Akira Hirakawa, *Index to the Abhidharmakośabhāṣya,* Tokyo: Daizo Shuppan Kabushikikaisha, 1973, p. IX, locates the date of Vasubandhu *circa* 400-480 A.D. All the mentioned authors consider that there was only one Vasubandhu. See below on Frauwallner's theory about the existence of two Vasubandhus. Cf. the book of A. Pezzali, the article of Pereira and Tiso quoted in previous note and the Introduction of L. de la Vallée Poussin's translation of the *Abhidharmakośa,* pp. XXIV-XXVII.

3. *Sarvāstivāda* was the first name of this school or sect; afterwards it received also the name of *Vaibhāṣikas.* The center of this sect was in Kashmir, although members of this sect were also found elsewhere. On the Sarvāstivāda school see A. Ch. Banerjee, *Sarvāstivāda Literature,* Calcutta: The World Press, 1979; the Introduction of L. de la Vallée Poussin's translation of the *Abhidharmakośa,* pp. XXIX-XLII; A. Bareau, *Les Sectes bouddhiques du Petit Véhicule,* Saigon: École Françaíse d' Extréme Orient, 1955, pp. 131-152; K.H. Potter and others (edd.), *Encyclopedia of Indian Philosophies, Vol. VII, Abhidharma Buddhism To 150 A.D.,* Delhi: Motilal Banarsidass, 1996; J. Takakusu, "Sarvāstivādins", in J. Hastings (ed.), *Encyclopaedia,* Vol. 11, pp.198-200; J. Takakusu, "On the Abhidharma Literature", in *Journal of the Pali Text Society,* 1905, pp. 67-146.

4. The fact that Vasubandhu favoured the theories of the Sautrāntikas in his *Abhidharmakośa,* could be considered as an antecedent of Vasubandhu's conversion to the Mahāyānist Yogācāra school, since among the Sautrāntika's doctrines there are some theses which are of idealistic tendency. And this would give another argument to the tradition that there was only one Vasubandhu.

The Sautrāntikas were a Hīnayānist school or sect essentially opposed to that of the Sarvāstivādins-Vaibhāṣikas. L.de la Vallée Poussin in J. Hastings, *Encyclopaedia,* Vol. 11, p.213, indicates which was the fundamental opposition between Sautrāntikas and Sarvāstivādins-Vaibhāṣikas: "The philosophers of the Little Vehicle (Hīnayāna...) were divided into two schools: on the one hand, the Vaibhāṣikas, who accepted the Abhidharma books of the Sarvāstivādins (the seven Abhidharmas) as 'revealed' scripture (*ipsissima verba*), and the commentary on them, *Vibhāṣā*, as the oldest and the most authoritative 'treatise' (*śāstra*); on the other hand, the Sautrāntikas, who considered the seven books simply as 'treatises' (*śāstra*) of human inspiration and therefore liable to error, who maintained that Buddha had not composed treatises dealing with Abhidharma or given indications for the composition of such treatises under his authority (a working hypothesis in Pali scholasticism) [note1 of the author: See, e.g., *Atthasālinī* (PTS: London, 1897, p.3)], but had taught Abhidharma doctrines in certain *sūtras* (or *Sutrāntas*) [note 2 of the author: *Abhidharmakośakārikās* and *Bhāṣya*, Tib. tr., ed. T. de Stcherbatskoi, *Bibl. Buddhica*, XX. (Petrograd, 1917); Tāranātha, *Geschichte des Buddhismus in Indien*, tr. A. Schiefner, do. 1869, p. 56; Tibetan text, do. 1868, p. 56]. According to these *sūtras*, the *Arthaviniśchaya*, etc., constitute 'the Basket of Abhidharma.' Hence their name Sautrāntikas, the philosophers who recognize the authority of the *sutrāntas* alone". Cf. A. Bareau, *Les Sectes bouddhiques*, 1955, pp. 155-159; A. Pezzali, *Il tesoro della metafisica*, pp. 27-29.

5. Cf. J. Takakusu, "La Sāṃkhyakārikā étudiée á la lumière de sa version chinoise", in *Bulletin de l' École Française d' Extrême Orient*, Hanoï, 1904, pp. 1-65.
6. According to M. Winternitz, *History of Indian Literature, Vol. II, Buddhist Literature and Jaina Literature*, New Delhi: Oriental Books Reprint Corporation, 1972, p.359, the mentioned work was a refutation not of Vindhyavāsin but of the *Sāṃkhyakārikās* of Īśvarakṛṣṇa.
7. See note 3.
8. All the works of Hīnayānist inspiration attributed to him by tradition.
9. All the works of Mahāyānist inspiration attributed to him by tradition. According to tradition Vasubandhu composed 500 Hīnayānist works and 500 Mahāyānist works, owing to which he received the surname of "Master of the 1000 treatises".

10. As for instance, S. Chaudhuri, *Analytical Study of the Abhidharmakośa,* Calcutta: Sanskrit College, 1976; L. Schmithausen, "Sautrāntika-Voraussetzungen in Viṃśatikā and Triṃśikā", in *Wiener Zeitschrift für die Kunde Süd-und Ost-Asiens,* 1967, p.110; A. Pezzali, *Il tesoro della metafisica,* p. 30 note 27. But many other scholars either do not accept Frauwallner's theory about two Vasubandhus or are sceptical about it, as for instance, P.S. Jaini, "On the theory of the two Vasubandhus", in *Bulletin of the School of Oriental and African Studies,* Vol. XXI, 1958, pp. 48-53; A. Wayman, *Analysis of the Śrāvaka-bhūmi,* Berkeley and Los Angeles: University of California, 1961, pp. 19 ff. According to H. Nakamura, *Indian Buddhism,* 1987, p. 268, Frauwallner's theory has not been accepted by Japanese scholars in general. For instance A. Hirakawa, *Index to the Abhidharmakośa,* p. VII, considers that "the author of the Kośa and the one belonging to the Yogācāra School and the younger brother of Asaṅga are the same person". Bhikkhu Pāsādika, "Once Again on the Hypothesis of Two Vasubandhus ", in *Prof. Hajime Nakamura Felicitation Volume,* edited by V.N. Jha, Delhi, 1991, corroborates Hirakawa's argumentation against the theory of two Vasubandhus pointing out Vasubandhu's leanings towards Mahāyāna in some passages of the *Abhidharmakośa.* It seems to us that Frauwallner's supposition creates many problems and much confusion in relation to Vasubandhu
11. *Tōhoku* (Indices), p.96 c, gives under the Tibetan name of Vasubandhu, *Dbyig-gñen,* 37 Tibetan translations of works attributed to Vasubandhu; and *Hōbōgirin, Répertoire,* p.147 b under his Japanese name, *Sheshin,* enumerates 36 Chinese translations of works attributed to Vasubandhu. A great part of the Sanskrit originals has not been preserved and these works are known to us only by their Tibetan and Chinese translations.
12. On Rāhula Sāṅkṛtyāyana see *Revista de Estudios Budistas,* México-Buenos Aires, N° 12, 1996; and, for a list of the manuscripts of Sanskrit texts he discovered in Tibet, see Frank Bandurski, "Übersicht über die Göttinger Sammlungen der von Rāhula Sāṅkṛtyāyana in Tibet aufgefundenen buddhistischen Sanskrit-Texte", in *Untersuchungen zur buddhistischen Literatur,* Göttingen: Vandenhoeck und Ruprecht, 1994, pp.9-126.
13. Cf. J. Takakusu's article mentioned in note 5, pp. 43 and 49; R. Garbe, *Die Sāṃkhya-Philosophie,* Leipzig: Verlag von H. Haessel, 1894, pp. 37-39.

14. It is our intention to publish in the future an English translation of this important treatise of Vasubandhu.
15. See note 12.
16. See S. Lévi, *Vijñaptimātratāsiddhi*, pp.XI-XVI, the history of the discovery of the manuscripts of the *Viṃśatikā* and of the *Triṃśikā*.
17. C.H. Hamilton gave a detailed analyśis of the treatise in his article "Buddhistic Idealism in Wei Shih Er Shih Lwen", in *Essays in Philosophy by 17 Doctors of Philosophy,* Chicago, 1929, pp. 99-115.
18. On the Yogācāra school in general see the *Introduction* of this book.
19. It could be said that this idealistic position is also a characteristic trait of Mahāyāna in general.
20. *Daśabhūmikasūtra, VIth Bhūmi,* p. 32, line 9 (P.L.Vaidya's edition): *cittamātram idaṃ yad idaṃ traidhātukam* (without the vocative). This text is also found in the *Pratyutpanna-buddha-saṃmukhāvasthita-samādhi-sūtra* without the vocative, Tibetan translation: *Khams gsum pa 'di dag ni sems tsam mo* (p. 36 Paul M. Harrison's edition, Tokyo, The Reiyukai Library, 1978) and Chinese translation (*Taishō* 416, p. 877 b, line 4). It is quoted with the vocative in *Subhāṣitasaṃgraha,* p. 393, lines 23-24 (C. Bendall's edition): *kathaṃ tarhi Bhagavatā cittamātraṃ bho jinaputrā yad uta traidhātukam ityuktam; by Advayavajra, in Advayavajrasaṃgraha (Tattvaratnāvalī),* p. 18, lines 1-2 (Haraprasada Shastri's edition): *cittamātraṃ bho jinaputrā!yad uta traidhātukam iti;* by Candrakīrti in *Madhyamakāvatāra* (Tibetan text), p. 181, line 11 (L. de la Vallée Poussin's edition): *khams gsum po ḥdi ni sems tsam,* and p. 182, line 3 *(ibidem): srid gsum rnam śes tsam du gaṅ rtogs pa.*
21. The three worlds are *kāmaloka (or kāmadhātu)* : the world of desire; *rūpaloka (or rūpadhātu)*: the world of form, and *arūpaloka (or arūpadhātu)*: the world of the formless. Different kinds of beings, humans, Gods, etc., dwell in these three worlds. The three worlds comprise all the empirical reality, the sphere of transmigrations. On this matter see J.R. Haldar, *Early Buddhist Mythology,* New Delhi: Munshiram Manoharlal, 1977, pp. 10-11; L. de la Vallée Poussin, "Cosmogony and Cosmology (Buddhist)", in J. Hastings (ed.), *Encyclopaedia of Religion and Ethics,* Edinburgh, T. and T. Clark, 1964, Vol. IV, pp. 133-137;

"Kosmologie und Kosmographie", in H.W. Haussig (ed.), *Götter und Mythen des indischen Subcontinents,* Stuttgart: Klett-Cotta, 1984, pp. 392-395; and W. Kirfel, *Symbolik des Buddhismus,* Stuttgart: Anton Hiersemann, 1959, pp. 21-31.

22. The case of the *taimirikas* is frequently employed by Buddhist authors as an example of visual perception without an external real counterpart. See for instance S. Yamaguchi, *Index to the Prasannapadā-Madhyamaka-vṛtti,* Kyoto: Heirakuji-Shoten, 1974, and his edition of Maitreya's *Madhyāntavibhāga,* Tokyo: Suzuki Research Foundation, 1966, Volume III; and T. Hirano, *An Index to the Bodhicāryāvatāra Pañjikā,* Chapter IX, Tokyo: Suzuki Research Foundation, 1966, under the word *taimirika.*

23. On the simile of dreams cf. M. Hattori, "The dream simile in Vijñānavāda treatises", in *Indological and Buddhist Studies,* Canberra: Faculty of Asian Studies, 1982.

24. Cf. Vasubandhu, *Abhidharmakośa* II, 34: *cittaṃ mano'tha vijñānam ekārtham; Saṃyuttanikāya* II, p.94 (PTS edition): *yaṃ ca kho etaṃ, bhikkhave, vuccati cittam iti pi, mano iti pi, viññāṇam iti pi...; Dīghanikāya* I, p.21 (PTS edition). On the synonymous value of these three terms see L. Schmithausen, "Sautrāntika-Voraussetzungen", pp. 119-121.

25. On more specific meanings attributed to the words *citta, manas, vijñāna* according to the different fullfiled functions, see *Abhidharma-Samuccaya,* ed. P. Pradhan, Santiniketan: Visva-Bharati, 1950, pp.11 (last line)-12 (line 12), p.16 (line 16) [=W. Rahula, *Le Compendium de la super-doctrine (Philosophie) (Abhidharmasamuccaya) d´Asaṅga,* Paris: École Francaise d' Extrême-Orient, 1971, pp.17-18, 24); Vasubandhu, *Abhidharmakośabhāṣya ad* II, 34 a-b and Yaśomitra *ad locum,* and L. de la Vallée Poussin's translation, I, p. 177, notes 1, 2, and 3. Cf. D.T. Suzuki, *Studies in the Lankavatara sutra,* London: Routledge and Kegan Paul, 1972, pp. 175-179.

26. On the mentioned schools of realistic inspiration see, besides the pertinent sections of histories of Indian philosophy and works of a general character as Max Müller, *The Six Systems of Indian Philosophy,* London: Longmans, 1919, Indian reprint, Varanasi: Chowkhamba, s.d., the following works of monographic character: on the Pūrva Mīmāṃsā: Gaṅgānātha Jhā, *The Prābhākara school of Pūrva Mīmāṃsā,* Delhi: Motilal Banarsidass, 1978; on the Nyāya-Vaiśeṣika: D.N. Shastri, *The*

Philosophy of Nyāya-Vaiśeṣika and its Conflict with the Buddhist Dignāga School (Critique of Indian Realism), Delhi: Bharatiya Vidya Prakashan, 1976; A. B. Keith, *Indian Logic and Atomism, an Exposition of the Nyāya and Vaiśeṣika Systems*, New York: Greenwood Press, 1968; K. H. Potter, (ed.), *Encyclopedia of Indian Philosophies, Vol. II Indian Metaphysics and Epistemology: The Tradition of Nyāya-Vaiśeṣika up to Gaṅgeśa*, Delhi: Motilal Banarsidass, 1977; K.H. Potter and S. Bhattacharyya, (edd.), *Encyclopedia of Indian Philosophies, Vol. VI Indian Philosophical Analysis: Nyāya-Vaiśeṣika from Gaṅgeśa to Raghunātha Śiromaṇi*, Delhi: Motilal Banarsidass, 1993; H.Ui. *The Vaiśeshika Philosophy according to the Daśapadārtha-Śāstra*, Varanasi: Chowkhamba, 1962; W. Halbfass, *On Being and What There Is*, New York: State University of New York Press, 1992; B. Faddegon, *The Vaiceṣika System described with the help of the oldest texts*, Wiesbaden: M. Sändig, 1969; on Sāṃkhya: G. L. Larson, *Classical Sāṃkhya*, Delhi: Motilal Banarsidass, 1969; A.B. Keith, *The Sāṃkhya System*, Calcutta: Y.M.C.A., 1949; R. Garbe, *Die Sāṃkhya-Philosophie*, Leipzig: H. Haessel, 1894, and *Sāṃkhya und Yoga*, Strassburg: K.J. Trubner, 1896; on Mādhava's system: S. Siauve, *La Doctrine de Mādhva, Advaita-Vedānta*, Pondichéry: Institut Francais d'Indologie, 1968.

27. For an exposition of the controversy between the realist schools and the Yogācāra school see A.K. Chatterjee, *The Yogācāra Idealism*, Delhi: Motilal Banarsidass, 1975 (Chapters III and IV) and *Facets of Buddhist Thought*, Calcutta: Sanskrit College, 1975, pp. 33-51; J. Sinha, *Indian Realism*, Delhi: Motilal Banarsidass, 1972, and the book of D.N. Shastri mentioned in the previous note. A manifestation of this conflict is found in Gotama's *Nyāyasūtras* IV, 2,26-37, and its commentaries, with direct references to Vasubandhu's argumentation in *Viṃśatikā* (ad IV, 2, 34, p.1085 *vārttika*, p.1086 *vārttika)*.

28. On the negation of an *ātman* or soul (*nairātmya*), the theory of the series or current or stream of consciousnesses (*vijñānasrotas)*, and in general the Buddhist conception of man see L. de la Vallée Poussin, *Boudhisme. Opinions sur l' Histoire de la dogmatique*, Paris: G. Beauchesne, 1925, pp. 156-185, and his translation of Vasubandhu's *Abhidharmakośa*, Vol. V, Preliminary note, pp. 227-229;

Sri Dhammananda, *What Buddhists believe*, Kuala Lumpur (Malaysia): The Buddhist Missionary Society, 1973, pp. 75-77; N. Dutt, *Early Monastic Buddhism*, Calcutta: Calcutta Oriental Book Agency, 1960, pp. 192-214 and 229-239; A.B. Keith, *Buddhist Philosophy in India and Ceylon*, Varanasi: Chowkhamba, 1963, pp. 75-95, and pp. 169-176; T.R.V. Murti, *The Central Conception of Buddhism*, London: G. Allen and Unwin, 1960, pp. 3-35; H. Oldenberg, *Buddha. Sein Leben, seine Lehre, seine Gemeinde*, München: W. Goldmann, 1961, pp. 237-246; P. Oltramare, *L´Histoire des idées théosophiques dans l´Inde II. La théosophie bouddhique*, Paris: P. Geuthner, 1923, pp. 199-221; J. Pérez Remón, The Hague: Mouton, 1980, and the reviews of this last book by T.Vetter in *Wiener Zeitschrift für die Kunde Südasiens*, Band XXVII, 1983, pp. 211-215, and of A. Solé Leris in *Buddhist Studies Review* (London), Vol. 5, 2, 1988, pp.176-182 (Spanish translation of this last review in *Revista de Estudios Budistas*, México-Buenos Aires, N° 3, pp.189-196; Pratap Chandra, *Metaphysics of perpetual change. The concept of Self in Early Buddhism*, Bombay: Somaiya Publications, 1978; L. Renou et J. Filliozat, *L 'Inde Classique*, Vol. II, Paris: Imprimerie Nationale, 1953, pp. 542-543; Th. Stcherbatsky, *The Central Conception of Buddhism*, Calcutta: Susil Gupta, 1961, pp. 21-23; D.T. Suzuki, *Outlines of Mahayana Buddhism*, New York: Schocken Books, 1973, pp. 31-32; J. Takakusu, *The Essentials of Buddhist Philosophy*, Delhi: Motilal Banarsidass, 1975, p. 14; F. Tola, "Tres concepciones del hombre en la filosofia de la India", in *Pensamiento*, No. 165, Vol. 42, Madrid, 1986, pp. 29-46; F. Tola and C. Dragonetti, "La doctrina de los *dharmas* en el Budismo", in *Boletín de la Asociación Española de Orientalistas*, Año XIII, Madrid, 1977, pp. 105-132 (Reprint in *Yoga y Mística de la India*, Buenos Aires: Kier, 1978, pp. 91-121); H. von Glasenapp, *Vedānta und Buddhismus*, Wiesbaden: F. Steiner, 1950 (=*Kleine Schriften*, pp. 238-255); Yamakami Sogen, *Systems of Buddhistic Thought*, Calcutta: University of Calcutta, 1912, pp. 16-28; Claus Oetke, *"Ich" und das Ich*, Stuttgart: Franz Steiner Verlag, 1988.

29. These cognitions, as anything else in Buddhism, are *dharmas* with all the specific characteristics they possess of unsubstantiality, impermanence, etc. On the *dharmas*, factors

or elements of existence, see Stcherbatsky's work and F. Tola's and C.Dragonetti's article on the doctrine of the *dharmas* (with bibliography), mentioned in the previous note; W.and M. Geiger, *Pali Dhamma vornehmlich in der kanonischen Literatur in Kleine Schriften zur Indologie und Buddhismuskunde,* Wiesbaden: F. Steiner, 1973, pp. 101-228; Jikido Takasaki, *An Introduction to Buddhism,* Tokyo: The Tōhō Gakkai, 1987, pp. 107-126.

30. On the important theme of efficiency from an epistemological point of view see Dharmakīrti, *Pramāṇavārttika* II, 1, 3 (R.C. Pandeya's edition, Delhi: Motilal Banarsidass, 1989), and *Nyāyabindu* I, 12-14 (F. Stcherbatsky's edition, Osnabrück: Biblio Verlag, 1970) with the commentaries of Manorathanandin for the first and of Dharmottara (pp. 12-14, Stcherbatsky's mentioned ed.) and of Vinītadeva (pp. 49-51, L. de la Vallée Poussin's edition of *Nyāyabindu,* Calcutta: The Asiatic Society, reprint1984) for the second, and Jñānaśrīmitra, *Kṣaṇabhaṅgādhyāya,* I, verse 1 (*sattā śaktir ihārthakarmaṇi),* quoted by Mādhavācārya, *Sarva-darśana-saṃgraha,* p.11 (Ānandāśrama ed., 1966). Cf. also B.K.Matilal, *Perception,* Oxford: Oxford University Press, 1986, pp. 320-321 and 370-371; M.D. Eckel, "The Concept of Reason in Jñānagarbha's Svātantrika Madhyamaka", p. 278, in B.K. Matilal and R.D. Evans (edd.), *Buddhist Logic and Epistemology,* Dordrecht: D. Reidel, 1986; E. Mikogami, "Some remarks on the Concept of *Arthakriyā*", in *Journal of Indian Philosophy,* Vol. 7, No. 1, 1979, pp. 79-94, and Vijaya Rani; *The Buddhist Philosophy as presented in Mīmāṃsā-Śloka-Vārttika,* Delhi: Parimal Publications, 1982, pp. 102-109.

31. In Buddhism as well as in Hinduism there is the belief in the existence of hells, where one can be reborn to atone for his bad deeds. The stay in hell is transitory and not at all eternal, as it happens to be in Christianity; it is a stage more in the series or chain of reincarnations. Once the punishment is over, one can be reborn anew as a human being to continue transmigrating according to the good and bad actions one has carried on. On the Buddhist hells see L. de la Vallée Poussin, "Cosmogony and cosmology (Buddhist)", in J. Hastings, *Encyclopaedia,* Vol. 4, pp. 133-134; E. J. Thomas, "States of the Dead (Buddhist)", *ibidem,* Vol. 11, pp. 829-833; J. R. Haldar, *Early Buddhist Mythology,* Chapter III; W. Kirfel, *Die Kosmographie der Inder,* Darmstadt: Wissenschaftliche

Buchgesellschaft, 1967, pp. 199-206; R. Spence Hardy, *A Manual of Buddhism in its modern development,* Varanasi: Chowkhamba, 1967, pp.26-28; R. Kloetzli, *Buddhist Cosmology,* Delhi: Motilal Banarsidass, 1983.

In this Section Vasubandhu will point out the causes due to which the beings condemned to hell see all of them at the same time the hell-guards and their instruments of torture, notwithstanding their being inexistent, mere creations of their minds.

32. Vasubandhu does not deny the existence of other consciousnesses besides one's own consciousness; he accepts the existence of a plurality of consciousnesses. That denial constitutes another type of solipsism. The existence of other minds, i.e. of a plurality of minds, was discussed in Buddhism. See Dharmakīrti's *Saṃtānāntarasiddhi* (*Tōhoku* 4219 = *Catalogue* 5716) with Vinītadeva's commentary (*Tōhoku* 4238 = *Catalogue* 5724). There is an English translation in *Papers of Th. Stcherbatsky,* Calcutta: Indian Studies Past and Present, 1969, pp. 81-121 (translated from Russian). Ratnakīrti's *Santānāntarasiddhidūṣaṇa (in Ratnakīrti-nibandhāvaliḥ,* A. Thakkur ed., Patna: K.P. Jayaswal Research Institute, 1975, pp. 145-149) maintains the thesis of solipsism (a single mind). Cf. Y. Kajiyama, "Buddhist Solipsism. A free translation of Ratnakīrti's Saṃtānāntaradūṣaṇa", included in his *Studies in Buddhist Philosphy,* Kyoto: Rinsen Book Co., 1989. Th. E. Wood, *Mind Only,* 1991, has an analysis of *Saṃtānāntara-siddhi* (pp. 107-131) and of *Saṃtānāntara-dūṣaṇa* (pp.149-159) and free renderings of both treatises (Appendix II and Appendix IV).

33. In Western philosophy, in a similar case, Berkeley has recourse to the idea of God as a means to overcome the solipsism in which his idealistic doctrine could incur.

We have here an example of how, in each culture, the philosophical systems, in order to overcome theoretical insuperable difficulties, ressort to hypothesis, principles or beliefs proper to the tradition to which they belong—as the ideas of *saṃsāra* and *karman* in Buddhist Philosophy, and of God and the soul in Western Philosophy. Cf.F. Tola, "Fundamental principles of Indian Philosophy", *Proceedings of the Fifth World Sanskrit Conference,* New Delhi: Rashtriya Sanskrit Sansthan, 1985, pp. 680-688 (Spanish version in *Revista Venezolana de Filosofia,* 19, 1985, pp. 89-101).

Hiuan tsang, *Tche' eng wei che louen (Taishō* 1585), p. 10 c lines 14-16 (= p. 135-136 L. de la Vallée Poussin translation) in order to explain the coincidence or identity of the mental creations has recourse only to the simile of the lamps: the light of each lamp is different from the light of the others, but their union creates a single light.

34. The orthodox Hīnayānist tradition affirmed that the *narakapālas* or *nirayapālas* (hell-guards) are a kind of beings with a *real* existence, to such an extent that many of these hell-guards received different names according to their physical aspect, as for instance *Kāla* (black), *Upakāla* (blackish). See *Jātaka,* Vol. VI, p. 248, lines 3 and 6 (V. Fausböll's edition, PTS, 1962-1964). The Theravāda sect was one of those that asserted the real existence as beings of the hell-guards. See A. Bareau, *Les Sectes,* p. 236, thesis No.192.

But, even before Vasubandhu, divergences of opinion did occur. The existence of hell-guards is one of the controverted points in *Kathāvatthu,* pp. 597-598 (PTS edition). And the Andhaka sect for instance, derived from the Mahāsaṃghika sect, affirmed (A. Bareau, *ibidem,* p. 97, thesis No. 62) that the hell-guards did not exist as such, as specific beings, that it was the *karman* of the beings condemned to hell that punished them, adopting the appearance of hell-guards.

Vasubandhu in *Abhidharmakośabhāṣya* III, 59 *pādas* a-c (cf. Yaśomitra's commentary *ad locum* and L. de la Vallée Poussin's note 3 in p. 152 of his translation of that treatise, Vol. II) deals with the question whether the hell-guards are *sattvas* (beings). Of course, Vasubandhu does not ask himself whether the hell-guards *really* exist, since the position of that treatise of Hīnayānistic inspiration is frankly realistic. Vasubandhu indicates that there exist two opinions in regard to that question: 1. Some think that the hell-guards are not *sattvas* (beings), that is to say (as Yaśomitra explains) that they are only "Great Elements and the product of the Great Elements" (*bhūtabhautikamātrā narakapālā iti).* These elements act (*ceṣṭante*) by virtue of the actions (*karman)* of the beings condemned to hell, in the same way as at the beginning of creation winds become active by virtue of the actions of those beings who are to be born, and provoke the arising of the worlds in which these beings will have experiences according to their merits or demerits.

2. Some think that the hell-guards are beings who by virtue of their cruel nature are reborn in hell as torturers and who in some further reincarnation will be reborn in hell to be punished for the suffering they have inflicted to those condemned to hell. Vasubandhu asks why these hell-guards are not burnt by infernal fire, and answers that that is so either because the force of the actions of the condemned to hell put a limit to the burning efficacy of fire or because those actions produce the arising of certain kind of Great Elements (*bhūtaviśeṣa*), that is refractory to fire and with which either the body of the hell-guards become refractory to fire or a protective coat for its protection is made.

The augumentation developed by Vasubandhu, the author of the *Viṃśatikā*, is based on the Buddhist belief in the existence of hells, hell-guards, condemned to hell and infernal tortures-belief to which he adheres. For Vasubandhu all that is simple mental creations; for his opponent all that is real. They agree in regard to their existence; they disagree in regard to the nature of that existence: *mental existence* for Vasubandhu, *real existence* for his opponent. If that belief is not accepted, Vasubandhu's demonstration loses its basis. This demonstration is valid if one partakes of that belief.

35. Paramārtha, in his Chinese translation of the *Abhidharmakośa* (*Taishō* 1559, p.216 a, line 25, cf. L. de la Vallée Poussin's translation, II, p. 154 note 1), asks: "If the hell-guards are not different from the condemned, how could they be hell-guards ?"

36. In *Kathāvatthu* XX, 4 is discussed the question of the existence of animals in heaven.

37. Vasubandhu, in the passage to which this note corresponds, expresses that the *vāsanā* dwells in the series of consciousnesses (*vijñānasantānasanniviṣṭa*). The *Karmasiddhiprakaraṇa* (paragraph 20) refers as a Sautrāntika opinion that a special virtuality (*nus pa,śakti*) is created (*bskyed pa*) in the series of consciousnesses (*sems kyi rgyud la=vijñānasantāna*). Dignāga in the *Ālambanaparīkṣā*, kārikā VIII a, expresses that the virtuality left by a cognition may dwell in the *rnam rig* (= *vijñapti*, synonym of *vijñāna*) and explains this term in the commentary by *rnam pa śes pa* (=*vijñāna*). It is remarkable that neither Vasubandhu in this passage of the *Viṃśatikā* nor Dignāga in the *Ālambanaparīkṣā* (VIII a) mention the

ālayavijñāna, but we think it is not erroneous to assume that both authors had in mind the *ālayavijñāna*.

38. See note 14 of *Ālambanaparīkṣā* in this same book.
39. The transformation (*pariṇāma*) of the consciousness into the empirical reality is a very peculiar (*viśeṣa*) process. Consciousness has as its essential characteristic inalterability (*ananyathātva*). Cf. *Trisvabhāva* 3. Therefore the transformation of consciousness is only an apparent one; for the person submerged in error consciousness appears as another thing, but without becoming another thing—as the rope in the obscurity appears as a snake without becoming a snake. An appropriate simile that clearly expresses the peculiarity of the *pariṇāma* of the consciousness is that of the ocean and its waves: there is not an essential difference between both, they are the same thing. Cf.*Laṅkāvatārasūtra* II verse 105, and *Mahāyānaśraddhotpādaśastra, Taishō* 1667, p.585 b lines 5-10.
40. On the *āyatana* and the arising of the sensorial act of cognition see Otto Rosenberg, *Die Probleme der buddhistischen Philosophie*, Heidelberg: O. Harrassowitz, 1924, Reprint: San Francisco: Chinese Materials Center, 1976, p. 139; F. Scherbatsky, *The Central Conception of Buddhism*, 1961, pp. 6-7, 46-48; and note 13 of the *Ālambanaparīkṣā*.
41. Buddha refers to the *āyatanas* in numerous texts of the Pali Canon (PTS edition). For references see the *Pali-English Dictionary of the PTS sub āyatana; A Critical Pali Dictionary II, 3 sub āyatana c.; and Pali Tipiṭakaṃ Concordance*, Part VI, pp. 330-331, *sub āyamati.*
42. See *Section K of Ālambanaparīkṣā* in the text and in our commentary thereon for a similar reasoning as the one developed in *Section XI* of the *Viṃśatikā* by Vasubandhu. In both cases the opponent adduces the words of the Buddha in order to refute his idealistic opponent: Buddha has referred to the internal *āyatana* (eye) and to the external *āyatana* (the visible object), affirming their existence; Dignāga and Vasubandhu, on maintaining the "only-mind"theory, that denies the existence of the external object, leave aside Buddha's teaching; therefore their theory cannot be accepted. Dignāga and Vasubandhu defend their position resorting to another interpretation of Buddha's words.
43. See F. Tola and C.Dragonetti, "The Conflict of Change in

Buddhism: the Hīnayānist Reaction", in *Cahiers d' Extrême-Asie,* 9, 1996.

44. On this matter see M. M. Broido, "Abhiprāya and Implication in Tibetan Linguistics", in *Journal of Indian Philosophy,* 12, 1, 1984, pp. 1-34, and "Intention and Suggestion in the Abhidharmakośa: Saṃdhābhāṣā Revisited", *ibidem,* 13, 4, 1985, pp. 327-382; L. de la Vallée Poussin, "Madhyamaka", in *Mélanges Chinois et Bouddhiques* 2, 1932-1933, pp. 47-48, and *Abhidharmakośa*'s translation, Vol. V, pp. 246-248 note; É. Lamotte, "La critique d' interprétation dans le Bouddhisme", in *India Antiqua,* Leyden, 1947, pp. 341-361; D. S. Lopez, Jr., *Buddhist Hermeneutics,* Honolulu: University of Hawaii Press, 1988 (where the mentioned article by É. Lamotte is included in English translation); and D.S. Ruegg, *La Théorie du Tathāgatagarbha et du gotra,* Paris: École Française d' Extrême-Orient, 1969, pp. 55-56, "Purport, Implicature and Presupposition: Sanskrit *abhiprāya* and Tibetan *dgoṅs pa/dgoṅs gźi* as Hermeneutical Concepts", in *Journal of Indian Philosophy,* 13, 4, 1985, pp. 309-325, "The Buddhist Notion of an 'Immanent Absolute' (tathāgatagarbha) as a Problem in Hermeneutics", in *The Buddhist Heritage,* Tring: Buddhica Britannica, 1989, pp. 229-245, "Allusiveness and Obliqueness in Buddhist texts: Saṃdhā, Saṃdhi, Saṃdhyā and Abhisaṃdhi", in *Dialectes dans les Littératures indo-aryennes,* C. Caillat ed., Paris, 1989.

45. There are four categories of beings as distinguished by their form of birth: *aṇḍaja*: born from an egg; *jarājuja (jalābuja* in Pali): born from a womb; *saṃsvedaja (saṃsedaja* in Pali): born from moist, and *upapāduka or aupapādika* (*opapātika* in Pali): spontaneously produced (i. e. without a perceptible cause) (*A Critical Pali Dictionary, sub voce*). The *opapātika/ upapāduka* are frequently mentioned in the Buddhist Sanskrit and Pali literatures (see references in *A Critical Pali Dictionary,* in *The Pali-English Dictionary* of the PTS, in the *Pali Tipiṭakam Concordance* of the PTS and in Edgerton's *Buddhist Hybrid Sanskrit Dictionary sub voce*). In Vasubandhu's *Abhidharmakośabhāṣya* they are referred to several times. See specially *ad* II, 14, p. 163; III, 8 c -d, and 9, pp. 401-405, VIII, p. 1207 (Swami Dwarikadas Shastri ed., Bauddha Bharati Series) and L. de la Vallée Poussin's translation, Vol. II, notes

on pp. 26-31, Vol. V, p. 258 note 2. For other references cf. A. Hirakawa, *Index to the Abhidharmakośabhāṣya*, 1973, Part one, *sub voce*.

In *Abhidharmakośabhāṣya* VIII, p.1207(quoted edition) Vasubandhu refers to the *Mānuṣyakasūtra* where the existence of an *upapāduka* being is admitted by Buddha. Vasubandhu accepts in this passage the existence of an *upapāduka* being in the meaning that Buddha in that Sūtra gives to the term: a series of *skandhas* designating a being able to be spontaneously born in another world (*paratropapādukasattvākhyaskandhasantāna)*.

46. Cf. Vasubandhu's *Abhidharmakośa*, III, 9 b-d (*nārakā upapādukāḥ/antarābhavadevāś ca)*. The *Bhāṣya* adds the Garuḍas among the *upapāduka* beings; a variant reading adds also the Nāgas.
47. On the *dharmas* see note 29.
48. On causality in Buddhism see A.Ch. Banerjee, "Pratītyasamutpāda", in *Indian Historical Quarterly* 32, 1956, pp. 261-264; H. Chatterjee, "A Critical Study of the theory of Pratītyasamutpāda", in *Journal of the Royal Asiatic Society of Great Britain and Ireland,* Bombay Branch, 1955, pp. 66-70; L. de la Vallée Poussin, *Théorie des douze causes,* 1913; N. Dutt, *Early monastic Buddhism,* 1960, pp. 215-228, and "The place of the Āryasatyas and Pratītyasamutpāda in Hīnayāna and Mahāyāna", in *Annals of the Bhandarkar Oriental Research Institute,* 1930, Part II, pp. 101-127; D. J. Kalupahana, *Causality: The Central Philosophy of Buddhism,* Honolulu: The University Press of Hawaii, 1975; É. Lamotte, "Die bedingte Entstehung und die höchste Erleuchtung", in *Beiträge zur Indienforschung. Ernst Waldschmidt zum 80. Geburtstag gewidmet,* Berlin: Museum für Indische Kunst, 1977 (English version: "Conditioned Co-production and Supreme Enlightenment", in *Buddhist Studies in Honour of Walpola Rahula,* London/Sri Lanka: G. Fraser/Vimamsa, 1980, pp. 118-132); B. C. Law, "Formulation of Pratītyasamutpāda", in *Journal of the Royal Asiatic Society of Great Britain and Ireland,* 1937, pp. 287-292; H. Oldenberg, *Buddha,* pp. 211-232; P. Oltramare, *La formule bouddhique des douze causes,* 1909; N. Tatia, "Paṭiccasamuppāda", in *Nava-Nalanda-Mahavihara Research Publications,* I, 1957, pp. 177-239; S. C h. Vidyabhusana, "Pratitya-samutpada or Dependent Origination", in *Journal of the Buddhist Text Society of India,* Calcutta, VII, 1, 1899, pp. 1-19; and bibliography

on *Pratītyasamutpāda* in *Buddhist Studies Review*, No. 1, London, 1983-1984, Editor's Notes, pp. 35-38.

49. This text comes from *Kṣudrakāgama* and is quoted in *Abhidharmakośabhāṣya*, VIII, p. 1203 (Bauddha Bharati Series ed., 1970).

50. On the mechanism of reincarnation on the basis of the series theory see F. Tola and C. Dragonetti, "Āryabhavasaṃkrāntināma-mahāyānasūtra: The Noble Sūtra on the Passage through Existences ", in *Buddhist Studies Review* (London) 1986, pp. 3-15.

51. Since its beginning Buddhism denied the existence of an *ātman* (soul) in the man. It is the *nairātmya* theory. See note 28. For Early and Hīnayānist Buddhism the *dharmas* (whatever exists and also the factors or elements of existence) were *real;* they had a true, objective existence, although they were conceived as unsubstantial and impermanent. Several Hīnayānist schools added to impermanence the instantaneity or momentariness: *dharmas* are not only impermanent, but also instantaneous, as soon as they arise, they disappear. But, anyhow, the *reality* of the *dharmas*, the *realistic position* was maintained. In the Introduction we have referred to the importance of this last characteristic for the coming forth of the idealistic inspiration of Mahāyāna.

The Mahāyāna abandoned the realistic position of the Hīnayāna and adopted an *idealistic* one. It denied the real existence of the *dharmas* (the constituents of reality); for it the *dharmas* are unreal, mere creations of human mind. The unreality of the *dharmas* is a consequence of their unsubstantiality which is designated with the term *śūnyatā*, Voidness (absence of an own being, *svabhāva*, absence of an existence in *se et per se).* The coming forth of this idealistic position, which since its origin coexisted in Buddhism with the realistic one, took place in several *sūtras* (like the *Laṅkāvatārasūtra*, the *Saṃdhinirmocanasūtra* etc.). It was systematized by the Mādhyamika and specially by the Yogācāra schools, Cf. J. Takasaki, *An Introduction to Buddhism*, pp. 126-127. On the Mādhyamika school see F. Tola and C. Dragonetti, *On Voidness, A Study on Buddhist Nihilism*, Delhi: Motilal Banarsidass, 1995.

52. Cf. note 29.

53. Cf. L. de la Vallée Poussin, "Extase et Spéculation (Dhyāna et Prajñā)", in *Indian Studies in Honor of Charles Rockwell*

Lanman, Cambridge Mass.: Harvard University Press, 1929, pp. 135-136 (Spanish translation in *Revista de Estudios Budistas*, 7, México-Buenos Aires, 1994, pp. 165-168); and *La Morale Bouddhique*, Paris: Nouvelle Librairie Nationale, 1927, pp. 98-117; D.T. Suzuki, *Outlines of Mahāyāna Buddhism*, pp. 76-86; and G. Bugault, *La notion de prajñā ou de sapience selon les perpectives du Mahāyāna. Part de la connaissance et de l' inconnaissance dans l' analogie bouddhique*, Paris: C.N.R.S. and É. de Boccard, 1968.

We think there is not any difference between the stages or degrees of knowledge as conceived in Buddhism and the stages or degrees of knowledge as conceived in Hinduism. The three stages or degrees we have mentioned in the text correspond to *śravaṇa, manana,* and *nididhyāsana* as indicated in Hindu texts. Cf. Dharmarāja, *Vedāntaparibhāṣā*, Adyar: The Adyar Library and Research Centre, 1971, pp. 159-166; *Vidyāraṇya, Vivaraṇaprameyasaṃgraha*, Kāśī: Acyutagranthamālā, saṃvat 1996, pp.4-8; O. Lacombe, *L' Absolu selon le Vēdānta*, Paris: P. Geuthner, 1966, pp. 349-350; V.P. Upadhyaya, *Lights on Vedānta*, Varanasi: Chowkhamba, 1959, pp. 210-216.

54. Cf. Vasubandhu, *Trisvabhāvanirdeśa* (or *Trisvabhāvakārikā*), included in this volume; Maitreya-Vasubandhu-Sthiramati, *Madhyāntavibhāgaśāstra*, Chapter I; Asaṅga's *Mahāyānasūtrālaṃkāra*, Chapter VI, 1; J. Masuda, *Der individualistische Idealismus der Yogācāra-Schulen. Versuch einer genetischen Darstellung*, Heidelberg: O. Harrassowitz, 1926, pp. 40-43; A.K. Chatterjee, *The Yogācāra Idealism*, Chapter VII; D.T. Suzuki, *Outlines of Mahayana Buddhism*, Chapter V.
55. On Buddhist Atomism cf. F. Tola and C. Dragonetti, *The Avayavinirākaraṇa of Paṇḍita Aśoka*, pp. XX-XXI with references to Buddhist authors and bibliography.
56. On the Vaiśeṣika atomism see the bibliography of note 6 of the *Ālambanaparīkṣā*. In the *Nyāyasūtras*, IV, 2, 18-25 and in its commentaries there is a defence of atomism against the *ānupalambhikas* who maintain that nothing exists (*sarvaṃ nāsti*). We find in this text several passages which contain references to Vasubandhu's argumentation in *Viṃśatikā*, as for instance *ad* IV, 2, 24 and 25 (p. 1064, *bhāṣya*; p. 1068, *vārttika*; p. 1069, *vārttika;* p. 1070, *vārttika;* p. 1071, *vārttika*).

57. The Early Buddhism not only did not include atomism in its doctrines, but even considered that Pakudha Kacchāyana, who maintained a doctrine that could be considered as an antecedent of the atomist theory, was one of the so called "Masters of Error", not accepted and criticized by Buddha. See C. Dragonetti, "Los seis maestros del error", in *Diálogos*, Puerto Rico, Año XI, N° 28, Abril 1975, pp. 71-94 (Reprint in F. Tola and C. Dragonetti, *Yoga y Mística de la India,* pp. 129-153) and C. Vogel, *The teachings of the Six Heretics,* Wiesbaden: F. Steiner, 1970.
58. On this subject see, Dignāga, *Pramāṇasamuccaya* (Pratyakṣa), M. Hattori's edition and translation, from *kārikā* 2 a-b to *kārikā* 7 a-b (pp. 176-181 for the text, pp. 24-27 for the translation, pp. 76-85 for the notes); Dharmakīrti, *Nyāyabindu* I, 4-6 with Dharmottara's and Vinītadeva's commentaries. Cf. also S. Chatterjee, *The Nyāya Theory of Knowledge. A Critical Study of Some Problems of Logic and Metaphysics,* Calcutta: University of Calcutta, 1965; B. Gupta, "Savikalpa pratyakṣa (Judgemental Perception) as viśiṣṭha jñāna", in *Our Heritage,* Vol. IV, Part I, Calcutta, 1956, pp. 107-114; B.K. Matilal, *Epistemology, Logic, and Grammar in Indian Philosophical Analysis,* The Hague: Mouton, 1971, pp. 34-39; Satkari Mookerjee, *The Buddhist Philosophy of Universal Flux,* Delhi: Motilal Banarsidass, 1980, pp. 273-299; D.N. Shastri, *The Philosophy of the Nyāya-Vaiśeṣika and its Conflict with the Buddhist Dignāga School (Critique of Indian Realism),* pp. 433-471, and "The distinction between Nirvikalpa and Savikalpa Perception in Indian Philosophy", in *Proceedings of All-India Oriental Conference,* Vol. 16, 1955, pp. 310-321; J. Sinha, *Indian Psychology, Cognition,* Calcutta: Sinha Publishing House, 1958; F. Th. Stcherbatsky, *Buddhist Logic,* 1962, Vol. I, pp. 146-153 and pp. 204-221; V.V. Tirupati, "A note on the *Nirvikalpa* and *Savikalpa* perceptions in Indian philosophy", in *Proceedings of Twenty-sixth Congress of Orientalists,* 1969, pp. 498-503; T.Vetter, *Erkenntnisprobleme bei Dharmakīrti,* Wien: Österreichische Akademie der Wissenschaften, 1964, specially pp. 37-41. For a modern exposition of the subject see Anonymous, "The effects of Marijuana on Consciousness"; W. James, *The Principles of Psychology,* New York: Dover Publications, 1950, Vol. II, Chapter XIX, and *Psychology: Briefer course,* New York: Collier Books, 1966, Chapter XX:; Ch. Solley

and Gardner Murphy, *Development of the perceptual world,* Chapter XIV, New York: Basic Books, 1960. On yogin's perception see Dignāga's, *Pramāṇasamuccaya* (Pratyakṣa), *kārikā* 6 c-d, and Dharmakīrti's *Nyāyabindu* I, 11 with Dharmottara's and Vinītadeva's commentaries, and *Pramāṇavārttika* II, 281-287 (Pandeya's edition). Patañjali, *Yogasūtra* I, 43 refers to the yogin's perception. See F. Tola's and C. Dragonetti's commentary on it, *The Yogasūtras of Patañjali,* Delhi: Motilal Banarsidass, second edition, 1991. It is noteworthy that Patañjali uses the word *nirbhāsā* and Dharmakīrti the word *avabhāsate.* See also J. Sinha, *Indian Psychology, Cognition,* Chapter XVII on "Supranormal Perception".

59. In the Introduction we have referred to the Hīnayānist theory of momentariness and to its importance as a factor promoting the idealistic theory. As it was obvious the thesis of the momentariness of the *dharmas* will prevail in the Mahāyāna. On the momentariness of the *dharmas* in Mahāyāna see for instance the following texts where the concept of momentariness is fully developed, and arguments for its demonstration are given: *Mahāyānasūtrālaṃkāra* XVIII, 82-91; Śāntarakṣita, *Tattvasaṅgraha (Sthirabhāvaparīkṣā)* 350-475, and Kamalaśīla *ad locum;* Dharmakīrti, *Hetubindu,* pp. 42-67, and the *ṭīkās* of Vinītadeva and Arcaṭa; Dharmottara, *Kṣaṇabhaṅgasiddhiḥ,* edition and translation by E. Frauwallner, *Wiener Zeitschrift für die Kunde des Morgenlandes,* 42, 1935, pp. 217-258 (=*Kleine Schriften,* pp. 530-571); Jñānaśrīmitra, *Kṣaṇabhaṅgādhyāya (in Jñānaśrīmitranibandhāvaliḥ,* ed. A. Thakkur, Patna: K.P. Jayaswal Research Institute, 1987) (English translation of Chapter 3, *Vyatirekādhikāra,* by A.C. Senape McDermott, Dordrecht: Reidel, 1969); Ratnakīrti, *Kṣaṇabhaṅgasiddhi (in Ratnakīrtinibandhāvaliḥ, ibidem,* pp. 67-95) and *Sthirasiddhidūṣaṇa (ibidem,* pp. 112-128 and in K. Mimaki, *La refutation bouddhique de la permanence des choses (sthirasiddhidūṣaṇa) et La preuve de la momentanéité des choses (kṣaṇabhaṅgasiddhi),* Paris: Institut de Civilisation Indienne, 1976); Ratnākaraśānti, Antarvyāptisamarthana; Jitāri, *kṣaṇajabhaṅga,* ed. Bühnemann, 1985, p. 11. For Dharmakīrti's treatment of the *kṣaṇabhaṅga* theory see E. Steinkellner, "Die Entwicklung des kṣaṇikatvānumāṇam bei Dharmakīrti", in *Beiträge zur Geistesgeschichte Indiens, Festschrift für Erich*

Frauwallner, Wien: Österreichische Akademie der Wissenschaften, 1968, pp. 361-377. For other sources see K. Mimaki's quoted book, *Introduction.* Cf. S. Mookerjee, *The Buddhist Philosophy of Universal Flux,* 1980, pp. 1-86; F. Th. Stcherbatsky, *Buddhist Logic* I, pp. 79-118; and A. von Rospatt, *The Buddhist Doctrine of Momentariness, A Survey of the Origins and Early Phase of this Doctrine up to Vasubandhu,* Stuttgart: F. Steiner, 1995.

60. The same idea about memory is expressed in Gotama's *Nyāyasūtra* IV, 2, 34 and its commentaries: memory has as its object something that has been previously perceived (*pūrvopalabdhaviṣaya),* as a consequence of their realistic position. Cf. J. Sinha, *Indian Psychology, Cognition,* 1958, pp. 376-383.

61. Cf. F. Tola and C. Dragonetti, "*Anāditva* or beginninglessness in Indian Philosophy", in *Annals of the Bhandarkar Oriental Research Institute,* 1980, pp. 1-20.

62. It is an application of the axiom, valid for the whole Indian culture and expressed in *Nyāyasūtra* IV, 2, 35, that "the destruction of wrong apprehension comes from knowledge of true reality" (*mythyopalabdhivināśas tattvajñānāt).* The wrong apprehension may be, according to Vātsyāyana's *bhāṣya ad locum,* perceiving a thing as being something else (*atasmiṃs tad iti jñānam),* the conception of things in a dream (*svapnaviṣayābhimāna°*), the illusory cognition of something created by magic, the cities of the Gandharvas, mirages (*māyāgandharvanagaramṛgatṛṣṇakāṇām...buddhayo),* and also, according to bhāṣya *ad* IV, 2, 1 (beginning), grasping what is not the *ātman* as the *ātman,* i. e. identifying the *ātman* with the body, the sense-organs, mind, feelings, cognitions (*anātmany ātmagrahaḥ...śarīrendriyamanovedanābuddhayaḥ*). For Vasubandhu the fundamental wrong apprehension is to conceive the world in which we exist as a really existing world and not as a mental creation with the status of a dream or a magical creation.

63. The features of the *jīvanmukta* (" liberated in life") of Hinduism correspond to the features of the person who has attained the world-transcending knowledge according to Vasubandhu. Cf. Vidyāraṇya, *Jīvanmuktiviveka,* and also G. Oberhammer, *La délivrance, dès cette vie (jīvanmuktiḥ),* Paris: É. de Boccard, 1994; S. Dasgupta, *A History of Indian Philosophy,* Vol. I, pp.

489-492, Cambridge: Cambridge University Press, 1963; T.M.P. Mahadevan, *The Philosophy of Advaita,* Madras: Ganesh and Co., 1969, pp. 282-285.

64. Cf. Vasubandhu, *Abhidharmakośa* II, 62 (p. 349 Bauddha Bharati Series edition=I, pp. 307-308 L. de la Vallée Poussin's translation); S. Chaudhuri, *Analytical Study of the Abhidharmakośa,* p. 114; L. de la Vallée Poussin, *Theorie des douze causes,* p. 53; D. J. Kalupahana, *Causality, The Central Philosophy of Buddhism,* 1975, pp. 165-166; Yamakami Sogen, *Systems of Buddhistic Thought,* p.310.
65. See F. Tola and C. Dragonetti, "The Buddhist Conception of reality", in *Journal of the Indian Council of Philosophical Research,* Volume XIV, Number 1, 1996, pp. 35-64, specially pp. 49-52.
66. Cf. *Dhammapada* stanza 176 and Dharmottara's *Paralokasiddhi,* edition of the Tibetan text and translation by E. Steinkellner, Wien: Arbeitskreis für tibetische und buddhistische Studien, Universiätt Wien, 1986 (review of this book in *Revista de Estudios Budistas* 4, México-Buenos Aires, 1993, pp. 175-177). Uddyotakara, *Vārttika ad* IV, 2, 34 (p. 1084, Calcutta edition), adduces also against the thesis of the inexistence of external real objects that this inexistence eliminates all difference between *dharma* and *adharma* (merit and demerit).
67. Uddyotakara (*Vārttika ad* IV, 2, 34, p.1084, Calcutta edition) attributes to his idealist opponent the idea that there is a difference between the dreaming and the waking states consisting in the different condition of the mind, since the *upaghāta* (weakness, sickness, morbid affection) produced by *nidrā* (sleep) creates a *vaikṛtya* (change, alteration, deterioration, degeneration) of the mind. The Calcutta edition indicates a variant reading for *nidropaghāta*: *siddhopaghāta,* that perhaps is a mistake for *middhopaghāta* which would correspond to the *middhenopahata* of Vasubandhu (*kārikā* 18c).
68. On the organ of life (*jīvitendriya*) see S. Chaudhuri, *Analytical Study of the Abhidharmakośa,* p. 97; Th. Stcherbatsky, *The Central Conception of Buddhism,* p. 91; Upali Karunaratne, "Indriya", in *Encyclopaedia of Buddhism,* 1993, Vol. V, fasc. 4, p. 561.

69. The term *ṛddhi* (in Sanskrit= Pali *iddhi*), denoting "supernatural powers", has in this passage a meaning much wider than the one it usually has in Buddhist canonical texts. The five *ṛddhis* as mentioned in Buddhist texts are for instance: the power to project mind-made images of oneself; to become invisible; to pass through solid things such as a wall; to penetrate solid ground as if it were water; to walk on water, to fly through the air; to touch the sun and the moon; to ascend into the highest heavens. Cf. S. K. Nanayakkara, "Iddhi", in *Encyclopaedia of Buddhism*, 1993, Vol. V, fasc. 4, pp. 508-510; L. de la Vallée Poussin, "Magic (Buddhist)", in J. Hastings, *Encyclopaedia*, Vol. 8, pp. 255-257.
70. On the dreams of Sāraṇa, see S.Lévi, "Aśvaghoṣa. Le Sūtrālaṃkāra et ses sources", *Journal Asiatique*, 1908, Juil.-Août, pp. 149 ff., and É. Chavannes, *Cinq Cents Contes et Apologues extraits du Tripiṭaka Chinois*, Paris: A.- Maisonneuve, 1962, Tome III, p. 23; and on the defeat of Vemacitra, King of the Asuras, see S. Lévi, "Notes indiennes", *Journal Asiatique*, 1925, Jaṇ.-Mars, pp. 17-26.
71. Cf. S. Lévi, "Notes indiennes", *Journal Asiatique*, 1925, Jan.-Mars, pp. 26-35.
72. The names of these forests are Daṇḍaka, Mātaṅga and Kāliṅga. On the incidents that occur in these forests see *Rāmāyaṇa, Uttarakāṇḍa* 71 and 72, critical edition, Baroda, 1975; Buddhaghosa's Commentary of the *Majjhimanikāya ad Upalisutta*, ed. by I. B. Horner, Part III, London: Pali Text Society, 1976, pp. 60-88; C.H. Hamilton, *Wei shih er shih lun*, New Haven: American Oriental Society, 1938, reprint 1967, p. 73 notes 153, 154, 155.
73. This power of the mind received the name of *cetaḥ-paryāya-jñāna* in Sanskrit, *cetopariyañāṇa* in Pali. It is one of the "special knowledges", *abhijñā* in Sanskrit, *Abhiññā* in Pali. Others *abhiññās* are: divine ear, divine eye, remembrance of former existences, etc. The *ṛddhis* mentioned in note 69 constitute also a kind of *abhijñā*. See H.G.A. van Zeyst, "Abhiññā", in *Encyclopaedia of Buddhism*, Vol. I, Fasc. 1, pp. 97-102.
74. The invocation to Mañjuśrī Kumārabhūta was taken by us from the Tibetan translation. S. Lévi does not include it in his "reconstruction" of the Sanskrit text.
75. S. Lévi, with the help of the Tibetan and Chinese translations,

made a "reconstruction" of the Sanskrit text from *mahāyāne traidhātukam* (in Section I) up to *tasmād arthābhāve deśakālā* (in Section III at the end), adding at the beginning the words: "*atha vṛttiḥ*". This part of the text was in the first page (that was not found) of the manuscript of Kathmandu (*kārikās* and commentary). As we have already said in the Introduction to the *Viṃśatikā*, after the discovering and publication of the incomplete manuscript of Kathmandu, another manuscript was found also in Kathmandu, but containing the *kārikās* alone, without the commentary. We give for this lost first passage the Sanskrit text "reconstructed" by Sylvain Lévi, but instead of including his "reconstruction" of the two first *kārikās* we give for them the text as published by the same Sylvain Lévi in *Matériaux pour l' étude du systēme Vijñaptimātra*, p.175, constituted on the basis of the last manuscript (*kārikās* alone) found in Kathmandu. In *kārikā* 1, *pāda d* we have introduced a textual change following *MTY-A*.
In what follows we give the text of the Tibetan translation (*Sde-dge* edition) and of the Chinese translation by Hiuan Tsang (*Taishō* edition) of this first passage missing in all the Sanskrit manuscripts.

Tibetan Text

ḥjam dpal gźon nur gyur pa la pḥyag ḥtshal lo/theg pa chen po la khams gsum pa rnam par rig pa tsam du rnam par bźag ste/mdo las/ kye rgyal baḥi sras dag ḥdi lta ste/khams gsum pa ḥdi ni sems tsam mo źes ḥbyuṅ baḥi phyir ro/sems daṅ yid daṅ/rnam par śes pa daṅ/rnam par rig pa źes bya ba ni rnam graṅs su gtogs paḥo/sems de yaṅ ḥdir mtshuṅs par ldan pa daṅ bcas par dgoṅs paḥo/tsam źes bya ba smos pa ni don dgag paḥi phyir ro/... (*kārikā* 1)... ḥdir ḥdi skad ces brgal te/... *(kārikā* 2)... ji skad du bstan par ḥgyur źe na/gal te gzugs la sogs paḥi don med par gzugs la sogs paḥi rnam par rig pa ḥbyuṅ ste gzugs la sogs paḥi don las ma yin na/ciḥi phyir yul la lar ḥbyuṅ la thams cad na ma yin/yul de ñid na yaṅ res ḥgaḥ ḥbyuṅ la thams cad du ma yin/yul daṅ dus de na ḥkhod pa thams cad kyi sems la ṅes pa med pa ḥbyuṅ la ḥgaḥ tsam la ma yin/ji ltar rab rib can ñid kyi sems la skra la sogs pa snaṅ gi/gźan dag la ni ma yin/ciḥi phyir gaṅ rab rib can gyis mthoṅ baḥi skra daṅ/ sbraṅ bu la sogs pas skra la sogs paḥi bya ba mi byed la/de ma yin pa gźan dag gis ni byed/rmi lam na mthoṅ baḥi bzaḥ ba daṅ btuṅ ba daṅ bgo ba daṅ dug daṅ mtshon la sogs pas zas daṅ skom la sogs paḥi bya ba mi byed la/de ma yin pa gźan dag gis ni byed/dri zaḥi groṅ khyer yod pa ma yin pas groṅ khyer gyi bya ba mi byed la/de ma yin pa gźan dag gis ni byed/ ḥdi dag don med par med du ḥdra na yul daṅ dus...

Chinese Text

(HIUAN TSANG'S TRANSLATION)

(*Taishō* 1590, Vol. XXXI, p. 74 b line 19-c line 13)

No.1590 [Nos. 1588, 1589; cf. 1591]

唯識二十論一卷

世親菩薩造

大唐三藏法師玄奘奉　詔譯

安立大乘三界唯識，以契經說三界唯心，心意識了名之差別，此中說心意兼心所，唯遮外境不遮相應，內識生時似外境現，如有眩瞖見髮蠅等，此中都無少分實義，即於此義有設難言，頌曰

若識無實境　則處時決定
相續不決定　作用不應成

論曰，此說何義，若離識實有色等外法，色等識生不緣色等，何因此識有處得生非一切處，何故此處有時識起非一切時，同一處時有多相續，何不決定隨一識生，如眩瞖人見髮蠅等，非無眩瞖有此識生，復有何因，諸眩瞖者所見髮等無髮等用，夢中所得飲食刀杖毒藥衣等無飲等用，尋香城等無城等用，餘髮等物其用非無，若實同無色等外境，唯有內識似外境生，

76. S. Lévi (*Matériaux*, p. 175): °*keśoṇḍrakādi*°. (S. Lévi, before the discovery of *MS2*, in his "reconstruction" of the lost first part of the text, had: °*keśacandrādi*°). This wrong reading still appears in several modern editions. *MTY-A*: °*keśoṇḍukādi*° which is a correct reading. Cf. F. Edgerton, *Dictionary sub voce*.
77. *MTY-B: daṇḍa deest.*
78. S. Lévi: *daṇḍa deest. MTY-B*: seems to have *daṇḍa*.
79 S. Lévi: *daṇḍa deest. MTY-B*: has *daṇḍa*.
80. S. Lévi: *daṇḍa deest. MTY-B*: has *daṇḍa*.
81. S. Lévi: *daṇḍa* after *samam. MTY-B*: no *daṇḍa*.
82. S. Lévi: the initial consonant blurred. *MTY-B: sva*°.
83. *MTY-B: sarveṣāñ.*
84. *MTY-B: kim.*
85. Our correction. S. Lévi: *satvā. MTY-B: satvā.*
86. *MTY-B:* °*balānāñ.*
87. *MTY-B: yātayatān.*
88. *MTY-B:* °*duḥkhañ.*
89. *MTY-B: nārake.*
90. *MTY-B* and *MTY-A: sambhavaḥ.*
91. S. Lévi: *na. MTY-B: na. MTY-A* and S. Lévi (*Matériaux*, p.175): *ca.*
92. *MTY-B* and *MTY-A: duḥkhan.*
93. *MTY-B: sambhavanti.*
94. *MTY-B: karmmaṇā.*
95. *MTY-B: sambhūtās.*
96. *MTY-B: caivan.*
97. *MTY-B: daṇḍa deest.*
98. *MTY-B: sambhavo.*
99. *MTY-B: teṣān.*
100. *MTY-B: karmmabhis.*
101. *MTY-B: sambhavanti.*
102. *MTY-B: yena* or *ye na* (this last possibility makes no sense).
103. *MTY-B: āganto.*
104. *MTY-B*: between *gacchanto* and °*vane* completely blurred. *Tibetan version: lcags kyi śal ma liḥi.*
105. S. Lévi: *ūrddha*° .*MTY-B: ūrdhva*°.
106. *MTY-B: sambhavanti.*
107. *MTY-B* and *MTY-A: karmmabhis.*
108. *MTY-B* and *MTY-A: sambhavas.*
109. *MTY-B: ne...* : the two last syllabes blurred. *MTY-A: neṣyate. Tibetan version: mi ḥdod.*

110. *MTY-B: karmmabhis.*
111. *MTY-B* and *MTY-A: karmmaṇo.*
112. *MTY-B: neṣyate* blurred. *MTY-A: neṣyate. Tibetan version: ḥdod mi bya.*
113. *MTY-B* and *MTY-A: kin.*
114. *MTY-B: karmmaṇā.*
115. *MTY-B: sambhavaḥ.*
116. S. Lévi: *tasya deest. MTY-B: tasya. Tibetan version: las deḥi.*
117. *MTY-B: karmmaṇo.*
118. *MTY-B*: between *vijñāna°* and *°sanniviṣṭā* blurred. *Tibetan version: rgyud la.*
119. *MTY-B: kin.*
120. *MTY-B: etat.*
121. *MTY-B: °janam. MTY-A: °janaṃ.*
122. Our correction. S. Lévi: *°satva°. MTY-B* and *MTY-A: °satva°.*
123. Our correction. S. Lévi: *satva. MTY-B: satva.*
124. *MTY-B: °santaty°.*
125. Our correction. S. Lévi: *satva. MTY-B: satva.*
126. *MTY-B: dharmmās.*
127. S. Lévi: *sahetukāḥ. MTY-B: sahetukā.*
128. *MTY-B: uktam.*
129. *MTY-B: daṇḍa* after *utpadyate.*
130. *MTY-B: pariṇāmaviśeṣād. Tibetan version: ḥgyur baḥi bye brag tu gyur paḥi.*
131. Our correction: no *daṇḍa* after *utpadyate.* S. Lévi: *daṇḍa. MTY-B: daṇḍa.*
132. S. Lévi: *tasyā. MTY-B: tasyāḥ.*
133. *MTY-B*: between *aya°* and *°prāyaḥ* manuscript destroyed. *Tibetan version: ḥdi ni ḥdir dgoṅs paḥo.*
134. *MTY-B: evam.*
135. *MTY-B*: double *daṇḍa* after *hi.*
136. *MTY-B*: between *dva°* and *°naṣaṭkaṃ* manuscript destroyed. *Tibetan version: gñis las rnam par śes pa drug.*
137. *MTY-B*: no *daṇḍa* after *pravartate.*
138. *MTY-B: punar* without following *daṇḍa. MTY-A: punaḥ* with following *daṇḍa.*
139. *MTY-B:* between *deśanā* and *°rātmyapraveśaḥ* manuscript destroyed. *MTY-A:* after *deśanā : dharmmanairātmyapraveśaḥ. Tibetan version: bstan pa chos la bdag med par.*
140. *MTY-B*: double *daṇḍa after °praveśaḥ.*

141. S. Lévi: no *daṇḍa*. *MTY-B: daṇḍa.*
142. *MTY-B: dharmma°.*
143. *MTY-B: °dharmma°.*
144: *MTY-B: dharmma°*; and between *dharmma°* and *°ti* manuscript destroyed. *Tibetan version: chos gaṅ yaṅ med par rig nas.*
145. *MTY-B: dharmmo.*
146 S. Lévi: *tahi*. *MTY-B: tarhi.*
147. *MTY-B: dharmmo.*
148. MTY-B: dharmma°.
149. *Our correction: bhavati.* S. Lévi: *mavati*. *MTY-B*: between *°praveśo* and *°pi tu* manuscript blurred. *Tibetan version: chos la bdag med par ḥjug par ḥgyur te.*
150. *MTY-B:* between *°pi tu* and *°tātmanā* manuscript blurred. *MTY-A: kalpitāmanā. Tibetan version: brtags paḥi bdag ñid kyis.*
151. S. Lévi: *dharmaṇāṃ*. *MTY-B: dharmāṇāṃ.*
152. *MTY-B: buddhānām.*
153. *MTY-B: evam.*
154. *MTY-B:* between *°pti°* and *°pi* manuscript blurred. *Tibetan version: rnam par rig tsam yaṅ.*
155. S. Lévi: *°praveśāt*. *MTY-B: °praveśād.*
156. *MTY-B: dharmmāṇāṃ.*
157. S. Lévi: *sarvathā deest*. *MTY-B: sarvathā. Tibetan version: rnam pa thams cad du.*
158. *MTY-B: °mātratvan.*
159. *MTY-B: yasmān* without following *daṇḍa*.
160. *MTY-A*: after *na* something written in the margin (?).
161. *MTY-B: uktam.*
162. *MTY-B: daṇḍa deest.*
163. *MTY-B: avayavebhyo* without following *avagraha*.
164. *MTY-B:* double *daṇḍa*.
165. *MTY-B: sambhavāt.*
166. S. Lévi and *MTY-B: parasparavyatirekād*. Our correction [according to the Tibetan and Chinese translation, and required by sense. See S. Lévi (*Matériaux*, p.52 note 3)]: *parasparāvyatirekād.*
167. *MTY-B: niravayatvāt* without following *daṇḍa.*
168. *MTY-B: daṇḍa deest.*
169. Our correction: *°vaibhāṣikāḥ* with following *daṇḍa*. S. Lévi: *°vaibhāṣikās*. *MTY-B: °vaibhāṣikās.*
170. *MTY-B: te.*

171. *MTY-B*: double *daṇḍa*.
172. S. Lévi (*Matériaux*, p.175) suggests "with the manuscripts": *asaṃyogāt*, but *MTY-B* and *MTY-A: asaṃyoge*.
173. *MTY-B*: without following *avagraha*. *MTY-A*: with following *avagraha*.
174. *MTY-B*: double *daṇḍa*.
175. *MTY-B*: *daṇḍa deest*.
176. *MTY-B: niravayatvāt*.
177. *MTY-B*: between °*bhyupa*° and °*ramāṇur* manuscript blurred or broken. *Tibetan version: khas mi len paḥi phyir ro/de bas rdul phra rab*.
178. *MTY-A*: before *digbhāgabhedo* some half erased words.
179. *MTY-B: tasyaikatvan*. *MTY-A: tasyaikatvaṃ*.
180. *MTY-B*: between *paramāṇoḥ* and *yāvad* manuscript blurred or broken. *Tibetan version: śar phyogs kyi cha*.
181. *MTY-B: iti digbhāga* °added in top margin.
182. *MTY-B: chāyā°*. *MTY-A: cchāyā°*.
183. *MTY-B*: small stroke after *vā*.
184. *MTY-B*: between *anyatra* and *bhavaty* °manuscript blurred. *Tibetan version: grib*.
185. *MTY-B: avagraha deest* after *pradeśo*.
186. *MTY-B: āvaraṇañ*.
187. *MTY-B*: between *cid* and °*ḥ (of paramāṇoḥ)* manuscript blurred. *Tibetan version: rdul phra rab gaṅ la yaṅ*.
188. *MTY-B: avagraha deest* after *parabhāgo*.
189. *MTY-B* : between °*mātraḥ* and/*kim evaṃ* manuscript blurred. *Tibetan version: ḥgyur te/de ni bśad zin to/*.
190. S. Lévi: *daṇḍa deest*. *MTY-B*: *daṇḍa* after *syātāṃ*.
191. *MTY-A*: between *kathaṃ (pāda c)* and this *na (pāda d)* reading not very clear. In lower margin of the manuscript an annotation: *nna* to complete *ce°(of cen na)*; and moreover something else written in this margin.
192. *MTY-B: yadi* and *nā°(of nānyaḥ)* blurred. *Tibetan version: gal te...gźan ma yin na*.
193. *MTY-B: siddham*.
194. *MTY-B: sanniveśa°*.
195. *MTY-B: eṣa* without following *daṇḍa*.
196. *MTY-B*: between *ana°* and °*tayā* blurred. *Tibetan version : bsam pa ḥdis*.
197. *MTY-B: lakṣaṇan*.

198. *MTY-B:* between *rūpā°* and *na* blurred. *Tibetan version: gzugs la sogs paḥi mtshan ñid ni ma bkag na.*
199. *MTY-B: kim.*
200. *MTY-B*: Our correction. S. Lévi and *MTY-B: daṇḍa deest.*
201. *MTY-B: nīläditvañ.*
202. *MTY-B: sampradhāryate.*
203. *MTY-B: kin.*
204. *MTY-B*: between *a°* (of *atha)* and *°d (of tad)* blurred. *Tibetan version: ḥon te.*
205. *MTY-B: kiñ.*
206. *MTY-B:* double *daṇḍa.*
207. S. Lévi: *°grahṛau. MTY-B* and *MTY-A: °grahau.*
208. *MTY-B*: between *nā°* and *°kam* manuscript blurred. The Tibetan version has: *ris su ma chad* for *avicchinnaṃ nānekam.* Hiuan tsang's version agrees with the Tibetan one. Both versions add to *viṣaya* adjectives of colour. Does these facts point to the existence of another recension of the Sanskrit text of the *Viṃśatikā* ?
209. Our correction. S. Lévi and *MTY-B: daṇḍa deest.*
210. *MTY-B:* between *°da°* and *°peṇa* manuscript blurred or broken. *Tibetan version: gom pa gcig bor bas.*
211. *MTY-B:* between *°gra°* and *yugapan* manuscript destroyed. *Tibetan version: ma zin.*
212. *MTY-B: syān* without following *daṇḍa.*
213. *MTY-B: grahaṇañ.*
214. *MTY-B: cāgrahaṇañ.*
215. *MTY-B: yuktaṃ.*
216. *MTY-B: nna.*
217. *MTY-B: ekan.*
218. *MTY-B: kathan.*
219. *MTY-B*: between *°vicche°* and *°te* manuscript destroyed. *Tibetan version: de dag ris su chad par ji ltar ruṅ.*
220. *MTY-B: katham.*
221. *MTY-B: prāptañ.*
222. *MTY-B: tābhyān.*
223. *MTY-B: sūkṣmāṇāñ.*
224. *MTY-B*: between *la°* and *°dād* manuscript destroyed. *Tibetan version: mtshan ñid tha dad pa ñid kyis.*
225. *MTY-B*: between *°tva°* and *°ti* manuscript destroyed. *Tibetan version: yul ñid du mi ḥgrub ste.*
226. *MTY-B: mātram.*

227. *MTY-B: sarveṣāñ.*
228. *MTY-B: prāṇānāṃ.*
229. *MTY-B: pratyakṣam.*
230. *MTY-B: °tha°* erased. *Tibetan version: ji ltar.*
231. S. Lévi: *budbhir. MTY-B: buddhir.*
232. *MTY-B:* between *bha* °and *pratyakṣam* manuscript destroyed. *Tibetan version: ḥbyuṅ.*
233. MTY*-B:* double *daṇḍa.*
234. *MTY-A: °buddhir.*
235. *MTY-B: daṇḍa* after *yathā.*
236. *MTY-B* and *MTY-A: avagraha deest* after *so.*
237. *MTY-A: katham.*
238. *MTY-B*: between *yad°* and *ca* erased. *Tibetan version: gaṅ gi tshe.*
239. Our correction: we suppress *na* after °*buddhir*, since it gives no sense. S. Lévi: °*buddhir na. MTY-B*: manuscript destroyed. Tibetan and Chinese translations have no negation.
240. *MTY-B*: between *pratyakṣa°* and *°tīdaṃ* manuscript destroyed. *Tibetan version: mṅon sum gyi blo de byuṅ ba.*
241 *MTY-B: avagraha deest* after *so.*
242. *MTY-B: daṇḍa deest.*
243. *MTY-B*: between *vi°* and *°na* erased. *Tibetan version: lhag par.*
244. *MTY-B*: between *kṣaṇika°* and *°yasya* manuscript destroyed. *Tibetan version*, seeming to follow another recension of the Sanskrit text, has: *skad cig mar smras bas*. Hiuan tsang's Chinese translation refers also to "those who hold the doctrine of momentariness". See note 208 of the Sanskrit text.
245. Our correction. S. Lévi and *MTY-B: daṇḍa deest.*
246. *MTY-B: °bhūtam.*
247. *MTY-B: smaryate.*
248. *MTY-B: smaraṇam.*
249. *MTY-B*: double *daṇḍa* after *vijñaptiḥ. MTY-A: vijñapti.*
250. *MTY-B: tathoktaṃ* with following double *daṇḍa.*
251. *MTY-B: smaraṇan.*
252. *MTY-B: °samprayuktā.*
253. *MTY-B: avagraha deest* after *jāgrato.*
254. *MTY-B: daṇḍa deest.*
255. *MTY-B: caivam.*
256. *MTY-B*: without following *daṇḍa.*

257. *MTY-B* and *MTY-A: svapnadṛg°*. Cf. S. Lévi, *Matériaux*, p.175, prefers *svapna.°MTY-A: °bhāvam.*
258. *MTY-A: avagraha deest* after *nāprabuddho.*
259. *MTY-B: artham.*
260. *MTY-B: °sammukhī°.*
261. *MTY-B: svasantāna°.*
262. Our correction. S. Lévi: *satvānām. MTY-B: °satvānām.*
263. *MTY-B: °dharmma°.*
264. *MTY-B: °satvānāṃ.*
265. *MTY-B: °deśanāyāñ.*
266. *MTY-B*: double *daṇḍa* after *mithaḥ. MTY-A: mitha.*
267. *MTY-B: satvānām.*
268. *MTY-B: santānā°.*
269. *MTY -B: santānā°.*
270. *MTY-B: evañ.*
271. *MTY-B: avagraha deest* after *jāgrato.*
272. *MTY-B: āyatyān.*
273. *MTY-B: daṇḍa deest.*
274. *MTY-B: °nopahatañ. MTY-A: °nopahataṃ.*
275. *MTY-B*: simple *daṇḍa. MTY-A*: double *daṇḍa.*
276. *MTY-B: avagraha deest* after *kāyo.*
277. *MTY-B: daṇḍa deest.*
278. Our correction according to the Tibetan (*gsod pa na)* and Chinese translations. S.Lévi and *MTY-B : anukramyamāṇānām.*
279. *MTY-B: maraṇam.*
280. *MTY-B*: double *daṇḍa.*
281. *MTY-A: maraṇa.*
282. *MTY-B: vemacitriṇaḥ parājayaḥ.*
283. *MTY-B: °santativicchedākhyam.*
284. *MTY-B: maraṇam.*
285. *MTY-B: ṛkopataḥ. MTY-A: ṛṣikopataḥ.*
286. Our correction. S. Lévi and *MTY-B: satvānāṃ.*
287. *MTY-B: daṇḍa deest.*
288. *MTY-B: daṇḍa deest.*
289. *MTY-B: daṇḍa deest.*
290. *MTY-B:* double *daṇḍa.*
291. *MTY-B:* simple *daṇḍa.*
292. *MTY-B: satvā.*
293. *MTY-B: karmmaṇā.*
294. *MTY-B: °daṇḍābhyām.*
295. *MTY-B: daṇḍa deest.*

296. *MTY-B: sattvānām* (?).
297. *MTY-B: kiñ.*
298. *MTY-B: daṇḍa deest.*
299. *MTY-B:* manuscript erased between *°nti* and *°racittavidāṃ. MTY-A: paracittavidāṃ. Tibetan version: śes na...gźan sems.*
300. *MTY-B: °jñānam.*
301. *MTY-B:* between *b°* and *°nāṃ* manuscript blurred. *Tibetan version: saṅs rgyas kyi.*
302. *MTY-B:* between *°vi°* and *°syā°* manuscript blurred. *Tibetan version: rnam par rtog pa.*
303. *MTY-B: daṇḍa deest.*
304. *MTY-B: daṇḍa* after *cintyā.*
305. *MTY-B: rkkā°* (?). *Tibetan version: rtog geḥi spyod yul ma yin paḥi phyir ro.*
306. *MTY-B:* simple *daṇḍa.*
307. *MTY-B: daṇḍa deest.*
308. *MTY-B:* double *daṇḍa.*
309. At the end of this Section Vasubandhu refers to the *saṃprayogas,* literally: " associations ", of the mind. With this word Vasubandhu is alluding to the *caittas* or mental phenomena that accompany all act of cognition, all state of consciousness: feelings, ideas, volitions, etc. The *caittas* are dealt with by Vasubandhu in *Abhidharmakośa* II, *kārikās* 23-24 (L. de la Vallée Poussin's translation, I, pp.149-178). See also Anuruddha's *Abhidhammattha Saṅgaha,* Part II (*Cetasikasangahavibhāga*) (Shwe Zan Aung's translation, PTS edition, pp. 94-110). Cf. Sukomal Chaudhuri, *Analytical Study of the Abhidharmakośa,* Calcutta: Sanskrit College, 1974, pp. 104-108.
310. *City of the Gandharvas*: An imaginary city created by magic.
311. The commentary in this passage, and in other similar ones, glosses some words, which are in the text of the *kārikās,* by means of other words which make clear their meaning. In this case we have included in the translation the words that are glossed.
312. *World of experience: bhājanaloka.* It is the world in which the being that reincarnates will receive the reward or the punishment corresponding to the good or evil actions he did in his or her previous lives.
313. *Abhiprāyavaśāt:* literally "by the power of (his) intention", "on account of, for the sake or purpose of, by reason of, (his) 'real' intention".

314. *Of its own*: This expression indicates the particular "seed" from which the cognition arises, that in some way "belongs" to it.
315. *In the same way up to*: With this expression the commentary indicates that what has been expressed in relation to the *eye* (and its object: *form-colour*) must be applied to the other sense organs: ear, nose, tongue, that are always enumerated between the *eye* (as the first sense organ) and the *body* (as the touch sense organ), this one being mentioned by this commentary as the last one of series of senses. In fact the last of the sense organs in this enumeration is always the *manas*, the mind, that has as its object the ideas, *dharmas*. See the commentary of *Section XIV (kārikā* 10) where the *set of six* sense organs and there respective functions (or cognitions) are referred to in the same elliptic way as here, being the mind (*manas*) and its act of cognition in the last place.
316. The body (*kāya)* is considered as the organ of touch.
317. *Pratyekam* in the text: each of the external *āyatanas* is the object of its corresponding cognition, i. e. the form-colour (*rūpa*) is the object of the visual cognition, and so on.
318. *So up to:* The idea is that all the regions of the space from East up to Nadir must be taken into account. Vasubandhu mentions only the first and the last one.
319. In *kārikā* 12 and its commentary a similar situation is dealt with.
320. The Sanskriṭ text has *sabhāgasaṃtati* that we have translated by "corresponding to one and the same series of consciousnesses", i. e. to the same individual.

Part III

THE *TRISVABHĀVAKĀRIKĀ* OF VASUBANDHU

To Víctor Massuh,
a true *kalyāṇamitra*

INTRODUCTION

The Sanskrit Original Text

Sylvain Lévi[1] found in Nepal in 1928 a manuscript of the Sanskrit text of this small treatise in verses. The manuscript attributes the work to Vasubandhu.

On Lévi's request, Susumu Yamaguchi published in 1931 that Sanskrit text. Yamaguchi's edition contains a critical *apparatus*, one of the two Tibetan translations that have been preserved (the one which attributes the work to Vasubandhu, see *infra)*, a Japanese translation and a commentary also in Japanese of his own.[2]

In 1932-1933 Louis de la Vallée Poussin published again the Sanskrit text on the basis of Yamaguchi 's edition. He added to his edition also a critical *apparatus*, the two Tibetan translations (the one which attributes the work to Vasubandhu, and the other which attributes it to Nāgārjuna, see *infra)* and a French translation.

In 1939 Sujitkumar Mukhopadhyaya published the Sanskrit text. In his Introduction, p. VI, Mukhopadhyaya expresses that Giuseppe Tucci received from Nepal a Sanskrit manuscript of this treatise and sent a transcription of it to Vidhushekhar Bhattacharya and that Bhattacharya gave to him that transcription in order to edit Vasubandhu's work. So Mukhopadhyaya's edition is based on Tucci's manuscript. Mukhopadhyaya's edition has also an introduction, a critical *apparatus*, the two Tibetan translations, an English translation, a rich selection of parallel texts, and Sanskrit and Tibetan word *indices*. It seems that Mukhopadhyaya did not know either Yamaguchi's or de la Vallée Poussin's editions.

The Two Manuscripts

The comparison of the two manuscripts, the one found by Lévi and Tucci's one, (as it is possible to judge from the editions of both by Yamaguchi and Mukhopadhyaya) allows us to think that the differences between them are not numerous and minor ones. That can easily be seen by a revision of our critical notes to the Sanskrit text, in which we have indicated those differences. G. Tucci, "A fragment from the *Pratītya-samutpāda-vyākhyā* of Vasubandhu", in *Journal of the Royal Asiatic Society,* 1930, pp. 611-623 (= G. Tucci, *Opera Minora,* Parte I, Roma: G. Bardi Editore, 1971, pp. 239-248), expresses p. 611= 239, that the *Trisvabhāvakārikā* is another work by Vasubandhu that has been found in Nepal and that S. Lévi and himself had copies of it, but without any indication that the copy he has is from the same manuscript found by S. Lévi or from some other one.

The Tibetan Translations

In the Tibetan Buddhist Canon, *Bstan-ḥgyur*, there are two metrical translations of a brief Sanskrit treatise. The first one: *Tōhoku* 3843 (*Sde -dge* ed.)=*Catalogue* 5243 (*Peking* ed.); the second one: *Tōhoku* 4058 (*Sde-dge* ed.)=*Catalogue* 5559 (*Peking* ed.).

The first translation (3843-5243) contains 40 *kārikās*. Its colophon attributes the work to Nāgārjuna (Klu-sgrub, in Tibetan). Its title is *Raṅ-bshin gsum la ḥjug paḥi sgrub pa (Svabhāvatrayapraveśa-sādhana, Sde-dge* ed., *Svabhāvatrayapraveśasiddhi, Peking* ed.).[3] This translation was done by Zla-ba grags-pa (K.).

The second translation (4058-5559) contains 38 *kārikās*. Its colophon attributes the work to Vasubandhu (Dbyig-gñen, in Tibetan). Its title is *Raṅ-bshin gsum ṅes-par bstan-pa (Trisvabhāvanirdeśa).* This translation was done by Shāntibhadra and Ḥgos Lhas-btsas.[4]

The comparison of these two Tibetan translations with the Sanskrit text, as found in Lévi's and Tucci's manuscripts, indicates that both are translations of that same Sanskrit original text. Nevertheless, the Tibetan tradition considers one of the two translations (3843=5243) as the translation of one of Nāgārjuna's works and locates it in the *Dbu-ma (Mādhyamika)* section of the Canon. The other translation (4058- 5559) is considered by the Tibetan tradition to be the translation of one of Vasubandhu's works and consequently it is located in the *Sems-tsam (Cittamātra)* section. Both Tibetan translations differ only in some minor points and in the fact that the first one (3843=5243) adds two *kārikās* that are not found in the second one (4058=5559). The first translation, which attributes the original work to Nāgārjuna, is sometimes more faithful to the original Sanskrit text that the second one, which attributes it to Vasubandhu.

Let us say that there is no Chinese translation of this treatise.

A Third Sanskrit Manuscript (MS3)

Katsumi Mimaki, Musashi Tachikawa and Akira Yuyama, in their already mentioned work, *Three Works of Vasubandhu in Sanskrit*

Manuscripts. The Trisvabhāvanirdeśa, the Viṃśatikā with its Vṛtti and the Triṃśikā with Sthiramati's Commentary, Tokyo: The Centre for East Asian Cultural Studies, 1989 (Bibliotheca Codicum Asiaticorum 1), edited in facsimile a Sanskrit manuscript of the *Trisvabhāva* treatise, which bears the name of *Trisvabhāvanirdeśa.* This manuscript belongs to the *National Archives* of Kathmandu, Nepal, and it comes from the *Durbar Library* of that country. All the manuscripts of the *Durbar Library* are now located in the stacks of the *National Archives.* In general the text of this manuscript and of those referred to as *MS1* (S. Lévi's manuscript) and *MS2* (G. Tucci's manuscript) are very similar. In the places where MS1 and MS2 have different readings, this third manuscript agrees sometimes with MS1 and sometimes with MS2. Very probably the manuscripts of S. Lévi and G. Tucci are copies of the manuscript edited by Mimaki, Tachikawa and Yuyama or derive from it.

We have indicated in the critical *apparatus* the readings of *MS3* that are different from those of Lévi's and Tucci's manuscripts.

Modern Editions and Translations of the Original Sanskrit Text

The three first editions that follow have been referred to in the first section of this Introduction with more complete indications about their contents.

S. Yamaguchi, *Shūkyō Kenkyū* (Journal of Religious Studies), 8, March-May 1931, pp.121-130 and 186-207.

L. de la Vallée Poussin, "Le petit traité de Vasubandhu-Nāgārjuna sur les trois natures", *Mélanges Chinois et Bouddhiques,* Vol. II, 1932-1933, pp. 147-161.

S. Mukhopadhyaya, *The Trisvabhāvanirdeśa of Vasubandhu, Sanskrit text and Tibetan versions edited with an English translation, introduction and vocabularies,* Visvabharati Series, No. 4, Calcutta, 1939.

S. Yamaguchi, *Bukkyō Gaku Bunshū* (Collection of Studies on Buddhism), Tōkyō, 1972-1973, pp. 119-162. This is a revised and enlarged edition of his previously indicated article. Specially it contains, as additional material, the Tibetan translation that attributes the work to Nāgārjuna and numerous references for each *kārikā* to parallel texts.

Thubtan Chogdub Śāstri and Rāmaśaṅkara Tripāṭhī, in Gaṅgānāthajhā Granthamāla, Vol. V, *Vijñaptimātratāsiddhiḥ (Prakaraṇadvayam) of Ācārya Vasubandhu,* Varanasi, 1972, pp. 449-458, edited the Sanskrit text of Vasubandhu's treatise, reproducing Mukhopadhyaya's edition, with a Hindi translation.

G. Nagao published in the *Daijō Butten* (Buddhist Scriptures of the Mahāyāna), Vol.15, *Sheshin Ronshū* (Collection of Vasubandhu's treatises), Tōkyō, 1979, pp. 191-213, a Japanese translation of the Sanskrit text, with a commentary of his own.

F. Tola and C. Dragonetti, "*Trisvabhāvanirdeśa*. Exposición acerca de las Tres Naturalezas Propias de Vasubandhu", *Boletín de la Asociación Española de Orientalistas*, Año XVIII, 1982, pp. 107- 138, edited the Sanskrit text of the treatise with a Spanish translation and a brief introduction.

Th. A. Kochumuttom, *A Buddhist Doctrine of Experience*, Delhi: Motilal Banarsidass, 1982, pp. 90-126, gives an English translation of the treatise with commentary, including in notes the Sanskrit text. He follows S. Mukhopadhyaya's edition of the text.

F. Tola and C. Dragonetti, "The Trisvabhāvakārikā of Vasubandhu", *Journal of Indian Philosophy* 11, 1983, pp. 225-266, published a critical edition of the Sanskrit text of the treatise with an English translation, an elaborate commentary, and numerous notes.

S. Anacker, *Seven Works of Vasubandhu, The Buddhist Psychological Doctor*, Delhi: Motilal Banarsidass, 1984, pp. 287-297 and pp. 464-466, published an English translation of the treatise based on the L. de la Vallée Poussin's edition, and added in *Appendix* the Sanskrit text.

Th. E. Wood, in *Mind Only, A Philosophical Analysis of the Vijñānavāda*, Honolulu: University of Hawaii Press, pp. 31-47, edited the Sanskrit text of the treatise with an annotated English translation. He does not indicate which text he follows. It seems that it is S. Yamaguchi's edition.

F. Tola and C. Dragonetti, "Trisvabhāvakārikā. Estrofas acerca de las tres naturalezas de Vasubandhu", in *Revista de Estudios Budistas* 4, México-Buenos Aires, 1992, pp. 139-160, published an annotated Spanish translation of the treatise.

In this book F. Tola and C. Dragonetti present a completely revised, corrected and augmented version of their previous work, mainly of the article published in *JIP* 11, 1983.

The Author of the Treatise

The Nepal manuscripts of the Sanskrit text attribute the work to Vasubandhu (*kṛtir ācāryavasubandhupādānām*).

Of the two Tibetan translations, one attributes the original work to Nāgārjuna, the other to Vasubandhu, as we have already said.

From the point of view of the contents of the treatise, it is possible to affirm without doubt that it cannot belong to Nāgārjuna, since it develops a doctrine which is neither his nor of his school. On the contrary, all the subjects developed in the treatise and specially the central topic of the three natures are characteristic of the philosophical idealistic school *Yogācāra* to which Vasubandhu belongs. Besides that, the same Vasubandhu treats in other works, as in the commentary (*bhāṣya)* of Maitreya's *Madhyāntavibhāga*, or the *Triṃśikā,* the theory of the three natures. It is then possible to say that the attribution of this work to Nāgārjuna by one of the Tibetan translations is wrong and the attribution to Vasubandhu indicated by the other is correct.

We think that the concordant testimonies of the two Sanskrit manuscripts and of the second Tibetan translation and the contents of the work, characteristic of the *Yogācāra* school, are sufficient to accept that we have in the *Trisvabhāvakārikā* an authentic work of Vasubandhu.

The modern editors and translators of the work that have been mentioned before accept that it is a genuine work of Vasubandhu. A.K. Chatterjee, *The Yogācāra Idealism,* Delhi: Motilal Banarsidass, 1975, p. 39 and P. S. Jaini, Introduction, p.128, of his edition of the *Abhidharmadīpa,* Patna : Tibetan Sanskrit Works Series, 1977, are of the same opinion.[5]

The Title of the Treatise

We indicate the titles under which this work appears in the colophons of the Sanskrit manuscripts and of the Tibetan translations :

Manuscript found by S. Lévi: Trisvabhāvakārikā; Trisvabhāvaḥ.

Manuscript of G. Tucci: Trisvabhāvaḥ; Trisvabhāvaḥ.

Third Manuscript: Trisvabhāvanirdeśa.

First Tibetan translation (3843=5243): Svābhāvatrayapraveśasādhana (3843), Svabhāvatrayapraveśasiddhi (5243).

Second Tibetan translation (4058=5559): Trisvabhāvanirdeśa (both editions).

Owing to the divergencies of the titles attributed to this work it is difficult to decide which was the original one. We prefer to adopt the title given by the manuscript found by Sylvain Lévi: *Trisvabhāvakārikā.*

Importance of the Subject of the Treatise

The theory of the three natures has special importance in the subject matter of the *Yogācāra* school. Extrinsically, that importance is manifested in the fact that the same subject is treated in many important works of the school and many references to it are found in them. Intrinsically the importance of the three natures' theory in the idealistic school is evident, since two of these natures, the "dependent" one (*paratantra*) and the "imaginary" one (*parikalpita*), constitute the empirical reality, and the third one, the "absolute" nature (pariniṣpanna), is the absolute reality, the Absolute. Thus to study these three natures means to study the empirical reality and the Absolute; to define the essence of these three natures is to define the essence of the empirical reality and of the Absolute; to establish the relation between the three natures is to establish the relation that unites the empirical reality and the Absolute, and to show the mechanism through which from the dependent nature the imaginary one is produced, is to show the process through which from the empirical mind and only from the empirical mind the perceptible world is created. In this way the essential problems of the *Yogācāra* school are reunited in the theory of the *trisvabhāva*.

Importance of the Treatise

The present work is not one of the most important works of Vasubandhu, because of its brevity (38 *kārikās*), because (and this is a consequence of the previous circumstance) it leaves aside, without treating them, several questions that have to do with the subject-matter and are developed in other treatises of the school (like the *Siddhi* of Hiuan Tsang, the *Mahāyānasaṃgraha* of Asaṅga, and the *Madhyāntavibhāgaśastra* of Maitreya, Vasubandhu and Sthiramati), and because no commentary of it has been found, neither by Vasubandhu nor by another author. But nevertheless the treatise is valuable and interesting, since it treats in a concise, clear and appropriate way the two principal aspects of the *trisvabhāva's* theory: their essence and their mutual relation. It constitutes an easy and sure introduction to the study of this important theory of the idealistic school, study that can be broadened with the help of other more developed works.

Some Works that Treat of the Theory of the Three Natures or in which References to it are Found[6]

Sūtras.

Saṃdhinirmocana, Chapters VI-VII;

Laṅkāvatāra, pp. 67-68 and 130-132 (Nanjio ed.) (= pp. 29, 53-54 Vaidya ed.).

Śāstras.

Asaṅga, *Mahāyānasaṃgraha*, Chapter II, paragraphs 1-4 and 15-34, Chapter III, paragraph 9 (Lamotte ed.);

Asaṅga, *Bodhisattvabhūmi, (Tattvārthapaṭala)*, pp. 37-38 (Wogihara ed.) (=pp.25-26 Dutt ed.);

Asaṅga, *Yogācārabhūmiviniścayasaṃgrahaṇī, Taishō,* Vol. XXX, pp.703 a ff.

Asaṅga, *Mahāyānasūtrālaṃkāra* XI, 13-30 and 38-41;

Maitreya (*kārikā*), Vasubandhu (*bhāṣya*) and Sthiramati (*ṭīkā*), *Madhyāntavibhāgaśāstra* I (*Saṅgrahalakṣaṇa*) 6, and III (*Mūlatattva*) 3 and *passim;*

Vasubandhu and Sthiramati (*bhāṣya*), *Triṃśikā,* stanzas 20-25, pp. 39-42 (S. Lévi ed.) (= pp. 300-339 Thubtan Chogdub Śāstri and R. Tripāṭhī edd.);

Hiuan Tsang (Hsüan tsang, Xuán záng), *Ch' eng wei shih lun, Taishō,* Vol. XXXI, No. 1585, p. 45 c, line 5-p. 48 b, line 5 (= pp. 514-561, L. de la Vallée Poussin, *Siddhi,* French trans.).

Some Modern Authors who Refer to the Trisvabhāva Theory

We indicate also some modern authors in whose works we find references to the three natures' doctrine.

E. Conze and Iida Shotaro, "Maitreya's questions in the *Prajñāpāramita", in Mélanges d'Indianisme ā la Mémoire de Louis Renou*, Paris: E. de Boccard, 1968, pp.229-242 (in E. Conze, *The Large Sūtra of Perfect Wisdom,* Berkeley: University of California Press, 1975, pp. 644-652, there is the English translation of the Sanskrit text edited by Conze and Shotaro); A.K. Chatterjee (1962), *The Yogācāra Idealism,* Delhi: Motilal Banarsidass, 1975, pp. 150-156; L. de la Vallée Poussin, "Philosophy (Buddhist)", in J. Hastings (1917), *Encyclopaedia of Religion and Ethics,* Edinburgh: T. and T. Clark, 1961, Vol. IX, pp. 850-851; L. de la Vallée Poussin, "Madhyamaka", in *Mélanges Chinois et Bouddhiques* II, 1932-1933, pp. 47-54; N. Dutt (1930), *Mahāyāna Buddhism,* Delhi: Motilal Banarsidass, 1977, pp. 281-285; M. Hattori, "Yogācāra", in *The Encyclopedia of Religion,* Mircea Eliade ed., Vol. 15, New York, Mcmillan Publishing Company, 1987, pp. 524, 527; Jay Hirabayashi and Iida Shotaro, "Another Look at the Mādhyamika vs. Yogācāra. Controversy Concerning Existence and Non-existence", in *Prajñāpāramitā and related systems, Studies in Honor of Edward Conze,* edited by L. Lancaster. L.O. Gómez, Berkeley: Berkeley Buddhist Studies Series, 1977, pp.341-360; E.W. Jones, "Buddhist Theories of existents: The Systems of two Truths", in *Mahāyāna Buddhist Meditation: Theory and Practice* edited by Minoru Kiyota,

Honolulu: The University Press of Hawaii, 1978, pp.3-45, specially pp. 29-39; A.B. Keith (1923), *Buddhist Philosophy in India and Ceylon,* Varaṇasi (India): The Chowkhamba Sanskrit Series Office, 1963 (The Chowkhamba Sanskrit Studies Vol. XXVI), pp.242-244; J. Kitayama (1934), *Metaphysik des Buddhismus. Versuch einer philosophischen Interpretation der Lehre Vasubandhus und seiner Schule,* San Francisco, U.S.A.: Chinese Materials Center, Inc., 1976, pp.121-131; Whalen W. Lai, "Nonduality of the Two Truths in Sinitic Mādhyamika: Origin of the "Third Truth"," in *Journal of the International Association of Buddhist Studies,* Vol. 2, 1979, No.2, pp.45-65, specially pp. 59-61; J. Masuda, *Der individualistische Idealismus der Yogācāra-Schule. Versuch einer genetischen Darstellung,* Heidelberg: O. Harrassowitz, 1926 (Materialien zur Kunde des Buddhismus, 10. Heft), pp.40-43; B.K. Matilal, "A critique of Buddhist Idealism", in *Buddhist Studies in Honour of I.B. Horner,* edited by L. Cousins, A. Kunst, and K.R. Norman, Dordrecht, Holland, Boston, U.S.A.: D. Reidel Publ. Co., 1974, pp. 139-169, specially pp.140 and 159; K. Mimaki and J. May, "Chudo", in *Hōbōgirin* V, pp. 467 *b*-470 *a*; Gadjin M. Nagao, "'What remains' in Śūnyatā: a Yogācāra Interpretation of Emptiness", in *Mahāyāna Buddhist Meditation,* already quoted, pp. 66-82, specially pp.71-78; G. Nagao,"The Buddhist World-View as elucidated in the Three-Nature Theory and its Similes", in *The Eastern Buddhist* 16, 1, 1983, pp.1-18; E. Obermiller, "The Doctrine of Prajñāpāramitā as exposed in the Abhisamayālaṃkāra of Maitreya", reprint from *Acta Orientalia* XI, 1932, pp.1-133, specially pp.97-98; Diana Y. Paul, *Philosophy of Mind in Sixth-century China, Paramārtha's 'Evolution of Consciousness',* Stanford (California): Stanford University Press, 1984, *Index under trisvabhāva, paratantra, parikalpita, pariniṣpanna;* L. Schmithausen, *Der Nirvāṇa-Abschnitt in der Viniścayasaṃgrahaṇī del Yogācārabhūmiḥ,* Wien: Österreichische Akademie der Wissenschaften, 1969, pp.106 c and 107 fn. i; Th. Stcherbatsky (1927), *The Conception of Buddhist Nirvāṇa,* London, The Hague, Paris: Mouton & Co. 1965 (Indo- Iranian reprints, VI), pp. 32-34; D.T. Suzuki (1963), *Outlines of Mahayana Buddhism,* New York: Schocken Books, 1973, pp.87-98; D.T. Suzuki (1930), *Studies in the Lankavatara Sutra,* London and Boston: Routledge & Kegan Paul Ltd., 1912, pp.157-163; Shōkō Takeuki, "Phenomena and Reality in Vijñaptimātra Thought. On the Usage of the Suffix 'ta' in Maitreya's Treatises", in *Buddhist Thought and Asian Civilisation. Essays in Honor of Herbert V. Guenther on his Sixtieth Birthday,* edited by L.S. Kawamura and K.

Scott, Emeryville-California: Dharma Publishing, 1977, pp.254-267; J.F. Tillemans, *Materials for the Study of Āryadeva, Dharmapāla and Candrakīrti,* Wien; Universität Wien, 1990, Vol. I, p. 1 fn.2, pp.55 and 116; F. Tola and C. Dragonetti, "La estructura de la mente según la escuela idealista budista (Yogācāra), in *Pensamiento* No.182, Vol. 46, Madrid, 1990, pp. 129-147 (reprinted in *Revista de Estudios Budistas* 4, México-Buenos Aires, 1992, pp.51-73); A.K. Warder, *Indian Buddhism,* Delhi: Motilal Banarsidass, 1970, pp.430-432; Th. E. Wood, *Mind Only, A Philosophical and Doctrinal Analysis of the Vijñānavāda,* Honolulu: University of Hawaii Press, 1991, pp.85-89; Sōgen Yamakami, *Systems of Buddhistic Thought,* Calcutta: University of Calcutta, 1972, pp.244-246; Yoshifumi Ueda, "Two main streams of Thought in Yogācāra Philosophy", in *Philosophy East and West,* 17, 1967, pp.155-165.

Adopted Text

For our translation we have adopted the text of Lévi's manuscript as it is presented by Yamaguchi's edition (1972-1973)[7], excepting some places in which we have followed another reading. In the critical notes we have indicated, in each case, the origin of the adopted reading and the reading whose place it takes. In these notes:

MS1=manuscript found by S. Lévi (as known to us by Yamaguchi's edition)

MS2=Tucci's manuscript (as known to us by Mukhopadhyaya's edition)

MS3=the third manuscript

N=Tibetan translation (3843-5243)

V=Tibetan translation (4058-5559)

Y=Yamaguchi (corrections)

Va=de la Vallée Poussin (corrections)

Mu=Mukhopadyaya (corrections)

corr.=correction

We follow MS1 as we know it through Yamaguchi's edition, whenever the contrary is not indicated. And also whenever the contrary is not indicated, MS2=MS1; Y and Va=MS1; Va=Y; and Mu=MS2; MS3=MS1.

We have divided the text into sections with subtitles. And we have adopted the same procedure in the translation and in our commentary on the text.

DOCTRINARY COMMENTARY OF TRISVABHĀVAKĀRIKĀ

Section I: Kārikās 1-5: The Three Natures

Kārikā 1 indicates that there are three natures, that is to say: three forms of being (*svabhāva*). Whatever exists, in the most comprehensive meaning of the word, falls under one of these three natures. They are: 1.the imaginary (*kalpita*) nature, 2. the dependent (*paratantra*) nature, and 3. the absolute (*pariniṣpanna*) nature. They constitute the object of the sage's knowledge.

The Dependent Nature, the Asatkalpa, the Mind

In *kārikā* 2 the author expresses 1. that the dependent nature is what appears and 2. that it is so called, because it exists depending on causes. Let us begin, for clearness sake, with point 2. The causes, on which the dependent nature "depends" are the *vāsanās,* mentioned in *kārikā* 7.[8]

Any representation, idea, cognition etc., which is produced in the mind, leaves in the "sub-consciousness" [9] (*ālayavijñāna*, term to which we shall refer afterwards) a *vāsanā*[10] It is sufficient for the moment to consider these *vāsanās* as something like a weak reproduction or copy of the representations, ideas, cognitions etc., which left them. These *vāsanās* remain in the "subconsciousness" in a latent, subliminal form, until, under certain conditions, they "reactualize" themselves, they pass into the consciousness, producing new conscious representations etc., similar to those by which the *vāsanās* were left or related to them in some way.

The dependent nature "depends" on these *vāsanās* in the sense that, if there are *vāsanās*, there is dependent nature, if there are no *vāsanās*, there is no dependent nature.

The author in *kārikā* 2 has said firstly that the dependent nature is "that what appears". He asks in *kārikā* 4 : what does appear ? and he answers: the *asatkalpa,*[11] term which we have translated by "unreal mental creation". This term designates the representations, ideas, cognitions etc. to which birth is given by the "reactualization" of the *vāsanās*.[12] These representations etc. are "what appears". The dependent nature is the whole of those representations etc. We must understand the expression "what appears" in two meanings: 1. those representations etc. are the only thing which appears, which manifests itself, i.e. which is known,[13] and 2. the empirical reality, which presents itself before us, is nothing else than those representations etc. There are only representations etc.; apart from them nothing appears, nothing exists, nothing is known.[14] This is the fundamental thesis of the *Yogācāra* school.

The *asatkalpa* (that is to say: the representations etc. under whose form the *vāsanās* reactualize themselves) is, according to ***kārikā*** 5, the mind.[15] Let us remember three facts. In the first place: those representations etc. are essentially of two classes: (1) subjective, of an ego who cognizes *(aham, vijñapti)* and (2) objective, simultaneous with the previous ones, of beings *(sattva)* and things *(artha)* that are known. In the second place: according to Buddhism, the mind has had no beginning, is *anādi*. And in the third place the mind is only a series of *vijñānas*, consciousnesses, cognitions, acts of knowledge. These acts of knowledge constitute the mind; there is no entity different from them. We must discard the substantialist conception of the mind according to which the mind is a permanent entity that knows something different from it. Consequently, the dependent nature or the *asatkalpa* or the mind is only the series of representations etc., some of an ego who knows, others of beings and things, which are produced by the *vāsanās* "reactualization" and which come from a beginningless eternity.[16]

Kārikā 5 explains why the mind is designated with the word *asatkalpa*. The mind, that is the series of representations etc., that are originated by the *vāsanās*, is an unreal mental creation, because of two reasons, indicated by the text:[17] (1) because the image that we have of the mind (*"as it is imagined"*) does not correspond to its true being, since it is conceived as a real ego which grasps an equally real object, although its true nature is (as we shall see later on) the *ab aeterno* inexistence of the subject-object duality; and (2)because the objects of those representations, which present themselves as real and external to the mind ("*as it imagines the object*"), do not exist as such, since they are only imaginations produced by the "reactualization" of the *vāsanās* without any real corresponding object.

To end this section we can indicate that, according to what has been expressed, *"dependent nature", "what appears", "asatkalpa", "mind", "representations, ideas, cognitions etc"*, provoked by the *vāsanās*' "reactualization", and *"vāsanās"* signify all the same thing under different points of view.

The Imaginary Nature

The imaginary nature, it is said in *kārikā* 2, is the form under which the dependent nature manifests itself, appears. And *kārikā* 4 expresses that the *asatkalpa*, which is the dependent nature appears with duality, that is to say: constituted by two elements.

In fact the dependent nature is, as we have said, the whole of the representations etc. originated by the *vāsanās*' "reactualization", the totality of the unreal mental creations which constitute it. Conceived in this way, the dependent nature necessarily presents itself always with duality, i.e. composed by a subject who knows opposed to an object which is known,[18] because this is the essence of all cognoscitive empirical processes, because this is the unavoidable form under which all cognoscitive empirical processes come to being.

And this second nature, according to *kārikā* 2, receives the name of "imaginary", because it is a mere unreal mental creation, since no true reality corresponds to the subject and to the object, which compose it, since they have not a counterpart, real, external to the mind, independent from it.

The Absolute Nature

The word *parinispanna,* used by the original, literally means "developed", "perfect", "real", "existent" (Monier-Williams, *Dict. sub voce*). We have translated it by "absolute" as it is usually translated.

Kārikā 3 indicates what is this third nature: it is the eternal not being so as it appears of that what appears. That which appears is of course the dependent nature, the *asatkalpa*, the mind. As the way in which the dependent nature appears is the subject-object duality, the absolute nature is only the eternal non-existence with duality of the dependent nature.

The same *kārikā* 3 explains why the third nature is called *parinispanna*: it is called so, because of its unalterability. It has always been, it is, and it will always be the same thing, the inexistence of duality. It has not begun, in a certain moment, to be inexistence of duality, and never will it cease to be inexistence of duality; and its relation with the dependent and imaginary natures do not implicate any change in its authentic and proper way of being.

In *kārikā* 4 the author asks what means the not being with duality (*tena*) of the dependent nature (*tasya*), in what consists the eternal non-existence, as it appears, of that nature-eternal non-existence with duality which, according to what has been said, is the definition of the absolute nature. That eternal not being with duality of the dependent nature is the fact that in it (*tatra*), i. e. in the dependent nature, the non-duality is the essence (*dharmatā*), that it has as essence the non-duality, in other words that its true and ultimate essence is the absolute nature which is the inexistence of duality.[19]

So from a beginningless eternity are opposed, on one side, the unreality constituted by the series of mental creations which manifest themselves under the form of duality and, on the other side, the absolute reality, about which it is only said, for the moment, that it is the inexistence of that duality.[20] See commentary of *kārikās* 13 and 25.

Section II: Kārikā 6: The Structure of the Mind[21]

The *kārikā* 6 indicates the two great"parts" of the empirical consciousness or mind, according to its being either cause or effect : the *ālayavijñāna*, receptacle-consciousness and the *pravṛttivijñāna*, function-consciousness.

The word *pravṛtti*, used to designate the second consciousness, means primarily 1. "*moving onwards, advance, progress*", but it also means 2. "*coming forth, appearance, manifestation*", and 3. "*activity, function*". We have translated it by " function" or "functioning", but on dealing with *pravṛtti-vijñāna* (function-consciousness), it is necessary to have always present in mind all the rich range of meanings that the word *pravṛtti* possesses, which are implied in the notion of *pravṛtti-vijñāna*: it is the consciousness as *evolving, manifesting itself, functioning*. The Tibetan versions translate *pravṛtti* by *ḥjug pa* which means: "to go in, to enter; to take place, to exist". The function-consciousness is divided into seven.

Of course we must not think that the consciousness is really divided into two "parts" and one of these into seven. The consciousness, although it is a complex entity, is only *one*. When we speak of its "parts" or "divisions", the only thing that we want to indicate is that it has diverse activities, diverse forms of manifestations, in the empirical reality-empirical reality that is created by the same consciousness when it manifests itself. It is not a real concrete division; it is only a theoretical division, a product of the conceptual analysis.

The Ālayavijñāna

One of the "parts" of the mind, one of its activities or forms of manifestation is the so-called *ālayavijñāna*, because the *vāsanās* are "deposited"[22] in it, until their "reactualization". Of course, we have here only metaphors, because neither the *vāsanās* are something that can be deposited in some place nor the *ālayavijñāna* is really something that can serve as a deposit. We shall try to give an idea of the true nature of the *ālayavijñāna* and of the *vāsanās*.

The Ālayavijñāna as a Series of Subliminal Representations, Ideas, Cognitions etc.

We have said that the consciousness or mind is a series, that comes from a beginningless eternity, of representations, ideas, cognitions, etc. The ālayavijñāna, as a "part" of the mind, shares the same nature; it is also a series, that comes from a beginningless eternity, of representations, etc..[23], but these representations etc. are of a certain type, they have a special characteristic: they are of subliminal nature.[24]

These subliminal representations etc. are psychological or mental facts or processes that are registered in the sub-consciousness without intervention of the consciousness. They are similar to the subliminal perceptions, which take place when one is perceiving something without being aware of it, to the images which are created in the mind on coming out from a swoon or from a state produced by a drug's application, to some states originated by hypnosis, or to some coma states.

The subliminal representations etc. are the vāsanās which "remain" in the ālayavijñāna or better said which constitute it—vāsanās because they are like the weak scent left in a flask by a perfume which evaporates, also called bījas, because they are like the seed from which a new representation etc. sprouts out, and shaktis, because they are the potentialities or virtualities which transform themselves into new actual acts of cognition.

These subliminal representations etc., these vāsanās however weak they may be, leave on their turn new vāsanās that replace them and which immediately become new subliminal representations[25]. In this way the series constituted by the subliminal representations (or what is the same, by the vāsanās) goes on without interruption.

The Ālayavijñāna as Cause

We have said that the dependent nature depends on the vāsanās; we can add now that it depends also on the ālayavijñāna, since this last one is nothing else than the ab aeterno succession of the vāsanās, i.e. of the subliminal representations etc. The ālayavijñāna is in this way the cause of the dependent nature (or in other words: of the mind). Besides that it is also the cause of the pravṛttivijñāna, since the vāsanās, which constitute the ālayavijñāna, through their "reactualization" produce the manifestation of the function- consciousness, that is to say:gives rise to the "conscious" representations, etc., in which the subject clearly knows the object as what it is.

"Reactualization" of the Vāsanās

According to what has been said, the process, to which we have applied metaphorically the words "reactualization of the *vāsanās*", consists in reality in the *conversion* of the subliminal representations etc. which constitute the *ālayavijñāna,* into new conscious representations etc. which constitute the *pravṛttivijñāna*, their *passage* from the subliminal level to the conscious level, the *replacement* of the subliminal manifestation of the *vāsanās* by their conscious manifestation[26].

The Importance of the Ālayavijñāna

The *ālayavijñāna* is most important, not only because of its preponderant function in the dynamics of the mind, since it provides the materials for the representations etc., that constitute the individual, but also because it is a brilliant anticipation of modern theory of the sub-consciousness.

The Pravṛttivijñāna

The *pravṛttivijñāna* is the totality of the conscious representations etc., into which the *vāsanās* are transformed. It has seven forms of manifestation.

The six forms of manifestation are the five types of sensorial cognition (visual etc.), and the mental cognition (*manovijñāna*), whose object are only ideas (*dharma*) in a broad sense. Any cognoscitive act adopts necessarily one of these six forms.

The Manas

The *manas* is the seventh aspect or theoretical part of the mind (*citta).* Of the seven aspects of the mind, it is the most difficult to define and explain.

The *vāsanās,* that are cognoscitive acts,as we have said, belong to the subliminal zone of the consciousness, to the *ālayavijñāna.* In them every element is unconscious(*asaṃvidita)*, undeterminate (*aparicchinna)*, subtle (*atisūkṣma*), weak: the subjective part of the cognition, the subject who has not a full and clear awareness of his condition as such; the objective part of the cognition, the object which is not clearly perceived in a determinate way *(idaṃ tat)* and consequently the cognition itself which is neither clear nor determinate. In a certain moment the *vāsanās* pass into the conscious zone of the consciousness; they are constituted, as before, by a subject who is in front of an object and cognizes it, but now that subject has a full awareness of this confrontation, he knows in a complete and determinate way what the object of his knowledge is, and has also a full awareness of his own cognoscent nature, that he is a subject, an ego which knows; now he is provided with the consciousness of himself, he possesses self-consciousness.

In the moment in which the transformation of the subliminal cognition into conscious cognition takes place, and in which the ego-consciousness, the self-consciousness is produced, the mind receives the name of *manas* or, what means the same thing: Its *manas*-aspect, its *manas*-function comes to being. The *manas* is in other words the self-consciousness, the ego-awareness. Of course this self, this ego is not a real entity, but only an idea, only a perishable element of the equally perishable cognition's act.

Simultaneity of the Indicated Processes

The transformation of the representations, etc. from subliminal into conscious (their passage from the *ālayavijñāna* to the *pravṛttivijñāna*), the arising of the ego-consciousness (*manas)* and the birth of one of the six types of cognition or consciousness (*cakṣur-vijñāna* or visual consciousness, etc.) are not successive; they are totally simultaneous, they take place at the same moment. And besides no one of the different aspects of the mind can exist without the others; they are mutually solidary.

Section III: Kārikā 7: Etymologies of Citta

Kārikā 7 gives two "etymologies" of the word '*citta*', the first one in relation to the *ālayavijñāna*, the second one in relation to the *pravṛttivijñāna*. The *ālayavijñāna is citta* because it is "accumulated" (*cita*), that is to say: full of *vāsanās*, and the *pravṛttivijñāna is citta* because it manifests itself under different (*citra*) forms.

These two etymologies are not valid from the linguistic point of view, but they have an important functional value. This kind of "functional" etymologies serves an author to justify a determined interpretation or doctrine on the basis that the word, which designates a certain phenomenon (in this case: the mind, *citta*), expresses in itself the theory that the author sustains in relation to that phenomenon (in this case: the division of the mind in a part considered as receptacle, where the *vāsanās* are accumulated, and in a part, which manifests itself under the form of diverse mental processes). In the present case of *citta*, the author, to give a basis to his thesis, arbitrarily associates with the word *citta*, that designates the phenomenon that interests him, two other words, *'cita'* and *'citra'*, which on one side present an external (phonetical) similarity with it, and which, on the other side, designate something that he is attributing, according to his theory, to that phenomenon.

This type of etymologies as a means of demonstration was used since the most ancient *Upanishads*.[27]

Of course the etymological explanation based on the apparent relation between *citta* and *cita*, and between *citta and citra* is not maintained in the Tibetan translation.

Section IV: Kārikās 8-9: Three Modes of Being of the Asatkalpa

Kārikā 8 indicates that the *asatkalpa* or unreal mental creation (in other words the dependent nature, the mind), as a whole, is of three modes; has three aspects, three attributes : (1) it is *vaipākika*, produced by "maturation" (*vipāka*), since the *asatkalpa* comes to existence and exists as the "fruit", effect or result of good or bad acts done in previous existences,[28] when the series of these acts is stopped, when, consequently, there is no more the necessity of their moral retribution, the *asatkalpa* ceases to be; (2) it is *naimittika*, produced by causes, since the *asatkalpa* belongs to the realm of causality, by opposition to the absolute nature that is beyond causality, that is *animitta (cf. kārikā* 32)[29] and (3) it is *prātibhāsika*, consisting of representations, because the *asatkalpa* is nothing else than a series of cognition's acts and (as it happens with all the cognition's acts), its essence are the mental representations.

Kārikā 9 expresses that the first (*prathama*) mode corresponds to the *mūlavijñāna (the vijñāna* that is the root or origin), another name for the *ālayavijñāna*, and it expresses also that the other (*anya*) mode, that is to say the third one (as we shall see), corresponds to the *pravṛttivijñāna*.

As regards the second mode or attribute, the *naimittika*, we think that it has not been treated by the author: (1) because the word *prathama*, which is in singular, can refer only to one of the three modes and this mode can only be the *vaipākika,* since this mode is the first in the enumeration of *kārikā* 8 and since *kārikā* 9 gives the reason why to the *mūlavijñāna* corresponds the *vaipākika* mode; and (2) because in the same way the word *anya,* which is also in singular, can refer only to one of the three modes and this mode can only be the *prātibhāsika* mode, since this mode is introduced in *kārikā* 8 by the same word *anya* and since *kārikā* 9 gives the reason why to the *pravṛttivijñāna* corresponds the *prātibhāsika* mode.

Now, in the same way as the *vaipākika* mode corresponds to the *ālayavijñāna* and the third one to the *pravṛttivijñāna,* to which consciousness corresponds the *naimittika* mode? We think that it corresponds to both, to the *ālayavijñāna* and to the *pravṛttivijñāna,* since both have to do with causes, since both constitute the empirical reality and consequently, as we have said, they belong to the conditional realm, being opposed as such to the absolute nature which is beyond causes (*animitta*). Moreover the author in *kārikā* 2 says that the dependent nature, that is the *asatkalpa,* depends on causes, i. e. is *naimittika.*

We do not agree with the idea that the *naimittika* mode must be included either in the word *prathama,* together with the *vaipākika* or in the word *anya,* together with the *prātibhāsika,* and consequently has been implicitly referred to by the author.[30]

Section V: Kārikā 10: "Coincidentia Oppositorum" in the Three Natures

Because the three natures participate (1) of being and non-being, (2) of duality and unity, and (3) because the essence of purity and the essence of impurity are not different, are identical, it is spoken about the difficulty of their being conceived and understood by a non trained mind.[31] It is necessary to relate this characteristic of the three natures with *kārikā* 1, that affirms that the three natures are the object of the sage's knowledge.

The Tibetan translation, which attributes the treatise to Vasubandhu (4058-5559), has *rab dbye bas* (omiting the negation existing in the Sanskrit compound *lakṣaṇa-abhedataś)* while the other Tibetan translation has *dbyer med phyir,* which corresponds to the Sanskrit original.

Kārikās 11-21 develop the ideas expressed in *kārikā* 10.

Section VI: Kārikās 11-13: Being and Non-Being

These *kārikās* explain in which way the three natures have as their characteristic existence and non-existence, i.e. how they participate in being and non-being. The participation in being and non-being of the three natures becomes clear and evident, if it is taken into account what they are, according to what has been explained in *Section* 1 of this commentary.

(1) *Kārikā* 11. The imaginary nature is the unreal mental creation of the subject-object duality. It is erroneously grasped as really existing, but it *exists* only with the illusory, unreal existence of that duality. It exists only as an illusion.
But it *does not exist,* since that duality lacks a true and real existence. It is not a true reality.

(2) *Kārikā* 12. The dependent nature, the *asatkalpa,* the mind, is a mere succession of unreal mental creations to which nothing real and external to the mind corresponds. It *exists* with the existence that is possessed by a succession of unreal mental creations, i.e. with the existence proper of an illusion, with a deceitful existence. It possesses a mental existence. But it *does not exist,* because it is not really so as it appears: as a real subject which grasps a real object. It has not the existence of a true reality.

(3) *Kārikā* 13. The absolute nature, which is (as *kārikā* 25 will say) "the existence of the inexistence of duality", *exists* as the existence of that inexistence. And it *does not exist,* in so far its essence is only an inexistence, the inexistence of duality. See commentary on *kārikā* 25.

The aspect *existence* of the three natures is related to duality, i. e. to the subject-object duality that occurs in the act of cognition. That existence lasts so long as there is the act of cognition and, therefore, the duality it implies. Thus that existence is provisional, transitory, non-permanent, dependent on conditions, liable to disappearance. It is not *true* existence, it is not an existence *in se et per se*. It belongs to the empirical level.

The aspect *non-existence* of the three natures is related to the *cessation of duality* that occurs when the act of cognition ceases and the non-dual nature of reality comes forth. Thus cessation of duality means the disappearace of the imaginary nature and of the dependent nature, and the exclusive remaining of the absolute nature whose essence is precisely the non-existence of duality. Thus affirming being and non-being in relation to the three natures does not imply at all a logical contradiction, since it concerns two different moments or situations.

Section VII: Kārikās 14-16: Duality and Unity

These *kārikās* explain in which way the three natures consist of duality and unity, i.e. participate in duality and unity.

(1) *Kārikā* 14. The imaginary nature is made of *duality,* because of the duality (says the text) of the imagined object. When the object appears in the mind and the cognitive act takes place, there occurs duality: the subject-object duality. It could be said that the object "creates" duality, that it is due to it that duality comes forth. The imaginary nature is made (*ātmaka*) of duality, since it is only the subject-object duality under which form the dependent nature appears. And it is also made of *unity,* because of the unity derived from the inexistence of duality (*tadasattvaikabhāvataḥ*). The imaginary nature is indeed only non-existent duality, (because the subject-object duality is only a mere mental creation without real existence); so it can be said that the imaginary nature is *really* non-duality, that is to say: unity.

(2) *Kārikā* 15. The dependent nature is made of *duality,* because the subject-object duality is its only form of manifestation, of existing in the empirical reality that it creates through its own manifestation. But its essence is also *unity,* because of the unity that derives from the fact that the subject-object duality is only an error, something that does not truly exist (*bhrāntimātraikabhāvataḥ*). When the error is eliminated and the illusion of the duality ceases, there remains only non-duality i.e. unity.

(3) *Kārikā* 16 says that the absolute nature is made of duality (*dvayātmaka*). The dependent nature always appears with duality, it is "made of duality", according to *kārikās* 3 and 4. The absolute nature is the *eternal* non-existence with duality of the dependent nature (the unreal mental creation, the mind), as such the absolute nature is the unalterable essence of the dependent nature, and, whenever it appears, *as* or *in* the empirical reality, it can only appear as the dependent nature, consequently "with duality", "made of duality".

This treatise gives indeed three definitions of the absolute nature in *kārikās* 3, 13 and 25. In *kārikā* 3 the absolute nature is defined as "*the eternal non-existence with duality of the dependent nature*", *kārikā* 13 says that the absolute nature "*exists with non-duality*", and *kārikā* 25 expresses that it is " *the existence of the non-existence of duality*". In these three definitions the notion of duality is always present. If we suppress that notion from these three definitions, *kārikā* 3 would say that the absolute nature is "*the eternal non-existence of the dependent nature*", *kārikā* 13 that the absolute nature "*exists*" and *kārikā* 25 that the absolute nature is "*the existence of non-existence*". Of these three resultant definitions, without the notion of duality, the first one and the third one would be inadmissible, since they constitute the total *apavādavāda*, that the *Yogācāras* attributed to Nāgārjuna's school but that they did not accept; and the second one does not define anything. It is the duality's notion that allows giving for the absolute nature a definition that does not limit itself to affirm either the existence or the inexistence. Thanks also to this notion of duality we can relate in an unique system the absolute nature, as the negation of duality, with the other two natures, that have to do with duality, even if this one is illusory. In this way duality is the element with reference to which it is possible to construct a definition of the absolute nature integrated in a system with the other two natures. Perhaps it is with this idea in mind that the author considered duality as the essence of the absolute nature.

On the other side, the absolute nature is also made of *unity,* because it is *only* inexistence of duality, i.e. unity.

The attribution of duality and unity to the three natures does not imply either any contradiction, because it also refers to two different moments or situations. When they are considered *as* or *in* the empirical reality, they are related in one way or another with *duality,* and the conceptual analysis can distinguish three separate entities, three natures. But, when they all are considered apart from the empirical reality, in their essence, *sub specie aeternitatis,* the imaginary nature and the dependent nature merge into the absolute nature and disappear since they are subordinate to duality that in this case ceases to be, and the absolute nature remains alone in its total and purest unity.

Section VIII: Kārikās 17-21: The Imaginary and the Dependent Natures=Impurity (Duality). The Absolute Nature=Purity (Non-Duality). Identity of the Three Natures

In *kārikā* 17 Vasubandhu only affirms that the imaginary and dependent natures are the essential characteristic or essence of impurity (*saṃkleśa)* and that the absolute nature is the essential characteristic or essence of purity. Impurity means duality; purity, non-duality. The first two natures constitute the realm of duality, of impurity; the third one the realm of non-duality, of purity.

In *kārikās* 18-21 Vasubandhu explains how there is no difference between the realms of impurity and purity, i.e. between the three natures.

(a) The absolute nature is not different from the imaginary nature (*kārikā* 18), because the first one is, by definition, inexistence of duality and the second one is in fact an inexistent duality, i.e. inexistence of duality, although apparently it is the subject-object duality.

At its turn the imaginary nature is not different from the absolute nature (*kārikā* 19), because the first one is in fact inexistence of duality and the second one is by definition non-duality.

(b) The absolute nature is not different from the dependent nature (*kārikā* 20), because the first one is not such as it appears i.e. it is not with duality, (which is the form which the absolute nature adopts in its manifestation as dependent nature), and the second one in fact is not as it appears, i.e. it is not with duality.

At its turn (*kārikā* 21) the dependent nature is not different from the absolute nature, because the first one is not such as it appears i.e. with duality, and the second one is, by definition, inexistent duality.

In conclusion we can say that strictly speaking there is not difference among the three natures. The impurity or duality is only the purity or non-duality wrongly grasped owing to ignorance. When error, i. e. the unreal mental creation of duality, disappears, there remains only what there has really always been: the absolute nature, the non-duality, the purity.[32]

Section IX: Kārikās 22-25: Distinction among the Three Natures

As *kārikā* 22 says, these *kārikās* indicate the distinctive marks of the three natures: 1. from the point of view of the empirical reality (activity or existence or experience), in relation to it, and 2. from the point of view of the understanding of the three natures, in relation to it. The distinctions among the three natures explained in *kārikās* 23 and 24-25 concerns the graduality *(krama)* involved in the processes described in these *kārikās*.

"The growth in knowledge" is of those who will receive and understand the teaching of the Three Natures. The Tibetan translation (4058-5559) attributed to Nāgārjuna has *slob maḥi ched du*: "for the sake of the disciple".

(1) *Kārikā* 23. From the first point of view, the imaginary nature is the *vyavahāra*, the empirical reality divided into a subject that knows and an object that is known. The dependent nature is the *vyavahartṛ*, i. e. the one engaged in or occupied with the *vyavahāra*. It is related to the *vyavahāra* as far as the *vyavahāra*, being the duality, is the form under which the dependent nature appears, and as far as the dependent nature, being the mind, is what produces the unreal imaginations, is what creates the empirical reality. The absolute nature is the destruction of the empirical reality, because when it is known, duality, i.e. the empirical reality, is abolished.

The Tibetan translation attributed to Vasubandhu has (*tha sñad) ḥdogs pa* : is attached to, is joined with, interests itself in (the *vyavahāra*), and the one attributed to Nāgārjuna has (*tha sñad) byed pa (ḥi)* : fabricates, effects, produces (the *vyavahāra*).

(2) *Kārikās* 24-25 refer to the second point of view. In the first stage of the path that leads to truth, one comes to know what the dependent nature really is : absence of the subject-object duality. One obtains the knowledge that there is no real ego, no *ātman*, a permanent and eternal subject of the cognitions' acts—it is the *pudgalanairātmya* conception; one obtains also the knowledge that beings and things, that are perceived, do not really exist—it is the *dharmanairātmya* conception. In a second stage one reaches the knowledge that it is the mind and *only* the *mind* which creates the beings and things that are perceived, that consequently beings and things exist only with the existence of mental creations, are mere illusions. Finally one acquires the knowledge of the absolute nature : if duality, under which form the dependent nature appears, does not exist really, the only "entity" that remains is the inexistence of duality i.e. the absolute nature.

Essential Identity between the Three Natures

In *kārikā* 24 it is said that the imaginary nature is *in* the dependent nature (*tatra*) and in *kārikā* 25 it is said that the absolute nature is also *in* the dependent nature (*atra*). The dependent nature "contains" in this way in itself the other two natures.[33] These *kārikās* repeat in other words the idea already expressed in *kārikās* 17-21, that the three natures are identical, since they have, as a common characteristic, being inexistent duality or inexistence of duality or non-duality.

Definition of the Absolute Nature

In *kārikā* 25 we have also the most complete definition of the absolute nature. See *kārikās* 3 and 13 and their commentary. *Kārikā* 25 defines the absolute nature as: " the existence of the non-existence of duality"[34] and it adds that "it is and it is not". We must understand this last expression as meaning that the absolute nature participates of being, of existence, in so far as in its essence there is the *existence* of the inexistence of duality, and it participates of non-being, non-existence, in so far as in its essence there is *inexistence* of duality.[35]

Section X: Kārikā 26: Common Characteristics of the Three Natures

This *kārikā* indicates two common characteristics of the three natures. The three natures are beyond duality, as it has been explained and consequently cannot *normally, empirically* be known. (1) The imaginary nature, which is posited as the subject-object duality, does not really exist and therefore it cannot be dual, and it cannot be grasped, because what is inexistent cannot be dual and cannot be known. (2) As regards the dependent nature, since it is not as it appears, i.e. as dual, with duality, it is in fact deprived of duality; and it cannot be grasped, since it is not as it appears (which is the only way in which it can be grasped) and consequently, when it is grasped, it is not known as it really is but only as it appears, which is different from its true form of being. (3) The absolute nature is beyond duality because its essence is the inexistence of duality, and it cannot be grasped because, without duality, without the opposition of a subject and an object, there cannot be knowledge, nothing can be known.

Section XI: Kārikās 27-30: Analogy between a Magical Creation and the Three Natures

To make clear the meaning of the three natures and the relation that unites them, Vasubandhu resorts to a comparison of the three natures with the magical creation of the illusion of an elephant. A magician, with the help of his *mantras,* creates a representation, an idea, a cognition in the spectator's mind. This representation etc. created in the spectator's mind is what the text designates with the words *'māyākṛta'* (made by magic, *sgyu ma byas pa* in Tibetan), *'ākāra,' 'ākṛti'* (form, shape, appearance, *rnam, rnam pa* in Tibetan). The *ākāra* that is produced in the spectator's mind has as its contents or object the illusory image of an elephant created by magic. The only thing we have in this case is an *ākāra*, representation, idea of an elephant; that is not a real elephant (*kārikā* 27).

In *kārikās* 28-30 Vasubandhu establishes the relations between the elements of his comparison with the three natures.

(1) The elephant (under or with whose form the magic creation appears in the mind: *hastyātmanā)* corresponds to the imaginary nature, i.e. to the subject-object duality (under or with whose form the dependent nature appears: *dvayātmanā of kārikā* 4). Without the elephant as contents or object of the act of cognition in the spectator's mind, there would be neither cognition nor the opposition subject-object. In the same way without duality, the dependent nature would be unable to manifest itself. Moreover the elephant and the duality are mere imaginary creations without real existence.

(2) What the magic produces, the *ākāra, ākṛti,* the representation, idea or cognition in the mind of the spectator corresponds to the dependent nature, to the mental creation (*vikalpa*) to which nothing real is related.

(3) The eternal inexistence of a real elephant in all this magical process corresponds to the absolute nature, to the *ab aeterno* inexistence of the duality (*kārikā* 28).

(4) The *mantra* corresponds to the *ālayavijñāna or mūlavijñāna* or *mūlacitta*, since by means of the *mantras,* coming from them, the magical illusion is created; and similarly by means of the *ālayavijñāna,* coming from it, the dependent nature; the *asatkalpa*, the mind manifests itself with duality. Of course here we have a reference to the process of the "reactualization" of the *vāsanās* which constitute the *ālayavijñāna*. See *Section B* of our commentary.

(5) The piece of wood, which the magician uses in his magic act (to "transform" it into an elephant or to superimpose on it the image of an elephant) corresponds to the *tathatā* or true reality, which is the absolute inexistence of duality, i.e. the *pariniṣpanna* or the absolute nature: in both cases there is only *one real thing,* the piece of wood in the case of the magical demonstration, the non-duality in the case of the three natures (*kārikās* 29-30).

In the *kārikā* 30 the notion of *tathatā,* "suchness", "the fact of being so" (*de bźin ñid* in Tibetan) is introduced as another designation of the absolute nature.

Section XII: Kārikās 31-34: Knowledge, Elimination, Obtention

Kārikās 31-32 explain what happens when one perceives the true nature of the object, that is to say when one knows that the object of the knowledge lacks a true reality and is only an idea, a mental creation, an hallucination, we can say.

The word *artha (kārikā* 31), that we have translated by "object", refers to any thing that is or can be an object of knowledge, i.e. to the whole empirical reality. The term *yugapad (kārikā* 31) expresses the simultaneity of the three processes indicated in *kārikā* 31, i.e. that they take place *at the same time* (cf. *kārikā* 34) Nevertheless this same *kārikā* points out that these three processes occur in the order in which they are presented (*yathākramam, cf. kārikā* 34), what means that there is a *sequence*. The simultaneity has to do with *time*, is a temporal notion; the order, the sequence has to do with *cause*, is a causal notion. There is no difficulty to accept that the three processes be produced together and notwithstanding have a causal relation among them, as it is asserted by Dignāga in *Ālambanaparīkṣāvṛtti, kārikā* VII and commentary. Cf. in this book *Section J: kārikā VII a-b* and *paragraphs 21-23* of our commentary on Dignāga's work, and the note 10 corresponding to it. The word *kriyā* in the compound *lakṣaṇakriyā* refers to the three processes: *parijñā, prahāṇa* and *prāpti*, that occur *in* the act of grasping the true nature of things (*arthatattva-prativedhe)*. The word *lakṣaṇa* has in *kārikā* 31 the meaning of *svabhāva* (see note 99). The presence in the compound of the word *lakṣaṇa (=svabhāva)* aims at indicating that the three processes are in relation to the three natures, correspond to each of them (as explained in *kārikā* 33).

(1) The process that corresponds to the imaginary nature is that *knowledge (parijñā)* which consists in an *anupalambha*, i.e. in a non-perception, in this case the non-perception of the subject-object duality (*kārikā* 32). As it is known *anupalambha* or *anupalabdhi* is considered by some schools of Indian philosophy as a special means of knowledge, *pramāṇa*, that ascertains the inexistence of something or (what is the same) the existence of the inexistence of that thing. *Anupalambha* or *anupalabdhi* is also called *abhāvapramāṇa, pramāṇāntara*. See Gupta, Brahmananda, "Story of the evolution of the concept of negation", in *Wiener Zeitschrift für die Kunde Süd-und Ostasiens*, Band XII-XIII, 1968/1969, pp. 115-118; Katsura, Shoryu, "Dignāga and Dharmakīrti on *adarśanamātra* and

anupalabdhi", in *Asiatische Studien* XLVI, 1, 1992, pp. 222-231; Randle, H. N., *Indian Logic in the Early Schools*, London: Oxford University Press, 1930, pp. 328 -338; Steinkellner, Ernst, "Bemerkungen zu Īśvarasenas Lehre vom Grund, in *Wiener Zeitschrift für die Kunde Süd-und Ostasiens*, X, 1965, pp. 73-85; Steinkellner, Ernst, "Lamotte and the concept of *anupalabdhi*", in *Asiatische Studien* XLVI, 1, 1992, pp. 398-410; and Steinkellner, Ernst, *Dharmakīrti's Hetubinduḥ*, Teil I, Wien: Österreichische Akademie der Wissenschaften, 1967, fn. V,4.

(2) The process that corresponds to the dependent nature is *elimination (prahāṇa, hāni)*, which is non-manifestation (*akhyāna)*, i. e. the non -manifestation of the dependent nature, the non-functioning of the mind, the stopping of the series of erroneous cognitive processes which constitute it, since it is now deprived of the only form it has to manifest itself : duality (*kārikā* 32).

And (3) the process which corresponds to the absolute nature is *obtention (prāpti)*, which is defined as an *upalambho 'nimittas* and also as a *sākṣātkriyā*. *Upalambho 'nimittas* designates a "perception beyond causes", a perception in which there is no intervention of any of the factors that usually give rise to *normal* knowledge, specially subject and object. *Sākṣātkriyā* means an intuitive knowledge which presents the true reality (the inexistence of duality) *tota et simul*, in its absolute integrity and not in a discursive way but in a simultaneous and punctual act (*kārikā* 32)

Kārikā 33 indicates that the non-perception of duality (imaginary nature) produces *ipso facto* the simultaneous disappearance of the *ākāra*, representation, idea, cognition (of duality) (dependent nature), which has that duality as the necessary condition of manifesting itself, and that with the disappearance of duality there remains only the total inexistence of duality (absolute nature), in the same way (says *kārikā* 34) as in the magic act we have simultaneously: (1) the non-perception of the illusory image of the elephant created by the magician (which corresponds to the imaginary nature), (2) the disappearance of the *ākāra*, representation, idea, cognition of elephant, which has been produced in the spectator 's mind (which corresponds to the dependent nature), and (3) the perception of the piece of wood, the only existing reality which remains after the disappearance of the elephant 's illusion (which corresponds to the absolute nature). Cf. *Section K. Kārikās 27-30* and our commentary thereon.

Section XIII: Kārikās 35-36: Traditional Arguments in Favour of the "Only-Mind" Thesis

To understand *kārikās* 35 and 36 it is necessary to refer to Hiuan Tsang, *Cheng Wei shih lun (Siddhi), Taishō*, Vol. XXXI, No. 1585, p. 39 a lines 8-22 (=pp. 421-423 of the L. de la Vallée Poussin's translation) and to Asaṅga, *Mahāyānasaṃgraha*, Chapter II, paragraph 14 (É. Lamotte's edition and translation including commentary and notes). We have here some of the arguments that were traditionally employed to establish the existence of the only consciousness.[36]

Mind is the cause of contradictory ideas.

According to traditional beliefs it was accepted that the same thing is perceived in a different manner by those damned, by men and by gods: what the damned people see as blood and pus, men see as clear water and gods as nectar.[37] This diversity in the perception of the same thing has its cause in the diversity of the *karmans* of each of these classes of beings. If one admits the existence of different perceptions of the same thing, then it is necessary to admit that there is not a real thing, which is perceived by damned, by men and by gods. If there were a real thing, it had to be perceived by them all in the same way. Blood and pus, water and nectar are mere mental creations, produced according to the *karman* of each of them and they are possible because of the sole existence of consciousness or mind, which is able to produce out of itself, in accordance with *karman*, those diverse creations.

The vision of unreal things

As it happens in dreams, hallucinations, mirages, magical illusions etc., it is possible that the mind functions without an external object, that there are in the mind representations without anything real corresponding to them, giving rise to them.[38]

The conformity (of things) with the three kinds of knowledge

Things manifest themselves to beings according to the kind of knowledge they have obtained in relation to the degree of spiritual development they have reached. These knowledges are of three kinds: (1) the *bodhisattvas* and the *dhyāyins*, who have obtained the power over thinking, transform things at their own will; objects manifest themselves to them according to their wishes; (2) to the *yogins* and to other people of great spiritual development, who have obtained serenity and practise the analysis of the *dharmas* or elements of existence, things manifest themselves at the moment of mind's concentration, with their general characteristics of impermanence, suffering etc; and (3) to wise people, who have obtained the intuitive knowledge, the fundamental wisdom which presents the true nature of things, and can remain established in that intuitive knowledge, things do not manifest themselves anymore to them.[39]

Liberation would occur without effort

If things really exist, they would be known by ignorant people as they really are; it would happen then that the knowledge of ignorant people reaches truth without effort and therefore this knowledge would produce liberation, since it is the true knowledge. Consequently no special training would be necessary to be in possession of the supreme intuitive knowledge, which according to Buddhism is the only one which grasps the true reality of things and in consequence is the only one that is able to produce liberation.[40]

These arguments oblige to accept the "only-mind" thesis, according to which the empirical reality (imaginary nature), which we perceive as something external to us and real, does not really exist; there are only ideas of beings and things, of ego-s and cognition acts,to which nothing real corresponds and under which form the empirical mind (dependent nature) manifests itself; the true essence of mind is non-duality (absolute nature). When it is accepted that only-consciousness exists in the above described manner, then it is known that objects created by that consciousness, do not exist as external and real objects; that there is no place for them in true existence. And with the knowledge that objects do not exist, it is known that the empirical consciousness also does not exist, because in our empirical reality consciousness cannot exist without the support of an object that functions as its contents.

Section XIV: Kārikās 37-38: Dharmadhātu; Vibhutva: Oneself's and Other's Good; The Supreme Enlightenment; The Three Bodies

Through the non-perception of the subject and object of cognition, one gets the perception of the *dharmadhātu*, the ultimate fundament or essence of *dharmas*,[41] of the totality of the empirical reality that is constituted by those *dharmas*. This essence is the non-existence of duality, the absolute nature. *Kārikā* 37 implicitly identifies the absolute nature, i. e. the absence of duality, with the *dharmadhātu*. Cf. *Section K. Kārikās 27-30*, paragraph (5) where the absolute nature is called *tathatā*.

And when the *dharmas'* ultimate essence, when non-duality is grasped, one gets *vibhutva*, sovereignty (*kārikā* 37).[42] By this last word we must understand the possession of several extraordinary powers as those possessed by the *bodhisattva*[43] (*kārikā* 37).

The words *upalambha* and *upalambhatā*, that we have translated by "perception", have been rendered by the Tibetan translators by *dmigs (pa)* and (once) by *dmigs pa ñid*. These Sanskrit words mean:"obtainment", and "perceiving". The term *'apprehension'* could cover those meanings. As to the Sanskrit word *vibhutva*, it means: "being everywhere, omnipresence; omnipotence, sovereignty". The Tibetan translation (4058-5559) renders it by *phun sum tshogs pa*: "perfection, excellence, superior good", evidently with reference to the meaning "excellent" of the Sanskrit word *vibhu*; the other Tibetan translation (3843-5243) renders it by *ḥbyor pa ñid*: "wealth, riches, goods, treasure", evidently with reference to the meaning "abundant, plentiful" which the Sanskrit word *vibhu* also possesses. G.M. Nagao, *An Index to Asaṅga's Mahāyānasaṃgraha*, Part I, Tokyo: The International Institute for Buddhist Studies, 1994, gives for *ḥbyor pa* the values of 1. *samṛddhi* and 2. *saṃpatti*. Cf. in the same Index *dbaṅ ḥbyor pa=vibhutva (kārikā* 37).

And the person who has obtained *vibhutva*, those extraordinary powers, realizes his own good, by the accumulation of merits; and also the good of other beings, who have not progressed as himself, helping them to become free from their passions, to accumulate merits and to get the appropriate personal conditions necessary to be liberated, making them able in this way to progress towards liberation. Then he gets the insuperable enlightenment (*bodhi*), i.e. the buddha's condition.

As a *buddha* he possesses the three bodies[44]: *nirmāṇakāya* i.e. the body or better said the bodies which he can create at his own will to appear in different places in order to teach the Doctrine according to the necessities and personal conditions of each class of beings; *saṃbhogakāya* i.e. the glorious body of excellent attributes which he adopts in order to reign in any of the buddhist heavens, surrounded by *bodhisattvas*, to whom he explains the Doctrine; and *dharmakāya*, the Doctrine body which is nothing else than another name for the Absolute, the non-duality, which is the ultimate essence of beings in its totality, concealed by ignorance and passions and which is revealed by knowledge (*kārikā* 38).

SANSKRIT TEXT

TRISVABHĀVAKĀRIKĀ

trisvabhāvakārikā ācāryavasubandhukṛtā
nevārākṣaralikhitā prācīnatāpatrodgatā
namo mañjunāthāya[45]

[Section I: Kārikās 1-5: The Three Natures]

kalpitaḥ paratantraś ca pariniṣpanna eva ca/
trayaḥ svabhāvā dhīrāṇāṃ[46] *gaṃbhīraṃ jñeyam*[47] *iṣyate //1//*
yat khyāti paratantro' sau yathā khyāti sa kalpitaḥ/
pratyayādhīnavṛttitvāt kalpanāmātrabhāvataḥ //2//
tasya khyātur yathākhyānaṃ yā sadāvidyamānatā[48]*/*
jñeyaḥ sa pariniṣpannaḥ svabhāvo[49] *nanyathātvataḥ //3//*
tatra kiṃ khyāty asatkalpaḥ[50] *kathaṃ khyāti dvayātmanā*[51]*/*
tasya kā nāstitā tena yā tatrādvayadharmatā[52] *//4//*
asatkalpo' tra[53] *kaś cittaṃ yatas tat kalpyate yathā*[54]*/*
yathā ca kalpayaty arthaṃ tathātyantaṃ na vidyate //5//

[Section II: Kārikā 6: The Structure of the Mind]

tad dhetuphalabhāvena cittaṃ dvividham iṣyate/
yad ālayākhyavijñānaṃ[55] *pravṛttyākhyaṃ*[56] *ca saptadhā //6//*

[Section III: Kārikā 7: Etymologies of Citta]

saṃkleśavāsanābījaiś citatvāc cittam ucyate/
cittam ādyaṃ dvitīyaṃ tu citrākārapravṛttitaḥ[57] *//7//*

[Section IV: Kārikās 8-9: Three Modes of Being of the Asatkalpa]

samāsato' bhūtakalpaḥ sa caiṣa trividho mataḥ/
vaipākikas tathā naimittiko' nyaḥ prātibhāsikaḥ //8//
prathamo mūlavijñānaṃ tad vipākātmakaṃ yataḥ[58]*/*
anyaḥ pravṛttivijñānaṃ[59] *dṛśyadṛgvittivṛttitaḥ //9//*

[Section V: Kārikā 10: "Coincidentia Oppositorum" in the Three Natures]

sadasattvād[60] *dvayaikatvāt saṃklesavyavadānayoḥ/*
lakṣaṇābhedataś[61] *ceṣṭā svabhāvānāṃ*[62] *gabhīratā //10//*

[Section VI: Kārikās 11-13: Being and Non-Being]

sattvena[63] gṛhyate[64] yasmād[65] atyantābhāva eva ca/
svabhāvaḥ kalpitas tena sadasallakṣaṇo mataḥ //11//
vidyate bhrāntibhāvena yathākhyanaṃ[66] na vidyate/
paratantro yatas tena sadasallakṣaṇo mataḥ //12//
advayatvena[67] yac cāsti dvayasyābhāva eva ca/
svabhāvas tena niṣpannaḥ sadasallakṣaṇo mataḥ //13//

[Section VII: Kārikās 14-16: Duality and Unity]

dvaividhyāt kalpitārthasya tadasattvaikabhāvataḥ[68]/
svabhāvaḥ kalpito bālair dvayaikatvātmako mataḥ//14//
prakhyānād dvayabhāvena[69] bhrāntimātraikabhāvataḥ /
svabhāvaḥ paratantrākhyo dvayaikatvātmako mataḥ //15//
dvayabhāvasvabhāvatvād[70] advayaikasvabhāvataḥ[71]/
svabhāvaḥ pariniṣpanno dvayaikatvātmako mataḥ //16 //

[Section VIII: Kārikās 17-21: The Imaginary and the Dependent Natures=Impurity (Duality). The Absolute Nature=Purity (Non-Duality). Identity of the Three Natures]

kalpitaḥ paratantraś ca jñeyaṃ samkleśalakṣaṇam[72]/
pariniṣpanna iṣṭas tu vyavadānasya lakṣaṇam[73]//17//
asaddvayasvabhāvatvāt tadabhāvasvabhāvataḥ/
svabhāvāt kalpitāj[74] jñeyo niṣpanno' bhinnalakṣaṇaḥ//18//
advayatvasvabhāvatvād dvayābhāvasvabhāvataḥ/
niṣpannāt kalpitaś caiva vijñeyo'bhinnalakṣaṇaḥ //19 //
yathākhyānam asadbhāvāt tathāsattvasvabhāvataḥ[75]/
svabhāvāt paratantrākhyān[76] niṣpanno' bhinnalakṣaṇaḥ[77] //20//
asaddvayasvabhāvatvād yathākhyānāsvabhāvataḥ /
niṣpannāt paratantro'pi[78] vijñeyo' bhinnalakṣaṇaḥ//21//

[Section IX: Kārikās 22-25: Distinction among the Three Natures]

kramabhedaḥ svabhāvānāṃ vyavahārādhikārataḥ /
tatpraveśādhikārāc ca vyutpattyarthaṃ[79] vidhīyate//22//
kalpito vyavahārātmā vyāvahartrātmako[80] paraḥ /
vyavahārasamucchedaḥ svabhāvaś[81] cānya iṣyate//23//
dvayābhāvātmakaḥ[82] pūrvaṃ[83] paratantraḥ praviśyate/
tataḥ praviśyate tatra kalpamātram asaddvayam[84]/24//
ato dvayābhāvabhāvo niṣpanno' tra[85] praviśyate/
tathā hyasau eva[86] tadā[87] asti nāstīti cocyate //25//

[Section X: Kārikā 26: Common Characteristics of the Three Natures]

trayo 'pyete[88] svabhāvā hi advayālabhyalakṣaṇāḥ[89] /
abhāvād atathābhāvāt tadabhāvasvabhāvataḥ //26//

[Section XI: Kārikās 27-30: Analogy between a Magical Creation and the Three Natures]

māyākṛtaṃ mantravaśāt khyāti hastyātmanā yathā /
ākāramātraṃ[90] tatrāsti hastī nāsti tu sarvathā[91] //27//
svabhāvaḥ kalpito hastī paratantras tadākṛtiḥ /
yas tatra hastyabhāvo' sau pariniṣpanna iṣyate //28//
asatkalpas tathā khyāti mūlacittād dvayātmanā /
dvayam atyantato nāsti tatrāsty ākṛtimātrakam[92] //29//
mantravan mūlavijñānaṃ kāṣṭhavat tathatā matā /
hastyākāravad eṣṭavyo vikalpo hastivad dvayam[93] //30//

[Section XII: Kārikās 31-34: Knowledge, Elimination, Obtention]

arthatattvaprativedhe[94] yugapal lakṣaṇakriyā[95] /
parijñā ca prahāṇaṃ[96] ca prāptiś ceṣṭā yathākramam[97] //31//
parijñānupalambho' tra[98] hānir akhyānam iṣyate/
upalambho'nimittas tu[99] prāptiḥ sākṣātkriyāpi sā//32//
dvayasyānupalambhena dvayākāro vigacchati/
vigamāt tasya niṣpanno dvayābhāvo' dhigamyate[100] //33//
hastino' nupalambhaś[101] ca vigamaś ca tadākṛteḥ[102] /
upalambhaś ca kāṣṭhasya māyāyāṃ yugapad yathā[103] //34//

[Section XIII: Kārikās 35-36: Traditional Arguments in Favour of the "Only-Mind" Thesis]

viruddhadhīkāraṇatvād[104] buddher[105] vaiyarthyadarśanāt/
jñānatrayānuvṛtteś ca mokṣāpatter[106] ayatnataḥ //35//
cittamātropalambhena jñeyārthānupalambhatā/
jñeyārthānupalambhena syāc cittānupalambhatā // 36//

[Section XIV: Kārikās 37-38: Dharmadhātu; Vibhutva: Oneself's and Other's Good; the Supreme Enlightenment; the Three Bodies]

dvayor anupalambhena dharmadhātūpalambhatā[107] /
dharmadhātūpalambhena[108] syād vibhutvopalambhatā //37//
upalabdhavibhutvaś ca svaparārthaprasiddhitaḥ[109] /
prāpnoty anuttarāṃ[110] bodhiṃ[111] dhīmān
kāyatrayātmikām[112] //38//

iti trisvabhāvaḥ[113] samāptaḥ kṛtir
ācāryavasubandhupādānām iti

TRANSLATION

KĀRIKĀS ON THE THREE NATURES

The *kārikās* on the three natures composed by Master Vasubandhu, written in Newāri characters, coming from an old manuscript.

Homage to Mañjunātha

Section I : Kārikās 1-5 : The Three Natures

1. *It is admitted that the three natures,*
the imaginary, the dependent and the absolute,
are the profound object
of the knowledge of the wise men.

2. *What appears is the dependent (nature);*
as it appears is the imaginary (nature);
(the first one being so called,)
because it exists subordinate to causes,
(the second one being so called,)
because its existence is only a mental creation.

3. *The eternal non-existence as it appears*
of what appears
must be known as the absolute nature,
because of its unalterability.

4. *And what does appear? The unreal mental creation.*
How does it appear? With duality.[114]
What is the non-existence with this (duality)
of that (dependent nature) ?
It is the fact that the essence (of the dependent nature)
is the non-duality in it.

5. *And what is the unreal mental creation ?*
The mind,
because as it is imagined
and as it imagines its object,
so it is not at all.

Section II: Kārikā 6: The Structure of the Mind

6. *It is admitted that mind is twofold,*
according to its being either cause or effect :
the consciousness that is called ālaya *(receptacle)*
and the (consciousness that is) called pravṛtti *(functioning)*
which (at its turn) is sevenfold.

Section III: Kārikā 7: Etymologies of Citta

7. *The first mind is called* 'citta' *(mind),*
because it is cita *(lit. accumulated=filled)*
by the seeds, i. e. the vāsanās, *of the impurities;*[115]
and the second one (is called 'citta', *mind),*
because of its functioning under citra *(diverse) forms.*

Section IV: Kārikās 8-9: Three Modes of Being of the Asatkalpa

8. *And this unreal mental creation,*
in a summary manner,
is considered to have three modes :
vaipākika *(produced by maturation),*
and also naimittika *(produced by causes);*
the other one is prātibhāsika *(consisting of representations).*

9. *The first (mode or aspect) is the root-consciousness,*
because its essence is maturation;
the other one is the functioning-consciousness,
because it exists
as object, subject and knowledge.

Section V: Kārikā 10: "Coincidentia Oppositorum" in the Three Natures

10. *It is admitted the profoundness of the (three) natures,*
because they are being and non-being,
because they are duality and unity,
and because of the identity of essence
of both purity and impurity.

Section VI: Kārikās 11-13, Being and Non-Being

11. *Since the imaginary nature*
is grasped with existence,
but it is only total non-existence,
therefore it is considered
as something whose essence[116] *is*
being and non-being.

12. *Since the dependent (nature)*
exists with the existence of an illusion,
(but) does not exist as it appears,
therefore it is considered
as something whose essence is
being and non-being.

13. *Since the absolute nature*
exists with non-duality,
but it is only non-existence of duality,
therefore it is considered
as something whose essence is
being and non -being.

Section VII: Kārikās 14-16: Duality and Unity

14. *The nature imagined by ignorants*[117]
is considered as something
consisting of duality and unity;
(duality) because of the twofoldness
of the imagined object,
(unity) because of its being one
due to the non-existence of that (duality).

15. *The nature that is called 'dependent'*
is considered as something
consisting of duality and unity;
(duality) because it appears
with the existence of duality,
(unity) because its being one
due to (duality being) a mere illusion.

16. *The absolute nature*
is considered as something
consisting of duality and unity;
(duality) because it is the (true) nature[118] *of duality,*
(unity) because its only nature is non-duality.

Section VIII: Kārikās 17-21:The Imaginary and the Dependent Natures=Impurity (Duality). The Absolute Nature=Purity (Non-Duality). Identity of the Three Natures

17. *It must be known that the imaginary (nature)*
and the dependent (nature)
are the essence[119] *of impurity;*
it is admitted that the absolute (nature)
is the essence of purity.

18. *It must be known that the absolute (nature)*
is not different[120] *from the imaginary nature,*
because the nature (of the last one)
is the inexistent duality;
because the nature (of the first one)
is the inexistence of that (duality).

19. *And it must be known that the imaginary (nature)*
is not different from the absolute (nature),
because the nature (of the last one)
is non-duality;
because the nature (of the first one)
is the inexistence of duality.

20. *The absolute (nature) is not different*
from the nature that is called 'dependent',
because of (the last one)
being non-existent as it appears;
because the nature (of the first one)
is not being so (as it manifests itself).

21. *And it must be known that the dependent (nature)*
is not different from the absolute (nature),
because the nature (of the last one)
is the inexistent duality;
because the nature (of the first one)
is not as it appears.[121]

Section IX: Kārikās 22-25: Distinction among the Three Natures

22. *The distinction, concerning graduality,*
among the (three) natures
is established in relation to the empirical reality
and in relation to their comprehension[122]
for the purpose of growth (in knowledge).

23. *It is admitted that the imaginary (nature)*
is the empirical reality [123]*;*
the following one (the dependent nature,)
is the creator[124] *of the empirical reality;*
and the other nature (the absolute,)
is the destruction of the empirical reality.

24. *At first, the dependent (nature),*
constituted by the non-existence of duality,

is comprehended;
then what is only imagination,
(which is found) there,
(and which is) inexistent duality,
is comprehended.

25. *Then the absolute (nature),*
(which is found) there,
and which is the existence
of the inexistence of duality,
is comprehended;
and so therefore it is said
that only it (= the absolute nature),
in that moment, "is and is not".

Section X : Kārikā 26: Common Characteristics of the Three Natures

26. *The three natures are also*
non dual and ungraspable,[125]
(the imaginary one),
because of its inexistence;
(the dependent one),
because it does not exist as (it appears),
(the absolute one),
because its nature is
the inexistence of that (duality).

Section XI : Kārikās 27-30 : Analogy between a Magical Creation and the Three Natures

27. *In the same way as a magic creation,*
due to the mantras *'power,*
appears as an elephant:
there is only a form there,
but a (real) elephant does not exist at all-

28. *The elephant is the imaginary nature,*
its form is the dependent (nature),
and the elephant's inexistence,
which is there,
is considered to be the absolute (nature)-

29. *In the same way the unreal mental creation,*
due to the root-mind,
appears with duality:

duality does not exist in any way,
there exists something that is only a form.

30. *The root-consciousness is like the mantra;*
the reality is considered as the log;
the mental creation is to be considered
as the elephant's form;
the duality is like the elephant.

Section XII: Kārikās 31-34: *Knowledge, Elimination, Obtention*

31. *It is admitted*
that in the (act of) intellectual penetration[126]
of the (true) reality of objects
(three) processes, corresponding to each nature,[127]
(take place), simultaneously, in their order:
knowledge, elimination and obtention.

32. *In relation to those (three processes)*
it is admitted that knowledge is non-perception,
elimination is non-manifestation,
and obtention is perception beyond causes -
assuredly it is intuitive perception.

33. *Through non-perception of duality,*
the form of duality disappears;
with its disappearance
the absolute inexistence of duality is obtained.

34. *in the same way as in the magical illusion*
there occur simultaneously
the non-perception of the elephant,
the disappearance of its form,
and the perception of the log.

Section XIII: Kārikās 35-36: *Traditional Arguments in Favour of the "Only-Mind" Thesis*

35-36 [128] *Through the perception of "only-mind"-*
because (mind) is the cause of contradictory ideas,
because of the intellect's vision of unrealities,
because of the conformity with the three knowledges,
and because of the production without effort of liberation-
there is the non-perception of the knowable object;
through the non-perception of the knowable object,
there is the non-perception of mind.[129]

Section XIV: Kārikās 37-38: Dharmadhātu; Vibhutva; Onself 's and Other's Good; the Supreme Enlightenment; the Three Bodies

37. *Through the non-perception of both,*
there is the perception of the fundament of the dharmas;
through the perception of the fundament of the dharmas
there is the obtention of sovereignty.

38. *And who has obtained sovereignty,*
through the realization
of his own good and the other's good,
reaches, wise, the Supreme Enlightenment
whose essence are the Three Bodies.

End of the *Trisvabhāva,* work of the Venerable Master Vasubandhu

NOTES FOR THE THIRD PART

1. Cf. Yamaguchi's and Nagao's Introductions to their editions and/or translations, and also L. de la Vallée Poussin, "Le petit traité", p.147.
2. See *infra* the bibliographical information about the publications mentioned in this section.
3. This title appears in the introduction of the Tibetan translation; the title of this text according to the colophon at the end of the translation (*Sde-dge* edition) is: *Mtshan ñid gsum la ḥjug pa*.
4. The Tibetan translations of this treatise are to be found of course in the different editions of the *Bstan-ḥgyur* and also in the quoted articles of Yamaguchi, de la Vallée Poussin, Mukhopadhyaya, and also in E. Teramoto's edition of the *Triṃśikā* of Vasubandhu, Kyōto 1933, Tokyo 1977. Teramoto adds a Japanese translation of both works of Vasubandhu.
5. *Abhidharmadīpa*, p. 282 (P. S. Jaini ed.) has a reference to the *trisvabhāva* theory in relation to Vasubandhu, the *kośakāra*, which perhaps may be used as an argument in favour of Vasubandhu's authorship of the present treatise. Cf. *ibidem*, p. 128 of the Introduction.
6. Cf. L. de la Vallée Poussin, *La Siddhi de Hiuan Tsang*, p. 514, note b, and É. Lamotte, *La Somme du Grand Véhicule (Mahāyānasaṃgraha), Notes et Références*, p. 17 *, Chapitre II,1.
7. We have adopted Yamaguchi's edition of 1972-1973, because it corrects misprints and mistakes of his former edition 1931, is more complete and offers the last opinion of Yamaguchi on this text.
8. Cf. Asaṅga, *Mahāyānasaṃgraha* II, 15, 1: gal te rnam par rig pa tsam don snaṅ baḥi gnas gźan gyi dbaṅ gi ṅo bo ñid yin na/ de ji ltar na gźan gyi dbaṅ yin la/ciḥi phyir na gźan gyi dbaṅ

źes bya źe na/raṅ gi bag chags kyi sa bon las skyes pa yin pas de lta bas na rkyen gyi gźan dbaṅ yin//skyes nas kyaṅ skad cig las lhag par bdag ñid gnas par mi nus pas na gźan gyi dbaṅ źes byaḥo/ (*"If the dependent nature* [paratantrasvabhāva] *is only mind* [vijnaptimātra], *support of the manifestation of the object* [arthābhāsāśraya], *why is it dependent, and why is it called 'dependent'?—Because it is born* [utpanna] *out of its own impregnations—seeds* [vāsanābīja], *it is dependent on conditions. Because after its birth, it is unable to subsist by itself* [svataḥ] *a single instant, it is called 'dependent'"* —from Lamotte's translation), and II, 17: gaṅ gis gźan gyi dbaṅ gi ṅo bo ñid la gźan gyi dbaṅ źes bya baḥi rnam graṅs gaṅ źe na / gźan gyi dbaṅ gi bag chags kyi sa bon las ḥbyuṅ baḥi gźan gyi dbaṅ gi phyir ro/ (*"In which sense the dependent nature is 'dependent'?—In so far as it depends on something else for being born: the impregnations—seeds* [vāsanābīja]" —from Lamotte's translation).

9. Cf.L. Grinspoon and J.B. Bakalar, *Psychedelic drugs reconsidered*, New York: Basic Books, Inc., Publishers, 1979, p. 146: "*But in any case they* (=experiences with LSD drug) *suggest how much of what we have felt and thought is registered permanently in the brain and accessible to consciousness in various transmutations*".
10. On the *vāsanās'* theory see Hiuan Tsang, *Cheng wei shih lun, Taishō*, Vol. XXXI, No. 1585, p. 8 a line 5-p. 10 a line 11 (= pp. 100-123 L.de la Vallée Poussin's translation); Asaṅga, *Mahāyānasaṃgraha*, Chapter I (Lamotte's edition and translation), and moreover J. Masuda, *Der individualistische Idealismus*, pp. 35-39; P.S. Jaini, "The Sautrāntika Theory of *Bīja"; Bulletin of the School of Oriental and African Studies* 22, (1959), pp. 236-249; D.T. Suzuki, *Studies in the Lankavatara-sutra*, pp. 178-179, 184. See also in this book Dignāga's *Ālambanaparīkṣāvṛtti, Section J: Kārikā VII a-b and paragraphs 21-23*, the text and our commentary.
11. It is also called, in this same treatise, *'abhūtakalpa' (kārikā* 8) and *'vikalpa' (kārikā* 30). In other texts it is also called '*abhūtaparikalpa*' like in Asaṅga, *Mahāyānasūtrālaṃkāra*, commentary *ad* XI, 15: tathābhūtaparikalpaḥ paratantraḥ svabhāvo veditavyaḥ ("*Thus it must be known that the unreal mental creation* [abhūtaparikalpa] *is the dependent nature*").

12. Cf. Vasubandhu, *Bhāṣya of the Madhyāntavibhāga ad* I,2, p.9, line13 (Pandeya's - edition): tatrā' bhūtaparikalpo grāhyagrāhakavikalpaḥ (*"The unreal mental creation is the imagination* [vikalpa] *of the object* [grāhya] *and the subject* [grāhaka] "); Sthiramati, *Ṭīkā ad locum*, p.11, penultimate line—p.12, lines 1-2 (Pandeya's edition): kaḥ punar asau (= abhūtaparikalpaḥ)?... viśeṣeṇa tu grāhyagrāhakavikalpaḥ/tatra grāhyavikalpo' rthasattvapratibhāsaṃ vijñānam/grāhakavikalpa ātmavijñaptipratibhāsam (*"What is this* [=abhūtaparikalpa=unreal mental creation] *?... but in a peculiar sense it is the imagination of the object and the subject. There the imagination of the object is the consciousness* [vijñāna] *appearing under the form of things and beings; the imagination of the subject is* [the consciousness] *appearing under the form of a self* [ātman] *and of knowledge* [vijñāpti] *"); Vasubandhu, *Triṃśikā* 21: paratantrasvabhāvas tu vikalpaḥ pratyayodbhavaḥ ("*But the dependent nature is the imagination arisen out of conditions* [pratyaya] "); and Sthiramati, *Bhāṣya ad locum*: atra vikalpa iti paratantrasvarūpam āha ("*There he calls the dependent nature* [paratantrasvarūpa=paratantrasvabhāva] *'imagination'* [vikalpa] *").
13. In other terms the only thing that comes to existence in the empirical (unreal) domain.
14. The *Ālambanaparīkṣā* of Dignāga explains very clearly in which way knowledge arises by the sole mechanism of the "re-actualization" of the *vāsanās*, although there is no external object of the cognition's act. See in this book the *Ālambanaparīkṣāvṛtti* of Dignāga.
15. Cf. Sthiramati, *Ṭīkā ad Madhyāntavibhāga* I, 2, p. 11, the last two lines (Pandeya's edition): kaḥ punar asau (= abhūtaparikalpaḥ)? atītānāgatavartamānā hetuphalabhūtās traidhātukā anādikalikā nirvāṇaparyavasānāḥ saṃsārānurūpāś cittacaittā aviśeṣeṇā-bhūtaparikalpaḥ ("*What is this* [abhūtaparikalpa=unreal mental creation]*? In a peculiar sense the unreal mental creation is the mind* [citta] *and the mental contents* [caitta] *past, future and present, being cause or effect, related to the three realms, beginningless in time, whose termination* [paryavasāna] *is nirvāṇa, following the form* [anurūpa] *of saṃsāra"*).
16. Cf. F. Tola and C. Dragonetti, "*Anāditva* or beginninglessness

in Indian Philosophy," *Annals of the Bhandarkar Oriental Research Institute,* 1980, Vol. LXI, Parts I-IV, pp. 1-20.

17. Cf. Sthiramati, *Ṭikā ad Madhyāntavibhāga* 1, 2, P.11, lines 31-33 (Pandeya's edition): abhūtavacanena ca yathā' yaṃ parikalpyate grāhyagrāhakatvena tathā nāstīti pradarśayati/ parikalpavacanena tv artho yathā parikalpyate tathārtho na vidyata iti pradarśayati ("*He shows with the word 'unreal'* [abhūta] *that as it* [=citta=the mind] *is imagined with the nature of object and subject, so it is not; and he shows with the word 'mental creation'* [parikalpa] *that as the object is imagined, so the object does not exist*").
18. Cf. Vasubandhu, *Bhāṣya* of the *Madhyāntavibhāga ad* I, 2, p. 9, line 13 (Pandeya's edition): tatrā 'bhūtaparikalpo grāhyagrāhakavikalpaḥ/dvayaṃ grāhyaṃ grāhakaṃ ca ("*There the unreal mental creation is the imagination of the object and the subject; object and subject are 'two'* [=duality]").
19. Cf. Sthiramati, *Ṭikā* of the *Madhyāntavibhāga ad* I, 6, p. 19, lines 20-22 (Pandeya's edition): sa (=abhūtaparikalpaḥ) eva grāhyagrāhakarūpeṇa svātmany avidyamānena prakhyānāt parikalpitaḥ/sa eva grāhyagrāhakarahitatvāt pariniṣpannaḥ ("*It* [=abhūtaparikalpa= the unreal mental creation] *is imaginary because of its appearing under the form of object and subject,* [form] *which does not exist in it; and it is absolute because of its being devoid of object and subject*"). Also Asaṅga, *Mahāyānasūtrālaṃkāra* commentary *ad* XI, 13: satataṃ dvayena rahitaṃ tattvaṃ parikalpitaḥ svabhāvo grāhyagrāhakalakṣaṇenātyantam asattvāt ("*The Reality* [tattva], *always devoid of duality, is imaginary nature, because of its non being at all provided with the marks of object and subject*").
20. Cf. F. Tola and C. Dragonetti, "*Anāditva* or beginninglessness in Indian Philosophy", pp. 1-2.
21. On the structure of the mind or consciousness according to the *Yogācāra* school see specially Hiuan Tsang, *Cheng wei shih lun, Taishō,* Vol. XXXI, No. 1585, p. 7 c line 12-p. 38 c line 13 (= pp. 94-415 L. de la Vallée Poussin's translation); Asaṅga, *Mahāyānasaṃgraha,* Chapter I (É. Lamotte's edition and translation); Maitreya-Vasubandhu-Sthiramati, *Madhyāntavibhāgaśāstra* I, 10; Vasubandhu, *Karmasiddhiprakaraṇa,*

Paragraphs 33-40 (É. Lamotte's edition and translation). Moreover see L. de la Vallée Poussin, "Note sur l' Ālayavijñāna", *Mélanges Chinois et Bouddhiques* 3, (1934), pp. 145-168; D. T. Suzuki, *Studies in the Lankavatara-sutra*, pp. 169-199; D.T. Suzuki, *Outlines of Mahayana Buddhism*, pp. 125-139; P. Masson-Oursel, "Tathāgatagarbha et Ālayavijñāna" *Journal Asiatique* 210, (1927), (*Mélanges*), pp. 295-302; E. Frauwallner, "Amalavijñānam und Ālayavijñānam.Ein Beitrag zur Erkenntnislehre des Buddhismus", *Festschrift Walther Schubring, Beiträge zur indischen Philologie und Altertumskunde*, Hamburg, 1951, pp. 148-159 (=*Kleine Schriften*, Wiesbaden : F. Steiner, 1982, pp. 637-648); J. Masuda, *Der individualistische Idealismus*, pp. 27-29; Yamakami Sōgen, *Systems of Buddhistic Thought*, pp. 210-216 and 236-244; A.K. Chatterjee, *The Yogācāra Idealism*, pp. 87-107; *Hōbōgirin* I, pp. 35-37 *sub Araya;* É. Lamotte, *Mahāyānasaṃgraha*, Tome II, *Notes et Références*, Chapitre 1, p. 3 *; S. Weinstein, "The Ālaya-vijñāna in Early Yogācāra Buddhism—A Comparison of Its Meaning in the Saṃdhinirmocana-sūtra and the Vijñapti-mātratā-siddhi of Dharmapāla—", *Kokusai Tōhō Gakusha Kaigikiyō*, 3, (1958), pp. 46-58; F. Tola and C. Dragonetti, " La estructura de la mente según la escuela idealista budista (Yogāchāra)", in *Pensamiento*, No. 182, Vol. 46 (Madrid, 1990), pp. 129 -147, reprint in *Revista de Estudios Budistas* 4, México-Buenos Aires, 1992, pp. 51-74.

22. Etymologies of *ālayavijñāna* in Sthiramati, commentary on the *Triṃśikā* 2; Vasubandhu, *Karmasiddhiprakaraṇa*, Paragraph 33 (É. Lamotte's edition and translation); Asaṅga, *Mahāyānasaṃgraha* 1, 2 and 3; Hiuan Tsang, *Cheng wei shih lun, Taishō*, Vol. XXXI, No. 1585, p. 7 c line 21 (= p. 96 L. de la Vallée Poussin's translation).

23. This is confirmed by the texts quoted in the next note, and by the fact that several *caittas* (*sparśa, manaskāra, vedanā, saṃjñā, cetanā*) accompany the *ālayavijñāna*, according to Vasubandhu, *Triṃśikā* 3 and Sthiramati, *Bhāṣya ad locum;* and also to Hiuan Tsang, *Cheng wei shih lun, Taishō*, Vol. XXXI, No. 1585, p. 11 b line 13-p. 12 *a* line 19 (= pp. 143-151 L. de la Vallée Poussin's translation). Sthiramati, *Bhāṣya ad Triṃśikā* 2 (in the beginning), giving the meaning of *ālayavijñāna*, says that it is *vijñāna* because it knows: vijānātīti vijñānam; and

Vasubandhu, *Triṃśikā* 4, explicitly says that the *ālavavijñāna "flows like the current of a river"* (tacca vartate srotasaughavat) ; cf. Sthiramati, *Bhāṣya ad locum* and Hiuan Tsang, *Cheng wei shih lun, Taishō,* Vol. XXXI, No. 1585, p. 12 b line 28-p. 12 c line 15 (= pp. 156-157 L. de la Vallée Poussin's translation).

24. Cf. Sthiramati, *Bhāṣya* of the *Triṃśikā* 2: yadi pravṛttivijñānavyatiriktam ālayavijñānam asti, tato 'syālambanam ākāraś ca vaktavyaḥ/na hi nirālambanaṃ nirākāraṃ vā vijñānaṃ yujyate/naiva tat nirālambanaṃ nirākāraṃ veṣyate/kiṃ tarhi? aparicchinnālambanākāram/kiṃ kāraṇam? yasmād ālayavijñānaṃ dvidhā pravartate/adhyātman upādānavijñaptitaḥ, bahirdhā' paricchinnākārabhājanavijñaptitaś ca/tatrādhyātman upādānaṃ parikalpitasvabhāvābhiniveśavāsanā sādhiṣṭhānam indriyarūpaṃ nāma ca/asyālambanasyātisukṣmatvāt *asaṃviditakopādisthānavijñaptikaṃ ca tat* /asaṃviditaka upādir yasmin asaṃviditakā ca sthānavijñaptir yasmin tad ālayavijñānam asaṃviditakopādisthānavijñaptikam/upādānam upādiḥ/sa punar ātmādivikalpavāsanā rūpādidharmavikalpavāsanā ca/ tatsadbhāvād ālayavijnānena ātmādivikalpo rūpādivikalpaś ca kāryatvenopātta iti tadvāsanā ātmādivikalpānāṃ rūpādivikalpānāṃ copādir ity ucyate/so 'smin idaṃ tad iti pratisaṃvedanākareṇāsaṃvidita ity atas tad asaṃvidītakopādīty ucyate/āśrayopādānaṃ copādiḥ/āśraya ātmabhāvaḥ sādhiṣṭhānam indriyarūpaṃ nāma ca/... tat punar upādānam idantayā pratisaṃvedayitum aśakyam ity ato' saṃvidita ity ucyate / sthānavijñaptir bhājanalokasaṃniveśavijñaptiḥ / sā' py aparicchinnālambanākārapravṛttatvād asaṃviditety ucyate (*"If the receptacle-consciousness* [ālayavijñāna] *is different from the function-consciousness, then it is necessary to point out its object* [ālambana] *and its form* [ākāra], *since it is not logically possible a consciousness without object or without form. It is not claimed* [by the Vijñānavādin] *that it is without object or without form. How then ? Its object and its form are undeterminate* [aparicchinna]. *Why ? Because the receptacle - consciousness evolves* [pravartate] *in two manners : inwards as knowledge of what is seized - and - held* [upādāna], *outwards as knowledge of the world of objects* [bhājana] *under an undeterminate form. There, inwards, 'what is seized -and-held'* [upādāna] *are the impregnations* [vāsanās] *of the attachment to the imaginary nature, the* rūpa *constituted by*

the sense organs [indriya, the physic component of man] *together with their abode* [adhiṣṭhāna, the body], *and the nāman* [name, the psychic component of man]. *Because of the extreme subtleness of its object* [Vasubandhu says :]
'that [=the ālayavijñāna] *is something in which there is an "unconscious"* [i.e. subliminal] *upādi and an* ["unconscious", subliminal] *knowledge of the locus* [sthāna].'
... *Upādāna* [means] *upādi. And this* [upādi=upādāna] *are the impregnations of the imagination of a self, etc., and the impregnations of the imagination of the* dharmas *form-colour, etc. Due to the existence of these* [impregnations], *the imagination of a self, etc., and the imagination of the form-colour, etc. are seized-and-held* [upātta] *as effects* [, in their state of effects,] *by the receptacle-consciousness; and consequently the impregnations of these* [imaginations] *are called the* 'upādi' *of the imagination of a self, etc., of the imagination of the form-colour, etc. It* [=the upādi] *in that* [receptacle-consciousness] *is "not-conscious"* [ly perceived] *under the form of an experience of the kind: 'This is that'; and consequently that* [receptacle-consciousness] *is called* [something] *in which there is an "unconscious"* [subliminal,] upādi'. *The* upādāna *[= what is seized-and-held] support* [āśraya] *is also* upādi. *The support is the* ātmabhāva [living body, individual], *the* rūpa *constituted by the sense organs together with their abode, and the* nāman... *And this* upādāna *cannot be consciously* [or clearly] *experienced as 'being that'* [i.e. in a determinate manner], *and consequently* [this upādi] *is called* ' *"unconscious"* [, subliminal]'. *'Knowledge of the locus' is the knowledge of the situation in the world of the objects. Also this* [knowledge] *is called' "unconscious"* [,subliminal,]', *because it takes place with an object and a form which are undeterminate."*). In this text the word *upādāna* and its synonym *upādi* have been translated by us with the words "what is seized and held". It could also be translated by "appropriation", but designating not the act of appropriating (seizing, holding, taking) something, but the *things* that are appropriated (seized, held, taken). This notion of *upādāna*, "appropriation", referred to in the text as the object of the subliminal cognition, is to be related to the notion of *ādāna-vijñāna*, "appropriating-consciousness", term which is applied

to the *ālaya-vijñāna*. In relation to this point, see *Saṃdhinirmocanasūtra,* Chapter Five, in Dharma Publishing edition of the Tibetan text, translated by John Powers, Berkeley, USA, 1994, pp. 68-71 :...daṅ por ḥdi ltar len pa rnam pa gñis po rten daṅ bcas paḥi dbaṅ po gzugs can len pa daṅ/mtshan ma daṅ miṅ daṅ rnam par rtog pa la tha sñad ḥdogs paḥi spros paḥi bag chags len pa la rten nas/sa bon thams cad paḥi sems rnam par smin ciṅ ḥjug la rgyas śiṅ ḥphrel ba daṅ yaṅs par ḥgyur ro/de la gzugs can gyi khams na ni len pa gñi ga yod la/gzugs can ma yin paḥi khams na ni len pa gñis su med do/ blo gros yaṅs pa rnam par śes pa de ni len paḥi rnam par śes pa źes kyaṅ bya ste/ḥdi ltar des lus ḥdi bzuṅ źiṅ blaṅs paḥi phyir ro/kun gźi rnam par śes pa źes kyaṅ bya ste/ḥdi ltar de lus ḥdi la grub pa daṅ bde ba gcig paḥi don gyis kun tu sbyor ba daṅ rab tu sbyor bar byed paḥi phyir ro /... (*"Initially, in dependence upon two types of appropriation-the appropriation of the physical sense powers associated with a support and the appropriations of predispositions which proliferate conventional designations with respect to signs, names, and concepts—the mind which has all seeds ripens; it develops, increases, and expands in its operations. Although two types of appropriation exist in the form realm, appropriation is not twofold in the formless realm.*

"Viśalamati, consciousness is also called the 'appropriating consciousness' because it holds and appropriates the body in that way. It is called the 'basis-consciousness' because there is the same establishment and abiding within those bodies. Thus they are wholly connected and thoroughly connected").

Also Vasubandhu, *Karmasiddhiprakaraṇa*, Paragraph 36: ḥo na deḥi dmigs pa daṇ/rnam pa ci yin zhe na/*dmigs pa daṅ/ rnam pa ma chad pa yin no* (" *Which is the object* [ālambana] *and the aspect* [ākāra] *of this knowledge? Its object and its aspect are imperceptible* [asaṃvidita]."—from Lamotte's translation). Also Hiuan Tsang, *Cheng wei shih lun, Taishō*, Vol. XXXI, No. 1585, p. 11 b lines 3-9=pp. 141-142 L. de la Vallée Poussin's translation (*"The ākāra (i.e. the darśanabhāga, the Vijñapti or act of knowledge) of the eighth Vijñāna is extremely subtle (aṇusūkṣma), therefore difficult to perceive.— Or the eighth Vijñāna is called asaṃvidita, because its internal object (the Bījas and the sense-organs that the eighth seizes-holds) is extremely subtle, because its external object (the receptacle-world), in its 'magnitude' is unfathomable."*—from de la Vallée Poussin's translation). Cf.L. de la Vallée Poussin, "Note sur l' Ālayavijñāna"; and A.K. Chatterjee, *The Yogācāra Idealism*, p. 89.

25. This is deduced from the nature (of being mental facts) and from the characteristics of the *vāsanās or bījas* (they are momentary; simultaneous with their fruits; they proceed in a continuous way; they are determinate; they depend on conditions and they produce their own fruit). Cf. the Chinese translation by Hiuan Tsang of the *Bhāṣya* of Asaṅga's *Mahāyānasaṃgraha, Taishō*, Vol. XXXI, No. 1597, p. 329 c lines 11-12, where it is said that *"the* bījas *of the* ālayavijñāna *produce only* ālayavijñāna".

26. According to this last explanation it is necessary to complete what we said before—that the *asatkalpa* or mind is composed by the representations etc. produced by the "reactualization" of the *vāsanās;* we must add now that the *asatkalpa* or mind is also composed by the subliminal representations etc., that constitute the *ālayavijñāna,* which is a part of the mind.

27. See J.Gonda, "The etymologies in the ancient Indian Brāhmanas", *Lingua,* Amsterdam, 1955 -1956, Vol. V, pp. 61-85.

28. In relation to this meaning of *'vaipākika'* cf. Hiuan Tsang, *Cheng wei shih lun, Taishō,* Vol. XXXI, No. 1585, p. 7 c lines 24-26=p. 97 L. de la Vallée Poussin's translation: (*It* [=the ālayavijñāna] *is the vipākaphala, the 'fruit of retribution' of good and bad actions, which project (āKṢIP-) an existence in a certain realm of existence, in a certain destiny, by a certain matrix (dhātu, gati, yoni)"* —from de la Vallée Poussin's translation); Sthiramati, *Bhāṣya ad Triṃśikā* 2, (ālayākhyaṃ vijñānam): sarvadhātugatiyonijātiṣu kuśalākuśalakarmavipākatvād vipākaḥ ([The consciousness called 'receptacle', 'ālaya':] *is maturation* [vipāka] *because of being the maturation of the good and bad actions in any realm* [dhātu], *destiny* [gati], *matrix* [yoni], *form of existence* [jāti]"). Besides that we can also understand that *ālayavijñāna* is *vaipākika* because the *vāsanās,* as germs (*bīja)* "remain" in it until they "mature" to transform themselves into new actual

representations or cognitions. So the *ālayavijñāna* is both the result of the necessity of a moral retribution and the means to realize that retribution.

29. In Śaṅkara's *Bhāṣya ad Vedāntasūtra* II, 2, 28; *Upadeśasahasrī* II, 2, 45, 46, 47, and 73 (S. Mayeda's edition, Tokyo: The Hokuseido Press, 1973) *naimittika* is employed with the meaning of "contingent", as opposed to "own being" (*svabhāva*); in Sureśvara, *Saṃbandhavārtika* 66 it is employed with the meaning of "caused" as opposed to *nimitta* "cause". We can also understand *naimittika* as "related to marks", "provided with marks". In this case, in *kārikā* 32 we must translate *animitta* by "deprived of marks". With this interpretation there remains anyhow the opposition between the *asatkalpa*, that, as a whole, is characterized by individualizing marks or distinctive signs or attributes, and the absolute nature, that is completely deprived of such.
30. This idea inspires the translations and interpretations of some translators.
31. "Trained mind" is the mind which has fulfilled the moral, intellectual and yogic discipline taught by the *Yogācāra* school and Buddhism in general, and thanks to which it is possible to get the intuition of the true nature of things.
32. Cf. texts quoted in note 19.
33. Cf. Sthiramati, *Ṭīkā* of Maitreya's *Madhyāntavibhāga ad* I, 6, p. 19 line 22 (Pandeya's edition): evañ cābhūtaparikalpa eva hetupratyayapāratantryāt paratantraḥ/sa eva grāhyagrāhakarūpeṇa svātmany avidyamānena prakhyānāt parikalpitaḥ/sa eva grāhyagrāhakarahitatvād pariniṣpannaḥ/ evam abhhūtaparikalpe trayaḥ svabhāvāḥ saṅgṛhītāḥ (*"Thus the unreal mental creation is dependent, because its being dependent on causes and conditions; it is imagined, because of its appearing under the form of object and subject that do not exist in it; it is absolute, because of its being deprived of object and subject. So the three natures are gathered in the unreal mental creation"*).
34. Cf. Maitreya, *Madhyāntavibhāga* I, 14: dvayā 'bhāvo hy abhāvasya bhāvaḥ śūnyasya lakṣaṇam (*"The inexistence of duality, the existence of inexistence, is the essence of Void"*); Vasubandhu *ad locum*: dvayagrāhyagrāhakasyā' bhāvaḥ/ tasya cābhāvasya bhāvaḥ śūnyatāyā lakṣaṇam... (*"The inexistence of*

both the object and the subject, and the existence of this inexistence is the essence of Voidness..."); Sthiramati *ad locum:* dvayasya grāhyasya grāhakasya cā 'bhūtaparikalpe' bhūtaparikalpena vā parikalpitātmakatvād vasturūpeṇa' bhāvaḥ/ tasya ca dvayābhāvasya yo bhāva etac chūnyatāyā lakṣaṇam (*"The inexistence of both the object and the subject with the condition of a thing* [occurs] *owing to the fact that their essence is imagined in the unreal mental creation or by the unreal mental creation; and the existence of the inexistence of duality is the essence of Voidness"*).

35. Cf. Sthiramati, *Ṭīkā* of Maitreya's *Madhyāntavibhāga ad* III, 3, last paragraph: pariniṣpannalakṣaṇaṃ sadasattattvataś ceti/ sadasac ca tattvaṃ pariniṣpannalakṣaṇam/dvayā' bhāvabhāvātmakatvāt sattvam /dvayā' bhāvātmakatvād asattvañ ca ("*'And the essence of the absolute* [nature] *is its being existent and non-existent'-the being existent and non-existent is the essence of the absolute* [nature] : *existence, because its essence is the existence of the inexistence of duality; and inexistence, because its essence is the inexistence of duality.*")

36. See other arguments in favour of the "only-mind" thesis in Dignāga, *Ālambanaparīkṣā,* who develops a strictly logical demonstration; Vasubandhu, *Viṃśatikā* and *Triṃśikā*; Hiuan Tsang, *Cheng wei shih lun, Taishō,* Vol. XXXI, No. 1585, p. 39 a line 4-p. 39 c line 29 (= pp. 419-432 L. de la Vallée Poussin's translation); Asaṅga,*Mahāyānasaṃgraha,* Chapter II, Paragraphs 7 -8 (É. Lamotte's edition and translation). Also A.K. Chatterjee, *The Yogācāra Idealism,* Chapters III and IV; D.T. Suzuki, *Studies in the Lankavatara Sutra,* pp. 267-276.

37. Cf. Sthiramati, *Tīkā* of Maitreya's *Madhyāntavibhāga ad* I, 4, p. 16 lines 14-16 (R. Pandeya's edition): tathāhi pretā apaḥ pūyapurīṣamūtrādipurṇā dhṛtadaṇḍapāṇibhir ubhayataḥ puruṣaiḥ saṃrakṣyamāṇāḥ paśyanti/manuṣyādayaḥ punaḥ svacchaśitalodakaparipūrṇā nirvibandhā ity upalabhante (*"Thus the pretas see the waters full of pus, excrement, urines, etc., watched over on both sides by men carrying sticks in their hands, on their turn men, etc., perceive [these same waters] full of pure and fresh water and free"*).

38. Vasubandhu, in his *Viṃśatikā* develops this argument.

39. This argument is based in the experiences and phenomena which take place during yogic concentration.

40. See in Sthiramati, *Ṭīkā* of Maitreya's *Madhyāntavibhāga ad* 1, 2, p. 11 line 10 (R. Pandeya's edition) another example of *prasaṅga* of liberation without effort (aprayatnena mokṣaprasaṅgaḥ).
41. Factors of existence, elements that constitute what exists. See F. Tola and C. Dragonetti, "La doctrina de los *dharmas* en el Budismo", *Boletin de la Asociación Española de Orientalistas,* Año XIII-1977, Madrid, pp. 105 -132 (= pp. 91-121 F. Tola and C. Dragonetti, *Yoga y Mística de la India,* Buenos Aires: Kier, 1978).
42. We think that *kārikā* 37 refers to the condition of *Bodhisattva* and the next one to the condition of *Buddha.* Cf. H. Dayal (1932), *The Bodhisattva doctrine in Buddhist Sanskrit Literature,* Delhi: Motilal Banarsidass, 1975; L. de la Vallée Poussin, "Bodhisattva", J. Hastings, *Encyclopaedia of Religion and Ethics,* Vol.II, Edinburgh: T. & T. Clark, 1964, pp. 739-753; D.T. Suzuki, *Outlines of Mahayana Buddhism,* Chapters XI and XII; "Bosatsu", *Hōbōgirin* II, pp. 136-142.
43. Like the powers mentioned e.g. by Asaṅga, *Mahāyāna-sūtrālaṃkāra* IX, 38-48, and *Mahāyānasaṃgraha* X, 5 and the Chinese translation of the *Bhāṣya* of this last text (done by Hiuan Tsang), *Taishō,* Vol. XXXI, No. 1597, p. 371 c line 23-p. 372 a line 21; and by *Upanibandhana, Taishō,* Vol. XXXI, No. 1598, p. 437 c line 18-p. 438 a line 26.
44. On the three bodies of Buddha see: D.T. Suzuki, *Outlines of Mahayana Buddhism,* Chapter X; *Studies in the Lankavatara Sutra,* pp. 308-338; P. Demiéville, "Busshin", *Hōbōgirin,* pp. 174 b-185 a; L. de la Vallée Poussin, "Note sur les Corps du Boddha", *Le Muséon,* 1913, pp. 257-290; P. Masson-Oursel, "Les trois corps du Bouddha", *Journal Asiatique,* 1913, pp. 581-618; Chizen Akanuma, "The triple body of the Buddha", *The Eastern Buddhist,* May-June, July-August, 1922, pp. 1-29; N.N. Dutt, *Mahāyāna Buddhism,* Chapter V.
45. MS2: *Trisvabhāvaḥ namo Mañjunāthāya;* Mu corr.: *trisvabhāvaḥ* unto *trisvabhāvanirdeśaḥ*; MS3: before *namo* illegible.
46. MS3: *dhīrāṇāṅ* .
47. MS2: *gambhīrajñeyam;* MS3: *gambhīraṃ jñeyam.*
48. MS2: *sadā 'vidyamānatā;* MS3: *sadā 'vidyamānatā* (?)
49. MS2: *parinispannasvabhāvo.*
50. *asatkalpaḥ*: Va corr.; MS1: *asaṅkalpaḥ*; MS2: *asatkalpaḥ;* MS3: *asatkalpaḥ.*

51. *dvayātmanā*: Va, Y 1972-1973 corr. (N: *gñis dag gis)*; MS1: *dvayātmatā;* MS2*: dvayātmanā;* MS3*: dvayātmanā.*
52. MS2: *tatrā 'dvayadharmatā;* MS3: *tatrā 'dvayadharmmatā.*
53. MS2: *asaṃkalpo 'tra;* Mu corr.*: asatkalpo' tra.*
54. MS2: *yatas taṃ kalpyate yathā;* Mu corr.*: yatas tena hi kalpyate.*
55. MS2: *ālayākhyaṃ vijñānaṃ;* MS3: *ālayākhyaṃ vijñānaṃ.*
56. MS2*: pravṛttyākhyañ;* MS3: *pravṛttyākhyañ.*
57. MS3: simple *daṇḍa.*
58. *yataḥ:* Va, Y 1972-1973 corr. (N: *gaṅ phyir*); MS1: *mataḥ*; MS2: *yataḥ;* MS3: *yataḥ.*
59. MS3: *°vijñānan.*
60. MS2: *medasattvād*; Mu corr.: *sadasattvād;* MS3: *sadasatvād*
61. MS1: has *lakṣaṇa°* according to Y 1931 and probably to Y 1972-1973 (critical annotation); Y corrects: *lakṣaṇā°*; MS2: *lakṣaṇā°;* MS3: *lakṣaṇā°.*
62. MS3*: svabhāvānāṅ.*
63. MS3: *satvena.*
64. MS1: has *rūte* (instead of *gṛhyate)* according to Y 1931, which Y and Va correct unto *gṛhyate,* but according to Y 1972-1973 MS1 has *gṛhyate;* MS2: *śaṃbṛte (śaṃbṛto?)*; Mu corr. : *gṛhyate;* MS3: *gṛhyate.*
65. MS1 has *yasmād* according to Y 1931, which he corrects unto *yat tad,* but according to Y 1972-1973 MS1 has *yat tad,* which he adopts: Va following the indication of Y 1931 adopts *yasmād* (N: *gaṅ phyir*); MS2*: yasmād;* MS3*: yasmād.*
66. MS3: *°naṃ* manuscript blurred.
67. MS3: between *a°* and *°tvena* manuscript broken.
68. *tadasattvaikabhāvataḥ*: Va corr. (N: *de yod ma yin*); MS1: *sadasattvaika°*; MS2: *sadasattvaika°*; Mu corr.: *tadasattvaika°*; MS3: *sadasatvaika°.*
69. MS2: *prakhyānadvayabhāvena;* Mu corr.*: prakhyānād dvaya°.*
70. Mu corr.*: dvayābhāva°.*
71. *advayaikasvabhāvataḥ:* Va corr. (V: *gñis su med par gcig gyur pas*); MS1: *advayaikatvabhāvataḥ;* MS2: *advayaikasvabhāvataḥ*; MS3: *advayaikatvabhāvataḥ.*
72. MS3: *°lakṣaṇaṃ.*
73. MS3: *°lakṣaṇaṃ.*
74. *kalpitāj*: Va corr.; MS1: *kalpito*; MS2: *kalpitāj*; MS3: *kalpitāj.*
75. MS2: *tathā 'sattva°;* MS3: *tathā 'satva°.*
76. *paratantrākhyān*: Va corr.; MS1: *paratantrākhyo*; MS2: *paratantrākhyān;* MS3: *paratantrākhyān.*

77. *niṣpanno' bhinnalakṣaṇaḥ*: Y, Va corr.; MS1: *niṣpannobhinna°*; MS2: *niṣpanno' bhinna°*; MS3: *niṣpannobhinnalakṣaṇaḥ*.
78. MS3: *pi* without preceding *avagraha*.
79. MS3: *°patyartham*.
80. MS2: *vyavaharttātmako*; Mu corr.: *vyavaharttrātmako*.
81. *vyavahārasamucchedaḥ svabhāvaś*: Va corr.; MS1 and MS2: *vyavahārasamucchedasvabhāvaś*; MS3 *vyavahārasamucchedasvabhāvaś*
82. *dvayābhāvātmakaḥ*: Va corr. (N: *gñis med bdag ñid*; V: *gñis po bdag med*); MS1 and MS2: *dvayabhāvātmakaḥ*; Mu corr. : *dvayā°*; MS3: *dvayabhāvātmakaḥ*.
83. MS3: *pūrvvaṃ*.
84. MS3: *°dvayaṃ*.
85. MS3: *tra* without preceding *avagraha*.
86. MS3: between *as°* and *tadā* manuscript blurred.
87. MS2: *tathā*; Mu corr.: *tadā*.
88. MS3: *py* without preceding *avagraha*.
89. MS2: *advayālambalakṣaṇāḥ*; MS3: *advayālambya°*.
90. MS3: *°mātran*.
91. MS3: *sarvvathā*.
92. MS3: *mātrakaṃ*.
93. MS3: *dvayaṃ*.
94. MS3: *°tatva°*.
95. Va corr.: *lakṣaṇatraye* (N : *mtshan ñid gsum la*; V. *mtshan ñid gsum*); Mu corr.: *°trayam*; MS3: *°kriyā*.
96. *prahāṇaṃ*: Va corr.; MS1: *prahāṇaś*; MS2 : *prahāṇañ*; MS3 : *prahāṇaś*.
97. MS3: *yathākramaṃ*.
98. MS2: *parijñā' nupalambho' tra*; MS3: *parijñā' nupalambho'* tra.
99. MS1 has *upalambho 'nipnagnas tu* according to Y 1931, which he corrects unto *upalambho' saddvayas tu* and Va unto *upalambho' nimittas tu* (following and correcting N : *dmigs pa dag ni mtshan ma ste)*, but according to Y 1972-1973 MS1 has *upalambho' saddvayas tu*; MS2: *upalambho nimagnas tu*; Mu corr.: *upalambhanimittā tu*; MS3: *upalambho nimagnas tu*.
100. MS3: *dhigamyate* without preceding *avagraha*.
101. *hastino' nupalambhaś*: Y, Va corr.; MS1: *hastinonupalambhaś*; MS2: *hastino' nupalambhaś*; MS3: *hastinonupalambhaś*.
102. *tadākṛteḥ*: Va, Y 1972-1973 corr.; MS1: *tadākṛtaḥ*; Y 1931 corr.: *tadākṛtiḥ*; MS2: *tadākṛteḥ*; MS3: *tadākṛteḥ*.

103. *yugapad yathā*: Va, Y 1972-1973 corr. (N: *dus gcig*); MS1: *gāyed yathā;* Y 1931 corr.: (*mār) gāyed yathā*; MS2 : *gāyad yathā;* Mu corr.: *yugapad yathā;* MS3: between *māyāyāṃ* and °*gapad* manuscript destroyed.
104. MS2: *viruddhadhīkāraṇatvād;* Mu corr. *viruddhadhīvāraṇatvād.*
105. *buddher.* Va, Y 1972-1973 corr.; MS1: *buddhair;* MS2 : *buddher;* Mu corr. : *buddhyā;* MS3: *buddher.*
106. MS2: *mokṣāpattir.*
107. MS3: °*dharmma*°.
108. MS3: °*dharmma*°.
109. °*prasiddhitaḥ*: Va corr.; MS1: °*prasiddhataḥ*; MS2 : °*prasiddhitaḥ*; MS3: °*prasiddhitaḥ*.
110. MS3: *anuttarām.*
111. MS3: *bodhin.*
112. MS3 *iti* at the end of the *kārikā.*
113. MS2: *Trisvabhāvaḥ*; Mu corr.: *Trisvabhāvanirdeśaḥ*; MS3: *Trisvabhāvasamāptaḥ* (without preceding *iti*).
114. *dvayātmanā*: instrumental of quality or attribute. Cf. Pāṇini II, 3, 21: *itthaṃbhūtalakṣaṇe (tṛtīyā)*. In the next *kārikās* there are others examples of this type of instrumental: *kārikā 4: tena; kārikā 11: sattvena; kārikā 12: bhrāntibhāvena; kārikā 13: advayatvena,* etc.
115. Cf. *kārikā* 17.
116. *lakṣaṇa*: characteristic mark, essential characteristic, essence.
117. This *kārikā* refers to the imaginary nature. Any one who, ignorant or wise, belongs to the empirical reality creates through his mind an illusory world of duality. The ignorant man attributes to that world externality and reality. The wise man, who knows the true nature of things, knows that the world is a mere mental creation.
118. Remark that the word *svabhāva* is used three times in this *kārikā*: it designates, on one side, the three natures and, on the other side, it indicates the nature, the way of being, the essence (of these three natures).
119. See note 123.
120. *abhinnalakṣaṇa*: lit. "whose *lakṣaṇa* is not different", "which possesses non-different characteristics".
121. *yathākhyānāsvabhāvataḥ:* lit, "because of its being a non (existing) nature as it appears".
122. *praveśa*: lit. "penetration", in the methaphorical meaning of "understanding", "comprehending ". Cf. Vasubandhu, *Viṃśatikā* 10.

123. *vyavahārātmā*: lit. "*ātman* of the *vyavahāra*". We prefer to understand that "the *kalpita* is the *ātman* of the *vyavahāra*" instead of: "the *kalpita* has as its *ātman* the *vyavahāra*", considering that in *kārikā* 17 it is said that the *kalpita* and the *paratantra* are the *lakṣaṇa* of the *saṃkleśa,* which is nothing else than the *vyavahāra*. But at bottom both translations point to the same idea: the identity of *kalpita* and *vyavahāra*. *Vyavahāra,* the empirical, practical or pragmatic reality is the totality of the unreal mental conceptions, expressed or not in conventional verbal formulations, to which nothing real corresponds, and which have duality as its essence. As such it is opposed to the absolute.

124. *vyavahartṛ,* is the conceiver of the unreal mental conceptions, the formulator of the conventional verbal formulations that constitute the *vyavahāra*. So we can translate this term by "creator of the empirical reality", without forgetting that the empirical reality has not a true existence and thinking that the empirical reality is "created" when the *vyavahartṛ,* the mind, conceives its unreal conceptions and formulates its conventional formulations.

125. *advayālabhyalakṣaṇaḥ*: lit. "whose *lakṣaṇa* is non-dual and un-obtainable (i.e. that cannot be perceived or known)".

126. *prativedha* : " (intellectual) penetration". (F. Edgerton, *Buddhist Hybrid Sanskrit,* Volume II: *Dictionary,* New Haven: Yale University Press, 1953).

127. *lakṣaṇa: svabhāva*. Cf. L. de la Vallée Poussin, translation of the *Siddhi,* p. 514 (a); *Mahāvyutpatti* 1662-1665; Asaṅga, *Mahāyānasaṃgraha* II, Paragraphs 1-4 (É. Lamotte's edition and translation).

128. We have united the translation of *kārikās* 35 and 36 to make clear their meaning.

129. *buddhi,* in the text synonym of *citta*.

REFERENCES*

Abhidharmadīpa, ed. P.S. Jaini , Patna: Tibetan Sanskrit Work Series, 1977.

Abhidharma-Samuccaya of Asaṅga , ed . P. Pradhan , Santiniketan: Visva-Bharati, 1950.

Abhidharmasamuccaya-bhāṣyam, deciphered and edited by Nathmal Tatia, Patna: K.P. Jayaswal Research Institute, 1976.

Advayavajrasaṃgraha, edited with an Introduction by M.H. Shastri, Baroda: Oriental Institute, 1927 (Gaekwad's Oriental Series No. XL).

Anaker S., *Seven Works of Vasubandhu, The Buddhist Psychological Doctor*, Delhi: Motilal Banarsidass, 1984.

Anonymous, "The effects of Marijuana on Consciousness", in Tart, Ch. T., *Altered states of consciousness.*

Anuruddha, *Abhidhammatha Saṅgaha*, PTS edition.

Asaṅga, *Mahāyānasūtrālaṃkāra, Exposé de la Doctrine du Grand Véhicule selon le Systẹme Yogācāra,* Edité et traduit d´après un manuscrit rapporté du Népal par S. Lévi, *Tome I.-Texte*, Paris: L. H. Champion, 1907.

Asaṅga, *Mahāyāna-Sūtrālaṃkāra, Exposé de la Doctrine du Grand Véhicule selon le Systẽme Yogācāra,* édité et traduit d´après un manuscript rapporté du Népal par S.Lévi, Tome I. Texte, Paris: Honoré Champion, 1907, *Tome II. Traduction*, Paris: Honoré Champion, 1911 (Bibliothèque de l´École des Hautes Études. Sciences Philologiques et Historiques, Fasc. 159, 190). Reprinted in Tōkyō: oRinsen Sanskrit Text Series, 1983.

Asaṅga, *Bodhisattvabhūmi (Being the XVth Section of Asaṅgapada's Yogācārabhūmi)*, edited by N. Dutt, Vol. VII, Patna: K. P. Jayaswal Research Institute , 1966 (Tibetan Sanskrit Works Series Vol. VII).

Asaṅga, *Bodhisattvabhūmi. A Statement of Whole Course of the Bodhisattva (Being Fifteenth Section of Yogācārabhūmi)*, edited by U. Wogihara, Tokyo. Japan: Sankibo Buddhist Store, 1971 (first edition, Tōkyō, 1930).

---

* These References do not contain the editions and translations of the three treatises included in this book neither of the other works attributed to Dignāga and Vasubandhu, bandhu, because they are mentioned in the respective Introductions.

Asaṅga, *Mahāyānasaṃgraha* =É. Lamotte (1938-1939), *La Somme du Grand Véhicule d' Asaṅga,* Tome I , *Versions Tibétaine et Chinoise (Hiuan Tsang)* , Louvain-la- neuve: Université de Louvain - Institut Orientaliste, 1973 (Publications de l 'Institut Orientaliste de Louvain, 8), Tome II, *Traduction et Commentaire,* Louvain -la -neuve: Université de Louvain-Institut Orientaliste, 1973 (Publications de l' Institut Orientaliste de Louvain, 8).

Bagchi, P. Ch., *Le Canon Bouddhique en Chine. Les traducteurs et les traductions* IIe, Paris: P. Geuthner, 1938.

Bandurski, F., "Übersicht über die Göttinger Sammlungen der von Rāhula Sāṅkṛtyāyana in Tibet aufgefundenen buddhistischen Sanskrit-Texte", in *Untersuchungen zur buddhistischen Literatur,* Göttingen: Vandenhoeck und Ruprecht, 1994.

Banerjee, A. Ch., "Pratītyasamutpāda", in *Indian Historical Quarterly* 32, 1956, pp. 261-264.

Banerjee, A. Ch, *Sarvāstivāda Literature,* Calcutta: The World Press Private Limited, 1979.

Bareau, A., "Trois Traités sur les Sectes Bouddhiques attribués á Vasumitra, Bhāvya et Vinītadeva", in *Journal Asiatique,* Vol. 242, Paris, 1954, pp. 229-266, and Vol. 244, Paris, 1956, pp. 167-200.

Bareau, A., *Les sectes bouddhiques du Petit Véhicule,* Saïgon: École Francaise d' Extrême Orient, Volume XXXVIII, 1955.

Bareau, A., *Die Religionen Indiens III, Buddhismus-Jinismus-Primitivvölker,* Stuttgart: W. Kohlhammer, 1964.

Bendall, C., see *Subhāṣita-Saṃgraha.*

Bhaduri, S., *Studies in Nyāya-Vaiśeṣika Metaphysics,* Poona: Bhandarkar Oriental Research Institute, 1947.

Bhāsarvajña, *Nyāyabhūṣaṇa,* Varanasi: Ṣaḍdarśana Prakāśana Pratiṣṭhānam, 1968.

Bhavasaṅkrāntiparikathā of Nāgārjuna, in *Bhavasaṅkrānti Sūtra and Nāgārjuna's Bhavasaṅkrānti Śāstra,* ed. N. Aiyaswami Sastri, Adyar: Adyar Library, 1938.

Bhikkhu Pāsādika, "Once Again on the Hypothesis of Two Vasubandhus", in *Prof. Hajime Nakamura Felicitation Volume,* edited by V.N. Jha, Delhi, 1991.

Broido, M.M., "Abhiprāya and Implication in Tibetan Linguistics", in *Journal of Indian Philosophy,* Vol. 12, N°1, 1984, pp. 1-34.

Broido, M.M., "Intention and Suggestion in the Abhidharmakośa: Saṃdhābhāṣā Revisited ", in *Journal of Indian Philosophy,* Vol. 13, No. 4, 1985, pp. 327-382.

Buddhaghosa, Commentary of the *Majjhimanikāya ad Upalisutta*, ed. I.B. Horner, Part III, London: PTS, 1976.

Bugault, G., *La notion de "prajñā" ou de sapience selon les perspectives du "Mahāyāna". Part de la connaissance et de l'inconnaissance dans l' analogie bouddhique*, Paris: Centre National de la Recherche Scientifique-E.É. de Boccard, 1968.

Bu-ston, *History of Buddhism (Chos-ḥbyung)*, Translated from Tibetan by E. Obermiller, Heidelberg: O. Harrassovitz, 1931-1932. Reprint: Suzuki Research Foundation, 1965.

Bu-ston, *The Collected Works of...*, Part 24 (Ya), edited by Lokesh Chandra, New Delhi : International Academy of Indian Culture, 1971.

Candrakīrti, *Madhyamakāvatāra=Madhyamakāvatāra, Introduction au Traité du Milieu de L' Ācārya Candrakīrti, avec le commentaire de l'auteur*, traduit d'aprés la version tibétaine par L. de la Vallée Poussin, in *Le Muséon* Vol. VIII (1907), pp. 249-358; (suite) in *Le Muséon* Vol. XII (1911), pp. 235-328.

Candrakīrti, *Madhyamakavṛtti*, edition of L. de la Vallée Poussin, Bibliotheca Buddhica, 4, St. Pétersbourg, 1913.

Catalogue=The Tibetan Tripitaka, Peking Edition-Kept in the Library of the Otani University, Kyoto. Edited by D.T. Suzuki, *Catalogue and Index*, Tokyo: Suzuki Research Foundation, 1962.

Chandra, P., *Metaphysics of perpetual change. The concept of Self in Early Buddhism*, Bombay-New Delhi: Somaiya Publications PTV. Ltd., 1978.

Chatterjee, H., "A critical study of the theory of pratītyasamutpāda", in *Journal of the Royal Asiatic Society of Great Britain and Ireland*, Bombay Branch (Bombay), 1955, pp. 66-70.

Chatterjee, S., *The Nyāya Theory of Knowledge. A critical Study of some problems of Logic and Metaphysics*, Calcutta : The University of Calcutta, 1965.

Chatterjee, A.K., *Facets of Buddhist Thought*, Calcutta: Sanskrit College, 1975.

Chatterjee, A.K., *The Yogācāra Idealism*, Delhi : Motilal Banarsidass, 1975.

Chaudhuri, S., *Analytical Study of the Abhidharmakośa*, Calcutta: Sanskrit College, 1976.

Chavannes, É., *Cinq Cents Contes et Apologues extraits du Tripiṭaka Chinois*, Paris : A.-Maisonneuve, 1962.

Chizen Akanuma, " The triple body of the Buddha", in *The Eastern Buddhist*, May-June, July-August, 1922, pp.1-29.

Cleary, Th., *The Flower Ornament Scripture*, Boston USA : Shambala Publications, 1993 (reissue).

Conze, E., *Abhisamayālaṅkāra*, Roma: IsMEO, 1954.

Conze, E., "Abhisamayālaṅkāra (1)", in *Encyclopaedia of Buddhism*, Vol. 1, fasc.1, pp. 114-118.

Conze, E. and Shotaro,I., "Maitreya's questions in the *Prajñāpāramitā*", in *Mélanges d' 'Indianisme à la Mémoire de Louis Renou*, Paris: E. de Boccard, 1968, pp. 229-242 (in E. Conze, *The Large Sūtra of Perfect Wisdom*, Berkeley: University of California Press, 1975, pp. 644-652, there is the English translation of the Sanskrit text edited by Conze and Shotaro).

Cox, C., "On the Possibility of a Nonexistent Object of Consciousness: Sarvāstivādin and Dārṣṭāntika Theories", in *The Journal of the International Association of Buddhist Studies*, Vol. 11, N° 1, 1988, pp. 31-87.

Daśabhūmikasūtra et Bodhisattvabhūmi. Chapitres Vihāra et Bhūmi, ed. J. Rahder, Paris-Louvain: P. Geuthner-J.B. Istas, 1926.

Daśabhūmikasūtra, ed. by P.L. Vaidya, Darbhanga (India): The Mithila Institute, 1967 (Buddhist Sanskrit Texts N° 7).

Daśabhūmīśvaro nāma Mahāyānasūtraṃ, ed. by Ryūkō Kondō, Kyoto: Rinsen Book Co., 1983 (reprint of the 1936 edition).

Dasgupta, S., *A History of Indian Philosophy*, Cambridge: University Press, 1963 (Volume I), 1965 (Volume II), 1961 (Volume III), 1966 (Volume IV), 1962 (Volume V).

Dayal, H., *The Bodhisattva doctrine in Buddhist Sanskrit Literature*, Delhi: Motilal Banarsidass, 1975.

de la Vallée Poussin, L., "Deux notes sur le pratītyasamutpāda", in *International Congress of Orientalists*, 14, 1905, pp. 193-205.

de la Vallée Poussin, L., "Note sur les Corps du Bouddha", in *Le Muséon*, 1913, pp. 257-290.

de la Vallée Poussin, L., *Bouddhisme. Études et Matériaux. Théorie des douze causes*, Gand: Librairie Scientifique E. Van Goethem- Luzac & Co., Londres, 1913 (Université de Gand. Recueil de travaux publiés par le Faculté de Philosophie et Lettres, 42 éme. Fascicule).

de la Vallée Poussin, L., *Bouddhisme. Opinions sur l' Histoire de la Dogmatique*, Paris: Gabriel Beauchesne, 1925.

de la Vallée Poussin, L., *La morale bouddhique*, avec une Préface de M.É. Senart, Paris : Nouvelle Libraire Nationale, 1927.

de la Vallée Poussin, L.,*La Siddhi de Hiuan-Tsang. Vijñaptimātratāsiddhi*, traduite et annotée par..., Tome I, Paris : Libraire Orientaliste Paul Geuthner, 1928 (Buddhica-Documents et travaux pour l' étude du Bouddhisme, Premiére Série: Mémoires-Tome I), Tome II, 1929 (Mémoires - Tome V).

de la Vallée Poussin, L., "Extase et Spéculation (*Dhyāna et Prajñā*)", in *Indian Studies in Honor of Charles Rockwell Lanman*, Cambridge Mass.: Harvard University Press, 1929, pp. 135-136.(Spanish translation in *Revista de Estudios Budistas*, 7, México-Buenos Aires, 1994, pp. 165-168).

de la Vallée Poussin, L., "Le petit traité de Vasubandhu-Nāgārjuna sur les trois natures", in *Mélanges Chinois et Bouddhiques* 2, 1932-1933, pp. 147-161.

de la Vallée Poussin, L., "Madhyamaka", in *Mélanges Chinois et Bouddhiques* 2, 1932-1933, pp. 1-146.

de la Vallée Poussin, L., "Note sur l' Ālayavijñāna", in *Mélanges Chinois et Bouddhiques* 3, 1934, pp. 145-168.

de la Vallée Poussin, L., *L' Abhidharmakośa de Vasubandhu*, Traduction et Annotations. Nouvelle édition anastatique présentée par Étienne Lamotte, Bruxelles: Institut Belge des Hautes Etudes Chinoises, 1971 (Tome I: Introduction, Chapitres 1 et 2), (Tome II: Chapitre 3), (Tome III: Chapitre 4), (Tome IV: Chapitres 5 et 6), (Tome V : Chapitres 7,8 et 9), (Tome VI: Fragment des Kārikās-Index-Additions). (Mélanges Chinois et Bouddhiques Volume XVI).

de la Vallée Poussin, L., "Bodhisattva", in *ERE*, Volume 2, pp. 739-753.

de la Vallée Poussin, L., "Cosmogony and Cosmology (Buddhist)", in *ERE*, Volume 4, pp. 129-138.

de la Vallée Poussin, L., "Magic (Buddhist)", in *ERE*, Volume 8, pp. 255-257.

de la Vallée Poussin, L., "Philosophy (Buddhist)", in *ERE*, Volume 9, pp. 846-853.

de la Vallée Poussin, L., " Sautrāntikas", in *ERE*, Volume 11, pp. 213-214.

Demiéville, P., "Busshin", in *Hōbōgirin, Dictionnaire Encyclopédique d' aprés les sources chinoises et japonaises*, Deuxième Fascicule, Tokyo: Maison Franco-Japonaise, 1930, pp. 174 b-185 a.

Dhammananda, K. Sri, *What Buddhists believe*, Jalan Berhala, Kuala Lumpur, Malaysia: The Buddhist Missionary Society, 1973.

Dharmakīrti, *Nyāya Bindu*, Banaras: Chowkhamba, 1954.

Dharmakīrti, *Pramāṇaviniścaya*, 1. Kapitel: *Pratyakṣam*, T. Vetter ed., Wien: Österreichische Akademie der Wissenschaften, 1966.

Dharmakīrti, *Nyāyabindu*, F. Stcherbatsky ed., Osnabrück: Biblio Verlag, 1970.

Dharmakīrti, *Nyāyabindu*, L. de la Vallée Poussin ed., Calcutta : The Asiatic Society (reprint of the 1913 edition), 1984.

Dharmakīrti, *Pramāṇavārttika*, R.C. Pandeya's edition, Delhi : Motilal Banarsidass, 1989.

Dharmarāja Adhvarindra, *Vedāntaparibhāṣā*, Adyar: The Adyar Library and Research Centre, 1971.

Dharmottara, *Kṣaṇabhaṅgasiddhiḥ*, ed. E. Frauwallner, in *Wiener Zeitschrift für die Kunde des Morgenlandes*, 42, 1935, pp. 217-258 (= *Kleine Schriften*, pp. 530-571).

Dharmottara, *Paralokasiddhi*, ed. E. Steinkellner, Wien: Arbeitskreis für tibetische und buddhistische Studien, Universität Wien, 1986 (review of this book in *Revista de Estudios Budistas* 4, México-Buenos Aires, 1993, pp. 175-177).

Dīghanikāya (1. Sīlakkhandha Vagga), General Editor Bhikkhu J. Kashyap, Bihar (India): Pali Publication Board, Bihar Government, 1958 (Nālandā-Devanāgarī-Pali-Series).

Dīgha Nikāya, edited by T.W. Rhys Davids and J. Estlin Carpenter, Vol. I, London: Luzac & Company, Limited, 1949.

Dignāga, *Pramāṇasamuccaya (Pratyakṣa)*, in Hattori, M., *Dignāga. On Perception.*

Dragonetti, C., *Udāna, La palabra de Buda*, Versión directa del Pali, introducción y notas de..., Barcelona (España): Barral Editores, 1972.

Dragonetti, C., "Los seis maestros del error", in *Diálogos*, Puerto Rico, Año XI, No. 28, Abril 1975, pp. 71-94. (Reprint in F. Tola and C. Dragonetti, *Yoga y Mística de la India*, pp. 129-153).

Dutt, N., "The place of the Āryasatyas and Pratītyasamutpāda in Hīnayāna and Mahāyāna", in *Annals of the Bhandarkar Oriental Research Institute*, Poona, Vol. XI, January 1930, Part II, pp. 101-127.

Dutt, N., *Early Monastic Buddhism*, Calcutta: Oriental Book Agency, 1960.

Dutt, N. (ed.), *Bodhisattvabhumi [Being the XVth Section of Asangapada's Yogacarabhumi)*, Patna: K.P. Jayaswal Research Institute, 1966.

Dutt, N., *Mahāyāna Buddhism*, Delhi : Motilal Banarsidass, 1977.

Eckel, M. D., "The Concept of Reason in Jñānagarbha's Svātantrika Madhyamaka", in B.K. Matilal and R.D. Evans (edd.), *Buddhist Logic and Epistemology*.

ed. *Peking=The Tibetan Tripiṭaka, Peking Edition*, Compiled and edited by D.T. Suzuki and S. Yamaguchi, Tokyo: Suzuki Research Foundation, 1955-1961.

Encyclopaedia of Buddhism, edited by G.P. Malalasekera, Sri Lanka: Government Press, 1961 ff.

ERE=Hastings, J., *Encyclopaedia of Religion and Ethics* edited by... Edinburgh: T. and T. Clark, 1964.

Faddegon, B., *The Vaisheṣika-System, described with the help of the oldest texts,* Wiesbaden: M. Sändig, 1969.

Frauwallner, E., "Amalavijñānam und Ālayavijñānam. Ein Beitrag zur Erkenntnislehre des Buddhismus", in *Festschrift Walther Schubring, Beiträge zur indischen Philologie und Altertumskunde,* Hamburg, 1951, pp. 148-159 (=*Kleine Schriften,* pp. 637-648).

Frauwallner, E., *On the date of the Buddhist Master of the Law Vasubandhu,* Roma : Is. M.E.O., 1951 (Serie Orientale Roma III).

Frauwallner, E., "Dignāga, sein Werk und seine Entwicklung", in *Wiener Zeitschrift für die Kunde Süd-und Ostasiens* III, 1959, pp. 83-164 (=*Kleine Schriften,* pp. 759-846)

Frauwallner, E., "Landmarks in the history of Indian logic", in *Wiener Zeitschrift für die Kunde Süd-und Ostasiens,* 5, 1961, pp. 125-148 (= *Kleine Schriften,* pp. 847-870).

Frauwallner, E., *Die Philosophie des Buddhismus,* Berlin: Akademie Verlag, 1969.

Frauwallner, E.,*Kleine Schriften,* herausgegeben von G. Oberhammer und E. Steinkellner, Wiesbaden: Franz Steiner, 1982.

Frauwallner, E., *Studies in Abhidharma Literature,* Albany: University of New York Press, 1995.

Gaṅgānātha Jhā, *The Prābhākara school of Pūrva Mīmāṃsā,* Delhi: Motilal Banarsidass, 1978.

Gangopadhyaya, M.K., *Indian Atomism. History and Sources,* Calcutta : K.P. Bagchi & Company, 1980 (Bagchi Indological Series I).

Garbe, R., *Die Sāṃkhya-Philosophie. Eine Darstellung des indischen Rationalismus nach den Quellen,* Leipzig: Verlag von H. Haessel, 1894.

Garbe, R., *Sāṃkhya und Yoga,* Strassburg: K.J. Trubner, 1896.

Geiger, W. und M., *Pali Dhamma, vornehmlich in der kanonischen Literatur,*Abhandlungen der Bayerischen Akademie der Wissenschaften, Philosophisch - philologische und historische Klasse, XXXI, Band, 1. Abhandlung, München, 1920=in *Kleine Schriften zur Indologie und Buddhismuskunde,* Wiesbaden : Franz Steiner Verlag GMBH, 1973 (Glasenapp - Stiftung, Band 6), pp. 101-228.

Golzio, Karl-Heinz, *Lankavatara Sutra,* München, 1996.

Gonda, J., "The etymologies in the Ancient Indian Brāhmaṇas", in *Lingua, International Review of General Linguistics,* Amsterdam: 1955-1956, Vol. V, pp. 61-85.

Gotama, *Nyāyadarśanam,* ed. by Taranatha Nyaya -Tarkatirtha and

Amarendramohan Tarkatirtha, Kyoto: Rinsen Book Company, 1982. Reprint of the Calcutta edition of 1936-1944.

Grinspoon, L. and Bakalar, J.B., *Psychedelic drugs reconsidered*, New York: Basic Books, 1979.

Gupta, B., "Savikalpaka pratyakṣa (Judgemental perception) as viśiṣṭajñāna", in *Our Heritage*, Vol. IV, Part I, Calcutta, 1956, pp. 107-114.

Gupta, Brahmananda, "Story of the evolution of the concept of negation", in *Wiener Zeitschrift für die Kunde Süd-und Ostasiens*, Band XII-XIII, 1968/1969, pp. 115-118.

Halbfass, W., *On being and What There is. Classical Vaiśeṣika and the History of Indian Ontology*, Albany: State University of New York, 1992.

Haldar, J.R., *Early Buddhist Mythology*, New Delhi: Manoharlal Munshiram, 1977.

Hamilton, C.H., "Buddhistic Idealism in Wei Shih Er Shih Lwen...", in *Essays in Philosophy by 17 Doctors of Philosophy*, Chicago, 1929, pp. 99-115.

Hamilton, C.H., *Wei Shih er Shih Lun or the Treatise in Twenty Stanzas on Representation-only by Vasubandhu, translated from the Chinese Version of Hsüan Tsang, Tripiṭaka Master of the T'ang Dynasty*, New Haven, Connecticut: American Oriental Society, 1938. Reprint: New York, 1967.

Hamlin, E., "Magical *Upāya* in the Vimalakīrtinirdeśasūtra", in *The Journal of the International Association of Buddhist Studies*, Vol. 11, N° 1, 1988, pp. 89-121.

Haribhadra, *Abhisamayālaṃkārālokā*, in *Aṣṭasāhasrikā Prajñāpāramitā*, Ed. P.L. Vaidya, Darbhanga: The Mithila Institute, 1960.

Harivarman, *Satyasiddhiśāstra*, edited and translated by N. Aiyaswami Sastri, Vol. I (1975), Vol. II (1978), Baroda: Oriental Institute.

Harrison, P. M., *Pratyutpanna-buddha-saṃmukhāvasthita-samādhi-sūtra*, Tokyo: The Reiyukai Library, 1978.

Harrison, P., *The Samādhi of Direct Encounter with the Buddhas of the Present*, Tokyo: The International Institute for Buddhist Studies, 1990.

Hastings, J., see *ERE*.

Hattori, M., *Dignāga, On Perception, being the Pratyakṣapariccheda of Dignāga's Pramāṇasamuccaya from the Sanskrit fragments and the Tibetan versions*, translated and annotated by..., Cambridge, Mass.: Harvard University Press, 1968 (Harvard Oriental Series, Volume Forty-seven).

Hattori, M., "The dream simile in Vijñānavāda treatises", in *Indological and Buddhist Studies*, Canberra: Faculty of Asian Studies, 1982.

Hattori, M., "Yogācāra", in *The Encyclopedia of Religion*, Mircea Eliade ed., Vol. 15, New York, Macmillan Publishing Company, 1987, pp. 524-529.

Haussig, H.W., (ed.), *Götter und Mythen des indischen Subcontinents*, Stuttgart: Klett-Cotta, 1984.

Hayes, R.P., "Diṅnāga's Views on Reasoning (*Svārthānumāna*)", in *Journal of Indian Philosophy*, Volume 8, N° 3, September, 1980, pp. 219-277.

Hirabayashi, J. and Shotaro, I., "Another Look at the Mādhyamika vs. Yogācāra. Controversy Concerning Existence and Non-existence", in *Prajñāpāramitā and related systems. Studies in Honor of Edward Conze*, edited by L. Lancaster-L.O. Gómez, Berkeley: Berkeley Buddhist Studies Series, 1977, pp. 341-360.

Hirakawa, A., *Index to the Abhidharmakośabhāṣya*, Tokyo: Daizo Shuppan Kabushikikaisha, 1973.

Hirano, T., *An Index to the Bodhicāryāvatāra Pañjikā*, Chapter IX, Tokyo: Suzuki Research Foundation, 1966.

Hiuan Tsang, *Siddhi*, see L. de la Vallée Poussin, *La Siddhi de Hiuan Tsang. Vijñaptimātratā-siddhi.*

Hiuan Tsang, Siddhi=*Chinese text in Taishō*, Vol. XXXI, N° 1585 (First edition 1925; reprinted 1970). *L. de la Vallée Poussin's translation: Vijñaptimātratāsiddhi. La Siddhi de Hiuan-Tsang*, traduite et annotée par L. de la Vallée Poussin, *Tomes I-II*, Paris: L.O.P. Geuthner, 1928-1929 (Buddhica. Documents et Travaux pour l étude du Bouddhisme, Première Série: Mémoires-Tomes I-V).

Hōbōgirin=Hōbōgirin, Dictionnaire Encyclopédique du Bouddhisme d' après les sources chinoises et japonaises, publié sous le haut patronage de L'Académie Impériale du Japon et sous la direction de Sylvain Lévi et J. Takakusu...,Rédacteur en chef P. Démiéville, 1929 and ss. See *Répertoire*.

Horner, I. B., *Milinda's Questions*, translated from Pali by..., Vol. I, Oxford: Pali Text Society, 1990.

Jacobi, H., "Atomic theory (Indian)", in *ERE*, Volume II, pp. 199-202.

Jaini, P.S., "On the Theory of the two Vasubandhus", in *Bulletin of the School of Oriental and African Studies*, vol. XXI/1958, pp. 48-53.

Jaini, P.S., "The Sautrāntika Theory of *Bija*", in *Bulletin of the School of Oriental and African Studies*, 22, 1959, pp. 236-249.

James, W., *The Principles of Psychology*, in two volumes, New York: Dover Publications, 1950.

James, W., *Psychology: Briefer course*, New York: Collier Books, 1966.

Jātaka (The), together with its Commentary being tales of the anterior births of Gotamo Buddha, for the first time edited in the original Pali by V. Fausböll, Vol. I-VII, London: PTS, 1962-1964.

Jha, M.G., *The Prābhākara School of Pūrva Mīmāṃsā*, Delhi: Motilal Banarsidass, 1978.

Jñānaśrīmitra, Kṣaṇabhaṅgādhyāya, in *Jñānaśrīmitranibandhāvali.*

Jñānaśrīmitranibandhāvali, A. Thakur ed., Patna: Kashi Prasad Jayaswal Research Institute, 1987. English translation of Chapter 3, *Vyatirekādhikāra*, by A.C. Senape McDermott, Dordrecht: Reidel, 1969.

Johnston, E. H. and Chowdhury, T. (edd.), *The Ratnagotravibhāga Mahāyānottaratantraśāstra*, Patna : The Bihar Research Society, 1950.

Jones, E.W., "Buddhist Theories of existents: The Systems of two Truths", in *Mahāyāna Buddhist Meditation: Theory and Practice* edited by Minoru Kiyota, Honolulu: The University Press of Hawaii, 1978, pp. 3-45.

Kajiyama, Y., "The Avayavinirākaraṇa of Paṇḍita Aśoka", in *Indogaku Bukkyōgaku Kenkyū ("Journal of Indian and Buddhist Studies")*, Tokyo, 9, 1961, pp. 371-366.

Kajiyama, Y., in *Daijō Butten* ("Buddhist Scriptures of the Mahāyāna"), Tōkyō, 1977, Vol. 15 *Sheshin Ronshū* ("Collection of Treatises of Vasubandhu"), pp. 5-30 (Japanese translation of the *Viṃśatikā*).

Kajiyama, Y., "Buddhist Solipsism. A free translation of Ratnakīrti's Saṃtānāntaradūṣaṇa", in his *Studies in Buddhist Philosophy*, Kyoto: Rinsen Book Co., 1989.

Kalupahana, D.J., *Causality: The Central Philosophy of Buddhism*, Honolulu: The University Press of Hawaii, 1975.

Karmasiddhiprakaraṇa, see Lamotte, É., *Le Traité de l' Acte de Vasubandhu.*

Kathāvatthu, PTS editon.

Kathāvatthu, General Editor Bhikkhu J. Kashyap, Bihar (India) : Pali Publication Board, Bihar Government, 1961 (Nālaṇḍā-Devanāgarī-Pali-Series). English translation: *Points of Controversy or Subjects of Discourse, being a translation of the Kathā-vatthu from the Abhidhamma-piṭaka* by Shwe Zan Aung and Mrs. Rhys Davids, London: Luzac & Company, Ltd., 1969.

Katsura, Shoryu, "Dignāga and Dharmakīrti on *adarśanamātra* and *anupalabdhi*", in *Asiatische Studien* XLVI, 1, 1992, pp. 222-231.

Keith, A. B., *The Sāṃkhya System, A History of the Sāṃkhya Philosophy,* Calcutta: Y.M.C.A. Publishing House, 1949.

Keith, A. B., *Buddhist Philosophy in India and Ceylon,* Varanasi (India): The Chowkhamba Sanskrit Series Office, 1963 (The Chowkhamba Sanskrit Studies Vol. XXVI).

Keith, A. B., *Indian Logic and Atomism, an Exposition of the Nyāya and Vaisheṣika Systems,* New York: Greenwood Press, Publishers, 1968.

Keśava Miśra, *Tarkabhāṣā,* Poona: Oriental Book Agency, 1953.

Kimura, T., "The date of Vasubandhu seen from the Abhidharma-Kośa", in *Indian Studies in honor of Charles Rockwell Lanman,* Cambridge Mass.: Harvard University Press, 1929.

Kirfel, W.,*Die Kosmographie der Inder,* Darmstadt: Wissenschaftliche Buchgesellschaft, 1967.

Kitayama, J., *Metaphysik des Buddhismus. Versuch einer philosophischen Interpretation der Lehre Vasubandhus und seiner Schule,* San Francisco (USA): Chinese Materials Center, Inc., 1976. Reprint of the 1934 edition.

Kochumuttom, Th. A., *A Buddhist Doctrine of Experience (A new Translation and Interpretation of the Works of Vasubandhu the Yogācārin),* Delhi: Motilal Banarsidass, 1982.

Lacombe, O., *L' Absolu selon le Vēdānta. Les notions de Brahman et d' Ātman dans les systémes de Shankara et Rāmānoudja,* Paris : Paul Geuthner, 1966.

Lai,Whalen W., "Nonduality of the Two Truths in Sinitic Mādhyamika: Origin of the 'Third Truth'", in *Journal of the International Association of Buddhist Studies,* Vol. 2, 1979, N° 2, pp. 45-65.

Lamotte, É., "Le Traité de l' Acte de Vasubandhu. Karmasiddhiprakaraṇa", in *Mélanges Chinois et Bouddhiques* IV, Bruges, 1936, pp. 151-288.

Lamotte, É., "La critique d' interprétation dans le Bouddhisme", in *India Antiqua,* Leyden, 1947, pp. 341-361.

Lamotte, É., *Le Traité de la Grand Vertu de Sagesse de Nāgārjuna (Mahāprajñāpāramitāśāstra),* Tomes I-V, Louvain: Publications Universitaires-Institut Orientaliste, 1949-1980 (Tomes I-II, Bibliothèque du *Muséon, Volume* 18; Tomes III-V, Publications de l 'Institut Orientaliste de Louvain, Volumes 2, 12, 24).

Lamotte, É., *L' Enseignement de Vimalakīrti (Vimalakīrtinirdeśa),* Louvain: Institut Orientaliste, 1962.

Lamotte, É., "Die bedingte Entstehung und die höchste Erleuchtung", in *Beiträge zur Indienforschung. Ernst Waldschmidt zum 80. Geburtstag gewidmet,* Berlin: Museums für Indische Kunst, 1977(English version: "Conditioned Co-production and Supreme Enlightenment", in *Buddhist Studies in Honour of Walpola Rahula,* London/ Sri Lanka: G. Fraser/Vimamsa, 1980, pp. 118-132).

Lamotte, É., *La Somme du Grand Véhicule,* see Asaṅga, *Mahāyānasaṃgraha.*

Laṅkavatara, edition B. Nanjio, Kyoto: Otani University Press, 1923.

Laṅkāvatāra=Saddharmalaṅkāvatārasūtram, edited by P. L. Vaidya, Darbhanga: The Mithila Institute of Post -Graduate Studies and Research in Sanskrit Learning, 1963 (Buddhist Sanskrit Texts-N° 3). B. Nanjio edition: Kyōto: Otani University Press, 1923.

Larson, G.J., *Classical Sāṃkhya. An interpretation of its history and meaning,* Delhi: Motilal Banarsidass, 1969.

Law, B. C., "Formulation of Pratītyasamutpāda", in *Journal of the Royal Asiatic Society of Great Britain and Ireland,* London, 1, 1937, pp. 287-292.

Lévi, S., "Aśvaghoṣa. Le Sūtrālaṃkāra et ses sources", in *Journal Asiatique,* 1908, Juil.-Août, pp. 149 ff.

Lévi, S., *Mahāyāna Sūtrālaṃkāra,* edité et traduit par..., Paris: Honoré Champion, 1911.

Lévi, S., "Notes indiennes", *Journal Asiatique,* 1925, Jan.- Mars, pp. 17-26.

Lévi, S., *Vijñaptimātratāsiddhi. Deux Traités de Vasubandhu. Viṃśatikā (La Vingtaine) accompagnée d' une explication en prose et Triṃśikā (la Trentaine) avec le Commentaire de Sthiramati,* original sanscrit publié pour la première fois d' après des manuscrits rapportés du Népal. *Ire. Partie.-Texte,* Paris : Honoré Champion, 1925 (Bibliothèque de l École des Hautes Études, 245)

Lévi, S., *Matériaux pour l ́Étude du Système Vijñaptimātra,* Paris: Honoré Champion, 1932 (Bibliothèque de l' École des Hautes Études).

Lopez, D.S., Jr., *Buddhist Hermeneutics,* Honolulu: University of Hawaii Press, 1988.

Lyssenko, V., "La doctrine des atomes (*aṇu, paramāṇu*) chez Kaṇāda et Praśastapāda. Problèmes d ́ interpretation", in *Journal Asiatique,* Tome 284, 1996, N° 1, pp. 137-158.

Mādhavācārya, *Sarva-darśana-saṃgraha,* Ānandāśrama ed., 1966.

Mahadevan, T. M. P., *The Philosophy of Advaita, with special reference to Bharatitīrtha-Vidyāraṇya,* Madras (India): Ganesh & Co., 1969.

Mahāprajñāpāramitopadeśa or *Mahāprajñāpāramitāśāstra*. See É. Lamotte, *Le Traité*.

Mahāvyutpatti, compiled by R. Sakaki, 2 vol., Kyoto, 1916-25; Tokyo, 1962 (Suzuki Research Foundation) (reprint).

Maitreya-Vasubandhu-Sthiramati, *Madhyāntavibhāga=Madhyānta-vibhāga-śāstra, Containing the Kārikās of Maitreya, Bhāṣya of Vasubandhu and Ṭīkā by Sthiramati*, Critically edited by R. Pandeya, Delhi: Motilal Banarsidass, 1971.

Majjhima-Nikāya, Edited by V. Trenckner, Vol. I, London: Oxford University Press, 1948 (Pali Text Society).

Masson-Oursel, P., "Les trois corps du Bouddha", in *Journal Asiatique* 1913, pp. 581-618.

Masson-Oursel, P., "L' Atomisme indien", in *Revue Philosophique (de la France et de l' étranger)*, Paris, 99, 1925, pp. 342-368.

Masson-Oursel, P., "Tathāgatagarbha et Ālayavijñāna", in *Journal Asiatique* 210, 1927 (*Mélanges*), pp. 295-302.

Masuda, J., "Origin and Doctrines of Early Indian Buddhist Schools", in *Asia Major*, II, 1925, pp. 1-78.

Masuda, J., *Der individualistische Idealismus de Yogācāra-Schule. Versuch einer genetischen Darstellung*, Heidelberg, O. Harrassowitz, 1926 (Materialien zur Kunde des Buddhismus, 10. Heft).

Matilal, B.K., *Epistemology, Logic and Grammar in Indian Philosophical Analysis*, The Hague: Mouton, 1971.

Matilal, B.K., "A critique of Buddhist Idealism", in *Buddhist Studies in Honour of I.B. Horner*, edited by L. Cousins, A. Kunst, and K.R. Norman, Dordrecht, Holland, Boston, U.S.A.: D. Reidel Publ. Co., 1974, pp. 139-169.

Matilal, B.K. and Evans, R.D. (edd.), *Buddhist Logic and Epistemology*, Dordrecht: D. Reidel, 1986.

Matilal, B.K., *Perception*, Oxford: Oxford University Press, 1986.

May, J.,*Candrakirti Prasannapada Madhyamakavrtti, Douze chapitres traduits du sanscrit et du tibétain, accompagnés d' une introduction, de notes et d' une édition critique de la version tibétaine par...*, Paris: Adrien-Maisonneuve, 1959 (Collection Jean Przyluski, Tome II).

May, J., "La Philosophie Bouddhique Idéaliste", in *Asiatische Studien* XXV, Bern, 1971, pp. 265-323.

Mikogami, E., "Some remarks on the Concept of *Arthakriyā*", in *Journal of Indian Philosophy*, Vol. 7, N° 1, 1979, pp. 79-94.

Milindapañho, being Dialogues between King Milinda and the

Buddhist sage Nāgasena, The Pali Text, edited by V. Trenckner, London: Luzac & Company Ltd., 1962 (Pali Text Society).

Mimaki, K., *La refutation bouddhique de la permanence des choses (sthirasiddhidūṣaṇa) et La preuve de la momentanéité des choses (kṣaṇabhaṅgasiddhi),* Paris : Institut de Civilisation Indienne, 1976.

Mimaki, K. et May, J., "Chūdō", in *Hōbōgirin, Dictionnaire Encyclopédique du Bouddhisme d' après les sources chinoises et japonaises,* Cinquième Fascicule, Paris-Tokyo: A. Maisonneuve-Maison Franco-Japonaise, 1979, pp. 467 b-470 a.

Mimaki, K., Tachikawa, M., and Yuyama, A., in *Three Works of Vasubandhu in Sanskrit Manuscript. The Trisvabhānirdeśa, the Viṃśatikā with its Vṛtti, and the Triṃśikā with Sthiramati's Commentary,* Tokyo : The Centre for East Asian Cultural Studies, 1989 (Bibliotheca Codicum Asiaticorum 1).

Mookerjee, Satkari, *The Buddhist Philosophy of universal Flux,* Delhi: Motilal Banarsidass, 1980.

Max Müller, K.M., *The Six Systems of Indian Philosophy,* Varanasi (India): Chowkhamba Sanskrit Series Office-The Vidya Vilas Press, reprint of the 1919 edition.

Murti, T.R.V., *The Central Philosophy of Buddhism. A Study of the Mādhyamika System,* London: G. Allen and Unwin Ltd., 1960.

Nagao, Gadjin M., "'What remains' in Śūnyatā: a Yogācāra Interpretation of Emptiness", in Minoru Kiyota, *Mahāyāna Buddhist Meditation,* Honolulu: The University Press of Hawaii, 1978, pp. 66-82.

Nagao, G., "The Buddhist World-View as elucidated in the Three-Nature Theory and its Similes", in *The Eastern Buddhist* 16, 1. 1983, pp. 1-18.

Nagao, G.M., *The Foundational Standpoint of Mādhyamika Philosophy,* New York: State University of New York Press, 1989.

Nagao, G. M., *Mādhyamika and Yogācāra. A Study of Mahāyāna Philosophies. Collected Papers of....,* Ed. by L.S. Kawamura in collaboration with G.M. Nagao, New York: State University of New York Press, 1991.

Nagao, G.M., *An Index to Asaṅga's Mahāyānasaṃgraha,* Part I, Tokyo: The International Institute for Buddhist Studies, 1994.

Nāgārjuna, *Mūlamadhyamakakārikās,* ed. L. de la Vallée Poussin, Osnabrück: Biblio Verlag, 1970 (reprint of the 1903-1913 edition).

Nakamura, Zuiryū, *A Study of Ratna-Gotra-Vibhāga-*

Mahāyānôttara-Tantra-Śāstra Based on a Comparison and Contrast between the Sanskrit Original and the Chinese Translations. Tokyo, 1967.

Nakamura, H., *Indian Buddhism. A Survey with Bibliographical Notes*, Delhi: Motilal Banarsidass, 1987.

Nanayakkara, S. K., "Iddhi", in *Encyclopaedia of Buddhism*, 1993, Vol. V, fasc. 4, pp. 508-510.

Nanjio=Nanjio B., *A Catalogue of the Chinese translation of the Buddhist Tripiṭaka, the Sacred Canon of the Buddhists in China and Japan*, San Francisco: Chinese Materials Center, 1975 (first published: 1883).

Nyanatiloka, "Dependent Origination (Paṭiccasamuppādo)", in *The Buddhist Review* V, 5-6, oct. dec. 1913, pp. 267-271.

Oberhammer, G., *La délivrance, dès cette vie (jīvanmuktiḥ)*, Paris: É. de Boccard, 1994.

Obermiller, E., "The Sublime Science of the Great Vehicle To Salvation being a Manual of Buddhist Monism", in *Acta Orientalia* IX, parts II, III and IV, 1930, pp. 81-306.

Obermiller, E., "The Doctrine of Prajñāpāramitā as exposed in the Abhisamayālaṃkāra of Maitreya", reprint from *Acta Orientalia* XI, 1932, pp. 1-33.

Obermiller, E., *Analysis of the Abhisamayālaṃkāra*, London : Luzac and Co., Calcutta Oriental Series 27, three fascicles, 1933, 1936 and 1943.

Oetke, Claus, *"Ich" und das Ich*, Stuttgart: Franz Steiner Verlag, 1988.

Oldenberg, H., *Buddha. Sein Leben, Seine Lehre, Seine Gemeinde*, München: Wilhem Goldmann Verlag, 1961.

Oltramare, P., *La formule bouddhique des douze causes. Son sens originel et son interprétation théologique*, Genève: L. Georg & Cie., 1909.

Oltramare, P., *L'Histoire des idées théosophiques dans l'Inde. La Théosophie Bouddhique*, Paris: Libraire Orientaliste Paul Geuthner, 1923.

Ono, G., "The date of Vasubandhu seen from the History of Buddhistic Philosophy", in *Indian Studies in honor of Charles Rockwell Lanman*, Cambridge Mass.: Harvard University Press, 1929, pp. 93-94.

Pali texts are quoted in their PTS editions.

Pandeya, R., *Madhyānta-vibhāga-shāstra*, see Maitreya.

Paṇḍita Aśoka, *Avayavinirākaraṇa*, see edition and translation of F. Tola and C. Dragonetti.

Paul, DianaY.,*Philosophy of Mind in Sixth-century China, Paramārtha's 'Evolution of Consciousness'*, Stanford (California): Stanford University Press, 1984.

Peking=*Peking* edition=*The Tibetan Tripiṭaka, Peking Edition,* Compiled and edited by D.T. Suzuki and S. Yamaguchi, Tokyo: Suzuki Research Foundation, 1955-1962.

Pérez Remón, J., *Self and Non-Self in Early Buddhism,* The Hague: Mouton, 1980.

Péri, N., "A propos de la date de Vasubandhu", in *Bulletin de l' École Française d' Extrême Orient,* 11, 1911, pp. 339-390.

Pereira, J. and Tiso, F., "The Life of Vasubandhu according to Recent Research", in *East and West,* Roma IsMEO, Vol. 37, Nos. 1-4, 1987.

Pezzali, A., *L' Idealismo Buddhista di Asaṅga,* Bologna: E.M. I., 1984.

Pezzali, A., *Il Tesoro della metafisica secondo il maestro buddhista Vasubandhu,* Bologna, EMI della Cooperative SERMIS, 1987.

Potter, K. H., *Bibliography of Indian Philosophies,* Delhi: Motilal Banarsidass, 1970 (American Institute of Indian Studies), Vol. I.

Potter, K.H., *Encyclopedia of Indian Philosophies, Vol. II, Indian Metaphysics.and Epistemology: The Tradition of Nyāya-Vaiśeṣika up to Gaṅgeśa,* Edited by..., Delhi: Motilal Banarsidass, 1977.

Potter, K. H., *Encyclopedia of Indian Philosophies, Vol. III, Advaita Vedanta up to Shamkara and His Pupils,* Edited by..., Delhi : Motilal Banarsidass, 1981.

Potter, K. H. and Bhattacharyya, S., (edd.), *Encyclopedia of Indian Philosophies, Vol. VI, Indian Philosophical Analysis: Nyāya-Vaiśeṣika from Gaṅgeśa to Raghunātha Śiromaṇi,* Delhi: Motilal Banarsidass, 1993.

Potter, K. H., and others (edd.), *Encyclopedia of Indian Philosophies Vol. VII, Abhidharma Buddhism to 150* A.D., Delhi : Motilal Banarsidass, 1996.

Powers, J., *Two Commentaries on the Samdhinirmocana-sutra by Asanga and Jnanagarbha,* Lewison/Queenston/Lampeter: The Edwin Mellen Press, 1992.

PTS=Pali Text Society editions.

Radhakrishnan, *Indian Philosophy,* Vol. I-II, New York-London: The Macmillan Company-George Allen & Unwin Ltd., 1962.

Rahula, W., *Le Compendium de la super-doctrine (Philosophie) (Abhidharmasamuccaya) d' Asaṅga,* Paris : École Française d'Extrême-Orient, 1971.

Rāmāyana=*The Vālmīki Rāmāyaṇa,* critical edition by G. H. Bhatt, Baroda: Oriental Institute, 1960 ff.

Randle, H.N., *Indian Logic in the Early Schools,* London: Oxford University Press, 1930.

Ratnakīrti, *Santānāntarasiddhidūṣaṇa,* in *Ratnakīrti nibandhāvaliḥ,* A. Thakkur ed., Patna: K.P. Jayaswal Research Institute, 1975.

Ratnakīrti, *Kṣaṇabhaṅgasiddhi,* in *Ratnakīrti-nibandhāvaliḥ,* A. Thakkur ed., Patna: K.P. Jayaswal Research Institute, 1975.

Ratnakīrti, *Sthirasiddhidūṣaṇam,* in *Ratnakīrti-nibandhāvaliḥ,* A. Thakkur ed., Patna: K.P. Jayaswal Research Institute, 1987.

Renou, L. et Filliozat, J., *L' Inde Classique. Manuel des Études Indiennes,* Tome II avec le concours de P. Démiéville, O. Lacombe, P. Meile, Paris: Imprimerie Nationale, 1953 (Bibliothèque de l' École Française d´Extrême-Orient, Volume III, Hanoi).

Répertoire=Répertoire du Canon Bouddhique Sino-Japonais. Édition de Taishō (Taishō Shinshū Daizōkyō), compilé par P. Demiéville, H.Durt, A. Seidel, Fascicule Annexe du Hōbōgirin, Paris-Tōkyō: A. Maisonneuve-Maison Franco-Japonaise, 1978.

Revista de Estudios Budistas, México-Buenos Aires, N° 12, 1996.

Ritter, J. (ed.), *Historisches Wörterbuch der Philosophie,* Vol. III, Darmstadt: Wissenschaftliche Buchgesellschaft, 1974.

Rosenberg, O., *Die Probleme der buddhistischen Philosophie,* Heidelberg: O. Harrassowitz, 1924 (Materialien zur Kunde des Buddhismus, 7/8. Heft). Reprint: San Francisco: Chinese Materials Center, 1976.

Ruegg, D.S., *La Théorie du Tathāgatagarbha et du Gotra, Études sur la Sotériologie et la Gnoséologie du Bouddhisme,* Paris: A. Maisonneuve, 1969 (Publication de l' École Française d' Extrême-Orient, Volume LXX).

Ruegg, D.S., *The Literature of the Madhyamaka School of Philosophy in India,* Wiesbaden: Otto Harrassowitz, 1981.

Ruegg, D.S., "Purport, Implicature and Presupposition: Sanskrit *abhiprāya* and Tibetan *dgoṅs pa/dgoṅs gźi* as Hermeneutical Concepts", in *Journal of Indian Philosophy,* 13, 1985, pp. 309 -325..

Ruegg, D.S., "The Buddhist Notion of an'Immanent Absolute' (tathāgatagarbha) as a Problem in Hermeneutics", in *The Buddhist Heritage,* Tring: Buddhica Britannica, 1989, pp. 229-245.

Ruegg, D.S., "Allusiveness and Obliqueness in Buddhist texts: Saṃdhā, Saṃdhi, Saṃdhyā and Abhisaṃdhi", in *Dialectes dans les Littératures indo-aryennes,* C. Caillat ed., Paris, 1989.

Saddharmapuṇḍarīkasūtra, edited by H. Kern and B. Nanjio, Osnabrück: Biblio Verlag, 1970.

Śālistambasūtra, see L. de la Vallée Poussin, *Bouddhisme*, 1913, and N.A. Sastri, 1950.

Saṃdhinirmocana=É. Lamotte, *L' Explication des Mystères (Saṃdhi- nirmocanasūtra, texte tibétain édité et traduit)*, Louvain: Recueil de l' Université de Louvain, 34, 1935; and John Powers, *Wisdom of Buddha. The Saṁdhinirmocana Sūtra*, Berkeley, U.S. A.: Dharma Publishing, 1995.

Saṃyutta Nikāya, Pali Text Society edition.

Saṃyutta Nikāya, General Editor Bhikkhu J. Kashyap, Bihar (India): Pali Publication Board, 1959 (Nālaṇḍā-Devanāgarī-Pali-Series).

Sancti Thomae Aquinatis, *Opera omnia*, Tomus XVI, New York: Musurgia Publishers, 1950, pp. 318-319 [Opusculum XXIII, "De aeternitate mundi contra murmurantes"].

Śaṅkara, *Vedāntasūtra=The Brahmasūtra Śaṅkara Bhāṣya*, ed. Anantakṛṣṇa Śāstrī, Bombay: Nirṇaya Sāgar Press, 1938.

Śaṅkara, *Upadeśasahasrī*, ed. S. Mayeda, Tokyo: The Hokuseido Press, 1973.

Śāntideva, *Shikshāsamuccaya. A Compendium of Buddhistic Teaching*, ed. by C. Bendall, The Hague: Mouton & Co., 1957.

Sastri, N.A., *Ārya Śālistamba Sūtra*, Adyar: Adyar Library, 1950.

Sastri, H., "The Northern Buddhism III", in *Indian Historical Quarterly* 1, 1925, pp. 464-472.

Schmithausen, Lambert, "Sautrāntika-Voraussetzungen in Viṃśatikā und Triṃśikā", in *Wiener Zeitschrift für die Kunde Süd-und Ostạsien*, Wien, 1967 (Archiv für indische Philosophie), pp. 109-138.

Schmithausen, L.,"Zur Literaturgeschichte der älteren Yogācāra-Schule", in *Zeitschrift der deutschen Morgenländischen Gesellschaft*, Supplementa I [XVII Deutscher Orientalistentag Juli 1968], 1969, pp. 811-823.

Schmithausen, L.,*Der Nirvāṇa-Abschnitt in der Viniścayasaṃgrahaṇī der Yogācārabhūmiḥ*, Wien: Österreichische Akademie der Wissenschaften, 1969.

Schmithausen, L., *Ālayavijñāna. On the Origin and the Early Development of a Central Concept of Yogācāra Philosophy*, Tokyo: The International Institute for Buddhist Studies, 1987.

Schmithausen, L., " On the Problem of the Relation between Spiritual Practice and Philosophical Theory in Buddhism", in *German Scholars in India*, Bombay, 1970, p. 247.

Sde-dge=Sde-dge edition=*Sde-dge Tibetan Tripiṭaka Bstan Ḥgyur-*

preserved at the Faculty of Letters, University of Tokyo-*Tshad ma* I, 276 (Ce), Tokyo: Tibetan Text Research Association-Sekai Seiten Kanko Kyokai (The World Sacred Text Publication Society), 1981.

Shastri, D.N. "The Distinction between Nirvikalpa and Savikalpa Perception in Indian Philosophy", in *Proceedings of the All-India Oriental Conference,* Vol. 16, 1955, pp. 310-321.

Shastri, D. N., *The Philosophy of Nyāya-Vaiśeṣika and its Conflict with The Buddhist Dignāga School (Critique of Indian Realism),* with a Foreword by S. Radhakrishnan, Delhi - Varanasi (India): Bharatiya Vidya Prakashan, 1976.

Siauve, S., *La doctrine de Madhva. Dvaita-Vedānta, Pondichéry* (India): Institut Français d'Indologie, 1968 (Publications de l' Institut Français d'Indologie No. 38).

Sinha, J., *A History of Indian Philosophy,* Volume I, Calcutta: Sinha Publishing House, 1956.

Sinha, J., *Indian Psychology, Cognition,* Vol. I, Calcutta: Sinha Publishing House, 1958.

Sinha, J., *Indian Realism,* Delhi: Motilal Banarsidass, 1972.

Snellgrove, D., *Indo-Tibetan Buddhism. Indian Buddhists & Their Tibetan Successors,* London: Serindia Publications, 1987.

Solley, Ch. and Murphy, G., *Development of the perceptual World,* New York: Basic Books, 1960.

Spence Hardy, R., *A Manual of Buddhism, in its modern development,* Varanasi: Chowkhamba Sanskrit Series Office, 1967 (The Chowkhamba Sanskrit Studies Vol. LVI).

Śrīdhara Bhaṭṭa, *Nyāyakandalī in Praśastapādabhāṣyam (Padārthadharmasaṃgraha)... Along with Hindi Translation,* Edited by Pt. Durgādhara Jhā, Varanasi (India), 1977 (Gaṅgānāthajhā-Granthamālā, Vol. 1).

Stcherbatsky, Ts., "Dignāga's Theory of Perception", in *Taishō Daigaku Gakuhō* (Journal of the Taishō University), 1930, pp. 89-130.

Stcherbatsky, F., *The Central Conception of Buddhism and the meaning of the word "dharma"*, Calcutta: Susil Gupta, 1961.

Stcherbatsky, Th., *Buddhist Logic,* New York: Dover Publications, *s.d.* (First edition: Leningrad, 1927).

Stcherbatsky, Th., *The Conception of Buddhist Nirvāṇa,* London: The Hague, Paris: Mouton & Co, 1965 (Indo-Iranian reprints, VI).

Stcherbatsky, Th., *Papers of Th. Stcherbatsky,* Calcutta: Indian Studies Past & Present, 1969.

Stcherbatsky, Th. and Obermiller, E., *Abhisamayālaṃkāra,* Leningrad: Bibliotheca Buddhica XXIII, 1929.

Steinkellner, E., *Dharmakīrti's Hetubinduḥ*, Teil I, Wien: Österreichische Akademie der Wissenschaften, 1967.

Steinkellner, E., "Die Entwicklung des kṣaṇikatvānumāṇam bei Dharmakīrti", in *Beiträge zur Geistesgeschichte Indiens, Festschrift für Erich Frauwallner,* Wien: Österreichische Akademie der Wissenschaften, 1968, pp. 361-377.

Steinkellner, E., "Lamotte and the concept of *anupalabdhi*", in *Asiatische Studien* XLVI, 1, 1992, pp. 398-410.

Steinkellner, E. und Much, M. T., *Texte der erkenntnistheoretischen Schule des Buddhismus,* Göttingen: Vandenhoeck und Ruprecht, 1995.

Steinkellner, E., "Bemerkungen zu Īśvarasenas Lehre vom Grund, in *Wiener Zeitschrift für die Kunde Süd-und Ostasiens,* X, pp. 73-85.

Sthiramati, *Ṭīkā,* see Pandeya R., Maitreya, *Madhyāntavibhāgaśāstra.*

Subhāṣita-Saṃgraha, an Anthology from Buddhist works compiled by an unknown author, to illustrate the Doctrines of Scholastic and of Mystic (Tantrik) Buddhism, Edited by C. Bendall, in *Le Muséon* N.S., IV. 1903, pp. 375-402, V. 1904, pp. 5-45 and 235-274.

Sundararaman, "Refutation of the Buddhist doctrine of Aggregates", in *Philosophical Quarterly,* Amalner, 16, 1940-1941, pp. 164-171.

Sureśvara, *Saṃbandhavārtika=The Saṃbandha-Vārtika of Sureśvara,* ed. T. M.P. Mahadevan, Madras: University of Madras, 1972.

Suzuki, D. T., *Studies in the Lankavatara Sutra, One of the most important texts of Mahayana Buddhism, in which almost all its principal tenets are presented, including the teaching of Zen,* London and Boston: Routledge & Kegan Paul Ltd., 1972.

Suzuki, D. T., *Outlines of Mahayana Buddhism,* Prefatory Essay by Alan Watts, New York: Schoken Books, 1973.

Taishō=Taishō Shinshū Daizōkyō (The Tripiṭaka in Chinese). Ed. by J. Takakusu and K. Watanabe, Tokyo: The Taishō Shinshū Daizōkyō Kanko kai, 1970.

Takakusu, J., "La Sāṃkhyakārikā étudiée a la lumière de sa version chinoise", in *Bulletin de l' École Française d' Extrême Orient,* Tome IV, Hanoï, 1904, pp. 1-65.

Takakusu, J., "The Life of Vasubandhu", in *T oung Pao Archives Series* II, Vol. 4-5, 1904.

Takakusu, J., "A Study of Paramārtha's life of Vasubandhu", in *Journal of the Royal Asiatic Society,* London, 1905, pp. 33-53.

Takakusu, J., "On the Abhidharma Literature", in *Journal of The Pali Text Society,* 1905, pp. 67-146.

Takakusu, J., "The date of Vasubandhu, the Great Buddhist

Philosopher ", in *Indian Studies in honor of Charles Rockwell Lanman*, Cambridge, Mass.: Harvard University Press, 1929, pp. 79-88.

Takakusu, J., *The Essentials of Buddhist Philosophy*, Delhi: Motilal Banarsidass, 1975.

Takakusu, J., "Sarvāstivādins", in *ERE*, Vol. 11, pp. 198-200.

Takasaki, J., *A Study on the Ratnagotravibhāga (Uttaratantra)*, Roma: IsMEO, 1966.

Takasaki, J., *An Introduction to Buddhism*, Tokyo: The Tōhō Gakkai, 1987.

Takeuki, Shōkō, "Phenomena and Reality in Vijñaptimātra Thought. On the Usage of the Suffix 'tā' in Maitreya's Treatises", in *Buddhist Thought and Asian Civilisation. Essays in Honor of Herbert V. Guenther on his Sixtieth Birthday*, edited by L.S. Kawamura and K. Scott, Emeryville-California: Dharma Publishing, 1977, pp. 254-267.

Tāranāthae de Doctrinae Buddhicae in India Propagatione Narratio. Contextum Tibeticum e Codicibus Petropolitanis. Edidit Antonius Schiefner, Petropoli: Academiae Scientiarum Petropolitanae, 1868. Reprint: Suzuki Research Foundation, Tokyo, 1966.

Tāranātha's Geschichte des Buddhismus in Indien, aus dem tibetischen übersetzt von A. Schiefner, St. Petersburg: Kaiserlichen Akademie der Wissenschaften, 1869. Reprint: Suzuki Research Foundation, Tokyo, 1966.

Tart, Ch. T., *Altered states of consciousness*, edited by..., New York: Anchor Books, 1972.

Tatia, N., "Paṭicasamuppāda (Causation in Pali Buddhism)", in *Nava-Nalanda-Mahavihara Research Publications* (Nalanda), I, 1957, pp. 177-239.

Tch' eng wei che louen. See L. de la Vallée Poussin, *La Siddhi*.

Thomas, E. J., "States of the Dead (Buddhist)", in *ERE*, Volume 11, pp. 829-833.

Thubtan Chogdub Śāstrī and Rāmaśaṅkara Tripāṭhi, *Vijñaptimātratāsiddhiḥ (Prakaraṇadvayam) of Ācārya Vasubandhu, Viṃśatikā, with an Auto-Commentary and Triṃśikā with the Commentary (Bhāṣya) of Sthiramati, Edited with The Gūḍhārthadīpanī Commentary and Hindi Translation by...*, Varanasi (India): Gaṅgānāthajhā-Granthamālā, Vol. V, 1972.

Tillemans, J. F., *Materials for the Study of Āryadeva, Dharmapāla and Candrakīrti*, Wien: Universität Wien, 1990.

Tirupati, V. V., "A note on the *Nirvikalpa* and *Savikalpa* perceptions in Indian philosophy", in *Proceedings of Twentysixth Congress of Orientalists*, 1969, pp. 498-503.

Tōhoku=A Complete Catalogue of the Tibetan Buddhist Canons (Bkaḥ-ḥgyur and Bstan-ḥgyur), edited by H. Ui, M. Suzuki, Y. Kanakura, T. Tada, Sendai, Japan: Tōhoku Imperial University-Saitō Gratitude Foundation, 1934.

Tola, F. and Dragonetti, C., "La doctrina de los *dharmas* en el Budismo", in *Boletīn de la Asociación Española de Orientalistas*, Año XIII, Madrid, 1977, pp. 105-132. Reprint in *Yoga y Mīstica de la India*, Buenos Aires: Kier, 1978, pp. 91-121.

Tola, F. and Dragonetti, C., *Yoga y Mīstica de la India*, Buenos Aires: Kier, 1978.

Tola, F. and Dragonetti, C., "Saṃsāra, anāditva *y* nirvāṇa", in *Boletīn de la Asociación Española de Orientalistas*, Año XV -1979, Madrid, pp. 95-114, and in *Filosofīa y Literatura de la India*, pp. 13-31.

Tola, F. and Dragonetti, C., "Anāditva or beginninglessness in Indian Philosophy", in *Annals of the Bhandarkar Oriental Research Institute*, 1980, Vol. LXI, parts I-IV, pp. 1-20.

Tola, F. and Dragonetti, C., *El Budismo Mahāyāna. Estudios y textos*, Buenos Aires: Kier, 1980.

Tola, F. and Dragonetti, C., "Nāgārjuna's conception of 'voidness' (śūnyatā)", in *Journal of Indian Philosophy* 9, 1981, pp. 273-282.

Tola, F. and Dragonetti, C.,*Filosofīa y Literatura de la India*, Buenos Aires : Kier, 1983.

Tola, F., "Fundamental principles of Indian Philosophy", *Proceedings of the Fifth World Sanskrit Conference*, New Delhi: Rashtriya Sanskrit Sansthan, 1985, pp. 680-688. Spanish version: "Principios Fundamentales de la Filosofía India", in *Revista Venezolana de Filosofīa*, N° 19, 1985, pp. 89-101.

Tola, F., "Tres concepciones del hombre en la filosofía de la India", in *Pensamiento*, Núm.165, Vol. 42, enero-marzo 1986, Madrid, pp. 29-46.

Tola, F. and Dragonetti, C., "Āryabhavasaṃkrāntināmamahāyānasūtra: The Noble Sūtra on the Passage through Existences", in *Journal of Buddhist Studies Review* (London) 1986, pp. 3-15.

Tola, F. and Dragonetti, C., *Nihilismo Budista. La doctrina de la Vaciedad*, México: Premiá, 1990.

Tola, F. and Dragonetti, C., "La estructura de la mente según la escuela idealista budista (Yogāchāra), in *Pensamiento* N° 182, Vol. 46, Madrid, 1990, pp. 129-147 (reprinted in *Revista de Estudios Budistas* 4, México-Buenos Aires, 1992, pp. 51-73).

Tola, F. and Dragonetti, C., *The Yogasūtras of Patañjali*, Delhi: Motilal Banarsidass, fourth edition, 2001.

Tola, F. and Dragonetti, C., *The Avayavinirākaraṇa of Paṇḍita Aśoka*, Tokyo: The International Institute for Buddhist Studies, 1994.

Tola, F. and Dragonetti, C., *On :Voidness. A Study on Buddhist Nihilism*, Delhi: Motilal Banarsidass, 1995. Second edition, 2002.

Tola, F. and Dragonetti, C., *Nāgārjuna's Refutation of Logic (Nyāya). Vaidalyaprakaraṇa, Zib mo rnam par ḥthag pa źes bya baḥi rab tu byed pa*, Delhi: Motilal Banarsidass, 1995. Second edition, 2002.

Tola, F. and Dragonetti, C., "The Conflict of Change in Buddhism: the Hīnayānist Reaction", in *Cahiers d' Extrême-Asie*, 9, 1996.

Tola, F. and Dragonetti, C., "The Buddhist Conception of reality", in *Journal of the Indian Council of Philosophical Research*, 1997.

Tucci, G., *On some aspects of the doctrines of Maitreya [nātha] and Asaṅga*, San Francisco: Chinese Materials Center, 1975 (reprint of the 1930 edition Calcutta).

Tucci, G., *Pre-Diṅnaga Buddhist Texts on Logic from Chinese Sources*, translated with an Introduction, Notes and Indices by..., Baroda: Oriental Institute, 1929. Reprinted by : Chinese Materials Center, San Francisco (U.S.A.), 1976.

Tucci, G., *Storia della Filosofia Indiana*, Bari: Editori Laterza, 1957.

Tucci, G., "A fragment from the *Pratītya-samutpāda-vyākhyā* of Vasubandhu", in *Journal of the Royal Asiatic Society*, 1930, pp. 611-623 (= G. Tucci, *Opera Minora*, Parte I, Roma: G. Bardi Editore, 1971, pp. 239-248).

Tucci, G., *Abhisamayālaṃkārāloka of Haribhadra*, Baroda: Gaekwad Oriental Series, 1932.

Tucci, G., *Opera Minora*, Parte I, Roma: G. Bardi, 1971 (Università di Roma, Studi Orientali pubblicati a cura della Scuola Orientale, Volume VI).

Tucci, G., *Minor Buddhist Texts*, Rome: IsMEO, 1956. Reprint: Delhi: Motilal Banarsidass, 1986.

Udayana, *Ātmatattvaviveka*, Benares: Chowkhamba, 1940.

Uddyotakara, *Vārttika*, in Gotama, *Nyāyadarśanam*.

Ueda, Y., "Two main streams of Thought in Yogācāra Philosophy", in *Philosophy East and West*, 17, 1967, pp. 155-165.

Ui, H., *Indo Tetsugaku Kenkyū* ("Studies in Indian Philosophy"), Tōkyō: Kōshisha, 1924-1930.

Ui, H., "On the Author of the Mahāyānasūtrālaṃkāra", in *Zeitschrift für die Indologie und Iranistik*, Leipzig, VI, 2, 1928, pp. 215-225.

Ui, H., "Maitreya as an historical personage", *Indian Studies in Honor of Charles Rockwell Lanman*, Cambridge, Mass.: Harvard University Press, 1929, pp. 95-101.

Ui, H., *Jinna Chosaku no Kenkyū* ("Studies of Dignāga's Works"), Tokyo, 1958.

Ui, H., *The Vaiśeshika Philosophy according to the Daśapadārtha-Śāstra, Chinese text with Introduction, Translation and Notes*, Varanasi (India): The Chowkhamba Sanskrit Series Office, 1962 (The Chowkhamba Sanskrit Studies, Vol. XXII).

Upadhyaya, V.P., *Lights on Vedānta. A Comparative study of the various views of Post-Śaṅkarites, with special emphasis on Sureśvara's doctrines*, Varanasi: The Chowkhamba Sanskrit Series Office, 1959 (The Chowkhamba Sanskrit Series, Studies Vol. VI).

Upali Karunaratne, "Indriya", in *Encyclopaedia of Buddhism*, 1993, Vol. V, fasc. 4, p. 561.

van Zeyst, H.G.A., "Abhiññā", in *Encyclopaedia of Buddhism*, Vol. I, Fasc. 1, pp. 97-102.

Vasubandhu, *Karmasiddhiprakaraṇa*=É. Lamotte, *Le Traité de l'Acte de Vasubandhu (Karma-siddhi-prakaraṇa)*, in *Mélanges chinois et bouddhiques*, Vol. IV, Bruges, 1936, pp. 151-288 (Tibetan and Chinese versions, and French translation).

Vasubandhu, *Abhidharmakośa*, P. Pradhan ed., Patna : K. P. Jayaswal Research Institute, 1967.

Vasubandhu, *Abhidharmakośa=Abhidharmakośa & Bhāṣya of Acharya Vasubandhu with Sphutārthā Commentary of Ācārya Yaśomitra*, S. Dwarikadas Shastri ed., Varanasi (India): Bauddha Bharati, 1970-1973 (Bauddha Bharati Series-5, 6, 7, 9).

Vasubandhu-Sthiramati, *Triṃśikā=Vijñaptimātratāsiddhi. Deux Traités de Vasubandhu, Viṃśatikā (La Vingtaine) accompagnée d' une explication en prose et Triṃśikā (La Trentaine) avec le commentaire de Sthiramati. Original sanscrit publié pour la première fois d' après des manuscrits rapportés du Népal par* Sylvain Lévi, Ire Partie.-Texte, Paris: L.A. Honoré Champion, 1925.

Vijñaptimātratāsiddhiḥ (Prakaraṇadvayam) of Ācārya Vasubandhu, Viṃśatikā with an auto-commentary and Triṃśikā with the commentary (Bhāṣya) of Sthiramati, edited with the Gūḍhārthadīpanī commentary and Hindi translation by Thubtan Chogdub Śāstri and R. Tripāṭhi, Varanasi: Gaṅgānāthajhā-Granthamālā, Vol. V, 1972.

Vetter, T., *Erkenntnisprobleme bei Dharmakīrti,* Wien: Österreichische Akademie der Wissenschaften, 1964.

Vidyāraṇya, *The Jīvan-mukti-viveka or The Path to Liberation-in-this-Life,* Edited with an English Translation by S. S. Shastri and T.R. Shrinivasa Ayyangar, Madras (India): The Theosophical Publishing House-Adyar, Diamond Jubilee, 1875-1935.

Vidyāraṇya, *Vivaraṇaprameyasaṃgraha,* Kāśī : Acyutagranthamālā-kāryālayaḥ, saṃvat 1996.

Vidyabhusana, S. Ch., "Pratītya-samutpāda or Dependent Origination", in *Journal of the Buddhist Text Society of India,* Calcutta, 7. 1, 1899, pp. 1-19.

Vidyabhusana, S. Ch., *A History of Indian Logic (ancient, mediaeval and modern schools),* Delhi: Motilal Banarsidass, 1971.

Vijaya Rani, *The Buddhist Philosophy as presented in Mīmāṃsā-Śloka-Vārttika,* Delhi: Parimal Publications, 1982.

Visuddhimagga of Buddhaghosācariya, edited by H.C. Warren, revised by Dh. Kosambi, Cambridge Mass. : Harvard University Press, 1950 (Harvard Oriental Series, Vol. 41).

Vogel, G., *The teachings of the Six Heretics,* Wiesbaden: F. Steiner, 1970.

von Glasenapp, H., *Vedānta und Buddhismus,* Wiesbaden: F. Steiner, 1950.

von Glasenapp, H., "Zur Geschichte der buddhistischen Dharma Theorie", in *Von Buddha zu Gandhi. Aufsätze zur Geschichte der Religionen Indiens,* Wiesbaden : Otto Harrassowitz, 1962, pp. 47- 80.

von Glasenapp, *Ausgewählte Kleine Schriften,* Wiesbaden: F. Steiner, 1980.

von Rospatt, A., *The Buddhist Doctrine of Momentariness, A Survey of the Origins and Early Phase of this Doctrine up to Vasubandhu,* Stuttgart: F. Steiner, 1995.

Vyomaśiva, *Vyomavatī,* commentary (*ṭīkā*) on the *Padārthadharmasaṃgraha* of Praśastapāda, edited by M. M. Gopīnath Kavirāj and P. D. Shāstri, Varanasi : Chaukhamba Amarabhati Prakashan, 1983.

Wang Sen, "Abhisamayālaṅkāra (2)", in *Encyclopaedia of Buddhism,* Vol. 1, fasc. 1, pp. 114-118.

Warder, A. K., *Indian Buddhism,* Delhi: Motilal Banarsidass, 1970.

Wayman, A., "Analysis of the Śrāvaka -bhūmi Manuscript", Berkeley and Los Angeles: University of California Press, 1961.

Wayman, A., "The Yogācāra Idealism", in *Philosophy East and West* 15, 1965, pp. 65-73.

Wayman, Alex and Hideko, *The Lion's Roar of Queen Śrīmālā*, Delhi: Motilal Banarsidass, 1990.

Weinstein, S., "The Ālaya-vijñāna in Early Yogācāra Buddhism—A Comparison of Its Meaning in the Saṃdhinirmocanasūtra and the Vijñapti-mātratā-siddhi of Dharmapāla", in *Kokusai Tōhō Gakusha Kaigikiyō*, Vol. 3, 1958, pp. 46-58.

Winternitz, M., *A History of Indian Literature. Vol. II: Buddhist Literature and Jaina Literature*, New Delhi: Oriental Books Reprint Corporation, 1972.

Wogihara, U., *Wogihara Unrai Bunshū* ("Collection of Unrai Wogihara's works"), Tōkyō: Taishō University, 1938.

Wogihara, U., "Vasubandhu", in *ERE* 12, pp. 595-596.

Wogihara, U. (ed.), *Bodhisattvabhūmi. A Statement of whole Course of the Bodhisattva (Being Fifteenth Section of Yogācārabhūmi)*, Tokyo: Sankibo Buddhist Book Store, 1971.

Wogihara, U., *Abhisamayālaṃkārāloka of Haribhadra*, Tokyo: Sankibo Buddhist Book Store, 1973 (reprint of the 1932-1935 edition).

Wood, Th. E., *Mind Only: a philosophical and doctrinal analysis of the Vijñānavāda*, Honolulu: University of Hawaii Press, 1991.

Yamaguchi, S. *Sthiramati Madhyāntavibhāgaṭīkā, Exposition Systématique du Yogacārāvijñaptivāda*, Nagoya: Librairie Hajinkaku, 1934. Reprint: Tōkyō: Suzuki Research Foundation, 1966.

Yamaguchi, S., *Index to the Madhyāntavibhāgaṭīkā*, Vol. III of the work cited immediately before this one.

Yamaguchi, S., *Index to the Prasannapadā Madhyamaka-vṛtti*, Part One: Sanskrit-Tibetan, Part Two: Tibetan-Sanskrit, Kyōto: Heirakuji-Shoten, 1974.

Yamakami Sogen, *Systems of Buddhistic Thought*, Calcutta: University of Calcutta, 1912.